Women and Aristocratic Culture in the Carolingian World

Valerie L. Garver

CORNELL UNIVERSITY PRESS
ITHACA AND LONDON

First published 2009 by Cornell University Press
First printing, Cornell Paperbacks, 2012

Printed in the United States of America

Library of Congress Cataloging-in-Publication Data

Garver, Valerie L. (Valerie Louise), 1972–
   Women and aristocratic culture in the Carolingian world /
Valerie L. Garver.
       p. cm.
   Includes bibliographical references and index.
   ISBN 978-0-8014-4771-6 (cloth: alk. paper)
   ISBN 978-0-8014-7788-1 (paper : alk. paper)
   1. Women—Europe—History—Middle Ages, 500-1500.
2. Upper class women—Europe—History—To 1500.
3. Carolingians.   4. Social history—Medieval, 500-1500.
5. Civilization, Medieval.   I. Title.

HQ1147.E85G37   2009
305.4094'09021—dc22

2009019277

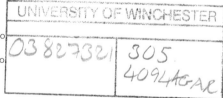
Cornell University Press strives to use environmentally responsible
suppliers and materials to the fullest extent possible in the publishing of its books. Such materials include vegetable-based, low-VOC
inks and acid-free papers that are recycled, totally chlorine-free, or
partly composed of nonwood fibers. For further information, visit
our website at www.cornellpress.cornell.edu.

Cloth printing   10 9 8 7 6 5 4 3 2 1
Paperback printing   10 9 8 7 6 5 4 3 2 1

For my parents
who first taught me history

WOMEN AND ARISTOCRATIC CULTURE IN THE CAROLINGIAN WORLD

CONTENTS

ILLUSTRATIONS

ACKNOWLEDGMENTS

This book has grown into its present shape because of the generous suggestions, time, and funding of many individuals and institutions. If I forget to mention any one of them, it is not out of a lack of gratitude.

Many individuals have helped me become a Carolingian historian. Lisa Bitel first sparked my interest in early medieval women, and time spent at the University of Groningen convinced me that I wanted to become a historian. I am deeply indebted to Tom Noble and to the late Jim Lang for sharing their enthusiasm for and knowledge of the Carolingian world. I am grateful to University of Virginia faculty and students, especially Paul Kershaw but also Peter Baker, Greg Hays, Ted Lendon, Erik Midelfort, Duane Osheim, Anne Schutte, Tony Spearing, Augustine Thompson, and Libby Thompson. I particularly want to thank Herwig Wolfram and Walter Pohl, who made it possible for me to spend a year in the rich intellectual atmosphere of the Institut für Österreichische Geschichtsforschung and the Forschungstelle für Geschichte des Mittelalters, Österreichische Akademie der Wissenschaften. For help and camaraderie I thank the writing workshop of Notre Dame's Medieval Institute.

At Northern Illinois University, I have benefited from the support and collegiality of my colleagues in the History Department. I continue to be impressed by their dedication to both research and teaching, and I remain extremely grateful to the senior colleague who took on an overload in order to give me a reduced teaching load for one semester. My fellow medievalists at NIU, particularly Nicole Clifton, Sue Deskis, and Ann van Dijk, provided me with sound advice and friendship.

I am profoundly grateful to Lynda Coon and Sandi Yandle, who read complete drafts of this book, and to the two anonymous readers for Cornell

University Press, who helped me to improve this book in countless ways. At Cornell University Press, I wish to thank my patient editor Peter Potter as well as Rachel Post, Irina Burns, and Susan Specter. Equally I am indebted to the individuals I thank elsewhere, who read complete or partial drafts. Any errors or omissions are of course mine.

Parts of this book appeared in slightly different form in earlier publications. I thank Verlag Walter de Gruyter for permission to reprint short portions of "The Influence of Monastic Ideals upon Carolingian Conceptions of Childhood," in *Childhood in the Middle Ages and Renaissance: The Results of a Paradigm Shift in the History of Mentality*, edited by Albrecht Classen (Berlin: de Gruyter, 2005), 67–85, in chapter 3 and the conclusion; and short portions of "Old Age and Women in the Carolingian World," in *Old Age in the Middle Ages and Renaissance: Interdisciplinary Approaches to a Neglected Topic*, edited by Albrecht Classen (Berlin: de Gruyter, 2007), 121–41, in chapters 1 and 4 and the conclusion. I also thank Dennis M. Kratz for permission to reprint several lines of his translation of the poem *Waltharius*, in *Waltharius and Ruodlieb*, edited and translated by Dennis M. Kratz (New York: Garland Publishing, 1984), in chapter 4. Short portions of "Learned Women? Liutberga and the Instruction of Carolingian Women," in *Lay Intellectuals in the Carolingian World*, edited by Patrick Wormald and Janet L. Nelson (Cambridge: Cambridge University Press, 2007), 121–38, appear in chapters 2, 3, 4, and 5.

The intellectual and financial support of many institutions made completion of this book possible. The University of Virginia Graduate School of Arts and Sciences and the Corcoran Department of History as well as the Northern Illinois University Division of Research and Graduate Studies, College of Liberal Arts and Sciences, and History Department provided funds for research and travel. I am also indebted to the Fulbright Commission of Austria and the University of Notre Dame Medieval Institute for financial support. I am grateful for the help of staff at Alderman Library, University of Virginia; Founders Library, Northern Illinois University; the Institut für Österreichische Geschichtsforschung; the Forschungsstelle für Geschichte des Mittelalters, Österreichische Akademie der Wissenschaften; the Österreichische Nationalbibliothek; the Fakultätsbibliothek für Katholische Theologie, Universität Wien; the Biblioteca Queriniana; the Archivio di Stato e Archivio Storico Civico Brescia; the Emeroteca e Basi Dati Brescia; the Musée des Tissus de Lyon, especially Marie-Jo de Chaignon; Hesburgh Library and the Medieval Institute, University of Notre Dame; the Library of Congress; the Vatican Library and Museum, especially Guido Cornini and Claudia Lega; the St. Afra Diözesanmuseum, especially Renate Mäder; the Bibliothèque Municipale, Arras; the Bibliothèque Nationale de France; the Koninklijke Bibliotheek van België; the Bibliothèque Municipale de

Douai; the Universitäts- und Landesbibliothek Düsseldorf; the Centrale Bibliotheek der Rijksuniversiteit Gent; the Koninklijke Bibliotheek Nederland; the Karlsruhe Landesbibliothek; the Bibliothèque de l'Université de Mons-Hainaut; and the Bibliothèque Municipale de Saint-Omer.

Among others from whom I received generous support, references, or advice were Stuart Airlie, Taylor Atkins, Cordelia Beattie, Scott Bruce, Caroline Walker Bynum, Cristina Cervone, Albrecht Classen, Richard Corradini, Amber Croy, Abe Delnore, Allyson Delnore, Max Diesenberger, Paul Dutton, Peter Erhart, Alberto Ferreiro, Mary Garrison, Pat Geary, Eric Goldberg, Sarah Hamilton, Yitzhak Hen, Marion Hoppe, Matthew Innes, Mayke de Jong, Bob Katz-Rühl, Annette Kern-Stähler, Lezlie Knox, Conrad Leyser, Felice Lifshitz, Amy Livingstone, Leslie Lockett, Jonathan Lyon, Louisa Mattozzi, the late June Mecham, Dimitri van Meenen, Rob Meens, Jinty Nelson, Catherine Nielsen, Helmut Reimitz, Jenny Ruff, Axel Stähler, Roland Steinacher, Rachel Stone, Amy Murrell Taylor, Patricia Werbrouck, Lara Diefenderfer Wulff, and Philip Wynn. I also thank Mildred Budny and Dominic Tweddle for permission to reproduce their photographs of the Maaseik embroideries. Mike Dawson saved me days of work with his expert technical advice. I am particularly thankful for the wonderful teachers at the Child Development Lab at NIU, whose care for my daughter made it possible for me to finish this book.

Words are hardly sufficient to thank my husband, Robert Feldacker, for his unfailing encouragement, support, and love. For the many hours he spent listening to me talk about the Carolingians and, most of all, for our beautiful daughter Rachael I am endlessly grateful. I am also fortunate to come from an extended family that has always prized learning. I am especially thankful for my grandparents, my brother Lee, and the entire Feldacker family. Finally, my greatest thanks goes to those who have always set an example of what it is to be good scholars, teachers, and people—my parents. It is to them that I dedicate this book.

ABBREVIATIONS

Primary Works

AASS	Acta Sanctorum
AB	*Annales S. Bertiniani*, in *Annales de Saint-Bertin*, eds. Félix Grat, Jeanne Vielliard, and Suzanne Clémencet (Paris, 1964).
AF	*Annales Fuldenses*, MGH SRG 7, ed. Friedrich Kurze (Hanover, Germany, 1891).
Agius, *Vita Hathumodae*	Agius, *Vita Hathumodae*, MGH SS 4 (Hanover, Germany, 1841), 166–75.
Alcuin, *LVV*	Alcuin, *Liber de virtutibus et vitiis*, PL 101.2, cols. 613–38.
BE	*Brevium exempla*, in *Capitulare de villis. Cod. Guelf. 254 Helmst. der Herzog August Bibliothek Wolfenbüttel*, ed. Carlrichard Brühl (Stuttgart, Germany, 1971).
CAC	*Cartulaire de l'abbaye de Cysoing et de ses dépendences*, ed. I. de Coussemaker (Lille, France, 1886).
CDLang	*Codex diplomaticus Langobardiae*, Historiae Patriae Monumenta 13, ed. Porro Lambertenghi (Turin, Italy, 1873).
CDLong	*Codice Diplomatico Longobardo*, Fonti per la storia d'Italia 63, ed. Luigi Schiaparelli (Rome, 1933).
CV	*Capitulare de villis. Cod. Guelf. 254 Helmst. der Herzog August Bibliothek Wolfenbüttel*, ed. Carlrichard Brühl (Stuttgart, Germany, 1971).
Dhuoda, *LM*	Dhuoda, *Handbook for her Warrior Son. Liber manualis*, ed. and trans. Marcelle Thiébaux (Cambridge, 1998).

Einhard, *VK*	Einhard, *Vita Karoli magni*, ed. Georg Heinrich Pertz and G. Waitz, MGH SRG 25 (Hanover, Germany, 1911).
Ermold, *In honorem*	Ermoldus Nigellus, *In honorem Hludowici*, in *Ermold le Noir. Poème sur Louis le Pieux et Epitres au roi Pépin*, ed. and trans. Edmond Faral (1932; repr., Paris, 1964).
Hincmar, *DLR*	Hincmar of Rheims, *De divortio Lotharii regis, Responsio 12*, MGH Conc. 4, suppl. 1, ed. Letha Böhringer (Hanover, Germany, 1992).
Hincmar, *OP*	Hincmar of Rheims, *De ordine palatii*, MGH Fontes 3, ed. and trans. Thomas Gross and Rudolf Schieffer (Hanover, Germany, 1980).
Hucbald, *Vita Rictrudis*	Hucbald of St. Amand, *Vita sanctae Rictrudis viduae*, AASS May 3, 79–89.
Huneberc, *Vita Willibaldi*	Huneberc of Heidenheim, *Vita Willibaldi episcopi Eischstetensis et vita Wynnebaldi abbatis Heidenheimensis*, MGH SS 15.1, ed. O. Holder-Egger (Hanover, Germany, 1887), 80–117.
IS	*Institutio sanctimonialium Aquisgranensis*, ed. Albert Werminghoff, MGH Conc. 2.1 (Hanover, Germany, 1908), 421–56.
Jonas, *Institutione*	Jonas of Orléans, *De institutione laicali*, PL 106, cols. 121–278.
Karolus Magnus	*Karolus Magnus et Leo papa. Ein Paderborner Epos vom Jahre 799*, eds. Helmut Beumann, Franz Brunhölzl, and Wilhelm Winkelmann, Studien und Quellen zur Westfälischen Geschichte 8 (Paderborn, Germany, 1966).
Liudger, *Vita Gregorii*	Liudger, *Vita Gregorii abbatis*, MGH SS 15.1, ed. O. Holder-Egger (Hanover, Germany, 1887), 63–79.
Mansi	Sacrorum conciliorum, ed. Giovanni Dominicus Mansi.
MGH	Monumenta Germaniae Historica
Capit.	Capitularia, *Capitularia Regum Francorum*, 2 vols. (Hanover, Germany, 1883–97).
Conc.	Concilia, 6 vols. (Hanover, Germany, 1893–1987).
Ep.	Epistolae, 8 vols. (Hanover, Germany, 1887–1939).
Ep. S	Epistolae selectae, 5 vols. (Hanover, Germany, 1916–1952).
Fontes	Fontes Iuris Germanici Antiqui in usum scholarum separatim editi, 15 vols. (Hanover, Germany, 1909–2000).
Libri mem.	Libri memoriales, 2 vols. (Hanover, Germany, 1970–2001).
Libri mem. N.S.	Libri memoriales et Necrologia, Nova series, 6 vols. (Hanover, Germany, 1979–2004).

SRG	Scriptores rerum germanicarum in usum scholarum separatim editi, 75 vols. (Hanover, Germany, 1871–2002).
SRM	Scriptores rerum Merovingicarum, 7 vols. (Hanover, Germany, 1885–1920).
SS	Scriptores, 38 vols. (Hanover, Germany, 1824–2000).
MS	Manuscript
Notker, *GK*	Notker, *Gesta Karoli*, MGH SRG 12, ed. Hans F. Haefele (Berlin, 1959).
Odo, *Vita Geraldi*	Odo of Cluny, *Vita sancti Geraldi Auriliacensis comitis*, PL 133, cols. 639–710.
PAI	*Polyptyque de l'Abbé Irminon avec des prolégomènes*, ed. Benjamin E. C. Guérard (Paris, 1844).
Paulinus, *LE*	Paulinus of Aquileia, *Liber exhortationis*, PL 99, cols. 197–282.
PCR	*Poetry of the Carolingian Renaissance*, ed. and trans. Peter Godman (Norman, Okla., 1985).
PL	Patrologia cursus completus, Series Latina, ed. J-P. Migne.
RCSBL	*Recueil des chartes de l'abbaye de Saint-Benoît-sur-Loire*, vol. 1, ed. Maurice Prou and Alexandre Vidier (Paris, 1907).
Rudolf, *Vita Leobae*	Rudolf, *Vitae Leobae abbatissae Biscofesheimensis*, MGH SS 15.1 (Hanover, Germany, 1887), 121–31.
Thegan, *Gesta*	Thegan, *Gesta Hludowici imperatoris*, MGH SRG 64, ed. and trans. Ernst Tremp (Hanover, Germany, 1995).
Theodulf, *Opus Caroli*	Theodulf of Orléans, *Opus Caroli regis contra synodum*, MGH Conc. 2, suppl. 1, ed. Ann Freeman (Hanover, Germany, 1998).
Vita Aldegundis	*Vita Aldegundis*, AASS January 2, 1040–47.
Vita Eusebiae	*Vita sanctae Eusebiae abbatissa Hammaticensi*, AASS March 2, 452–55.
Vita Herlinde et Renulae	*De sanctis virginibus Herlinde et Reinula*, AASS March 3, 386–92.
Vita Liutbirgae	*Vita Liutbirgae virginis*, in *Das Leben der Liutbirg*, ed. Ottokar Menzel, MGH Deutsches Mittelalter. Kritische Studientexte 3 (Leipzig, Germany, 1937).

Secondary Works

Coon, *SF*	Lynda L. Coon, *Sacred Fictions: Holy Women and Hagiography in Late Antiquity* (Philadelphia, 1997).
EME	*Early Medieval Europe*.

FG, vol. 7	Werner Affeldt and Annette Kuhn, eds., *Frauen in der Geschichte VII. Interdisziplinäre Studien zur Geschichte der Frauen im Frühmittelalter. Methoden—Probleme—Erbebnisse* (Düsseldorf, Germany, 1986).
FL	*Il futuro dei Longobardi. L'Italia e la costruzione dell'Europa di Carlo Magno*, eds. Carlo Bertelli and Gian Pietro Brogiolo (Milan, 2000).
FS	*Frühmittelalterlichen Studien.*
GEMW	*Gender in the Early Medieval World: East and West, 300–900*, eds. Leslie Brubaker and Julia M. H. Smith (Cambridge, 2004).
Herlihy, *OM*	David Herlihy, *Opera Muliebria: Women and Work in Medieval Europe* (Philadelphia, 1990).
JMH	*Journal of Medieval History.*
Kunst	*Kunst und Kultur der Karolingerzeit. Karl der Große und Papst Leo III. in Paderborn*, vols. 1–2, eds. Christoph Stiegemann and Matthias Wemhoff (Mainz, Germany, 1999).
Le Jan, *FP*	Régine Le Jan, *Famille et pouvoir dans le monde France (viie-xe siècle). Essai d'anthropologie sociale* (Paris, 1995).
LICW	*Lay Intellectuals in the Carolingian World*, eds. Patrick Wormald and Janet L. Nelson (Cambridge, 2007).
Ludwig, *TB*	Uwe Ludwig, *Transalpine Beziehungen der Karolingerzeit im Spiegel der Memorialüberlieferung. Prosopographische und sozialgeschichtliche Studien unter besonder Berücksichtigung des Liber vitae von San Salvatore in Brescia und des Evageliars von Cividale* (Hanover, Germany, 1999).
NCMH 2	*The New Cambridge Medieval History*, vol. 2, ed. Rosamond McKitterick (Cambridge, 1995).
PP	*Past and Present.*
Schilp, *NW*	Thomas Schilp, *Norm und Wirklichkeit religiöser Frauengemeinschaften im Frühmittelalter. Die Institutio sanctimonialium Aquisgranensis des Jahres 816 und die Problematik der Verfassung von Frauenkommunitäten* (Göttingen, Germany, 1998).
Settimane	*Settimane di studi sull'alto medioevo.*
Stafford, *QCD*	Pauline Stafford, *Queens, Concubines and Dowagers: The King's Wife in the Early Middle Ages* (Athens, Ga., 1983).
TRHS	*Transactions of the Royal Historical Society.*

Un village	*Un village au temps de Charlemagne. Moines et paysans de l'abbaye de Saint-Denis du viie siècle à l'an mil* (Paris, 1988).
Wemple, *WFS*	Suzanne Wemple, *Women in Frankish Society: Marriage and the Cloister 500 to 900* (Philadelphia, 1981).
WFSME	*Women, Family and Society in Medieval Europe*, ed. A. Molho (Providence, 1995).
WLFM	*Weibliche Lebensgestaltung im frühen Mittelalter*, ed. Dagmar B. Baltrusch-Schneider and Hans-Werner Goetz (Cologne, Germany, 1991).

WOMEN AND ARISTOCRATIC CULTURE
IN THE CAROLINGIAN WORLD

Introduction
WOMEN AND CAROLINGIAN SOCIETY

"For there are four reasons why men desire women: family, prudence, wealth, and beauty."[1] Thus wrote the Carolingian cleric Jonas of Orléans in his *De institutione laicali*, composed in the 820s to explain to laymen how they could lead a virtuous life. On the surface Jonas's list seems self-explanatory, a list of attributes that men doubtless have long desired in women. In fact, his choices mirror an earlier list of wifely characteristics in Isidore of Seville's *Etymologies* (c. 560–636),[2] who in turn drew upon ancient prescriptions concerning women's traditional roles. Since the early Christian era, prudence in women, for example, referred to domestic virtue. Resting upon old Roman ideals of the *matrona*, a woman was to bear children, care for her family, remain at home spinning, and maintain the good reputation of her husband and household. Yet it is safe to say that when Jonas wrote these words in the early ninth century he did so with the specific social conditions of his own day in mind. Certain cultural attributes were prized by the Carolingian elite, and each of Jonas's characteristics—beyond being desirable for centuries—reflect the expectations men had for women during the Carolingian rule.

In this book I argue that women, specifically elite women, were active participants in shaping and perpetuating the behaviors, beliefs, and practices that marked the culture of the Carolingian lands between c. 700 and c. 925. Their contribution to that culture remains very much in the background of texts

---

1. "Quatuor quippe sunt, quibus feminae viris appetibiles fiunt, genus, prudentia, divitiae, et pulchritudo." Jonas, *Institutione*, 2.12, col. 188.
2. "In eligenda uxore quattuor res inpellunt hominem ad amorem: pulchritudo, genus, divitiae, mores." Isidore of Seville, *Etymologiarum*, vol. 1, 9.7.29.

from that era, but by examining the rhetoric concerning aristocratic women it becomes clear that their actions were recognized and valued. Churchmen expected that elite women would participate in the dissemination of Christian reform, especially because women communicated regularly with those with whom clerics probably had the least contact: other women, children, and social inferiors. Aristocratic women had ample opportunity to transmit religious ideals and to persuade others to act with Christian virtue. According to her *vita*, the Saxon recluse Liutberga explained appropriate behavior to other women in her local community. Just as clerical authors of mirrors for laymen taught them how to pray, Liutberga instructed an aristocratic woman Pia to pray.[3] In this respect, expectations of women's participation in the Carolingian renaissance reflected clerical male understanding of women's positions and actions.

Carolingian women were participants not just in religious matters but also in the wider political, social, and cultural spheres of their day. In this regard women in both the religious and secular worlds had a great deal in common. Rather than separating women into these two categories, as has often been the case in early medieval scholarship, I explore the many similarities that linked elite female experience, regardless of profession, in the Carolingian world. Clerical and lay aristocratic values often intersected with respect to women. Ecclesiastical leaders recognized the need to make some allowances for the lay elite. Religious men tolerated certain potentially sinful behaviors, characteristics, or possessions that marked high status among laywomen so long as those women cultivated a domestic virtue in order to prevent a life of excess (*luxuria*). Thus aristocratic women could employ an opulent appearance to demonstrate familial wealth and prestige and to enhance the status of men as members of the elite.

Jonas gives us one way to think about early medieval women; modern scholarship offers a different approach. In the quarter century since the publication of Suzanne Wemple's groundbreaking *Women in Frankish Society*, historians have increasingly turned to gender as an analytic tool for examining the ways that women in the early Middle Ages participated in and changed the broader society around them.[4] Following the lead of this scholarship, I present a gendered investigation of women's experiences in Carolingian lands that considers both ideals and social practices. Strictly dividing "ideal" and "reality" is impossible; indeed it is useful to consider the two notions together as they

---

3. *Vita Liutbirgae*, chap. 35, 41.
4. Wemple, *WFS*; Smith, "The Problem of Female Sanctity in Carolingian Europe c.780–920"; idem, "Did Women Have a Transformation of the Roman World?"; Nelson, *The Frankish World*; Le Jan, *Femmes, pouvoir et société dans le haut Moyen Âge*; and the essays in *GEMW*.

emerge from the sources. Stephanie Hollis, Clare Lees, and Gillian Overing have argued, for example, that clerics in Anglo-Saxon England sometimes obscured contemporary women's roles in society because they emphasized a view of women based on earlier traditions.[5] Nevertheless these scholars argue that it is possible to learn about Anglo-Saxon women by examining those ideals, their variations, and their deviations. Such an approach can be usefully applied to Carolingian sources as well.

Though not all scholars agree on a single definition of gender, most acknowledge that gender relies upon norms and beliefs, not upon objective observations of men and women.[6] In this book I use gender to refer to the social and cultural expectations of men and women and the ways in which perceived differences of femininity and masculinity affected social relations. The relative degree to which gender influenced early medieval women has been the subject of some debate, but gender was fundamental in forming female identity in the Carolingian world.[7] From the moment a girl was born, her femininity shaped her expectations and her ability to work in her own interests, though naturally status, religious estate, age, and kinship affected her perception of herself as well as others' assessment of her. Gender also influenced the society around her, especially with respect to how the Carolingian elite often measured the power and success of individual men and women upon their ability to embody idealized masculinity and femininity.[8]

In some ways this book hearkens back to Eileen Power's efforts in the 1920s and 1930s to examine seemingly ordinary aspects of women's lives.[9] Power demonstrated that the everyday experiences of women provided rich context for the social, economic, political, and religious understanding of the Middle Ages. Few scholars immediately followed up on Power's insights, but a burst of scholarship in the first half of the 1980s initiated the concentrated interest in early medieval women that has persisted in the United States.[10] Although

5. Hollis, *Anglo-Saxon Women and the Church*; Lees and Overing, *Double Agents*.
6. Smith, "Gender and Ideology in the Early Middle Ages," 52–53; idem, "Introduction: Gendering the Early Medieval World," 4–8.
7. Goetz, "Frauenbild und weibliche Lebensgestaltung im fränkischen Reich," 41–43; McNamara, "Women and Power through the Family Revisited," 24–25.
8. Here I rely upon Joan W. Scott's seminal idea of gender as a way to "signify relationships of power," but I do so as a means to make the active participation of women in the Carolingian elite visible. "Gender: A Useful Category of Historical Analysis," 1067, 1075.
9. Eileen Power, *Medieval Women*; idem., *Medieval People*. Prior to Power's work, Lina Eckenstein's *Women Under Monasticism* was practically the only work available in English on medieval women.
10. For relevant bibliography, see Miri Rubin, "A Decade of Studying Medieval Women, 1987–1997," and the annual bibliographic updates of Chris Africa in the *Medieval Feminist Forum*.

this scholarship was critical in laying the basis for the study of early medieval women, one of its fundamental conclusions—that women became increasingly restricted to the household and convent in the Carolingian period—no longer seems so certain. Relying mainly on prescriptive evidence, these historians sometimes overlooked the opportunities that women had to influence those around them.[11] They also tended to see a strict division between lay and religious women. In recent years, scholars of the early Middle Ages have increasingly found innovative ways to tap into the lives of women using a wider range of textual sources.[12] It is becoming clear in the process that the experiences of elite women, religious and lay, often overlapped. Specifically, I argue that their common efforts to create and perpetuate aristocratic culture linked them.

I realize that to some it may seem that this book is advancing a traditional agenda—making the actions of the female elite visible. However, when studying early medieval women, it is the aristocratic women who are consistently visible in surviving sources.[13] Lisa Bitel's recent survey of early medieval women makes a commendable effort to focus upon "ordinary" as well as powerful women.[14] Yet the extant sources limit the areas of women's lives one can examine. The most poorly documented women of the early Middle Ages are those numbered neither among the powerful elite nor among the peasants listed in inventories of estates. This lack of evidence pertaining to the countless free women who lived on Carolingian lands makes any discussion of them relatively conjectural.

Hans-Werner Goetz has suggested two avenues by which to approach the study of early medieval women: the ideal way others thought women should conduct their lives and the reality of how they could lead their lives.[15] My study takes both approaches into consideration while arguing that we can learn a great deal about women's preservation and transmission of elite culture by concentrating on the ways in which clerical discourse and social

---

11. McNamara and Wemple, "Marriage and Divorce in the Frankish Kingdom"; Jane Tibbetts Schulenburg, "Sexism and the Celestial *Gynaeceum*—from 500 to 1200"; idem, "Strict Active Enclosure and Its Effects on the Female Monastic Experience (ca 500–1100)"; idem, "Women's Monastic Communities, 500–1100"; McNamara, *Sisters in Arms*, esp. 149–51.

12. Stafford, *QCD*; Ennen, *Frauen im Mittelalter*; Goetz, *Frauen im frühen Mittelalter.* Also see the collected essays in *FG*, vol. 7, and *WLFM.*

13. Evidence for the lower strata of early medieval society is both more opaque and less abundant. Kuchenbuch, "Trennung und Verbindung im bäuerlichen Werken des 9. Jahrhunderts," 230–37; Affeldt, "Lebensformen für Frauen in Frühmittelalter," 68; Obermeier, "Ancilla"; Devroey, "Femmes au miroir des polyptyques."

14. Bitel, *Women in Early Medieval Europe, 400–1100.*

15. Goetz, "Frauenbild und weibliche Lebensgestaltung," 7–8, 41.

practice shaped one another. All early medieval people contended with substantial social, economic, and political conventions that affected their ability to act as they might wish.[16] Some of these constrictions were gendered. Early medieval aristocratic women certainly had their own *Lebensform* (way of life) because of their gender and particularly because of their reproductive capacity and the biological differences in life expectancy, aging, and relative maturity between men and women.[17] Nevertheless, elite women created a way of life for themselves through the very constrictions placed upon them.

There is a relatively large corpus of work on royal women in the early Middle Ages, but this book widens the focus to include all female members of the Carolingian elite.[18] Far more direct evidence remains concerning queens or the daughters, sisters, and mothers of kings than other women, but because royal women often came from aristocratic families or married into them, differentiating sharply between royal and aristocratic women would obscure the continuum along which all elite Carolingian women ranged. Religious women have received even greater scholarly attention.[19] Distinguishing between lay and religious disguises the fact that status and gender gave women common experiences. When powerful abbesses and queens worked in their own interests, for instance, clerics and other writers often reacted adversely. They believed that such actions were not in keeping with female virtue—early medieval women were rather to work for the benefit of their spiritual and natal families.

The Carolingian era was transformative in European history for both men and women. The map of modern Europe began to take shape during the ninth century, following the 843 Treaty of Verdun by which Charlemagne's grandsons divided the empire in three. The erudition of Carolingian scholars changed European culture. Their synthesis of Roman, Christian, Germanic, and Hebrew traditions in nearly all aspects of life resulted in the composition of a rich body of texts, construction of beautiful buildings that made statements of power, fabrication of fine artworks ranging from manuscripts to metalworks to ivories, and the development and spread of religious learning

---

16. Werner, "Les femmes, le pouvoir et la transmission du pouvoir," 372.

17. Herlihy, "The Natural History of Medieval Women," 57.

18. Konecny, *Die Frauen des karolingischen Königshaus*; Nelson, "Queens as Jezebels"; idem, "Women at the Court of Charlemagne"; Stafford, *QCD*; idem, *Queen Emma and Queen Edith*; de Jong, "Exegesis for an Empress."

19. Muschiol, *Famula Dei. Zur Liturgie in merowingischen Frauenklöstern. Beiträge zur Geschichte des alten Mönchtums und des Benediktinertums*; Nolte, *Conversio und Christianitas*; Schulenburg, *Forgetful of Their Sex*; Schilp, *NW*.

throughout western Europe.[20] During the late eighth and ninth centuries, clerics under royal patronage wrote various texts and helped to formulate laws at church and secular councils meant to bring about increased consistency in practice and belief.[21] Reformers concerned themselves with issues ranging from acceptable rules for the religious life to mandatory recitation of the Creed and Lord's Prayer by the laity, from prohibitions of work on Sundays and holidays to the regulation of marriage; from chastisements for immoral behavior by priests, abbesses, monks, nuns, and laypeople to attempts to improve clerical education.[22] Almost nothing escaped their purview.[23] These comprehensive, organized efforts reveal great ambition even if they ultimately never gained full implementation.[24] Indeed the fruits of these reforms and the artistic and literary revival that accompanied them merit the title of renaissance.[25]

The originality of the Carolingian renaissance rested upon an ability to draw from older texts and traditions while applying them to contemporary exigencies. Carolingian rulers, especially Pippin the Short, Charlemagne, and Louis the Pious, worked to implement a degree of religious uniformity in Carolingian-controlled lands, and the sons and grandsons of Louis the Pious carried on smaller-scale programs of reform within their own kingdoms. A Frankish-papal alliance developed in the mid-eighth century between Carolingian rulers, who desired papal legitimacy after their usurpation of kingship from the Merovingian family, and popes, who wanted Frankish protection from the Lombards. Over time, Charlemagne and his heirs gained access to many important manuscripts through their alliance with the papacy. They also engaged the papacy in major theological debates, but popes did not direct Carolingian rulers to make specific reforms, and textual evidence reveals inconsistencies in papal and officially sanctioned Carolingian views on certain Christian practices.[26] Furthermore, great variety marked ideas of reform: rulers

---

20. See among other works Riché, *The Carolingians*, and Hageneier, Laudage, and Leiverkus, *Die Zeit der Karolinger.*

21. Among the many works on this subject, see McKitterick, *The Frankish Church and the Carolingian Reforms;* Wallace-Hadrill, *The Frankish Church*, 162–389; and the relevant essays in *NCMH* 2.

22. Carolingian capitularies and records of synods and councils are full of such legislation. For examples, see *Concilium Vernense*, 32–37; *Admonitio generalis*, 52–62; *Admonitio ad omnes regni ordines*, 303–7; *Capitulare Olonnense*, 316–17, all in MGH Capit. 1; *Capitulare Carisiacense*, MGH Capit. 2.2, 285–91. Also see Meens, "Religious Instruction in the Frankish Kingdoms."

23. John J. Contreni, "Learning in the Early Middle Ages," 9.

24. Sullivan, "The Carolingian Age."

25. Jean-Jacques Ampère first coined the term "Carolingian renaissance" in 1839. *Histoire littéraire de la France avant le XIIᵉ siècle*, 32–35.

26. For some discrepancies in liturgical texts see Hen, *The Royal Patronage of Liturgy in Frankish Gaul to the Death of Charles the Bald (877)*, 84–89, and in images see Noble, *Images, Iconoclasm, and the Carolingians.*

and clerics promoted learning and cultural activity quite broadly—efforts that produced diverse results.[27] Some of the changes this Carolingian renaissance brought were quite practical: the propagation of schools and scriptoria, where manuscripts could be copied in a new uniform script, Caroline miniscule; reforms to church liturgy so that ideally one could hear the same mass throughout Carolingian lands; and an effort to build a system of standardized legal and administrative practices in the empire, especially through church councils and the issuing of capitularies, prescriptive lists of acts, edicts, and instructions on nearly every topic imaginable.

Carolingian reformers contended with many cultural, social, religious, legal, political, and economic issues in direct response to the world around them. Reflecting their broad desire that reform respond to perceived needs, ecclesiastical leaders encouraged women to spread good Christian practice and demonstrate virtue to others.[28] Of all the Carolingian reforms, the ideas concerning this female role had perhaps the greatest effect upon women's lives. Women therefore participated in the Carolingian renaissance but not always in the same ways or to the same degree as men. Clerical demands that elite women be moral exemplars found fruition, for example, in the aristocratic laywoman Dhuoda's composition of a book of advice for her absent son William in the early 840s. Female participation in the vibrant literary production of this era allowed for some of their contributions to the Carolingian renaissance.[29] Religious women produced manuscripts that responded to the wider reforms in script, Latin grammar, and dissemination of texts. Some religious women copied texts, and some may have written original texts themselves. If the *Prior Metz Annals* were produced at the double monastery of Chelles where Charlemagne's sister Gisela was abbess, it is possible a woman (or women) wrote them.[30] A number of women wrote letters including various Carolingian queens, the abbess Leoba, and Charlemagne's daughters, who displayed their love of learning by asking the court scholar Alcuin (735-804) to write a commentary on the Gospel of John for them.[31] Nonetheless relatively few have investigated women's contributions to these changes, particularly the ways in which religious rhetoric touched upon women.

---

27. Contreni, "Inharmonious Harmony," 83.

28. Nelson, "Les femmes et l'évangélisation au ixe siècle."

29. Contreni, "The Carolingian Renaissance," 716–17.

30. Beumann, "*Nomen imperatoris*. Studien zur Kaiseridee Karls des Grossen," 529; Hoffman, *Untersuchung zur karolingischen Annalistik*, 53–61; Nelson, "Perceptions du pouvoir chez les historiennes du haut Moyen-Âge," 80–82. For a good summary of the debate over the authorship of the *Prior Metz Annals*, see Fouracre and Gerberding, *Late Merovingian France*, 337–39.

31. MGH Ep. 4, ed. Ernst Dümmler (Berlin, 1895), no. 342, 25–7.

Carolingian clerical views of women were often ambivalent, neither consistently negative nor wholly positive. When Carolingian churchmen advocated marriage as a beneficial institution among the laity, they echoed the works of earlier thinkers, but they recognized the ways wives could act constructively within their families. Compared to many of their late antique and eleventh- and twelfth-century counterparts, some Carolingian theorists can come across as less misogynist.[32] The Carolingian renaissance and traditional expectations nevertheless limited opportunities for women. Ecclesiastical leaders believed laywomen should focus on the domestic sphere, explaining how they should best be wives, mothers, and heads of households and estates, similarly to the ways they described the duties and actions of abbesses in hagiographical texts. The late ninth-century abbess of Gandersheim Hathumoda, for example, looked after her flock with great care, tended the sick, including her elderly aunt, and ensured the religious instruction of the girls in her charge.

Male lay aristocratic necessities and desires sometimes came to be reconciled with the goals of Carolingian religious reform. In the *Liber exhortationis* of c. 795, a book of advice for the layman Eric of Friuli, Paulinus of Aquileia described hell as the elite world turned upside down. Using examples that would make an impression upon a male lay aristocrat, Paulinus writes that hell is a place

> where there is not any honor, or recognition of closest kin, but unremitting sorrow and pain; where death is desired and is not given; where there is no esteem of the older man and king, nor is the lord above the servant, nor does the mother love son or daughter, nor does the son honor the father; where all evil, and the anger and stench and acrimony of all abound.[33]

Paulinus emphasized social bonds, underlining their importance in the Carolingian world. A hierarchy of personal relations regulated the well-ordered aristocratic world, and elite men wished to gain offices and recognition that could maintain and promote their power and authority. Men conceived of and wrote about women in ways that reflected their desire that women aid them in these tasks; though highly idealized, the specific female actions and expectations, which Carolingian texts encouraged or took for granted, reflect the activities women either undertook or conceivably could undertake. Notice that Paulinus discusses a mother's love and a father's honor; other clerics also assumed the prominence of parent–child relations among lay aristocrats, particularly singling out the mother for her nurturing role. This passage

---

32. Heene, *The Legacy of Paradise*, 266–67.
33. Paulinus, *LE*, chap. 49, col. 253.

helps to reveal one reason why ecclesiastical leaders emphasized motherhood: the laity prized it. Paulinus equates the repercussions of the rupture of these personal bonds with the torments of hell in order to convey to his aristocratic audience how terrible damnation is. As did Jonas of Orléans in his *De institutione laicali*, Paulinus exhorted the laity to behave in a Christian manner, but molded his ideas to conform to lay life. In great part, these two bishops understood the demands and contingencies of the lay world because they were born into it and because they remained part of the aristocratic milieu beyond consecration.

Examining these predominantly male texts, one can see that the rhetoric concerning elite women and reform changed over the period of Carolingian rule, but by the reign of Louis the Pious (814-840) it had begun to stabilize. The models of the first third of the ninth century remained influential at least into the early tenth century. This development had repercussions for the long-term history of Western women, for it marked a key period in reshaping older perceptions of women in lasting ways. During the rule of Pippin the Short and more notably under his son Charlemagne, men began to write about women in new ways. Although virtuous wives and mothers had long been associated with worthy households, in the early ninth century reformers began to spell out that role more clearly. For example, the bishops at the Council of Meaux-Paris in 845 insisted that noble men and especially noble women look after the morality of their households.[34] In other words, women had an active role in propagating and maintaining a Christian society. In this regard, the Carolingian renaissance shaped the Western perception of women as exemplary models and informal teachers for children, other women, and individuals of inferior status.

The experiences of Carolingian women can be seen as part of the ongoing project of remaking classical culture north of the Alps. Carolingian rhetoric concerning women drew from the Roman and sometimes (through late antique intermediaries) the Greek past. When Theodulf of Orléans argued in the *Opus Caroli* (792–93) that women ought not teach publicly, he drew upon not only Paul of Tarsus but also upon the same classical idea of woman as weaker vessel that had influenced Paul.[35] The holy woman Liutberga studied scripture, hymns, and psalms, becoming so learned that were it not for the "weakness of her sex" she could have taught well.[36] She did, however, help

---

34. Canon 77, MGH Conc. 3, ed. Wilfried Hauptmann (Hanover, 1984), 63–132, at 124. Of course, looking after one's household had its limits. The bishops at Meaux-Paris were careful to stipulate that sinful inferiors be sent to priests for correction.

35. Theodulf, *Opus Caroli*, 3.13, 388–89.

36. *Vita Liutbirgae*, chap. 5, 13.

other women develop piety and domestic virtue. At the same time Carolingian writers continued to associate ancient gendered practices such as textile work with morality. Penelope wove and unraveled in her husband Odysseus's absence in order to preserve her virtue. Carolingian nuns engaged in textile work to prevent idle gossip.

Ecclesiastical leaders molded their exhortations to women in ways that reflected contemporary social practice, consciously interpreting ancient models in ways that conformed to the needs of their own time. This delineation of female duties contributed to the transformation of Christian culture under the Carolingians as secular and ecclesiastical leaders worked to bring increased order and harmony to religious practice. Numerous sources offer evidence that women carried out the activities that churchmen advocated. For example, Queen Emma gave a belt to a bishop, a prominent example of fulfilling clerical demands that women provide textiles to churches. Old models helped to shape the ways women could act, offering boundaries that women sometimes transgressed. Dhuoda, for instance, instructed her child in Christian practices such as praying and giving alms just as men had long expected that mothers should, but she asserted her authority to do so in written form, inserting her words and her presence at the royal court, where her son was a hostage. She instructed her son on ostensibly male affairs advising him to exercise caution in dealing with powerful men.

This book reveals that women had agency to affect both their society and their own presentation in contemporary texts. Churchmen wrote all but a handful of these sources to address other topics, providing us with a masculine and elite vision of Carolingian society that reflects the clerical view of monks and priests. Ninth-century advice books for men, for instance, have passages that often touch upon women and their social roles.[37] Though I employ texts not typically associated with the history of women and gender, the evidence for both cultural expectations and activities of women displays relative consistency and quantity across many source types. Prescriptive texts offer regulations concerning women; annals and other historical works sometimes comment upon the actions of queens or abbesses; and hagiography and literature present rather idealized pictures of aristocratic women.[38]

This evidence poses certain problems. First, only rare Carolingian sources provide a woman's voice; Dhuoda's handbook for her son is the best known.

---

37. There are no Carolingian advice books for women.

38. I have excluded some sources that reveal little about social practice. Penitentials, for example, probably do not reflect everyday sexuality. Brundage, *Law, Sex, and Christian Society in Medieval Europe*, 152–75; Meens, *Het Tripartite Boeteboek*, 276–84, 561–62.

Employing gendered analysis helps to overcome this difficulty; nevertheless we are primarily left with the male view of women. Furthermore, these sources reflect only the experiences and ideas of the elite. By addressing the subject of aristocratic culture, my hermeneutic position can help to overcome both of these problems for I address a subject of profound concern to the elite, including many male clerical writers. Rather than addressing a topic beyond the scope of these sources, such as female friendship or women's attitudes to marriage, this study embraces the limitations of the sources, making them the subject of study. So long as I account for its genre, author, audience, models, and purposes, I can often use the asides or incidental details of a text to help to reveal information concerning women. When these elements do not come from an earlier model or advance the purposes of a text, it is frequently possible to assume that they reflect contemporary norms and practices.

I take an interdisciplinary approach, examining a wide range of sources: textiles, exegesis, archaeological remains, poetry, liturgy, letters, inventories, lay mirrors, charters, polyptychs, capitularies, church councils, hagiography, and memorial books. In addition to examining material evidence, I address written mentions of material culture. Cemetery remains, for example, help to support estimates of female longevity based upon written works. Elite women's control over and organization of goods marked their daily activities and affected their presentation in sources. Lay and religious aristocratic women frequently had responsibility for acquiring, commissioning, and producing textiles. As such, they were both fabricators and patrons of this art form.[39]

In order to gain the most evidence, I cast my net widely, examining sources from all areas ruled by the Carolingians from the beginning of the eighth century to the first decades of the tenth century. The phrase "Carolingian women" therefore refers not only to women of the Carolingian ruling family but to all elite women living under their rule. "Membership" in the aristocracy remained fluid throughout premodern Western history, with individuals attaining and losing recognition as members of the elite from generation to generation.[40] In the Carolingian Empire status as a magnate or aristocrat depended heavily on: access to and display of wealth, especially land; ability to exert power over others; close proximity to the king (Königsnähe); a respected

---

39. Only a handful of studies address early medieval female production of textiles and integrate that work into the general historical picture. Budny and Tweddle, "The Maaseik Embroideries"; Herlihy, *OM*; Budny, "The Byrhtnoth Tapestry or Embroidery"; Goldberg, "*Regina nitens sanctissima Hemma*."

40. For the early Middle Ages, see the essays in Reuter, *The Medieval Nobility*, and Le Jan, *La royauté et les élites dans l'Europe carolingienne*. For the rest of the Middle Ages see Reynolds, *Fiefs and Vassals*. For the early modern period see the essays in Bush, *Social Orders and Social Classes in Europe since 1500*.

family background, close bonds with other members of the elite; appointment to royal offices; and the status of women with whom men associated. Writers either directly identified or implied that numerous women of wealth, good family, and learning were aristocratic.

Noble markers and participation in the activities of the elite constitute what I will term aristocratic culture—the set of knowledge, practices, beliefs, and behaviors that helped individuals identify themselves as members of the elite and aided others in recognizing them as such. To be sure, aristocratic culture refers to a modern understanding of past beliefs and ideas; early medieval people did not write specifically about such a conception. Some historians might question whether an aristocracy existed at all in the eighth and ninth centuries. By aristocracy, I mean an open elite, with a membership defined by certain cultural practices and understandings. Scholars have increasingly sought to determine the markers and self-understanding (*Selbstverständnis*) or self-awareness (*Selbstbewußtsein*) of an aristocrat. Because men and women shared this elite culture, men also transmitted it to others, and their activities are at the forefront of many sources. Less clear have been the ways women helped to produce and perpetuate aristocratic culture. Their duties concerning the instruction of children and domestic management gave them increased opportunity to convey practices, beliefs, behaviors, and knowledge to others. Because women—aristocratic, free, half-free, or unfree—often transmitted their status to their children, others may have expected women to transmit the culture that defined their rank.[41] Association with male aristocrats indicated a woman's membership in the elite. The daughters, wives, mothers, and sisters of magnates and kings were aristocratic as were those accepted into the circles of the powerful in the Carolingian world, and contemporaries recognized as noble those holding extensive lands, moveable wealth, or high office, such as abbesses. Women identified as aristocratic in this book therefore had one or more of these status markers.

As in much history of the poorly documented past, this study relies on relatively sparse evidence, but its conclusions are grounded in careful readings of the Carolingian texts mentioning women. Employing a disciplined imagination offers one way to deal with the sometimes intractable sources related to Carolingian women. By a disciplined imagination, I mean an approach to texts that takes careful account of the strictures of convention, earlier models, and contemporary circumstances in order to suggest highly probable female actions and behavior. For this reason, this book is to some degree speculative

---

41. Some free women, who married unfree men, and their families may, however, have had to negotiate the freedom of their future children. Rio, "Freedom and Unfreedom in Early Medieval Francia," 17–21.

and I cannot claim to offer definitive conclusions concerning female actions much less purport to have reconstructed ninth-century social reality. In order to study some areas, particularly household management, I suggest the activities for which women almost certainly had responsibility based on the existing evidence. For example, according to prescriptive texts, gardening seems a probable activity of religious and lay aristocratic women, and the discovery of a watering can at an excavation of the convent of Herford helps to bolster the veracity of that impression. By employing this methodology, this book explores little studied areas of female life, especially commemorative prayer, beauty, textile work, and domestic management. Rather than ignoring evidence of a problematic nature, I employ difficult sources, sometimes offering speculative readings when no other analysis is possible. It is better to address these subjects in this manner than not to address them at all. In other cases, I have gleaned asides and remarks from many sources by paying rigorous attention to the details of texts. Because I am interested in perceptions and discourse, I consider as evidence letters composed in Anglo-Saxon England that ended up in Carolingian hands and *vitae* written about Merovingian women in the ninth and tenth centuries. Such prescriptive sources can reveal the responsibilities and actions of women as well as the ideals that others urged upon them. Individual prescriptions did not necessarily demand actions or behaviors that did not already occur; they could be meant to reinforce or shape them. Because the audience for female *vitae*, mirrors, and letters consisted mainly of women and laymen, it is hardly surprising that they promote domesticity and feminine virtue.[42]

Many sources, but especially hagiography, provide circumstantial details revealing women's roles in aristocratic culture. The authors of *vitae* hoped mainly to demonstrate that an individual was worthy of veneration. In order to accomplish this task, they often borrowed heavily from earlier *vitae*, making some Carolingian *vitae* highly formulaic. Furthermore, hagiographic texts frequently employed topoi, sometimes making it difficult to determine whether the events they relate have much bearing upon social practice. When certain information is incidental or does not appear in other *vitae*, they quite possibly provide circumstantial details about Carolingian life. The *Vita Liutbirgae* twice mentions that the aristocratic woman Gisla had to travel among her estates.[43] These passing references corroborate other evidence for female supervision of family lands.

Conscious selection marked each author's or scribe's choice of certain words or motifs. One ought not to dismiss tropes, ideals, and repetition of

---

42. Smith, "The Problem of Female Sanctity," 25, 35; Coon, *SF*, 147–51.
43. *Vita Liutbirgae*, chaps. 3, 4, 11, and 13.

earlier texts as mere copying of earlier models. To reject the content and connotation of topoi and passages of older texts is as much a mistake as taking them literally. Ernst Curtius identified many topoi and formulae but never dismissed their potential resonance for a contemporary audience.[44] Examining antique and earlier medieval texts circulating in the Carolingian world proves helpful at times to understanding views and social practices of eighth- and ninth-century women. Earlier texts exerted a profound influence on portrayals of early medieval women in historical texts and emphasized virtue in depictions of both lay and religious women.[45] Topoi also frequently reflected the needs of aristocratic families and society. Poetry employed traditional motifs that reveal male expectations and sometimes provide supporting evidence for behaviors or practices described elsewhere. Royal and aristocratic women in poems are always beautiful in similar ways—richly adorned, white skinned, they display the wealth and power of their families, helping to clarify why Jonas of Orléans mentioned beauty as a desirable characteristic in his lay mirror. One can read topoi in reverse, finding in disapproval of women the ideal characteristics men desired. For example, Regino of Prüm wrote that an aristocratic woman, Friderada contributed to the deaths and problems of her successive husbands through lack of virtue.[46] Her case is similar to the better-known and better-documented queens of the mid-ninth century, such as Judith and Theutberga, who suffered accusations of sexual immorality.

Approaching Carolingian sources broadly reveals the relatively wide scope women had to act in their society despite the legal and social constrictions. Official limitations did not restrict women as closely as once thought; Carolingian women sometimes attained their objectives within those bounds. In fact, the institution of such limits reveals a concern on the part of Carolingian clerics and rulers with the ways women helped to promote the power and prestige of aristocratic families. Had women been strictly confined to their religious houses or to their households, they might not have been able to preserve portions of the family patrimony as easily or promote the careers of their husbands and sons as successfully. The letter Lull, archbishop of Mainz, wrote to Suitha in 754 chastising her and her fellow nuns for ignoring their religious duties and enjoying lay delights reveals that some tried to enforce such legislation. Suitha and her sisters were to go as penitents, consuming only bread and water and abstaining from meat and drinks they enjoyed.[47] Though

---

44. Curtius, *European Literature and the Latin Middle Ages*, 149–50, 161–62, 175–76, 202.
45. Portmann, *Die Darstellung der Frau in der Geschichtsschreibung des frühen Mittelalters*.
46. Regino of Prüm, *Chronicon*, 121.
47. *Die Briefe des Heiligen Bonifatius und Lullus*, 265–66.

we do not know what became of Suitha and her sisters, this letter suggests that ideas concerning strict claustration represented more than empty rhetoric. In contrast to some earlier scholarship on Carolingian women, I examine the particular ways women acted in their own interests within the contours of their specific bounds rather than try to define precisely where those limits lay. A number of scholars have noted in the last twenty years that such boundaries were in any case permeable and fluid.[48]

Many women were aware of clerical exhortations that they lead upright lives. Those women who were literate surely read texts concerning virtuous behavior.[49] Religious women in particular could have attained some knowledge of Latin grammar and writing as some of them produced manuscripts or wrote texts.[50] In the religious life female teachers instructed young girls; a letter from one of these pupils to her *magistra* even survives.[51] Extant evidence suggests that the lay elite enjoyed many of the same texts and artworks as did their religious counterparts. For example, the ninth-century magnate Eberhard of Friuli and his wife Gisela owned a rich library, containing theological, historical, and practical books.[52] Similarly, some learning allowed laywomen to instruct their young children and to inculcate virtue in their households. Clerics rarely discussed such instruction explicitly, rather mentioning it in asides in texts on other subjects. Rather than preventing women from learning, churchmen encouraged them to attain the knowledge necessary to be a virtuous Christian. Oral transmission of ideas was a prime part of Carolingian women's lives; that relative informality may help to explain the lack of discussion of female instruction in surviving sources.[53] Mothers' care for children contributed to the dynamics of early medieval aristocratic families.[54] According to the early tenth-century anonymous *Vita Aldegundis*, the saint's mother provided an inverse model: when the young Aldegund ran out of alms to distribute to the poor, she thought that she ought to give

---

48. In this regard, my approach draws heavily from the works of Hans-Werner Goetz, Régine Le Jan, Janet L. Nelson, Julia M. H. Smith, and Pauline Stafford.

49. Most arguments pertaining to literacy depend heavily upon the definition being used, but many aristocratic women almost certainly had some familiarity with Latin even if they could not compose Latin or read complex Latin texts. McKitterick, *The Carolingians and the Written Word*; idem, "Women and Literacy in the Early Middle Ages."

50. Bernhard Bischoff, "Die Kölner Nonnenhandschriften und das Skriptorium von Chelles"; Lifshitz, "Gender and Exemplarity East of the Middle Rhine"; idem, "Demonstrating Gun(t)za."

51. *IS*, canon 22, 452; Universitäts- und Landesbibliothek Düsseldorf B3, fol. 308ᵛ.

52. *CAC*, no. 1, 4.

53. Nelson, "Women and the Word in the Earlier Middle Ages," 68–70.

54. Stafford, *QCD*, 143–74; Nelson, "Family, Gender and Sexuality in the Middle Ages"; Le Jan, *FP*, 56, 348–49.

away the money that her mother, Bertilla, hid. Naturally, the holy Aldegund resisted this temptation.[55] This saintly act also speaks to female supervision of wealth.

Our understanding of early medieval social relations should better account for women's roles. Wives contributed more to their marital families than producing and instructing heirs, though broader Carolingian scholarship tends to emphasize these two duties. Although early medieval marriage had legal, social, and economic consequences for both partners, a woman's efforts in perpetuating aristocratic culture brought some intangible benefits to her marriage. The beauty and social competence that men sought in women contextualizes the more material aspects of elite unions. A wife may have squandered wealth and family connections without an eye for effective display.

Women contributed to the collective memory of the Carolingian aristocracy. Their acts of remembrance connected them to others, especially their spiritual and religious families, and made them cognizant of their membership in the elite. Maurice Halbwachs argued that all memory is reconstructed based on common recollection.[56] His conception of memory is applicable to consideration of female commemorative acts within a larger social context during the eighth to ninth centuries. A goal of early medieval commemoration was to create bonds among the living and between the living and the dead, but it also served to help individuals recall their noble backgrounds and connections to other members of the elite.[57] This conception of these female actions conforms to Rosamond McKitterick's premise that the memory and commemoration of the past in the written record was a means for Carolingians to develop identities.[58] Annals, histories, and letters provide information on the gendered nature of medieval memory: both men and women worked to preserve memory in a variety of ways. Elite women helped their families remember and construct identities that made them and others aware of their high status. Their participation in commemoration helped them retain bonds to their kin, to other families, and to institutions such as monasteries and churches.[59] When women at the convents of Remiremont and San Salvatore in Brescia kept copies of charters and maintained their memorial books—which contained lists of the living and the dead for whom they were to pray by employing the liturgical texts also recorded in the codices—they participated

---

55. *Vita Aldegundis*, chap. 17, 1044.
56. Halbwachs, *The Collective Memory*, esp. 31–33.
57. Such social memory is similar to many of the examples discussed in Fentress and Wickham, *Social Memory*, esp. 87–172.
58. McKitterick, *History and Memory in the Carolingian World*, esp. 7 and 282.
59. Geary, *Living With the Dead in the Middle Ages*; idem, *Phantoms of Remembrance*; van Houts, *Memory and Gender in Medieval Europe*; Innes, "Keeping It in the Family."

in developing an "archival" or historical memory, that is the (re)collection of past events.[60] As Mary Carruthers argued, medieval people did not separate oral and literate forms of memory, often understanding books as devices to help in recalling. Like most individuals prior to the Renaissance, they experienced the written word by listening to a reader.[61] Hearing the names listed in these memorial books probably produced visual images in the minds even of women who had no direct contact with those texts. Furthermore, participation in liturgical rites of commemoration helped the women to recall the past and relate it to the present.[62]

Exploring women's various economic and social roles clarifies political relations in the Carolingian world, providing a gendered vantage often missing in much early medieval political history. Men and women needed every possible advantage to help them successfully navigate elite society. The landholding and related bonds and alliances that governed that world shifted frequently. Disputes over land were frequent. Early medieval society was highly litigious, though the many remaining eighth- and ninth-century charters reveal only those cases that involved the religious institutions that preserved the documents. Furthermore, the late eighth and ninth centuries witnessed a number of rebellions against the Carolingian ruler; shifts in alliances among aristocratic families were relatively frequent and sometimes resulted in bloodshed.[63] No male aristocrat, including the king, could assume his power would remain secure.[64] Succeeding in this arena required political acumen, the ability to negotiate alliances with and among other aristocrats, and awareness of the behaviors, beliefs, and possessions that marked a member of the elite. Women could aid men in these areas of expertise with appropriate conduct, demeanor, and appearance.[65] Just as scholars have noted incipient aspects of knighthood, nascent forms of courtesy or courtliness appear in Carolingian sources, showing that these later movements had roots in the early Middle Ages and late antiquity.[66]

---

60. For this form of memory see Nora, "General Introduction: Between Memory and History," 7–10.

61. Mary Carruthers, *The Book of Memory*, 16–18.

62. On the importance of rites in social memory, see Connerton, *How Societies Remember*, esp. 41–71.

63. Brunner, *Oppositionelle Gruppen im Karolingerreich*; Fouracre, "Attitudes Towards Violence in Seventh- and Eighth-Century Francia"; Nelson, "Violence in the Carolingian World and the Ritualization of Ninth-Century Warfare."

64. Airlie, "Narratives of Triumph and Rituals of Submission," 25.

65. For male-oriented examinations of these issues see Koziol, *Begging Pardon and Favor*; Nelson, "Peers in the Early Middle Ages," 28–31.

66. On knighthood see Leyser, "Early Medieval Canon Law and the Beginnings of Knighthood"; Nelson, "Ninth-Century Knighthood."

As the Carolingian Empire gradually fragmented during the ninth century, elite families came increasingly to imitate the royal family, and women had greater opportunity than before to advance their own interests and those of their families. Carolingian texts reflected the need to employ expected behaviors, such as female hospitality, in order to develop those bonds. According to an early ninth-century *vita*, the abbess of Pfalz Addula provided hospitality to the missionary Boniface and used the opportunity to advance the interests of her grandson, Gregory of Utrecht.[67] Queens and women at court had access to the goods of the household, giving them opportunities to shape the provision of hospitality. Such female labor involved humble but necessary tasks such as the recycling of wax, which could allow for the provision of light or for lining containers to store or serve food and drink.[68] Despite many scholarly attributions of responsibility for household management to early medieval aristocratic women, no one has yet systematically explored female supervision of labor.[69] Bringing such efforts to light places women squarely in the current historical discourse concerning the early medieval economy.

"Family, prudence, wealth, and beauty" in women provided advantages to aristocratic men, both lay and clerical, explaining why Jonas of Orléans emphasized them. I begin my study with the two seemingly most self-explanatory characteristics—beauty and family. These are traits determined greatly by birth, though women found ways to improve upon or surpass what birth had provided them. Some clerics wrote about female beauty as a possible indication of female virtue, but in lay society it could serve to display the status of male kin. Women could alter their appearance using material items to enhance or create a pleasing impression. Men also had their female kin connect them to other families, including the royal family, through marriage and through religious communities making those women members of marital and spiritual families.

Prudence and wealth offered women ample opportunity to act and were therefore less accidents of birth than tools women could employ. Each offers new opportunities to consider how men understood female social practice. Defining precisely what Jonas meant by *prudentia* is difficult, but it is the only characteristic in his list that alludes to female actions. Carolingian aristocratic women possessed a social competence, that is a knowledge of the actions and behaviors that allowed them to instruct their children, act as moral

---

67. Liudger, *Vita Gregorii*, chap. 2, 67–68.
68. *Vita Aldegundis*, chap. 16, 1044.
69. Herlihy, *OM*, 43; Kuchenbuch, "*Opus feminile*"; Bitel, "Reproduction and Production in Early Ireland," 72.

exemplars to those around them, supervise households and estates, make shrewd decisions concerning the management of resources and the advancement of their kin, and find ways to exert power despite the legal, social, and political constraints that bound them. Heiresses brought wealth and status to their spouses, while women's management of household and convent helped to preserve the wealth of those institutions. Women, along with men, held and transmitted land, a principal marker of an aristocrat. Their possession and donation of that land helped to preserve the memory of their families and ensure the commemoration of their kin as did female prayer and participation in the liturgy of commemoration. Laywomen almost certainly organized rich, appealing display in household and court. Their supplying of fine textiles to religious houses allowed for rich decoration in those institutions. Extant Carolingian sources reveal that their authors took account of these conventional female roles in aristocratic culture, at the same time shaping and being shaped by them.

Textile work unites Jonas's characteristics. Aesthetic considerations were crucial to fabrication and display of cloth in both liturgical and lay settings: not least clothing could profoundly affect contemporaries' assessment of a woman's beauty. Supervision of a household necessitated knowledge of textile work because textiles comprised essential components of the material culture that marked Carolingian aristocrats. Traditional ideas, advanced especially by male clerics, and female work on textiles built upon each other to give cloth and clothing crucial roles in Carolingian aristocratic culture. Through their association with textiles women could advance the interests of their families and convents, demonstrate their virtue, and play a vital economic role. Each of these acts related to textiles required the exercise of women's prudence.

Female social practices and related rhetoric concerning women were essential to the political, social, economic, and cultural transformations of the Carolingian era, and indeed influence the heirs of the Carolingians in the West to this very day. Men had similar expectations of the behavior and abilities of lay and religious women, who had far more in common with each other than with their male counterparts. Carolingian reforms often reveal that clerics understood the lives of aristocratic women, and they promoted expectations of women that encouraged them to cultivate their virtue and to use their conventional duties for broader purposes. This book argues for the many prominent ways in which women produced, maintained, and shaped elite culture in the Carolingian world. Because of the nature of both the sources and traditional historical approaches, this role has too often been absent in studies of both early medieval women and aristocratic culture. Crisscrossing and comparing disparate sources rarely employed in conjunction with each other allows exploration of much new territory and re-evaluation of seemingly well-examined subjects. These efforts not only produce a new image of elite women as producers and transmitters of the culture that marked the Carolingian aristocracy but also demand re-evaluation of the male-dominated world in which they lived.

Chapter One
BEAUTY
Appearance and Adornment

When men and women at the Carolingian court heard or read the description of Charlemagne's sister from the epic panegyric poem *Karolus Magnus et Leo papa*, composed after either Pope Leo's visit to Paderborn in 799 or the imperial coronation in 800, they doubtless appreciated its interlocking meanings concerning female beauty.[1]

> Gisela followed them in shimmering white,
> Accompanied by the band of virgins she gleams along with the golden
>   offspring. Covered in a mallow colored cloak she shines,
> Her supple veil of purple thread has a reddish glow,
> Voice, face, hair shimmer with radiating light.
> Her white neck shines, lit with a rosy blush,
> Her hand appears to be made from silver, her golden brow flashes,
> And the lights of her eyes conquer the great Phoebus.[2]

Gisela's physical appearance conveys brightness, light, and wealth. Contemporary readers at court would immediately have understood that Gisela's shining, beautiful appearance revealed her inner virtue because of the color symbolism.[3] For late antique and early medieval audiences, such symbolism

---

1. Ratkowitsch, *Karolus Magnus—alter Aeneas, alter Martinus, alter Iustinus*, 9–10; Banniard, "La réception des *carmina* auliques," 48–49.

2. *Karolus Magnus*, 76, lines 229–38.

3. Bede's tract on the symbolic meaning of colors and stones enjoyed relatively wide dissemination and influence across early medieval western Europe. Eleven extant manuscripts from Carolingian monasteries and nine mentions of the work in ninth-century Carolingian

made the invisible visible.[4] White and silver symbolized purity and virginity. The association of gold with faith, love, and wisdom meant "her golden brow" complimented Gisela, a learned abbess who corresponded with perhaps the greatest of her brother's court scholars, Alcuin. The purple of her veil and cloak would have been extremely costly, and purple was associated with humility, a highly appropriate virtue for an abbess.[5]

This description also conveys more concrete meanings. Gisela physically appears to be treasure—golden, silver, and shimmering. As abbess of Chelles, she was not supposed to wear jewelry or clothes embroidered with valuable materials, but the poet has made her physical being as rich as the opulent adornment associated with elite laywomen in Carolingian poetry. Those lavish depictions conveyed the wealth and power of the court and the king. Aristocratic male display of richly adorned, lovely women gave them prestige and a means of marking their own high status and power. Thus, the description's sumptuousness points to the potent connection between beauty and splendid display. In the poem Gisela had come out with Charlemagne's female relatives to see off a hunting party, an opportunity to flaunt the royal family's wealth and power. At the same time, the reference to Phoebus reveals the poet's reliance upon antique models and ideals of appearance and rich adornment, which remained highly influential into the Carolingian era. Discerning some of the specific meanings for Carolingian audiences in such literary passages reveals both a rich discourse on female beauty and certain practical realities that made the presence of attractive women an expected part of aristocratic culture.

Both lay and religious women shared the burden of living up to these expectations. As an external, visible characteristic, appearance immediately caused others to identify women in particular ways. A woman's dress, bearing, and physicality almost immediately indicated her lay or religious status. Veiling, for example, demonstrated a woman's consecration whereas a pregnant body suggested another's fulfillment of the lay duty of biological motherhood. Yet men believed that beauty in both lay and religious women demonstrated similar qualities—aristocratic status, access to wealth, and internal virtue. Their lovely demeanor adorned both their lay households and religious communities. This heretofore unexamined but highly significant quality of early

---

booklists indicate its popularity among the Franks. Laistner, *A Hand-List of Bede Manuscripts*, 5, 10–14, 25–30. Among the late antique and Carolingian writers who addressed these issues were Cassiodorus, Gregory the Great, Isidore of Seville, Alcuin, Raban Maur, and Walafrid Strabo. Haupt, *Die Farbensymbolik in der sakralen Kunst des abendländischen Mittelalters*, 51–117.

4. Ladner, *God, Cosmos, and Humankind*, 2.

5. Haupt, *Die Farbensymbolik*, 68–69, 78, 113.

medieval women demands detailed examination, not pat assumptions that male beliefs concerning female appearance remained relatively unchanging in the West. Clerical discourse allows glimpses of women's beauty through a male gaze. Of all the characteristics that Jonas mentioned, this one is most difficult to study: learning anything about women's actions through their appearance is nearly impossible. Female beauty is the most external quality whose history has been shaped primarily by men.

Although Carolingian conceptions of female beauty rest firmly within a longer history of its association with wealth and virtue, the particular ways writers described or addressed women associated with powerful men reveal much about contemporary understanding of those conventional norms. Eighth- and ninth-century sources contain frequent references to the beauty of royal and aristocratic women, especially saints and queens, as do antique and later medieval texts, but scholars have taken their loveliness for granted, often assuming it was merely a trope or an obvious male desire. Precisely because such an expectation in aristocratic women seems self-explanatory, it demands attention. What made a woman attractive was no more self-evident in the Carolingian world than in different places and periods. Conceptions of beauty are constructed, not innate. Beauty certainly mattered to the Carolingian elite; various sources touch upon theological and philosophical ideas concerning aesthetics and male desire for pretty women. Eighth- and ninth-century men expected and appreciated the pleasing physicality and rich adornment of women for their contribution to the status of the men to whom those women were related or married. The clothing, jewelry, and other adornments associated with aristocratic women in this era were costly items that demonstrated the wealth of women and their families. Clerics understood that beauty mattered on all of these levels: its role in aesthetics; a connection between physical attractiveness and virtue in the highly religious and aristocratic; and a recognition of lay desire for rich and lovely display in female kin.

Ecclesiastical leaders took an interest in female appearance, for it provided a means to think about the larger issues of the morality of both the laity and the religious. The connection between beauty and goodness allowed writers to reinforce an image of domestic virtue associated with women through their textile work, moral exemplarity, rearing of children, and preservation of family bonds. Clerics warned, however, that beauty did not always indicate virtue. Religious men wrote against the sin of vanity, and they warned that a pretty woman could blind men to her faults. They recognized that women had long created and maintained desirable personal appearances. In order to promote Christian behavior among both the lay and religious elites and to prevent men and women from falling into sin or error, they frequently wrote about the proper place of female appearance in aristocratic society.

To be sure only some women were physically attractive regardless of their dress or adornment, but all aristocratic women probably were aware of the ways they could enhance their own appearance through right comportment and rich display. Discussions of female vanity indicate that, though the descriptions of panegyric cannot be accepted at face value, contemporary women did, in fact, adorn themselves in an effort to create a pleasing appearance. Late antique and Merovingian women had dressed themselves richly, drawing in part from Roman traditions of displaying treasure. As the early church developed ideas of decoration and use of treasure that emphasized the connection of gold with the divine, such displays began to take a Christian role. A saint who had rejected worldly vanities, for example, could be depicted in heaven adorned with gems indicative of her virtue and new status.[6] Gisela therefore shone with a natural, pious beauty, not the cultivated looks of a laywoman. Among the items the Merovingian queen Radegund (c. 525–587) distributed to the poor upon entering the religious life was her jewelry, and she heaped other personal riches upon an altar.[7] In making such donations, she put the vanities of the world to fitting Christian use. Embroidery in the form of jewelry adorns the "chasuble of Chelles," the remains of a seventh-century chemise associated with another Merovingian queen Balthild (d. c. 680).[8] Archeological artifacts from Merovingian sites include necklaces, bracelets, hairpins, brooches, and fasteners found with female remains; these items often seem to mark the status of the buried women.[9] Carolingian aristocratic women continued to adorn themselves with expensive clothing and jewelry, though contemporary sources rarely directly address the mechanisms of this social practice. That conventional female act must nevertheless have affected the way clerics and others discussed female vanity and acknowledged the ability of beauty to affect others.

Moving from the discursive to the practical aspects of female beauty permits understanding of the ways biblical and antique ideals affected everyday concerns in the Carolingian world. A cursory examination of how some ecclesiastical leaders at this time commented upon the issue of aesthetics will provide a foundation for understanding why and how Carolingian theologians and scholars concerned themselves with beauty and its effects more broadly conceived. A variety of texts touch upon female appearance, and bishops wrote the majority of them. At the same time that these learned men were

6. Janes, *God and Gold in Late Antiquity*, 75–82, 165–69.

7. Fortunatus, *De vita sanctae Radegundis*, 1.13, 369.

8. Laporte, "La chasuble de Chelles," 1–29.

9. Halsall, "Female Status and Power in Early Merovingian Central Austrasia," 5–6, 23; Müller, *Die Kleidung nach Quellen des frühen Mittelalters*, 263–64.

concerned with perhaps the greatest controversy of their era, the long debate concerning images, they often wrote for and about the laity. As scholars they engaged in theological debate; as priests they performed liturgical acts and interacted with lay peers and inferiors. Their comments on beauty reflect their broad range of interests. To examine in isolation the various texts they wrote risks missing the ways in which discourse on sensible or material beauty touched upon understanding not only of women but also of Christian society as a whole. In the West, loveliness had long carried an implication of virtue especially in descriptions of the highly religious and aristocratic, and an examination of different texts—exegesis, hagiography, panegyric, mirrors, and historical works—demonstrates that the precise strength of that connection varied depending upon the audience for and function of these particular genres. Lay aristocrats probably conceived of female beauty in the rather concrete terms of rich display and attractive physicality that helped them to demonstrate their wealth and status. It is in the approbations against vanity, display, and desire for pretty women that one can discern the integral role that female beauty played in aristocratic culture.

Carolingian Aesthetics

The early medieval controversy over images began in the Byzantine Empire in the mid-eighth century, and by the late eighth century, the papacy, the Carolingians, and the Anglo-Saxons among others were engaged in an ongoing debate on the proper understanding and use of images. One particularly important cause of this wide-ranging discussion was a faulty papal translation of the Greek proceedings of the Second Council of Nicaea in 787; it erroneously indicated that the Byzantines had advocated the adoration (*adoratio*) of images. The papacy sent this inaccurate Latin translation to Charlemagne's court and unleashed "a storm of controversy."[10] From the late eighth to mid-ninth centuries, in response to the arguments of Second Nicaea and ensuing debates, clerics produced various texts concerned mainly with images that remarked on decoration and the power of beauty to influence the observer. Because it was a cause célèbre of their era, the image controversy affected the ways clerics understood sensible beauty whether in terms of aesthetics or of female appearance. Carolingian theologians did not write extensively about aesthetics per se, but their texts provide essential background to Carolingian clerical thought concerning female beauty. Naturally, one cannot

---

10. Freeman, introduction to Theodulf, *Opus Caroli*, 1.

equate a liturgical vessel or image with a living, breathing woman; nevertheless, when discussing attractive women, men frequently described them as the means of displaying expensive objects that projected male power and/or they presented an ideal image of women, rather than providing an objective observation of female appearance. Particularly in panegyric, as seen in the description of Gisela above, poets sometimes described women as a form of treasure, and lay mirrors indicate that men desired women for their pleasing physicality. In hagiography and exegesis, idealized female beauty results from internal virtue, and clerics expected that such loveliness could influence the observer, sometimes inspiring piety or, in the case of Judith and Holofernes, arousing lust. An examination of Carolingian aesthetics helps to demonstrate more fully how contemporaries understood the potential effects of beauty.

Texts concerning images and those addressing female good looks drew upon a common intellectual heritage. Through antiquity and the earlier Middle Ages, numerous Western and Eastern philosophers and theologians had examined beauty, and Carolingian writers drew in large part from this classical and late antique tradition, often through writers such as Cassiodorus (c. 490–580), Gregory the Great (c. 540–604), and Isidore of Seville (c. 560–636).[11] Plato's ideas, for example, naturally shaped conceptions of beauty in the Carolingian era, but only through the works of intermediate authors.[12] Augustine's writings exerted a direct influence on these Carolingian clerics; alongside Pseudo-Dionysus, he remained one of the principal authorities on aesthetics throughout the Middle Ages.[13] In Augustine's view, art could have an anagogical effect because artworks are the product of God filtered through the artist. Particularly in his earliest writings, he argued that beauty resulted from a piece's mathematical qualities: harmony, symmetry, number, unity, and proportion. Artworks, literature, or music with such characteristics delighted the observer. He reiterated these ideas in his later texts, putting increased emphasis on art's anagogical possibilities: beauty (*forma*), he insisted, is inseparable from its God-given existence. Delight in art could lead a person to further knowledge of God, therefore serving a valuable purpose.[14] Carolingian clerics concerned themselves with this idea when they worked to understand how aesthetically pleasing objects affected people. In their

---

11. Eco, *Art and Beauty in the Middle Ages*, 15–16, 92.

12. Plato argued that all virtues come from the highest plane of his world of ideas where Goodness and Beauty are one. This relation between the good and the beautiful continued into the Christian era. Ladner, *God, Cosmos, and Humankind*, 183.

13. Weitmann, *Sukzession und Gegenwart*, 20.

14. Harrison, *Beauty and Revelation in the Thought of St. Augustine*, 21–39, 54.

works regarding images they drew from forerunners such as Augustine but developed their own ideas, including discussions of aesthetics and beauty.[15]

The best known of these texts is the *Opus Caroli regis* of 792–93, in which Theodulf of Orléans argued that images were not worthy of veneration. The *Opus Caroli* reveals an opinion at Charlemagne's court, but after its completion it did not circulate widely.[16] Although Theodulf argued against their veneration, he asserted that images could be used to decorate and commemorate; he did not, however, argue that they should be used for those purposes.[17] He maintained that art was permissible, not that it was necessary. He probably appreciated beautiful ornament in adorning churches, as evidenced by the apse mosaic in Germigny-des-Prés, which he had built.[18] Yet Theodulf thought that the visible did not necessarily lead the soul to God; rather an individual could make spiritual progress only by grasping the invisible.[19] Scholars may disagree about whether Theodulf thought images could be instructive, but at the very least they agree he privileged the written word over images.[20]

Despite his preference for the written word Theodulf argued that some objects had a place in Christian worship. He made allowances for sacred vessels, which were necessary for consecrating the wine and host of communion. Other items that created a hallowed atmosphere—images, holy water and oil, incense, and lights—were not necessary to consecration, but he did not suggest banning these items from sacred places. Theodulf separated the maker from the object. Painters could evoke the memory of events, but images did not necessarily provide truthful representations. An artist could be pious or impious; his images could depict pious or impious events or creatures; but his work could not be either.[21] The value of a piece of art lay in its materials and the skill of the artist.[22] Individual pieces could exhibit beauty and therefore have a high value, but that worth did not arise from the image itself.

---

15. Noble, *Images, Iconoclasm, and the Carolingians*, addresses many of these issues.

16. Following the Colloquy of Paris in 825, Theodulf's work disappeared into the palace archive and had little immediate influence, not resurfacing until Jean du Tillet's 1549 anonymous edition of the single surviving 850/860 manuscript. Freeman, introduction to Theodulf, *Opus Caroli*, 11–23; Weitmann, *Sukzession und Gegenwart*, 198–203, 216.

17. Theodulf, *Opus Caroli*, 2.21, 273–75.

18. Nees, "Art and Architecture," 818.

19. Theodulf, *Opus Caroli*, 1.18, 189–92, where Theodulf quotes Romans 8:24. Freeman, "Scripture and Images in the *Libri Carolini*," 163–88.

20. A key passage is Theodulf, *Opus Caroli*, 2.30, 303. For the argument that Theodulf thought images were instructive, see Freeman, introduction to Theodulf, *Opus Caroli*, 31–32, and for a contrary opinion, see Noble, *Images, Iconoclasm, and the Carolingians*, 222–23.

21. Theodulf, *Opus Caroli*, 2.29, 302; 3.22–3, 438.

22. Ibid., 2.27, 3.15, 3.16, 4.19; 294–95, 399–400, 410, 535. Freeman, "Scripture and Images in the *Libri Carolini*," 164–65.

In his brief discussion of images of pretty women, Theodulf noted that female appearance could be as ambivalent as beauty in its other forms. If one had two images of lovely women, one of Mary and one of Venus, made with the same colors and materials, until Mary's image received an inscription, he argued, no one would have reason to believe that image had the power to refer prayers to Mary any more than the image of Venus.[23] Theodulf wished to refute the idea that on its own, an image of Mary with Jesus could inspire worship. Beauty's presence did not necessarily indicate the concurrent presence of piety, holiness, or goodness, nor could it lead individuals to more devout belief or behavior. In the *Opus Caroli*, then, Theodulf reveals an ambivalent understanding of beauty, neither condemning nor advocating its possible effects.

Other Carolingian theologians reveal similar thoughts on aesthetics, beauty, liturgical objects, and women, but they often placed more value on the commemorative and decorative worth of objects than Theodulf. Although the Carolingian court was wary of venerating images, some believed that lovely items could serve useful purposes in church settings, and they understood that appearance could influence the ways people thought. Most of these other works appeared after the Paris Colloquy of 825, at which participants addressed the issue of images once again.[24] No fewer than five texts on images appeared after the Colloquy.[25] For the purposes of a discussion of Carolingian aesthetics, the most pertinent of them is the *Libellus synodalis Parisiensis*, a work in which those who attended the Colloquy carefully balanced the views of the Franks, Byzantines, and papacy on images. The *Libellus synodalis* offered, among other arguments, the idea that images could elevate the mind and teach.[26] Its authors wrote that liturgical vessels were holy only because they serve God in sacraments; intrinsically they do not demand worship.[27] In making the former argument, the authors went farther than Theodulf did in advocating the instructive benefits of images, but in the latter they maintained his principal argument that images should not be venerated, noting, as he had, that the necessity for some decorated religious objects did not make them worthy of adoration.

---

23. Theodulf, *Opus Caroli*, 4.16, 528–29.

24. The colloquy was a response to an 824 letter from the Byzantine emperor Michael II. He mentioned debate over images though it was not his main concern. Some of the most influential theologians of the day, including Jonas of Orléans, Freculf of Lisieux, Jeremias of Sens, Amalar of Metz, and Halitgar of Cambrai, came to discuss the issue and formulate a response to the renewed questions about images. Boshof, *Erzbischof Agobard von Lyon*, 140–41.

25. Noble, *Images, Iconoclasm, and the Carolingians*, 287.

26. *Libellus synodalis Parisiensis*, MGH Conc. 2.2, no. 44, chap. 76, 505–21.

27. Ibid., chap 61, 500. Here they quote Augustine and support his argument on this count. Noble, *Images, Iconoclasm, and the Carolingians*, 274.

These ideas did not go unchallenged. Following his investment in 817/8, Bishop Claudius of Turin allowed the destruction of images in his diocese. Louis the Pious had excerpts of Claudius's writings distributed to Jonas of Orléans and Dungal for refutation. Each produced a treatise. Jonas wrote *De cultu imaginum* over two periods—first between c. 825 and Claudius's death in 827, when the purpose of the treatise seemed moot, and again from c. 840 because Charles the Bald requested that he finish the work and because some of Claudius's disciples had become active.[28] The text addresses Claudius's major arguments against both the veneration and utility of images, and does not extensively address aesthetics. Jonas agreed with Claudius that images were not worthy of adoration, but he went significantly further than Theodulf in advocating their use. In a section in which he defended images from destruction while insisting they should not be venerated, Jonas wrote that images were made for decoration and commemoration, even repeating this idea as though to emphasize it.[29] Dungal, head of the school at Pavia, in his 827 *Responses* to Claudius, mentioned the unhappiness Claudius's policies had produced in the people of the region.[30] Dungal argued more strongly than Jonas for the utility of images. Citing Gregory the Great, he wrote that images were useful for the "unlettered" and the "ignorant," giving them what the literate could obtain directly from scripture. Using biblical evidence, he argued that pictures, which exist only to recall history and to praise and honor God, should not be destroyed.[31] Both Jonas and Dungal advocated the use of decoration, but they left open the question of the effect of the objects' beauty, arguing instead for their historical value.

In the mid-ninth century, Walafrid Strabo brought decoration and its effects on viewers to the forefront of the ongoing discussion of images in his handbook of liturgical history, *De exordiis et incrementis quarundam in observationibus ecclesiasticis rerum*, written sometime between 840 and 842.[32] The chapter "On Images and Pictures" offered a brief history of the image controversies. He began by arguing that pictures could be used to increase the splendor of churches, just as vestments and hanging cloths (*cortinae*) did. Even

---

28. Theutmir, the abbot of Psalmody and a former student of Claudius, wrote to him to object to this destruction. After 824, in response to Theutmir's criticisms, Claudius wrote the *Apology and Response of Bishop Claudius of Turin against Abbot Theutmir*, from which the excerpts come. Theutmir had sent that text on to the royal court. Noble, *Images, Iconoclasm, and the Carolingians*, 287–94.

29. Jonas of Orléans, *De Cultu Imaginem*, PL 106, at col. 318.

30. Dungal, *Responsa contra Claudium*, 2. The *Responsa* survives in two early ninth-century manuscripts. Zanna, introduction, xxiv.

31. Dungal, *Responsa*, chap. 16, 26–30.

32. Harting-Correa, introduction to Walafrid Strabo, *Libellus et incrementis*, 21–22.

though images should not be venerated, he argued, they should not be suppressed. He maintained that nothing could be so lovely that it would lead everyone astray. Although the ignorant may easily be deceived by the beauty and elegance of an object, that effect should not necessitate its destruction. The learned should know better, and Walafrid believed that pictures could serve as the literature of the illiterate, just as Gregory the Great and Dungal had argued. He believed that images were necessary for the practice of devotion and to attract the unlettered to unseen matters.[33] Thus, Walafrid brought the commemorative and instructive functions of images, emphasized by Jonas and Dungal, to the fore again. Given his pastoral interests, Walafrid took a moderate stance on images that allowed for their benefit to the laity in particular.[34] For Walafrid, pretty objects could help to instruct others—their very beauty could act as a means to attract those who could not fully understand things not visible to them.

Thus, in texts concerning images, a range of opinions marked the subjects of aesthetics, beauty, and decoration throughout the late eighth and ninth centuries. During that time most of those who wrote about images did not concern themselves much with decoration, though Jonas touched upon it.[35] Yet, by the second half of the ninth century, scholars seem to have established that liturgical objects, though not holy in and of themselves, served necessary functions. Furthermore, their potential splendor did not necessarily harm and might aid worshippers in their devotions. These writers offered relatively ambivalent conceptions of aesthetics, ideas that were remarkably similar to those concerning female appearance. Just as an image could depict a holy subject or a profane one, a pretty woman could be virtuous or sinful. Just as an attractive image could lead one astray or have the anagogical effect of bringing one closer to God, Carolingian texts depict pretty women leading men into error and lovely saints inspiring virtue in others. Given the antique and biblical models upon which men drew in addressing appearance, it is hardly surprising to find such consonance in their opinions.

Just as views concerning aesthetics varied in Carolingian texts on images, so too did specific meanings of beauty differ depending on the individual text, its purposes, and its audience. Descriptions of attractive women provide an idealized image of aristocratic culture in Carolingian lands. Although the textual realities constructed by Carolingian authors suggest the physical appearance of women, they do not offer concrete evidence for it. Only in the twelfth

---

33. Walafrid Strabo, *Libellus et incrementis*, chap. 8, 72–80.
34. Harting-Correa, introduction to Walafrid Strabo, Libellus, 14–15, 228.
35. For example, Agobard of Lyons' *Liber de imaginibus* (PL 104, cols. 199–228) did not touch upon decoration. See also Boshof, *Erzbischof Agobard von Lyon*, 139–58.

century, especially with the development of romances, can one find detailed accounts of individual appearance. Carolingian texts offer few details about corporeal human characteristics, making it impossible to discern what made a woman lovely or a man handsome. The textual realities constructed by Carolingian men suggest the physical features of women; they do not offer concrete evidence for them. Although we cannot travel through time to witness the appearance of that world, contemporary texts provide an opportunity to examine expectations and models that reveal the importance of a female presence in that world. A woman's attractiveness and the ways in which she might use that appearance for good or ill reflected not only upon herself but also upon her family. In particular the potential connection of female beauty with virtue and/or wealth made women an especially effective means of connoting textual images that conveyed wealth and power, and those textual images reveal contemporary expectations of female behavior and conduct.

Vanity and Wealth

Beauty obviously mattered on a theological and philosophical level, but it also had a crucial social role in helping to identify some women as members of the elite. Annals, hagiography, mirrors, and poetry from the period describe many aristocratic and royal women as beautiful. Good looks served equally as a sign of status and privilege for religious women and for laywomen. Both suffered accusations of vanity, and attractiveness made men associate both groups of women with certain attributes, especially virtue and wealth. In fact, female beauty was a powerful social force. Surely some women were lovely, but these references to beauty probably reveal more about expectations and flattery than reality. When Jonas of Orléans echoed Isidore of Seville, admitting that men pursued women for their beauty, he indicated that aristocratic men—like others in all times and places—found this attribute in women highly desirable.

Beyond sexual attraction and a desire to have a wife whom other men admired, some men pursued pretty women for material reasons. Female beauty and riches often went hand in hand because wealth may have been necessary to looking lovely. Although a woman could be born with natural good looks, she could enhance and maintain her appearance with sufficient wealth for opulent dress and a knowledge of how to adorn and comport herself. Thus, female physical desirability could be created as much as embodied. When providing hospitality to others on family estates or when at court, a pretty wife or daughter gave a man an opportunity to display the good fortune of his household. An attractive woman could literally wear her husband's wealth on her body as a marker of his status at occasions for the formation of aristocratic bonds. Such opportunities may have been especially important for those whose rank was not as clear as that of the royal family or the wealthiest elite. Men who wished to have others recognize them as aristocrats may have needed their female relatives richly adorned when attending court or going to church on a major religious feast, two key opportunities to be seen by other men in positions of power. The idealized images of the sources indicate certain practical concerns.

Affluence made beauty associated with rich adornment possible and further helped to identify certain Carolingian women as aristocratic. Scholars have long realized that high status for medieval men required wealth. Land provided the resources necessary to exert power, and opportune marriages to heiresses constituted one means by which men acquired property and goods.[36] Women often took donations of land with them into the religious life for the spiritual and material benefit of their family members. Thus, women transmitted land from family to family and from family to religious house, but they sometimes held land on their own: through gifts from their parents, husbands, or both at the time of marriage; as unmarried heiresses; and as widows. Wellborn Carolingian women possessed another asset, moveable goods, including rich clothing and jewelry. Moreover, they played a major part in looking after their households' financial matters. Thus, possession or control of substantial wealth constituted a principal characteristic that distinguished an aristocratic woman from her counterparts of lower status. Descriptions of richly adorned, lovely women called attention to their access to fortune.

Unfortunately, sources reveal little that indicates precisely what women and men actually wore in the Carolingian world. Manuscript illuminations and textual descriptions of dress are often drawn from antique sources and were meant to convey certain religious, political, and social messages more than describe dress through accurate observation.[37] Furthermore, few illuminations depicted women. One appears in the Bible of San Paolo fuori le Mura, produced during the reign of Charles the Bald (840–877), who is depicted in the Bible with two female figures. These women wear veils, chemises, and long tunics adorned with golden bands. Their only visible jewelry are long dangling golden earrings. Although it is possible to argue that they are figurative representations of the provinces paying tribute to the emperor, the poem at the bottom of this portrait mentions that Charles's "noble wife, beautiful as always" is to his left. The other woman may be her attendant. If this is the queen, her depiction is highly unusual; the artist probably included her in the

---

36. Reynolds, "Carolingian Elopements as a Sidelight on Counts and Vassals"; Schmid, "Heirat, Familienfolge, Geschlechterbewusstsein," 137.

37. Müller, *Die Kleidung nach Quellen*, 55–60.

portrait both to underline Charles's proper rule over his wife and household and, as the dedicatory poem indicates, to ask for God's help in ensuring that she would bear the king heirs.[38] Regardless of the identity of the women, their depiction conveys the wealth and power of Charles's court. Although most descriptions, like manuscript illuminations, of dress in the Carolingian world are idealized, we nevertheless know that women attended to their appearance from clerical denunciations of female vanity and the rejection of adornment by female saints. The challenge of promoting their own good looks, and by extension the beauty and prosperity of their households and religious houses, argues for an expectation of social competence among aristocratic women. Attentive household supervision sustained beauty and wealth through production of fine clothing and careful management of resources. Churchmen made choices based on cultural and social norms when describing the clothing, jewelry, and general appearance of women. While Carolingian sources provide relatively little direct evidence of female agency in employing their physical appearance for gain, they do indicate an expectation that women could use their beauty for their own or their families' benefit.

Clerical denunciations of vanity reveal that some men and women wished to maintain a pleasing appearance. These concerns were longstanding. The Hebrew Scriptures noted the danger of vanity; it could keep one too much in the present world without thought for God and others.[39] The influential early Christian writers Tertullian (160–220) and Jerome (c. 347–419/20) both criticized the ways Roman women adorned themselves, though presumably those women dressed a certain way in order to fulfill a traditional female role among the elite.[40] In his letters Alcuin frequently admonished his male religious correspondents to be modest in dress and avoid vanity.[41] In a letter to his former pupil Eanbald, who had just become archbishop of York, he shows a pronounced concern with male clerical vanity: "Do not seek needless adornment in dress. It is better for the servants of God to adorn the soul with the fashions of the church than to clothe the body as the laity do with vain show."[42] In Alcuin's opinion, some priests' dress conveyed their vanity and perhaps too strong an attachment to the luxuries of the lay world. At times

---

38. Kantorowicz, "The Carolingian King in the Bible of San Paolo fuori le Mura," 288, 291–94; Diebold, "The Ruler Portrait of Charles the Bald in the S. Paolo Bible," 7, 9, 12.

39. Psalms 119:37; Ecclesiastes 1:2, 12:8; Hosea 5:11.

40. Coon, *SF,* 37–8.

41. He directed his admonitions beyond his recipients urging them not only to have his letters read aloud but also to share his letters. The large surviving corpus of Alcuin's letters attests to his influence in the ninth century. Garrison, "Alcuin's World through His Letters and Verse," 23–36; Bullough, *Alcuin: Achievement and Reputation,* 35–105.

42. MGH Ep. 4, no. 42, 86.

Figure 1. A queen and her attendant? This rare depiction of Carolingian laywomen consists of two female figures who appear to the lower right of Charles the Bald (840–877) in his ruler portrait in the Bible of San Paolo fuori le Mura, folio 1ʳ. Reproduced by permission from Istituto Poligrafico e Zecca dello Stato.

Alcuin associates these faults with women, for vanity was a sin particularly linked with women in the Carolingian world. Such a connection had precedent in the Old Testament. A passage from Jeremiah (4:30) makes explicit the futility of adorning oneself: "And you, desolate one, what will you do? Why will you dress in scarlet? Why will you adorn yourself with ornaments of gold, and paint your eyes with a *stibium*? You will array yourself in vain."[43] Women were not to please others but rather God who cared little for worldly vanity: "Charm is deceitful, and beauty is vain, but a woman who fears the Lord is to be praised."[44] In their commentaries the early church fathers often understood dress in the Old Testament as an outward sign of an individual's piety. They associated male clothing with power and women's clothing with debauchery or the distance it created between humanity and God.[45] For these reasons, religious women especially began to dress modestly. Bishop Caesarius of Arles (c. 470–542), for example, insisted on humble dress in his rule for religious women.[46]

Carolingian writers continued this association of female adornment with vanity and sin. In a letter to Bishop Higbald, Alcuin wrote: "When he has taken care to forbid ostentation and costly clothing to women, how much more unseemly vanity in clothing is in men."[47] In letters to his female correspondents, he also urged restraint in dress. Writing to Gisela in c. 792 Alcuin stated:

> Your glorious bridegroom is illustrious, and seeks no other adornment in you than that of the spirit—no twisted plaits of hair, but straight conduct, no vain outward splendor of clothes, but a noble grandeur of purity within.[48]

His words echo Paul's first epistle to Timothy (2:9–10): "[I desire] also that women in decorous attire should adorn themselves with modesty and moderation, not with braided hair or pearls or costly clothing but with that which suits women, professing devotion through good works." In another letter to Charlemagne's daughters, Alcuin similarly wrote: "Dear daughter let proper conduct, works of mercy, and purity of life adorn you. Remember your rank, and may you be praised more for upright behavior than a display of shining gold."[49] The *Institutio sanctimonialium* of 816—a rule for religious women—expressly

---

43. See also Ezekiel 16:15–18.
44. Proverbs 31:30.
45. Coon, *SF,* 31–40.
46. Caesarius of Arles, *Regula virginum,* chap. 28, 206.
47. MGH Ep. 4, no. 21, 58–9.
48. Ibid., no. 15, 41.
49. Ibid., no. 164, 266.

forbade love of display, especially in the form of adornment, in religious women: "Transfer love of necklaces and gems and silk clothes to the knowledge of scripture."[50] In a later canon, the authors exhorted religious women to give up "silk clothes" and "pompous vanities."[51] In the late ninth century Agius wrote that Hathumoda (c. 840–874) mocked vanity and was contemptuous of anything that was not useful.[52] In the eyes of clerics throughout the eighth and ninth centuries, the ostentatious dress, jewelry, and hairstyles that only aristocratic and royal women could afford presented particular danger. These same sources hint that lay and religious women sometimes desired the same rich forms of adornment, an indication of cultural similarity despite a difference in profession.

Even the lay author Dhuoda mentioned female vanity in her book of advice for her son William. Urging him to consider her advice carefully, she compared the way he should regard her handbook to women gazing at themselves in mirrors in order to clean their faces so that they may appear radiant and beautiful to their husbands.[53] In so doing she turned the idea of female vanity on its head, first because her book was a mirror (*speculum*). She suggests in a rather humble and ironic manner that, because women are especially skilled with using mirrors, her femininity gives her authority to produce one of her own.[54] Second, she laid the blame for female vanity at the doorsteps of men who desired lovely wives, recognizing that social pressures may have led women to engage in activities that made them appear vain as a result of their efforts to please men.

A variety of sources reveals that those individuals recognized as aristocratic indeed looked different than their lower status counterparts, giving some clues as to what constituted a lovely or at least rich appearance. References to the beauty of women of unknown status are quite rare.[55] Surely aristocratic women looked different from women of lower status because they had a better diet and did not work outside or perform hard labor with their hands. Elite women's hands would have been relatively unblemished, and both aristocratic men and women would have had uncalloused feet because they consistently wore

---

50. *IS*, canon 3, 432.

51. Ibid., canon 7, 442.

52. Agius, *Vita Hathumodae*, chap. 2, 167.

53. Dhuoda, *LM*, Prologue, 46–48.

54. Dhuoda, *Handbook for William*, 115, note 33.

55. One episode may imply that a woman was pretty, without reference to good family, wealth, or virtue. In 882, Louis III, "because he was a youth," chased a girl identified as the "daughter of a certain Germund" on horseback into her father's house and struck his head so hard on the door lintel that he died. Conversely, this forceful attention or possible rape probably had less to do with female beauty than with male exertion of power. *Annales Vedastini*, 52.

shoes or boots.[56] In a mid-ninth–century poem, Sedulius Scottus described the white hands of Irmingard, wife of Lothar I.[57] Huneburc of Heidenheim, in her *Vita Willibaldi et vita Wynnebaldi* composed sometime between 761 and 786, wrote that people in the marketplace of a Syrian town stared at Willibald and his brother Wynnebald because "they were young and handsome and dressed well in decorated clothing."[58] In an early ninth-century poem, Theodulf of Orléans described a prelate who disguised himself as a peasant by putting on rough clothing and heavy shoes.[59] When one of Lothar's men traveled to Bologna to stop Adrebald, abbot of Flavigny, from delivering a letter from Pope Gregory IV to Louis the Pious in 837, Adrebald borrowed clothes from one of his men so that he looked like a beggar. His disguise allowed him to cross the Alpine passes that Lothar was watching.[60] Though these examples have concerned men, similar differences in clothing doubtless marked the status of women. A correlation between beauty and wealth existed in the Carolingian world, and the denunciations of vanity found in these texts indicate that ecclesiastical leaders recognized the danger of that combination.

Beauty and Virtue

The ways in which Carolingian men came to terms with the idea of female beauty as related to virtue clarify social expectations of aristocratic women and further demonstrate the striking parallel in expectations of women in both the lay and religious estates. Joining virtue to the immediately attractive aspects of good looks and rich display brought together contemporary concerns and the ancient idea that beauty indicated internal virtue. Anticipation that elite women be lovely was therefore intertwined not only with status and wealth but also with upright female behavior. The degree to which beauty and virtue went together, however, depended upon the genre and goals of the texts in question. Exegesis and panegyric display more direct correlations between the two than lay mirrors. For that reason, the former sources are most useful

56. Concerning what peasants might have worn see *Un village*, 185, 347–48; Sirat, "Le costume dans le Haut Moyen Âge," 114–15. The wealthy sometimes gave not only clothing but also shoes to the poor. Odo, *Vita Geraldi*, chap. 14, 308; *Statutes of Adalhard*, no. 5, 355–56.

57. Sedulius Scottus, Carmen 20, MGH Poetae 3, ed. Ludwig Traube (Berlin, 1886), 186–87, line 28.

58. Huneberc, *Vita Willibaldi*, chap. 4, 94.

59. Theodulf of Orléans, Carmen 17, MGH Poetae 1, ed. Ernst Dümmler (Berlin, 1881), 473, lines 19–28.

60. Astronomer, *Vita Hludowici imperatoris*, chap. 56, 512.

for revealing how Carolingians thought about beauty, while the latter may inform us about the practical nature of female appearance.

For many ninth-century Carolingian writers, an ancient topos of good looks reflecting inner worth extended to both sexes and to all ages in the case of individuals who were well-born, held a high office, or were saints. The idea that physical attractiveness reflects the internal goodness or worth of an individual reaches back at least to the Hellenistic period.[61] Late antique Christianity adopted this understanding of corporeal appearance, and martyrs, saints, and the devoutly religious were almost always described as good looking. Augustine thought that an inner beauty of mind or character could radiate from within, making a person, no matter how physically ugly, appear to be lovely.[62] As for female beauty specifically, Augustine recognized that pretty women could be wicked, but he also believed that female beauty was one of God's goods. Because bodily attractiveness was temporal and mortal, however, beauty of soul was more worthy.[63] Both male and female Carolingian saints were described in terms of high birth, good character, virtue, and pleasing appearance. These criteria reflect the late antique models from which Carolingian hagiographers drew and the perpetuation of certain motifs prominent in Merovingian *vitae*. In fact, Walter Berschin has noted that the ideal of good looks in a saint was so ingrained in the Carolingians that when Hathumoda had her visions of St. Martin, he appeared to be beautiful despite the fact that Sulpicius Severus had described him as being "*deformis.*"[64]

Vitae of Carolingian female saints routinely employed a *Tugendkatalog* or catalog of virtues; their subjects were almost always described as well-born and attractive. The eighth-century abbess Leoba's appearance was "angelic" (*angelica*).[65] As a young girl, the recluse Liutberga attracted the attention of her future patroness because she "stood out among the other [girls] in beauty (*forma*) and intelligence."[66] Her mid-ninth–century hagiographer describes the young girls she later educated as beautiful (*elegans*).[67] In the early tenth century, Hucbald of St. Amand described Rictrud as shining "like a star of very magnificent beauty (*venustus*)."[68] The good looks of female saints and

---

61. Berschin, "Die Schönheit des Heiligen," 74.

62. Here one can recognize the influence of Platonic ideas upon Augustine, especially through Plotinus. Harrison, *Beauty and Revelation*, 36–37, 190.

63. Ibid., 153.

64. Berschin, "Die Schönheit des Heiligen," 71. Agius, *Vita Hathumodae*, chaps. 13–14, 171. Sulpicius Severus, *Vita Martini*, chap. 3, Sources Chrétiennes 133, 258. See also chap. 9, 270–72.

65. Rudolf, *Vita Leobae*, chap. 11, 126.

66. *Vita Liutbirgae*, chap. 3, 12.

67. Ibid., chap. 35, 44.

68. Hucbald, *Vita Rictrudis*, chap. 5, 82.

their male counterparts, which appeared in conjunction with other virtues, demonstrated their inner worth and piety. Their holy beauty indicated these women were extraordinary in a religious sense.

As these examples illustrate, Carolingian clerics employed a variety of descriptive words for beauty or beautiful, including but not limited to *elegans, venustus, pulcher, forma, praepulcher, decorus,* and *speciosa.* Most of these terms do not have a consistent, particular connotation in the texts examined beyond conveying the idea of an attractive appearance, with the exception of *decorus.* It nearly always occurs in conjunction with *virtute* or implies concurrent virtue. The most common term for beauty, however, is *pulchritudo* and for beautiful *pulcher.* The Vulgate as well as Carolingian hagiographical, epistolary, advice, biographical, historical, poetic, and exegetical texts all employ the term, sometimes also in relation to men or to inanimate objects. Yet the terms themselves seem less revealing of specific meanings than their textual contexts.

Biblical exegesis of the time further reveals how Carolingian writers associated a woman's lovely appearance with virtue, good character, and internal worth. In commentaries on books that mention female beauty—Judith, Esther, and Song of Songs—writers explained the presence and function of beauty, not its nature per se. Frequently, they equated loveliness or strongly associated it with the church (*ecclesia*) and Christian virtue. The wealthy and powerful who saw pretty women at court or on estates could have been exposed to these ideas. Religious men and women in particular had access to biblical exegesis in their monastery and church libraries, but some well-educated elite women and men almost certainly read or heard of exegetical commentaries.

In his *Expositio in canticum canticorum,* which circulated in two "somewhat different versions" starting sometime around the second quarter of the ninth century, Alcuin used beauty to discuss the church.[69] He naturally identifies the Beloved as the church.[70] When beauty comes up, as it frequently does, it designates virtue, pure heart, faith, and chastity.[71] In explaining verse 1.4, Alcuin wrote in the person of the Beloved: "I am black in the afflictions of persecution, but lovely in the beauty of virtue. That is, I appear black in the eyes of persecution but before God, adorned with the beauty of virtue, I shine."[72] Alcuin associated beauty with the virtues of a beleaguered church. The female figure representing the church is lovely because of the church's innate goodness. Such passages associate female attractiveness almost exclusively with

69. Bullough, *Alcuin,* 8.
70. Janes, *God and Gold in Late Antiquity,* 84–85.
71. Alcuin, *Compendium in Canticum Canticorum,* PL 100, cols. 644–45.
72. Ibid., col. 643.

virtue, greatly reflecting Augustine's view that women's beauty was one of God's goods. Raban Maur, abbot of Fulda (822–842), explored similar ideas in his commentaries on Judith and Esther.

Written in the early 830s to comfort the empress Judith and offer her guidance in a time of trouble, Raban Maur's commentaries presented *imitabiles* to a beleaguered queen. Raban associated both Judith and Esther with a besieged church, an appropriate analogy for a period when the Carolingian Empire was in turmoil.[73] The book of Judith explains how Judith, a lovely Hebrew widow, was able to trick and kill Holofernes, the general of the Assyrian army, who had come to conquer the Israelites. She dressed beautifully one evening, went to Holofernes's camp, and promised to help him to defeat the Israelites. After a few days he invited her to dinner in his tent with the intention of seducing her, but she encouraged him to become drunk and then beheaded him, thereby saving her people. In his commentary on Judith, Raban only touched upon beauty; he unsurprisingly skips some biblical passages that focused on Judith's good looks as her appearance was not his main concern. Because her attractiveness, in addition to her cunning, allowed her close access to Holofernes, it is, however, pivotal to the book. Furthermore, the empress Judith was known to be pretty, which may have made this commentary especially apt. After deciding to murder Holofernes, the biblical Judith cast aside her widow's clothing, bathed, and adorned herself more appropriately to seduce him. Because God knew that her efforts stemmed from virtue, not desire, he enhanced Judith's appearance before she went to the Assyrian camp. Raban uses notions of beauty to explore other issues. When commenting upon these passages, Raban equates her preparations to the way the church becomes lovely through its virtues. "The holy Church adorns herself with all these ornaments, because she strives to adorn herself with the beauty of all virtue."[74] In this passage and throughout his commentary on Judith, when Raban discusses her stunning good looks, he associates them with virtue. By doing so, he lends Judith's beauty and adornment a moral value beyond their ability to entice Holofernes, whose perverse nature causes him to mistake virtue for desire in Judith's appearance.[75] Rather than seeing vanity, which such preparations might reveal in an average woman, Raban appreciates Judith's efforts to appear lovely as intimately linked to her moral exemplarity.

The book of Esther concerns another beautiful woman, the Jewish wife of the Perisan king Artaxerxes, who also saved her people from death. Artaxerxes

---

73. de Jong, "The Empire as *ecclesia*," 207; de Jong, "Exegesis for an Empress," 92, 97.

74. Raban Maur, *Expositio in librum Judith*, PL 109, col. 565.

75. Ibid., col. 571.

married Esther after rejecting his wife Vashti, who had disobeyed him. He ordered his men to find the most lovely women in all the provinces so that he could select one to be his new queen; he chose Esther. Haman, one of the king's courtiers, eventually became jealous of the advancement of Esther's foster father Mordecai at court and hatched a plot to kill all the Jews, especially Mordecai. Haman convinced the king to issue a decree that on a certain day all Jews in his land were to be killed. Once Esther discovered this plan, she tried to stop it. After praying, Esther went to her husband, dressed in her best clothing and jewels and asked that he and Haman attend a banquet she would prepare. At that banquet she convinced her husband to have Haman hanged; following Haman's death she persuaded the king to allow the Jews to defend themselves against any who followed Haman's orders, thereby saving the Jews from destruction.

As in the other exegetical texts, Raban's commentary on Esther links beauty with the church and its virtue. "For then mystically, Esther, that is, the Church, ... with the beauty of virtue seemed lovely in the eyes of all."[76] Raban associates her with a newly converted church while Vasthi, the former queen, stands for the old Synagogue.[77] In his commentary, Esther's good looks are a reflection of her metaphorical Christian state. Raban associates her beauty with the besieged church just as Alcuin correlates the Beloved with the church in his commentary on the Song of Songs. Here again, Raban's commentary does little to illuminate the nature of female beauty, but he firmly connects it to Christian virtue. Although all these exegetical texts concerned beauty and virtue, they never addressed explicitly the issue of whether a physically attractive appearance implies moral worth. Biblical exegetes understood that virtue could make something or someone appear lovely. Other sources that concern less holy subjects indicate that physical beauty was not necessarily understood as a sign of internal virtue.

Portraits of women in court poetry drew from late antique panegyric when maintaining the ancient association between external good looks and internal virtue. In late antique poetry rulers and their families were invariably handsome. Moral portraits such as these lived on into the Carolingian period and beyond and over time became more schematized and stylized. These Carolingian poetic scenes indicate ways the clerical and secular elite thought about female beauty, but they reveal little about the actual appearance of those described. Early medieval poets revealed few or no individual characteristics of their subjects. Deeply influenced by late antique panegyric and the poems of Venantius Fortunatus (c. 530–c. 603), poetry emanating

---

76. Maur, *Expositio in librum Esther,* col. 648.
77. Ibid., cols. 642–43, 645.

from Charlemagne's court praised the king and his family in expected ways.[78] Carolingian poets nevertheless creatively employed motifs, lines, and even entire scenes from ancient and late antique poetry to advance an image of a powerful and worthy ruler presiding over a well-run and cultured court.[79] Readers and listeners would have appreciated the explicit references to earlier royalty and others worthy of praise.

A series of three epistolary court poems by Angilbert, Alcuin, and Theodulf of Orléans dated between 794 and 796 heaps praise upon the Carolingian family. Such poems were read aloud at court and their authors, conscious of possible performance, wrote with such recitation in mind. Alcuin's poem offers no mention of female beauty, but Angilbert, in his poem "To Charlemagne and His Entourage" (794–95), notes the combination of physical good looks and moral qualities among Charlemagne's daughters:

> Rotrud, a maiden of reknowned intellect, loves poetry;
> A very beautiful maiden celebrated for her conduct....
> Speak now with me, Muses, in praise of the extraordinary maiden Bertha,
> May my poetry please her,
> For the girl is worthy of the Muses' songs.
> Rise, pipe, and make sweet verses for my dear ones.
> Let my pipe now also praise you, girls,
> Tender in years, but mature in kind character
> whose upright life surpasses their extreme beauty.[80]

In this passage Angilbert notes the combination of the sisters' attractive appearances with their comportment. Rotrud, though "very beautiful," is also "celebrated for her conduct." Angilbert emphasizes that she exhibited not merely beauty but a moral character implying that the one did not automatically indicate the other. Aside from good looks, Bertha has discernment in regard to poetry, and Angilbert worries about her reception of the poem because she had enough experience of court poetry to tell a fine poem from a poor one.[81] Bertha's appearance does not automatically entail cultivation, but Angilbert implies that it can make a woman more attractive. Angilbert

---

78. Portmann, *Die Darstellung der Frau*, 52; Cizek, "Das Bild von der idealen Schönheit in der lateinischen Dichtung des Frühmittelalters," 7.

79. Introduction to *PCR*, 8–10.

80. Angilbert, "To Charlemagne and His Entourage," in *PCR*, no. 6, 114–17, lines 43–54. All translations of poetry are my own unless otherwise noted but are sometimes drawn from Godman's translations.

81. Doubtless, Angilbert especially wished to please Bertha because she was his lover and the mother of his two sons.

furthermore points out that all the daughters conduct themselves in a kind and upright manner, and that this virtuous behavior surpasses even their "extreme beauty." Throughout this passage Angilbert continually tempers admiration for beauty by calling attention to virtue, implying that such a combination was particularly praiseworthy. Although these depictions of Charlemagne's daughters reveal little about them individually, those at court expected and readily understood a literary combination of physical desirability, upright character, and intelligence in royal women. Certainly, Charlemagne's learned daughters would have understood the flattery inherent in such depictions.

Theodulf of Orléans's poem "On the Court" (796) also combines a sense of virtue with loveliness and reveals some of the components of beauty when describing Charlemagne's daughters.

> Let the king's fiery gaze now turn to them,
> may he now look upon the throngs of maidens on either side
> of the gathering of young girls lovelier than any other
> in dress, bearing, beauty, figure, heart and faith:
> that is Bertha and Rotrud and Gisela as well;
> she is one of the three beautiful sisters, even if the youngest.[82]

When Theodulf writes that Charlemagne's daughters were lovely (*pulchra*) in "dress, bearing, beauty, figure, heart and faith," he implies a link between beauty and virtue. Faith (*fide*) and heart (*corde*) imply an inner disposition that found reflection in the royal women's outward appearance. Dress (*veste*) and bearing (*habitu*) as outward characteristics depended to some degree upon wealth and instruction. In a chapter admonishing laymen not to think that they are, by nature, better than those less fortunate than themselves, Jonas of Orléans wrote about the importance of men's demeanor (*cultus*). He stated that, even if men could recognize that others were not their social equals because of their appearance and wealth (*cutis et opes*), they should nevertheless understand that they are by nature their peers.[83] Being well-born, wearing fine clothes and jewelry, and training in courtly graces may equally have helped others to perceive beauty (*specie*) in women; certainly Theodulf's reference to their *corpore*, figure or more literally body, indicates a purely physical beauty. Though pleasing, the women's good looks are tied to their virtue, an internal characteristic that can find expression through action. Theodulf immediately

---

82. Theodulf of Orléans, "On the Court," in *PCR*, no. 15, 154–55, lines 77–82. This translation is Godman's.

83. Jonas, *Institutione*, 2.22, col. 215. See also Nelson, "Peers in the Early Middle Ages," 30–31.

followed this passage on Charlemagne's daughters with a description of the king's future wife Liutgard.

> The lovely virago Liutgard is joined by [Charlemagne's daughters];
> Her character shines with acts of devotion.
> Beautiful in her refinement but more lovely in her fitting actions,
> She pleases all the people and magnates.[84]

Liutgard's fitting actions enhanced her cultivated beauty (*pulchra satis cultu*), letting her delight the whole court, not just her future husband. Loveliness in this passage does not automatically imply virtue; upright character enhances it. Liutgard "pleases" those at court not only by her lovely appearance but also by her right actions. The ways women carried themselves, their gestures and acts, influenced how others perceived them, and at times they may have taken advantage of these expectations to influence others. The resonance of such a description helped it to work effectively; it was not an empty trope but a meaningful one. Once rich dress marked a woman as a member of the elite, her gestures had implications for relations among the powerful.

Fine clothes and jewelry were components of the image of royal or aristocratic women that, in poetry, promoted a certain vision of wealth, beauty, and virtue. A case in point are the lavish descriptions of Charlemagne's female relatives' clothing and jewelry in *Karolus Magnus et Leo papa*.

> The beautiful woman adorned with clothing with varying stones,
> Her brooch glitters with the colorful light of many gems
> Her cloak is decorated with crysolite gems.[85]

A literal reading of this passage would ignore both the poem's ancient and late antique models and the Christian overtones implicit in mentioning the gems.[86] Charlemagne's daughter's jewels give her an aspect similar to that of women in Venantius Fortunatus's poetry and to descriptions of Justinian's family.[87] A combination of colorful gems implied a complementary set of virtues and meanings, even if the poet does not list the gem types. Though each gem and color had a specific meaning in the early Middle Ages, readers understood

---

84. Theodulf of Orléans, "On the Court," 154, lines 83–86.
85. *Karolus Magnus*, 74, lines 226–28.
86. Meier, *Gemma Spiritalis*, 27–138.
87. For example, Venantius Fortunatus described Brunhild by using a series of gems to demonstrate her virtue and nobility; he even called her a new gem of Hispania. Carmen 6.1, *Venance Fortunat. Poèmes*, vol. 2, ed. and trans. Marc Reydellet (Paris, 1998), 48, lines 110–1.

that they were meant to balance and set off one another.[88] Crysolite in both ancient and early medieval texts usually symbolized wisdom.[89] Therefore, again beauty and prudence appear in combination in court poetry.

Men in the same poems were also frequently described as physically good-looking, but descriptions of their attire differ in meaning and emphasis from those of female dress. For example, while Theodulf of Orléans praises Charlemagne's daughters' beauty, character, and learning in his poem "On the Court," he praises the king's appearance and intelligence.

> Chest, legs and feet: nothing in Charlemagne is not worthy of praise.
> All is in beautiful health; all looks fitting,
> and how lucky is he who listens to your very beautiful, wise utterances
> in which you surpass all, and none surpasses you.[90]

Health and wise words accompany Charlemagne's good looks, and it is his physical body and speech that are "lovely," not his adornment. Nevertheless, as in the descriptions of his daughters, the idea that physical beauty reflects inner worth remains. Descriptions of his sons' accoutrements later in the poem show a marked contrast to his descriptions of the daughters' attire.

> Let Charles swiftly take up his father's double cloak or smooth gloves
> for his hands, and may Louis take his sword.[91]

In this short description, Charlemagne's sons Charles and Louis ideally stand ready for action; their accessories are items useful for either hunting or warfare. By implying that Charlemagne's sons will be worthy and capable heirs, Theodulf suggests the vitality of the Carolingian dynasty.[92] In comparison, in a longer passage concerning the attire of Charlemagne's daughters, Theodulf emphasizes the emperor's wealth and the way the women serve as ornaments to the court.

> [His daughters'] appearances differ, but their beauty is one and the same.
> The one gleams with gems, the other shines with gold and purple,
> the one is resplendent with sapphires, the other with rubies.

---

88. Janes, *God and Gold in Late Antiquity*, 86.
89. Kitson, "Lapidary Traditions in Anglo-Saxon England," 77.
90. Theodulf of Orléans, "On the Court," 150, lines 19–22.
91. Ibid., 154, lines 93–94.
92. Sedulius Scottus later wrote poems that similarly praised Carolingian kings as well as the magnate Eberhard of Friuli for their manly actions. See for example Carmen 25, 190–92; Carmen 39, 202–3; Carmen 53, 212–13.

One wears a brooch, a decorative border adorns the other,
Armbands adorn one, a becoming necklace another.
A dark-red dress suits one, a dress of yellow the other,
one wears a snow-white bodice, another a bodice of red.[93]

This description displays Christian imagery and reliance on late antique and early Frankish models similar to those in *Karolus Magnus et Leo papa*. It also emphasizes the riches at court, evident in what Charlemagne's daughters wear, and certain virtues that the colors of their clothing and the particular gemstones imply. Gold indicated the daughters' faith, love, and wisdom while the purple emphasized their humility. Sapphires represented the blue of heaven and hence the love of all that was heavenly, especially as made manifest on earth through miracles, and rubies, like other red precious stones, probably indicated joy in the passion.[94] Such descriptions were feasts of imagery and allusion, creating a picture of an opulent court.

Because these passages concerning Charlemagne's children follow descriptions of the court chapel, "a beautiful building with a wondrous cupola," and the "lofty palace residence," they stress the wealth of the Carolingian court and the possibilities for ostentatious display following the Avar conquest of 796.[95] The capture of Avar gold, mentioned in lines 33–36 of "On the Court," made construction of the impressive palace complex at Aachen possible and may well have financed and made believable the fine clothes and jewels of Charlemagne's daughters.[96] Despite the verisimilitude of such a description in light of the recent Carolingian windfall, the description remains far more an ideal than a representation of reality. Though Charlemagne's daughters probably wore fine clothes and jewelry, these passages cannot stand as evidence of what they actually did wear. Theodulf of Orléans wrote "On the Court" while away from court, and like the author of *Karolus Magnus et Leo papa*, he borrowed descriptions of gems and clothing from Virgil's *Aeneid*.[97] These depictions conveyed the image of a cultured court that was in part created through the appearance of the emperor's daughters.

During the reign of Charlemagne's son Louis the Pious (814–840), the poet Ermold the Black provided a flattering image of the empress Judith at court. Ermold wrote his epic poem "In Honor of Louis" while away from court (826–28), but for some passages he probably drew from his own prior

---

93. Theodulf of Orléans, "On the Court," 154–55, lines 100–106.
94. Haupt, *Die Farbensymbolik*, 68–69, 103–4, 113–14.
95. Theodulf of Orléans, "On the Court," 152, lines 63–64.
96. Einhard, *VK*, chap. 13, 16.
97. Introduction to *PCR*, 11–13.

experiences at court. As most other writers of the time did, Ermold the Black described Judith as lovely in the poem.[98] In his account of a hunt, he drew especially from Virgil's *Aeneid* as well as from *Karolus Magnus et Leo papa*. When he described Judith's appearance at the start of the hunt, he offered less detail than the earlier Frankish poem, but the sentiment of beauty, wealth, and virtue is similar.

> Then Judith, the pious, very beautiful wife of the emperor,
> Mounted her horse splendidly dressed and marvelously arrayed.[99]

Ermold notes her beauty in conjunction with her piety and adornment. Judith's clothing enhanced her well-known natural good looks, and presumably her piety contributed to her attractive appearance.

Sedulius Scottus (active c. 840–c. 860) employed earlier motifs in his panegyric for Charlemagne's grandsons, often reusing the images of other poets. Like other Carolingian poets he continued to connect beauty both with feminine virtue and with a display of wealth and male power. In his poem for Irmingard, wife of Lothar I, he wrote: "For presently your seemly beauty, character, reputation, and powerful family are unrivaled among all the Franks."[100] Here again loveliness accompanies character and reputation; on its own it is not enough to recommend the queen, but Sedulius nevertheless offers a rich description of Irmingard's appearance.

> Your fair head is crowned with golden hair,
> A pattern of crisolite encircles your head entirely;
> Like a brilliant sapphire, glittering with luster,
> Great charm illuminates your features,
> Your milk-white neck is adorned with shining beauty,
> It gleams like lilies or ivory.
> Plentiful grace thus abounds in your white hands,
> For they sow on earth what they shall reap in heaven.[101]

In this passage, Irmingard shines, her appearance reflecting not only the wealth of Lothar's court but also her own virtue. Sedulius often wrote of the dazzling and glowing of his subjects, including men.[102] Sedulius associates

---

98. Ermold, *In honorem*, 170, line 2241.
99. Ibid., 182, lines 2378–79.
100. Sedulius Scottus, Carmen 20, 186–87, lines 13–4.
101. Ibid, lines 23–29.
102. Sedulius Scottus, Carmen 14, 82–83, lines 27–28; Carmen 54, 212–13, lines 1 and 15; Carmen 66, 220, line 5.

Irmingard with gems, crisolite and sapphire, that indicate her wisdom and piety. Sedulius further notes Irmingard's grace or charm (*gratia*). Her actions, behavior, and demeanor enhance her beauty. In a poem in honor of Empress Irmingard, he again described Irmingard in similar terms, writing that even as a small girl, she was lovely, prudent, and gentle.[103] Later in the same poem, he praises her learning and wisdom.[104] Her good looks are part of a collection of virtues.

Irmingard's daughter Bertha was the subject of similar descriptions in at least three poems by Sedulius Scottus. Because Bertha had entered the religious life at the time he wrote about her, Sedulius emphasized her piety and devotion to Christ, her spiritual spouse.[105] In this regard he offered a complement to his portrayal of Bertha's mother as a faithful wife and worthy queen, whose beauty and adornment served to demonstrate the wealth of her husband. Bertha's faith and piety made her worthy for the spiritual life. Unsurprisingly his poems also emphasized the laudable characteristics that Bertha inherited from her parents. Sedulius wrote that Bertha was "equal to her mother and entirely like her father."[106] Here he praised her parents, who were among his principal patrons. Sedulius further extolled Irmingard's family background in his poetry: he wrote as though beauty and good birth ought to accompany one another.[107] Bertha resembled her parents (and other subjects of panegyric) because she shone as they did, and, like Irmingard, Bertha rivaled the beauty of precious stones whose mention in the poem served to indicate her various virtues.[108] Sedulius wrote that Bertha was "reddish gold like a silver dove" and that she was like electrum.[109] In associating her with a white dove and the gleam of metals, Sedulius indicates Bertha's purity, faith, and wisdom. As earlier poets had, Sedulius offered lavish descriptions of royal women that conveyed their virtue in addition to their wealth and good birth. From these poems and the description of Abbess Gisela it is clear that panegyric praised elite religious women in similar ways to their lay counterparts. Sedulius extolled female beauty while associating it with appropriate behavior and internal virtue, whether describing women in the lay or religious estates.

Throughout the ninth century, poetic descriptions of women reveal a common understanding of female beauty. The continuation of these motifs and

---

103. Sedulius Scottus, Carmen 24, 189–90, lines 15–16.
104. Ibid., lines 21–24.
105. Sedulius Scottus, Carmen 43, 208; Carmen 61, 217–18; Carmen 78, 228; Carmen 79, 229.
106. Carmen 61, 217–18, line 20.
107. Carmen 20, lines 13–14; Carmen 24, 189, lines 13–5.
108. Carmen 43, 208, line 5; Carmen 61, 218, line 22, Carmen 78, 228, lines 1–3.
109. Carmen 43, 208, lines 2–3.

ideas resulted from borrowing passages from earlier works, but these poets made choices to please their contemporary patrons. Though royal patrons may have appreciated references to past texts, they equally wanted poems to respond to their present desire for praise, which might cause others to appreciate their wealth, good fortune, and power and to accept the legitimacy of the Carolingian line. Even if panegyric cannot offer reliable observations of women at court, these poetic passages reflect common, longstanding ideas concerning female beauty. Fewer poetic descriptions of women survive from the mid- to late ninth century than from the reigns of Charlemagne and Louis the Pious, perhaps because of changes in patronage by Carolingian kings and the lack of equivalent "court schools" producing poetry.[110] Other sources from that later period nevertheless suggest the continuing importance of female appearance.

The rich dress of aristocratic women in late ninth and early tenth-century hagiography conveys a similar concern with the meaning of clothing, but the desired message is rather different. When describing Rictrud's actions after taking up the religious life following her husband's death, Hucbald of St. Amand wrote in his early tenth-century *vita:*

> However, so that she could appear outwardly as she bore herself inwardly, she changed the clothing of her body just as she changed her state of mind. She threw off the ostentatious clothes which adorned her in marriage when she thought about worldly things, how she might please her husband.[111]

This passage reflects competing aristocratic and clerical value systems. A change of dress (*habitus*) could reflect the change in one's internal disposition (*habitus*). Hucbald described her rejection of the worldly, external habit for a spiritual, internal one. Here Rictrud casts away her old life and duties and takes up the religious life with its goals, more in line with her virtuous nature much as Radegund had done when she gave her jewelry to the poor. Hucbald clearly believed that Rictrud was a virtuous and pious woman prior to entering the religious life, but to reflect her new consecrated status, she had to abandon her rich secular clothing as earlier holy women had. This passage indicates the continuing importance of appropriate dress; like most social markers, garments revealed a great deal about their wearer. Ermold the Black had similarly described Harold the Dane and his followers adopting new Frankish clothes following their baptism.[112] Further, Hucbald, like Theodulf in his description

---

110. Introduction to *PCR*, 56–63.
111. Hucbald, *Vita Rictrudis*, chap. 15, 84–85.
112. Ermold, *In honorem*, 176, lines 2308–13.

of Liutgard and Dhuoda in her discussion of women's use of mirrors, believed that women dressed in certain ways to please men, particularly husbands. Rictrud's choice of adornment attested to her husband's wealth and station, and it connected her to him, much as a consecrated woman's veil connected her to her heavenly bridegroom. It may also have contributed to the perception of her beauty. In this respect this passage is similar to the descriptions of Charlemagne's daughters in court poetry. Their dress served their family's purposes, and the poet doubtless envisioned the daughters' "choice" of dress as a means to create a certain image that would please their father.

In the *Vita Hathumodae*, when explaining Hathumoda's girlhood rejection of worldly vanities, Agius reveals some of the ways an aristocratic girl or woman may have made herself appear beautiful.

> She did not desire nor did she want to have the gold and precious finery, which children desire, albeit innocently, because it is beautiful. For she burned with disdain toward the clothing adorned with gold, female headgear, head bands, hair pins, earrings, necklaces, bracelets, adornments, chaplets, and perfumes which many women either had or wanted, and when they were spontaneously offered, in accordance with the wealth and rank of her parents, she refused to take them, and when they were imposed upon her against her will, she lamented anxiously and wept vehemently.[113]

This passage bears a strong resemblance to Isaiah 3:18–23, but it differs enough that it seems to reflect what others expected a Carolingian woman to wear. Agius spins Isaiah's statement that God will strip the haughty daughters of Zion of their finery and sets Hathumoda in contrast to those women. God need not strip her of vanities; she freely gave them up at a young age. Hathumoda rejects a long list of adornments that "many women either had or wanted." These accessories would furthermore have indicated her "wealth and rank" as well as that of her family. The variety of ways in which women could enhance their beauty stands out in this passage, as does the expectation that women don such accoutrements and take pleasure in them. Adornments, which created an attractive appearance, were appropriate to the wealth and rank of an aristocratic woman and almost certainly communicated her status to others. That Hathumoda received gifts of finery and was sometimes forced to wear them reveals how important the looks of a laywoman could be to her family, whose status she reflected. Agius's *vita* may seem to criticize such lay concerns by positively portraying Hathumoda's rejection of these

---

113. Agius, *Vita Hathumodae*, chap. 2, 167.

accoutrements as vanity, but despite the *vita*'s instructive purposes, he does not insist that other, less extraordinary women ought to give up these items. He may have recognized the potential mix of lay and religious audiences for this *vita* and offered an implicit compromise. His references to dress indicate an expectation that elite secular women should be richly, though not flamboyantly, dressed, while religious women should adopt a modest appearance suppressing their desire for finery. These hagiographic examples are significantly later in date than the poetic examples above, but despite their distance in time the two types of sources convey a similar ambivalence about the relationship between beauty and virtue. These *vitae* and poems recognized the social importance of female beauty, especially when created through dress and adornment that also displayed familial wealth, and both texts acknowledged that loveliness did not necessarily imply the presence of virtue.

A similar, though rather more practical, view of beauty emerges in Jonas of Orléans's *De institutione laicali*. Because his text was directed to laymen, not clerics, he is more of a pragmatist about female good looks. In his discussion of the model aristocratic laywoman, in particular a wife, he explicitly admitted that a lovely and wealthy woman was not necessarily virtuous, although a combination of good looks, wealth, and virtue was optimal. He acknowledged that men sought beauty and riches in a wife, but insisted that virtue was more important:

> And so [men] ought to consider, as the aforesaid examples indicate, that the external beauty and the carnal pleasure of wives in no way should be preferred to their [wives'] chaste interior love. For [men] must not so much seek riches and beauty in wives but rather virtue and good character.[114]

Beauty, then, did not necessarily imply either moral probity or a lack of it but rather was an external quality set in opposition to the internal quality of chaste love. Jonas explicitly acknowledges that the two could conflict. His description of a wife's attractive appearance was more ambivalent than that presented in the portraits of holy or royal women in hagiography and panegyric. Giving practical advice to laypeople, Jonas observed that beauty, though still a preferred characteristic in women, was not the most important desideratum. Like Augustine before him, he understood that beauty could incite a desire to possess.[115] Female good looks could accomplish some of the lay goals mentioned earlier: they could impress, please, and reflect well upon men. Jonas understood that wealth, though hardly a virtue in itself, appealed greatly to

---

114. Jonas, *Institutione*, 2.5, col. 179.
115. Harrison, *Beauty and Revelation*, 271.

laymen.[116] Wealth in a future wife was similar to beauty because it could help a layman attain certain aims; it offered possibilities for social, political, and economic advancement. Again, however, internal attributes trumped the external qualities of loveliness and riches. Jonas exhorted laymen to consider virtue above all other attributes no matter how attractive.

An example from Hucbald of St. Amand's *Vita Rictrudis* supports the continuing importance of Jonas's emphasis on female virtue in Carolingian lands. Hucbald wrote this *vita* in 907 at the request of the monks and nuns of Marchiennes, where Rictrud had been abbess.[117] According to Hucbald, Vikings had burned Marchiennes in 879, destroying her original *vita* and leaving Hucbald with no other version to consult.[118] He relied on the oral testimony of individuals who had read the earlier *vita*, and he borrowed episodes from a number of other *vitae*. Hucbald also drew from both Isidore of Seville's *Etymologies* and Jonas's *De institutione laicali* when addressing marriage in the *vita*.[119] About Rictrud and her husband Adalbald, he observed:

> In both of them, those things which people customarily expect in choosing husband or wife were combined. The man had strength, good birth, good looks, and wisdom which made him most worthy of love and affection. And the wife had good looks, good birth, wealth, and good character which should be sought above all else.[120]

Though he was ostensibly describing two individuals, Hucbald notes that these qualities are "customarily expected." This passage did not concern one particular marriage but reflected wider expectations. Both husbands and wives ought to have the good birth and good looks (*genus* and *pulchritudo*), which went together in panegyric and hagiography. The spouses' first two characteristics especially recall panegyric in which well-born women were good-looking, and well-born laymen ready for masculine pursuits that required strength. However, following Jonas, Hucbald emphasizes that good character or morality (*mores*) should take precedence over the other desirable aspects of

---

116. For Jonas's views on charity (a virtue wealth helps make possible) and greed (a vice that it can engender), see *Institutione*, 1.20, cols. 163–66.

117. Hucbald, *Vita Rictrudis*, chap. 2, 81.

118. L. van der Essen, "Hucbald de saint Amand (c. 840–930) et sa place dans le mouvement hagiographique médiéval," *Revue d'histoire ecclésiastique* 19 (1923): 333–51, 342; *Chronicle of Marchiennes*, chap. 20, PL 132, col. 849.

119. Smith, "The Hagiography of Hucbald of Saint-Amand," 535; idem, "A Hagiographer at Work," 154–56.

120. Hucbald, *Vita Rictrudis*, chap. 9, 83. My translation follows very closely *The Life of Rictrud*, in *Sainted Women of the Dark Ages*, ed. and trans. Jo Ann McNamara and John E Halborg (Durham, N.C., 1992), 203.

women and men; again beauty does not automatically imply accompanying inner qualities of wisdom and upright disposition, here treated as separate attributes. Jonas (and later Hucbald) needed to emphasize the lack of a direct correlation between beauty and virtue because he recognized the attractions of lovely women. Although acknowledging that good looks are understandably desirable, he reminds his readers that the best wife is virtuous, regardless of her appearance. He offered this advice not only with Christian morality in mind but also with an understanding that magnates wished to avoid marriage to wives who might engage in sexual indiscretions that could threaten their lineage and reputation.

Jonas's and Hucbald's presentations of female (and male) beauty, virtue, and wealth reflect both the continuity of general cultural values and expectations in the West and the ongoing concern with women's behavior and the means of attaining and promoting female virtue throughout the ninth century and beyond in Carolingian lands. In antiquity, at least rhetorically and perhaps in reality, a good wife could contribute to a man's power, because concord within the Roman household undergirded a husband's position in public life. With the development of Christian, elite ideals, a competing ideal of virginity began to gain ground over the high value placed upon harmony in marriage.[121] Female virtue obtained a specifically Christian aspect, and negative views of marriage appear in late antique Christian writings, most famously those of Augustine. During late antiquity and into the Merovingian era (c. 300–c. 750), hagiographers especially emphasized domestic virtue in their subjects, often portraying women in powerful roles rendered acceptable by actions appropriate to women.[122] By the Carolingian period, although great value was still placed upon virginity, marriage received relatively positive treatment.[123] The continuing promotion of virtue in women may have contributed to and drawn from this more favorable view. Hucbald did not merely parrot Jonas any more than Jonas parroted Isidore; both writers drew from earlier texts in order to emphasize the concerns of their own times. Jonas wrote at the height of Carolingian reform, when clerics hoped to inculcate the laity with Christian ideals and behavior. Hucbald, particularly given his access to rich libraries, was well aware both of Frankish history and of relatively recent events.[124] His versions of older lives, especially the *Vita Rictrudis* for which he had no earlier model, allowed him to bring the past to bear on present problems, both because the *vitae* included old ideas that still had currency and because Hucbald presented

---

121. Kate Cooper, *The Virgin and the Bride*, 3–19.
122. Coon, *SF*, 95–141.
123. Toubert, "La théorie du mariage," 276–79; Heene, *The Legacy of Paradise*, 111–13.
124. Smith, "A Hagiographer at Work," 154–63.

material in new ways to reflect on recent events.[125] In "updating" these *vitae*, he worked to make the subjects' lives relevant for the audiences. Given the succession problems of the Carolingian dynasty in this era and the relative instability in West Francia, the desire that women embody an identity, which rested upon fulfillment of conventional roles, could reflect a desire for stability.

Similar concerns are apparent in a number of Carolingian historical texts. Because many were written under royal patronage, they show an unsurprising concern with the stability of the realm, which is sometimes reflected in their depictions of women. In these sources, women were ideally to be virtuous mothers passing on their illustrious lineage or at least daughters who do not produce competing heirs. Making known the ancestry of any woman marrying into the Carolingian family was conventional.[126] Because it was not the most important female attribute in historical texts, beauty made infrequent appearances in histories and annals. In perhaps the most famous historical text of the Carolingian era, the *Life of Charlemagne* (825–26), Einhard took little interest in anyone's physical appearance, except that of the king himself. His two-chapter description of Charlemagne emphasizes his physical strength and ability to rule, similar to the depictions of men at court in the poetry discussed above.[127] He portrayed Charlemagne's daughters as being very beautiful, when explaining why they did not marry despite their good looks and cultivation.[128] Detailing their appearance, however, was not part of his plan; to call them lovely was sufficient. In fact, historical texts rarely offer more about female beauty than passing references. The empress Judith, wife of Louis the Pious, to whom Raban Maur dedicated his exegetical texts on Judith and Esther, was known to be pretty. Thegan, in his biography of Louis the Pious, and the author of the *Prior Metz Annals* both credit her beauty with causing Louis to choose her at a supposed bride show, but modern scholars suspect that her eastern origin made her a strategic choice.[129] The allusion to a bride show that probably never occurred was rather meant to associate Judith with Esther, who had been selected as king's bride in that manner.[130] Thegan does not mention the appearance of other women; Hildegard, wife of Charlemagne and mother of Louis the Pious, is *beatissa regina* (blessed queen),

125. Platelle, "Le thème de la conversion à travers les oeuvres hagiographiques d'Hucbald de Saint-Amand," 516–18; Smith, "The Hagiography of Hucbald," 540.

126. Thegan, *Gesta*, chap. 4, 178–80, chap. 28, 216; Astronomer, *Vita Hludowici*, chap. 8, 306–8, chap. 34, 404.

127. Einard, *VK*, chaps. 22–23, 26–28.

128. Ibid., chap. 19, 25.

129. Thegan, *Gesta*, chap. 26, 214; *Annales Mettenses priores*, 95. Ward, "Caesar's Wife," 208.

130. de Jong, "Bride Shows Revisited."

and he takes pains to trace her noble lineage.[131] The Astronomer similarly describes Hildegard as very noble (*nobilissima*) and very pious (*piissima*) or, in the Vienna manuscript containing the biography, very pure (*purissima*), but he never referred to Judith as beautiful.[132]

Like other ninth-century annals, the *Annals of St. Bertin* rarely mention women other than queens. Its description of the Synod of Ponthion in the summer of 876 offers a hint of royal women's adornment. The queen Richildis along with her husband, Charles the Bald, received papal envoys and letters. The next day she accepted a papal gift of "rich garments and jewel encrusted armlets."[133] The ninth-century *Annals of Fulda* provide no mentions of female appearance.

Historical works rarely mention non-royal women, much less provide descriptions of them, but in his *Chronicle* Regino of Prüm devoted the last part of his entry for 883 to an account of some recent violence among a few magnates. In the passage, he seems to use the beauty of the woman Friderada to explain her successive marriages to two powerful men: Engilram, count of Flanders, and the "noble and faithful" Bernard. Another man kills Bernard and immediately marries Friderada. Regino does not appear to find Friderada an entirely innocent party in the episode, noting that her daughter's husband would eventually have his wife beheaded for "commission of the same dishonor."[134] Regino both uses female appearance as an excuse for male conflict and addresses the idea of beauty as a dangerous attribute. Concerns that a lovely and wealthy woman might not be appropriately virtuous as wife and mother were perennial. The Hebrew Scriptures presented the dangers of such a wife; if David could fall prey to the beauty of Bathsheba (2 Samuel 11:2–5), other men could easily yield to similar temptations. In fact, David's family presented the ambivalence of physical beauty: Tamar's beauty attracted Amnon who later raped her (2 Samuel 13:1–14) and the rebellious Absalom was known for his beauty. "Then in all Israel there was no man as beautiful as the exceedingly handsome Absalom; from the sole of his foot to the crown of his head there was no blemish in him."[135] In the end, Absalom's thick, long hair, of which he was excessively proud, proved his undoing. Riding out to meet his father's army, his hair caught in an oak tree, making it possible for Joab to kill him with a spear while he hung from the branches (2 Samuel 18:9–15). Charlemagne's nickname was David, and the association of the Carolingian

---

131. Thegan, *Gesta*, chap. 2, 176.

132. Astronomer, *Vita Hludowici*, chap. 2, 286. Ernst Tremp believes the *purissima* in ÖNB MS 529 is probably an error.

133. *AB*, yr. 876, 204.

134. Regino of Prüm, *Chronicon*, 121.

135. 2 Samuel 14:25.

family with that of David gave particular significance to these events from the Hebrew Scriptures. The royal family had a strong interest in preventing such temptations among its members in order to ensure the legitimacy of heirs. Women therefore helped to shape family identity by demonstrating virtue and purity; they were meant to reassure others that an unbroken Carolingian line continued. Other aristocratic families doubtless had similar concerns; the recognition in annals and histories about the importance of family legitimacy suggests that ecclesiastical leaders recognized this elite interest, which affected clerical ideas concerning the relationship between female beauty and virtue.

In the same way that the authors of lay mirrors, especially Jonas of Orléans and Paulinus of Aquileia, could compromise between the ideal ascetic Christian life and the realities of the lay world, other Carolingian churchmen throughout the ninth century may equally have recognized the importance of secular concerns, such as a beautiful wife. Moreover, they found ways to work them into their admonitions to the laity and into texts, such as the *Vita Rictrudis*, whose readers and listeners may have been familiar with such lay conventions. These male clerical authors also expected that religious women could be tempted to adorn themselves, revealing their low opinion of women's ability to resist such sins as well as their understanding that religious women came from the same milieu as their lay counterparts and were shaped by similar expectations of beauty. Ecclesiastical leaders therefore noted that religious women were not to cultivate an attractive appearance, but female saints and royal women might reflect their internal virtue through their loveliness. As for laymen, seeking a pretty wife or encouraging a daughter to learn to adorn herself were fine, as long as these ideas did not lead to vanity or the potentially misleading idea that such beauty necessarily implied morality. Rather women (and men) needed to strive to be virtuous.

The Carolingian Gaze

Although determining how Carolingian women actually looked remains impossible, this chapter has suggested what members of aristocratic society expected to see in women and how they interpreted female beauty. Evidence for female appearance is unfortunately not nearly as rich as for male appearance. Descriptions of men, such as Einhard's passage concerning Charlemagne's physical demeanor and clothing, offer more details than those concerning women. In addition, manuscript illuminations, coins, and the equestrian statue of Charles the Bald offer what appear to be depictions of specific people with individual features, though they are highly stylized and draw from earlier sources. The common characteristics of idealized beauty evident in remaining sources, however, suggest the sort of female appearance the Carolingian gaze may have anticipated, even desired. These attributes do not indicate what people saw, but they provide an opportunity to think about the ways people understood the women upon whom they looked and the effects that gaze may have had upon women. Although men writing about women in the late eighth and ninth centuries provided practically no objective, observed details, they demonstrated the clear expectation that women could create or embellish their own loveliness. Their descriptions of women's physicality may reflect the characteristics that men found sexually appealing. Clerics wrote most panegyric, and that genre gave them an opportunity to write about a subject not normally appropriate for their texts—female corporeal beauty—that may have given them pleasure. Considering these attractive attributes provides a glimpse into an aspect of Carolingian aristocratic culture that contemporaries only rarely addressed directly—the desire or admiration that a person's outward appearance could arouse. These expectations also mattered for women: the perceived loss of good looks as women aged was accompanied by a loss of social status. Though determining what constituted natural or bodily beauty within aristocratic society remains difficult, the texts and illuminations examined thus far have provided numerous clues concerning female adornment.[136]

Carolingian texts rarely touch upon specific corporeal attributes of female appearance. The texts that mention the good looks of the empress Judith, wife of Louis the Pious, for example, seem to assume either that the audience will understand what made her lovely or that such "natural" beauty is best left to the imagination. Yet, the texts discussed in this chapter have offered a few hints about the physical features others found attractive in elite women. Furthermore, although manuscript illuminations usually offer depictions of women derived from earlier models, they nevertheless indicate an appearance others may have expected in women. To return to the first example in this chapter, Charlemagne's sister Gisela shone. Her white neck and the rosy blush of her cheeks suggest fair skin, even if those two descriptions were rather common in early medieval panegyric.[137] The "silver" of her hand and her "golden brow" further indicate a desire for light skin. When Sedulius Scottus wrote that Irmingard was a "spotless dove" or Bertha "a silvered or

---

136. All of the following examples, unless noted, appear earlier in the chapter where their citations may be found.

137. Both Venantius Fortunatus and Sedulius Scottus used similar descriptions. See for example, Venantius Fortunatus, Carmen 4.26, 156, line 22, and Carmen 6.1, 48, line 107; Sedulius Scottus, Carmen 20, 186, lines 21, 27–28, and Carmen 24, 190, lines 27–8.

silver dove," he may have meant to convey their fair appearance.[138] Fair skin may have not only indicated freedom from outdoor toil and therefore relative wealth but also been a highly desirable component of female beauty. Men doubtless considered long hair an attractive attribute in women. Almost all Carolingian illuminations depict women with long hair; in fact, it is often a key characteristic for determining their gender. Stipulations in earlier Germanic law concerning women's hair take for granted that women's hair was long. Men could be fined for pulling a free woman's hair or undoing her headband so that her hair fell down, and both women and men could be fined for cutting a woman's hair.[139] Furthermore, women needed relatively long hair in order to twist or plait it, a practice Alcuin and Agius, echoing Paul of Tarsus, argued against. This condemnation may also have resulted from the pleasure women may have taken in dressing their hair, possibly a social activity because elite women throughout history often wore hairstyles possible only with the help of another individual. Such complex hairdos further demonstrated that these women had the wealth and power to obtain such assistance. Unfortunately, both textual descriptions and illuminations offer little indication of any sort of desirable weight or height, eye or hair color, build or body type. Though Sedulius Scottus described Irmingard's golden blonde hair, it is difficult to know if that was the most desirable color.[140] Furthermore, available texts offer practically no indication of standards of ugliness. Without such information the ideal components of physical beauty in Carolingian society remain elusive.

The available evidence offers relatively rich information on expectations of adornment among the Carolingian female elite. Rictrud clearly wore the dress of an aristocratic laywoman, which she set aside upon entering the religious life. References to the queens Judith and Richildis offer examples of what such accoutrements may have been. When Ermold the Black wrote that Judith "mounted her horse splendidly dressed and marvelously arrayed," he suggests that elite women wore impressive clothing when on public view. The papal gift of "rich garments and jewel encrusted armlets" to Richildis reflected anticipation that queens wear such items.

Manuscript illuminations further indicate that men believed important women should be richly attired. The illumination of Charles the Bald, Richildis's husband, with his queen and her attendant in the Bible of San Paolo

---

138. Sedulius Scottus, Carmina 24, 189, line 17; 43, 208, line 2; and 78, 228, line 1.

139. *Pactus legis Salica*, 104.1–3, in *The Laws of the Salian Franks*, trans. and ed. Katherine Fischer Drew (Philadelphia, 1991), 147. See also *Lex Baiuwariorum*, 33.1–5, 45; 92.1–4, 82, in *The Burgundian Code*, trans. and ed. Katherine Fischer Drew (1949; repr., Philadelphia, 1988).

140. Carmen 20, 186–87, line 23.

fuori le Mura confirms such an expectation. The two figures wear decorated clothing and long golden earrings. Such lavish female clothing may often have been of silk.[141] The *Institutio sanctimonialium* of 816 twice forbade silk clothing to religious women in its canons, and the shining attributes of a number of women in court poetry may reflect the sheen of their silken clothing in addition to the glow of their skin and the brightness of their jewelry. *Karolus Magnus et Leo papa* has many descriptions of the shining clothing and jewelry of women. Gisela, Charlemagne's sister was dressed in "shimmering white" and her purple veil glowed. Bertha, dressed in gems, shone. Rotrud gleamed with gems and adornment as she led her sisters to the hunt.[142] In fact, the entire "crowd of girls," dressed in gems and silk, shimmered.[143] Theodulf of Orléans also described the splendid, sometimes shining attire of Charlemagne's daughters in his poem, "On the Court." Purple cloth, gold, and gems made the women gleam. He even described the colors of their clothing: yellow, dark-red, and snow-white. Though hardly literal descriptions, these passages suggest that the Carolingian elite expected to see richly dressed women, who though perhaps not quite so resplendent, shone with what silken clothing and jewelry they had. Specific lay garments remain impossible to reconstruct. Hathumoda rejected clothing adorned with gold, and Theodulf's description of Charlemagne's daughters mentions dresses and bodices. Both descriptions are rather vague. Gisela wore a cloak and veil, but she was an abbess, and the clothing of the religious is easier to reconstruct because more evidence for it survives than for lay clothing.[144]

Jewelry and hair adornments received more attention in Carolingian texts, perhaps because unlike clothing, a necessity for anyone in northwestern Europe, they were a more common source of vanity. Archeology has provided many rich examples of Merovingian jewelry. Found in 1959 in a tomb in Saint-Denis, dated to c. 570 and probably from the burial jewels of the Merovingian queen Arnegond, wife of Clothar I (511–561), pieces such as the pair of gold and electrum veil pins and the large gold, silver, and garnet pin help to suggest the kinds of items to which writers referred in discussing female accoutrements.[145] The large pin may have provided a means for twisting up a woman's long hair. In his rendition of the text of the judgment concerning the uprising at the convent at Poitiers in 590, Gregory of Tours mentioned a *vitta*

---

141. The European elite increasingly wore silk clothing throughout the early Middle Ages. Fleming, "Acquiring, Flaunting and Destroying Silk in Late Anglo-Saxon England," 133–42.

142. *Karolus Magnus*, 74, lines 213–18.

143. Ibid., 78, lines 258–65.

144. Müller, *Die Kleidung nach Quellen*, 137.

145. M.A.N. 87429 and M.A.N. 87425, both at the Louvre Museum.

aura exornata, meant for the abbess' niece to wear at her engagement party, and the Carolingian poem *Karolus Magnus et Leo papa* used the term *vitta*.[146] In a passage describing Charlemagne's daughter Rotrud, she wears a *vitta* in her hair.[147] The other passage mentioning a *vitta* from the same poem reveals the problems of interpreting a single type of adornment:

> The queen sets out from this august bedchamber having lingered
>   a long while,
> With a great throng gathered around
> Charles' very beautiful wife Liutgard.
> Their flashing necks shine taking on a rosy color;
> Indeed splendid purple yields to her encircled hair;
> Her shining locks are wreathed appropriately with purple headbands (*vittis*);
> Golden threads close her cloak, and she wears a beryl upon her head;
> Her diadem gleaming with bright metal
> Shines, and her purple attire of twice-colored linen;
> Their shining necks are adorned with various stones.[148]

Determining precisely what constituted a *vitta* is probably impossible; but because Charlemagne's wife Liutgard and daughter Rotrud wear *vittae* in this poem and because the word occurs most frequently in panegyric, the ornament doubtless helped to denote high status.[149] Though the word may not indicate precisely what Carolingian women wore, it suggests that others expected elite women to adorn their heads. Perhaps a *vitta* resembled the gold braids found in so many Anglo-Saxon female graves.[150]

Other texts provide an equally ambiguous guide to female accoutrements. Theodulf in describing Charlemagne's daughters in "On the Court," mentions brooches, necklaces, and armbands. Naturally, the many references to gems have far more to do with religious imagery than reality, but it suggests the desire that women adorn themselves as richly as possible. Religious women were not to keep jewelry, which the *Institutio sanctimonialium* banned, or the kinds of adornment Hathumoda rejected in her *vita*. Most of these items would have been worn about the head. Hathumoda rejected hair pins, perhaps similar to Arnegond's pins as well as "female headgear, head bands,... earrings,

---

146. Gregory of Tours, *Decem libri historiarum*, chap. 10.16, MGH SRM 1.1, ed. Bruno Krusch and Wilhelm Levison (Hanover, Germany, 1951), 505.

147. *Karolus Magnus*, 74, line 215.

148. Ibid., 72, lines 182–91.

149. Ibid., 72, line 187.

150. Elisabeth Crowfoot and Sonia Chadwick Hawkes, "Early Anglo-Saxon Gold Braids," *Medieval Archaeology* 11 (1967): 42–86, 61–62.

necklaces, bracelets, adornments, chaplets." Although this passage relies heavily on Isaiah 3:18–23, two items differ—adornments (*destraliola*) and chaplets (*strophia*)—while the others represent items with which women throughout Western history had dressed themselves and would continue to wear for centuries to come. Agius left off some of the items in this biblical passage suggesting that he may have recalled the passage only in part as he wrote the *vita*, was unconsciously influenced by it, or consciously chose items from it. Specifically he left off Isaiah's torques, anklets (*periscelidas*), small necklaces (*murenulas*), rings (*annulos*), gems hanging from one's front (*gemmas in fronte pendentes*), capes (*mutatoria*), mantles or veils (*palliola*), linen cloths (*linteamina*), needle (*acus*), mirrors (*specula*), silken cloth (*sindones*), and summer garments (*theristra*). Some of these words, such as *mutatoria* and *periscelidas* occur quite rarely in the Latin corpus; Agius may have left them off if he thought his readers were not familiar with them. Some other terms, *palliola*, *linteamina*, and *sindones*, occur relatively frequently in Carolingian texts; they identify what were probably common items. Agius may not have considered these items generally as vain but rather worried that opulent clothes posed a greater problem. Alcuin urged Charlemagne's daughters in a letter to show their rank through their behavior, not through "a display of shining gold," a turn of phrase that encapsulates the various ways in which laywomen could adorn themselves with the sorts of golden jewelry and ornamentation that Agius later mentioned.

Adornment did not merely consist of physical items but of other means of changing or enhancing one's appearance. Hathumoda rejected perfumes, which suggests that the Carolingian elite expected women to smell pleasant. Also, cultivation and behavior could enhance a woman's appearance by the way in which she carried herself. After all Angilbert noted that the bearing of Charlemagne's daughters contributed to their beauty. When Sedulius wrote two of his poems for Bertha, daughter of Lothar and Irmingard, he described her mother as embodying "graceful beauty" when she was young and as being "noble in disposition."[151] It seems that aristocratic men expected a certain level of grace among their female peers.

Men associated youth with beauty. Old women probably lost social position as their ability to appear pretty in the male gaze faded. A woman's lovely appearance attracted men and served as an elite marker, but it could not last. Raban Maur in his commentary on the third chapter of Ecclesiastes discussed some repercussions of female aging. "The beautiful woman, who attracts bands of adolescents, her countenance will be drawn into furrows: and first she is regarded with love, afterwards with disgust. For the orator preeminent

---

151. Carmen 24, 189, line 15; Carmen 78, 228, line 8.

among the Greeks writes that the beauty of the body is destroyed by time and consumed by listlessness. Her precious beauty therefore dries out and fails."[152] The loss of a woman's youthful beauty served as a visible reminder of her passing years and, for Raban, of the ephemeral nature of physical good looks.

Determining what constituted female old age may help us understand its repercussions for beauty, but the paucity and types of relevant sources prevent precise conclusions. Late antique and early medieval people do not seem to have defined old age chronologically for women. The paradigm of the ages of man was an ideal model that applied to men, not women.[153] Carolingian clerics did not employ mentions of old women to convey certain ideas in the same way that they sometimes used the old man (*senex*), especially in poetry. Rather, two approaches prove more fruitful to understanding female old age in the Carolingian era. The first is a demographic or biological approach, focused on determining about how long a woman could expect to live and the possible reasons for that longevity. The obstacles to obtaining clear results with such a methodology, however, prevent knowing the precise age at which a woman was considered old, therefore complicating the second approach: examining how others expected old women to function in society.[154] Ninth-century data from polyptychs indicate that men may have outnumbered women and possibly lived longer than they did, but the variety of possible explanations for this discrepancy makes uncertain all generalizations about the female versus the male lifespan and the number of men compared to women in the early Middle Ages.[155] Women in religious communities, who bore no children and who sometimes had a more dependable food supply, probably lived longer than laywomen, to an average of 56.5 to 60 years.[156] The death of the ninth-century abbess of Gandersheim, Hathumoda, in an epidemic, however, demonstrates that they fell prey to some of the same dangers as their lay counterparts.[157] Unfortunately, the two memorial books that survive from female monasteries at Remiremont and San Salvatore in Brescia do not provide sufficient information for a demographic study.[158]

---

152. Raban Maur, *Commentario de Ecclesiastes*, PL 109, col. 858.

153. For a Carolingian example, see Raban Maur, *De universo*, chap. 7.1, PL 111, cols. 179–81.

154. Garver, "Old Age and Women in the Carolingian World," 123–24.

155. Polyptychs list low status individuals. For the possible explanations for the gender difference see Devroey, "Femmes au miroir," 238–44.

156. Schulenburg, *Forgetful of Their Sex*, 365–76.

157. Agius, *Vita Hathumodae*, chap. 22, 173.

158. The memorial book from Remiremont contains necrologies that might help with a relative date of death, but it contains no clear information on the women's entry into the religious life as is found in the memorial book from San Salvatore in Brescia, which contains an oblation list but no comprehensive necrologies of the nuns.

Royal women in the early medieval world could live as long as their male counterparts: to 60 or 70, an age at which many kings died naturally.[159] For Carolingian queens, the average age at death was probably around 35, with an average life expectancy of 40.5 after very early childhood, but the high rate of death in childhood and the increased risks of death during childbearing years pull these averages down.[160] The relative lack of iron in the early medieval diet meant that the critical need for this mineral among pregnant and nursing mothers went unmet, and many early medieval laywomen probably had severe anemia that left them more susceptible to death in the form of disease and injury.[161] Nevertheless, women in the early Middle Ages could survive into their sixties and sometimes seventies; the relative lack of information about old women results more from the nature of the sources and Carolingian views of old women than from their high death rates earlier in life from problems related to childbearing.

Measuring old age on the basis of having reached a certain age is highly problematic even in the case of men. Medieval people recognized that aging could be a gradual and individual process. What constituted old age for women in the Carolingian world related far more to social, familial, and individual circumstances than reaching a specific birthday. In particular, the loss of fertility marked a new stage in life for laywomen. Miscarriages, stillbirths, and other complications from pregnancy and childbirth must have taken their toll, rendering medieval women infertile at younger ages than women in the modern era.[162] The age medieval medical authorities maintained for the onset of menopause suggests that Carolingian women most often may have reached menopause between 40 and 50.[163] When referring to an early medieval woman as old, therefore, I use the term in relative, not precise terms. Women in the religious life highlight the impossibility of being exact about female old age in the Carolingian world because fertility was not an issue for them. Within monastic communities, however, members recognized the aged as a group with greater needs than other adult members.

The paucity of detail in histories and annals suggests that narrative texts such as hagiography and literary works such as poetry may reveal more vividly the past views of female old age. When explaining the foundation of Conques around 800 in *In Honor of Louis*, Ermold the Black describes a pivotal event in the life of Datus, a man thought to be the first inhabitant of

159. Stafford, *QCD*, 144–45.

160. Dutton, *Charlemagne's Mustache and Other Cultural Clusters of a Dark Age*, 158–59 and appendix 3. See also Wemple, *WFS*, appendix, 199–201.

161. Bullough and Campbell, "Female Longevity and Diet in the Middle Ages," 317–25.

162. Shahar, *Growing Old in the Middle Ages*, 12–13, 19.

163. Post, "Ages at Menarche and Menopause."

Conques and eventually a brother at that monastery. The wealthy Datus lived with his mother, who, Ermold notes, was fortunate, "sospite matre."[164] In describing her as "fortunate," he suggests that she had reached an age at which ill health, frailty, or family neglect may not have been unexpected. Although Ermold never uses a word that clearly indicates the age of Datus's mother, his account implies that others probably considered her to be old. Datus is a mature man, an indication that his mother must at least be approaching forty. Furthermore, Datus makes a decision concerning his mother's fate that implies that she had outlived her relative usefulness to her son and possibly to society as a whole. Accompanied by followers, an outsider named Maures invaded the Rouergue, immediately established a fortification, and proceeded to seize Datus's household goods as well as his mother. Gathering his arms and his companions, he immediately set out by horseback to find Maures. Upon reaching his fortification, Datus prepared to break through the gate, but Maures did not want to face Datus in battle. The "young Maures" jeered at him from the rampart, telling him he must give up his beloved horse for his goods and mother. Otherwise he promised to kill her right before Datus's eyes.[165] Datus replied: "Give my mother a funeral; I don't care. For you shamelessly demand this horse of which I will never deem you worthy; by no means is it fitting to give its reins to you."[166] Without hesitation, Maures killed Datus's mother and then held her head aloft to taunt her son. Datus instantly regretted his decision, and the profound sorrow that he had allowed his mother to die caused him to give up arms and become a hermit.[167]

This semi-legendary episode reveals far more about expectations and perceptions than about any sort of historical reality. Ermold placed this anecdote in his poem to offer a counterexample of a good leader, not to comment on old age. The episode relates a reverse model; laymen ought not to behave as Datus who loved worldly goods and specifically his horse so much that he allowed a defenseless kinswoman to die. Datus realized only too late that he loved his mother or at least regretted his complicity in her death. Datus's mother functions in the tale as a figure who allows the poet to make his point; she does not even have her own name. Ermold does not explain why Datus may have valued his horse more than the woman who gave birth to him. Yet Datus may not have been unusual for initially believing his horse to be worth

---

164. Ermold, *In honorem*, 24, line 245.
165. Ibid., 24–6, lines 246–75.
166. Ibid., 26, lines 277–79.
167. Ibid., 26, lines 280–91.

more than a woman whose childbearing years presumably were past and whose immediate utility may not have been apparent. The above-mentioned emphasis on family and reproduction meant that the youth, which indicated fertility, was a probable component of beauty. The Carolingian male gaze expected young women, still capable of bearing heirs and attracting attention. If we recall Dhuoda's words about women and their mirrors, we realize male pressure to be beautiful probably became ever more untenable for women as they aged. All the more reason they needed to employ their experience and social competence to exert some agency.

The male Carolingian gaze then expected to observe young, fair skinned, and pleasantly scented laywomen with long hair, wearing richly decorated silk clothing, jewelry, and various hair adornments. In many respects this description is little different than that of beautiful women throughout much of Western history. Though that continuity results partly from the classical, biblical, and late antique sources upon which Carolingians drew, it reflects the phenomenon that, because of these longstanding expectations, women continued to conform to these ideas. Thus, continuity in the ideals of female appearance came to be reflected in reality just as the available types of clothing, jewelry, and adornment affected the ideal appearance that men wrote about. Men saw female beauty through the prism of earlier traditions and ideals, but one cannot escape the sexual and gender implications inherent in these ideas. Women did not merely display wealth; they scented themselves, dressed and adorned themselves to be physically attractive to men, to show others that they were women, and perhaps to please themselves. Though the biblical Judith provides our only concrete example of a woman using her beauty to achieve a goal, other evidence, such as Regino of Prüm's discussion of Friderada, suggests that the Carolingians believed lovely women could seduce men and convince others of their good intentions. Beauty may have been a powerful tool for Carolingian women, though the sources provide little direct evidence for specific female actions in this regard. More obvious are the ways in which men's ideals put pressure on elite women to promote a certain appearance, much as the women Dhuoda describes gazing in their mirrors to catch the imperfections that might displease their husbands. Women did not shape notions of loveliness so much as those conceptions impinged female social practices, yet cultivation of beauty in response to male demands influenced female portrayals in remaining sources. Although this glimpse of the Carolingian gaze is fleeting, it suggests that clerical ideals almost certainly influenced the ways men perceived the appearance of the women around them and the ways women responded to these male expectations.

Female Beauty in the Carolingian World

Ecclesiastical leaders writing throughout the late eighth and ninth centuries in Carolingian lands appreciated the power of beauty—whether of images, objects, or people—to affect the perceptions of viewers. Just as those men addressing the image controversy understood that a pretty object might not necessarily lead a viewer to a worthy path, so too did writers addressing female appearance recognize that a lovely woman might not be virtuous despite the ancient trope that made that connection. Rather, clerics took a complex set of views regarding beauty, often depending upon the genre of their particular works, their audiences, and their goals. Beauty mattered in the Carolingian world because it identified some women as aristocratic and confirmed their social prestige. Ideally, it also indicated virtue, but this correlation remained consistent only in exegesis, hagiography, and panegyric. Good looks in women or female figures automatically implied virtue in exegetical texts and hagiography, while in panegyric poets made efforts to note the presence of both beauty and virtue, as if to imply that such a combination was especially laudable. The concern in annals and histories not with women's appearance but with their noble lineage demonstrates the reason others valued such a combination; it potentially contributed to the stability of the family. In his mirror, Jonas separated good looks and morality more explicitly, warning that virtue was a woman's most important quality and beauty, though desirable, was not as crucial. In letters and hagiography religious men warned of the vanity that too much concern with appearance could produce. These texts indicate that women and their families and husbands must have been concerned with their outward appearance, even if these texts present images, rather than actual observations, of women.

The repetition of this theme of beauty demonstrates its importance in Carolingian aristocratic culture. Rather than merely reflecting the fact that women through the ages have been appreciated for their loveliness, a pretty wife or daughter benefited a man, adding to his status, because she may have been part of the rich display of his household or a prize to show off at court. Adorned women acted as another marker of the male aristocrat, and indeed cultivation of personal physical beauty and rich display in the lay world marked women as members of the elite. Men expected that religious women should be lovely, too. Their virtue meant that their piety should be reflected in their unadorned good looks. Their appearance also denoted the rank of the men to whom they were related; the religious women Gisela and Bertha, for example, helped to mark the royal status of Charlemagne and Lothar, respectively. Attractive female saints, such as Liutberga or Leoba, contributed to the prestige of their religious communities. According to both lay and clerical value systems, women could exhibit beauty in similar ways and yet convey multiple meanings. The richly dressed, beautiful wife of an aristocrat demonstrated his power and wealth at the same time suggesting her own virtue. Ideally, a wife or daughter, like Liutgard in Theodulf's poem, would be "more lovely in her fitting actions" than her physical beauty and rich adornment alone could allow. In so doing, she served the interests and needs of the male Carolingian elite, lay and religious alike. Yet male desire that she cultivate her beauty put her at risk of an accusation of vanity, and the male gaze anticipated features that old women did not have—no longer considered beautiful, they especially needed to employ their social competence. Expectations of beauty must therefore have made demands that some women could not meet.

Chapter Two

FAMILY

Bonds and Memory

The case of Gisela, daughter of Eberhard of Friuli and his wife Gisela, dem-onstrates the convergence of family bonds, land, and memory in the expec-tations and actions of female members of aristocratic families in the ninth century. Her name recalled both her mother and her mother's aunt, Gisela, the abbess of Chelles and sister of Charlemagne, for the youngest Gisela was the granddaughter of Louis the Pious and his second wife, Judith. Thus, through her name, Gisela bore the memory of her mother's illustrious family, but she also preserved the memory of her father and his family. Gisela entered the religious community of San Salvatore at Brescia, where her father's name, but not her mother's, was entered along with hers in the oblation list of the community's memorial book, put together under the tenure of abbess Amal-berga (first notice 837).[1] Her family almost certainly endowed her with lands, thereby providing the oblation offering that was usually necessary for entry into a religious community and some security for part of the family patri-mony. Furthermore, San Salvatore's memorial book, containing lists of the living and the dead for whom the members were to pray, included young Gisela, her mother and father, and her brothers.[2] Gisela herself would have participated in the liturgical commemoration of her family; texts for such cele-brations were recorded in the memorial book as well as the lists of names. Later, in their will her parents bequeathed two books to her.[3] Clearly, their bond with their daughter continued beyond her consecration and indeed

---

1. MGH Libri mem. N.S. 4, 183, fol. 43ᵛ.
2. Ibid., 148, fol. 8ʳ.
3. *CAC*, no. 1, 4.

beyond their own deaths. Gisela's situation was far from unusual; in fact her case demonstrates how women helped their families to shape a familial identity, to gain and maintain prestige and power, and to ensure spiritual benefit for their souls.

Female maintenance of memory and land as well as their commemoration of the dead contributed to lasting, crucial bonds between women, whether lay or religious, and their families. The early medieval family has undergone concentrated study for at least the past fifty years, but that scholarship has failed to account adequately for Carolingian women's critical contributions to family identity. Most early medieval women must be studied as members of kin networks and the religious and spiritual communities in which they lived. By focusing on female dependency and familial relations, the degree to which families and kin relationships obscure individual women becomes moot.[4] Charters, memorial books, and liturgy offer evidence of other women who, like Gisela, helped to preserve their families' memories and patrimonies. Elite women therefore sometimes had agency to aid their family's situation, though having powerful kin from the beginning of life was mainly an accident of birth.

Preserving memory here means not only the retention of knowledge about kin both living and dead but also participation in specific acts of remembering, praying for, and celebrating the deceased and the living, thereby shaping others' knowledge and impression of particular kinship groups.[5] As the social anthropologist Paul Connerton has argued, the performance of rites constitutes a key means of creating social memory.[6] The Carolingian elite more generally employed the written word to construct a common identity by shaping the memory of a shared past.[7] Some women also received portions of their families' patrimonies, giving their natal families another means to retain some control over that land, perhaps to use it as a way to draw upon the resources of their female relatives' marital or spiritual kin. Calling a son-in-law to help defend family interests or asking for the prayers of the convent in which a daughter resided could be another means to gain a desired level of power. For these reasons, women often had a relatively high degree of flexibility in preserving family bonds and memory. In particular, women's personal commemoration of the dead in liturgical acts and their prayers for the dead and living listed in the two female memorial books from the Carolingian

---

4. For an explication of this problem see Smith, "Gender and Ideology," 51.

5. Memory was a collective act, based upon identification with, definition of, and membership in particular social groups. Halbwachs, *The Collective Memory*, 23; Fentress and Wickham, *Social Memory*, 144–72.

6. Connerton, *How Societies Remember*, 40 and passim.

7. McKitterick, *History and Memory*, 7.

period contributed significantly to lasting bonds between aristocratic women and their families. Although clearer evidence remains for liturgical commemoration by religious women, laywomen also maintained familial lands and memory as charters, wills, Dhuoda's handbook for William, and letters demonstrate. The elder Gisela ensured commemoration of her kin at the family monastery of Cysoing in addition to the prayers carried out at San Salvatore in Brescia. Women sometimes donated land, a principal means of guaranteeing prayer for one's family and a continuing bond with a major religious institution.

Religious women often remained physically close to their birth families, contributing to the strength of their bonds with natal kin. Clerics and monks could and often did travel more widely and frequently than their religious sisters. Though often retaining close associations with their natal families, men generally had a greater capacity to act in their own interests. Women had to rely on the help of others in looking after lands and even their own security. Religious women sometimes kept control over their own estates.[8] Such compromise allowed them to help maintain part of their families' patrimonies while creating a bond between their families and religious houses. Some evidence indicates that women could leave monastic institutions for marriage or other purposes that benefited their families without suffering severe repercussions. Their proximity to their families allowed their kin easier access to them than to their male relatives in the religious life.

Aristocratic families valued the sorts of bonds women could create, but modern scholars have not yet appreciated how that aim conflicted at times with the ideas of clerics and the royal family. Aside from cultivating the virtue clerics urged upon them, women needed to try to fulfill the material and spiritual promise their relatives may have seen in them. Churchmen often railed against women's actions outside the spheres of family and cloister and urged strict enforcement of claustration because of women's continuing familial bonds. Clerics encouraged religious men and women alike to sever their ties to their kin in order to pursue a life wholly devoted to God at the same time that they increasingly argued for the indissolubility of marriage.[9] Nevertheless, their reforms involved compromise with the demands of aristocratic families, who needed flexibility in their relations with female relatives in the religious life. Irrevocably cutting ties with a daughter would have defeated many of her family's purposes in providing her with oblation offerings so that she could enter a convent. Although genuine desire for monastic reform played no small role in church and imperial legislation, Carolingian

---

8. Schilp, *NW*, 177–78.
9. Toubert, "Le moment carolingien," 355–56.

rulers may have supported these specific clerical reforms in their capitulary legislation in part because they recognized that weakening female bonds with their families might give rulers greater power over magnates. If aristocratic families could not maintain some control over the pieces of their family patrimonies that they preserved at their female relatives' religious communities and if they had greater restrictions upon their foundation and control of female religious houses, it could decrease their ability to compete with the royal family. Suzanne Wemple and others have argued that these clerical and royal efforts constricted women's influence.[10] Yet these censures signal just how crucial women's activities were.

During the Carolingian period a tension developed between the secular desire to maintain a family patrimony and produce heirs through advantageous marriage and the church's efforts to curb sexuality and confine it to monogamous procreation within marriage. Clerics believed that marriage was necessary for the good of lay society because it allowed the laity to lead virtuous lives.[11] Jonas of Orléans, for example, began the second book of *De institutione laicali*, which concerned marriage, by expounding upon marriage's principal purpose of procreation.[12] Without a wife, a layman's material and spiritual well-being was in some jeopardy, particularly because he needed legitimate children. Only some men could afford wives: a bar against marriage constituted a marked loss of status. Such a prohibition served sometimes as punishment for men, revealing that a wife was crucial to power and influence in the Carolingian lay world. Stripping men of sanctioned access to sex also contributed to their penitent state.[13] Through marriage to a woman of higher rank, a man could raise his own status and that of his heirs (who usually inherited the mother's social position), thereby increasing his ability to exert power.[14] Having a family furthermore helped to guarantee a man's own commemoration and that of his relatives and ancestors. Through remembrance of marital relatives, mothers could create strong bonds with their children's paternal kin, from whom their offspring might profit through inheritance or patronage. In the long run such preservation may have benefited the mothers, who often became dependent upon male children for means of influence, but contemporaries seem to have expected women to do this regardless of any potential advantage.

---

10. Wemple, *WFS*, 123; idem, "Female Monasticism in Italy," 291–310; Schulenburg, "Strict Active Enclosure and Its Effects," 51–86; idem, "Women's Monastic Communities," 261–92; McNamara, *Sisters in Arms*, 148–75.

11. Toubert, "La théorie du mariage," 245.

12. Jonas, *Institutione*, 2.1, cols. 167–68.

13. Leyser, "Early Medieval Canon Law," 58–60.

14. Rio, "Freedom and Unfreedom," 20–21.

This chapter offers a brief overview of the rich secondary literature on memory and family before presenting new evidence for the ways women provided many benefits to their natal, marital, and spiritual families through bonds and memory. The variation and flexibility that characterized the family in the Carolingian world helps to explain the kinds of memorial commemoration that marked that era. Case studies of three royal foundations—San Salvatore at Brescia, Remiremont, and Fulda—reveal that female bonds to royal monasteries helped allow families to exert power and provided social cohesion within the Carolingian elite. These three examples concern rather different areas of the Carolingian Empire—northern Italy, the borderland between West Francia and Lotharingia, and Saxony—demonstrating relative unity of social practice throughout the empire in this regard. Women found ways to preserve familial memory through male foundations such as Fulda, not only through female houses. A range of other cases across time and space contextualizes that evidence and reveals a common cultural pattern of female commemoration.

The Family and Memorial Commemoration in the Carolingian World

Although kinship was a key means of marking one's membership in the Carolingian elite, the exact working out of kin relations and their relative weight versus other bonds remains a complex topic. Recent scholarship has stressed the dynamism and flexibility of the family in Carolingian lands rather than attempting to provide any strict definition.[15] A common term for household, *familia*, could vary in its connotations. Centered on the conjugal couple, a *familia* usually consisted of the nuclear family while the kinship group (*Sippe*) included all those who believed themselves to be related to each other by blood or marriage. In addition to the conjugal couple and any children, a household at times included extended kin, servants, and retainers, located at a certain residence (*domus*), though in the early Middle Ages *domus* sometimes referred to a lord's household members or to a family without reference to place.[16] Although a nuclear family centered on the conjugal couple usually superseded any extended kin group or *Sippe* in importance among the elite, especially with the palpably increased insistence on monogamy in the Carolingian era, each individual case presents a different set of variables. Families

---

15. See particularly the bibliographies in Nelson, "Family, Gender and Sexuality," 153–76, and Le Jan, *FP.*

16. Le Jan, *FP,* 429; Réal, *Vie de saints,* 97–98, 315.

needed to cultivate and use broader kin relations. Though more prominent in the eighth century, even in the ninth century horizontal kinship played a significant role in the working out of bonds among the elite, particularly those to the royal family. The Pippinids gained power in the Frankish world during the eighth century in part through those on the margins of their kin group, making the Carolingian family well aware that others could employ similar bonds to gain power at their expense.[17] Ian Wood, for example, has noted that the Pippinid line emphasized cognatic ties when it suited them: strategic exogamous marriages and stressing connections to certain female relatives were essential to this family's identity and power.[18]

Anthropologists have argued for the impossibility of separating any "kinship domain" from the religious, political and economic.[19] In the Carolingian world, the lack of distinction between public and private further supports an examination of family, kinship, and memory within that wide context. Households participated in a network of links among families, religious institutions, the royal family, and their various followers. That web of relations complicates any picture of the family beyond the conjugal unit. Multiple, and sometimes conflicting, bonds could influence a person in the early Middle Ages. Some cut across family relations. Rifts and competition could cause discord, but marriage helped to regulate bonds and maintain peace in the Carolingian world by creating equilibrium among kin groups.

Carolingian women contributed to both the equilibrium and competition among the elite by facilitating or hindering the development of certain bonds and by preserving familial memory and patrimony. They were hardly alone in their actions: contemporary Anglo-Saxon and Lombard women and tenth-century women in Saxony also commemorated their families and protected family lands through membership in religious communities.[20] Because aristocratic families lacked single seats of power at this time, they often focused their loyalties on a religious foundation, which widows, younger sons, or daughters usually led.[21] The purposes of these institutions reflect religious women's strong affinity with the interests of the aristocracy. One religious rule allowed women to hold their own land even after consecration and to maintain relatively extensive contact with their families. A product of reforms set in place by Louis the Pious and his advisers, the *Institutio sanctimonialium Aquisgranensis,*

---

17. Le Jan, *FP,* 227–28, 399–401.
18. Wood, "Genealogy Defined by Women," 234–56.
19. Goody, *The European Family,* 9.
20. Fell, *Women in Anglo-Saxon England,* 109–28; Baltrusch-Schneider, "Klosterleben als Alternative Lebensform zur Ehe?" 47–48; Lees and Overing, *Double Agents,* 37; Nelson, "Making a Difference," 173–74; Leyser, *Rule and Conflict,* 49–73.
21. Goetz, "Social and Military Institutions," 470.

was issued at the Aachen imperial synod of 816. Those attending the synod stipulated that religious women in the Carolingian Empire had to choose to live under either the *Institutio sanctimonialium* or the Benedictine rule, which would supersede all earlier religious rules for women.[22] Although the authors of the *Institutio sanctimonialium* insisted upon strict enclosure, they allowed women leeway to pursue family interests. Religious women generally retained stronger ties to their natal families than men.[23] When Liutberga, for example, wished to become a recluse, her patron helped to install her at a monastery led by his sister.[24] Yet depending upon each individual case, female interaction with their birth families varied. The patterns of female memorial activity were fluid.

The complex subject of the relationship between the living and the dead has engaged scholars since Gerd Tellenbach first began to notice patterns in the lists of names in *libri memoriales* or memorial books.[25] Rather than random or indecipherable collections of names, the lists consist of groups, including families, confraternity groups, and other individuals associated by bonds of blood or friendship (*amicitia*). Through investigation of these memorial books, scholars have been able to make connections among various religious institutions and powerful families of early medieval Europe. Charters and other records of land donation further indicate that these relationships continued over many generations, with the giving and taking back of the same lands. This exchange helped to ensure that the religious institution would pray for and liturgically commemorate the family's dead while the family reconfirmed the religious institution's possession of land from its patrimony. These continual negotiations of land and memory created networks or communities of donors.[26]

Memorial activity had wide social, political, cultural, and religious implications because it forged new and preserved existing bonds. With roots in antiquity, Christianity and contemporary conditions affected its forms and meanings in the early Middle Ages. The act of commemoration established a relationship among the living, the dead, and their descendants while helping to ensure eternal life through assurances of continual prayer.[27] For women,

---

22. Schilp, *NW,* 13–16.

23. Smith, "The Problem of Female Sanctity," 25; de Jong, *In Samuel's Image,* 65–66.

24. *Vita Liutbirgae,* chap. 15, 20.

25. Gerd Tellenbach, *Zur Bedeutung der Personenforschung für die Erkenntnis des früheren Mittelalters,* Freiburger Universitätsreden N.F. 25 (Freiburg, 1957), 10–14. Excellent bibliographies are found in the most recent four MGH editions of the memorial books from Reichenau, Regensburg, Remiremont, and Brescia.

26. Rosenwein, *To Be the Neighbor of St. Peter,* 48.

27. Wollasch and Schmid, "Die Gemeinschaft der Lebenden und Verstorbenen in Zeugnissen des Mittelalters," 368–70. See also the essays in Schmid and Wollasch, *Memoria.*

such activities not only served their families' needs and goals but also reflected their virtue because remembering the dead and taking care of the sick and of bodies constituted acts of piety. One means of guaranteeing commemoration was to found a family church or religious community, which a relative led.[28] Through donation of land, an individual often ensured that her name and those of her family and *amici* were entered in a monastery's memorial book. The land provided for the material needs of the religious community, which could spend its time praying. Such donations of land provided the names of living heirs, to demonstrate their permission for the gift, and of the dead, frequently those from whom the donor had inherited land. Care for and remembrance of the dead provided a means to control a family's past.[29] Commemoration defined the family: memorial prayers named members of kin groups. By ensuring such acts an aristocratic family set itself into a wider kin group, while at the same time it emphasized parents and grandparents in memorial documents, demonstrating the greater consequence of more immediate family and the conjugal couple.[30]

Use of land and bonds varied. Different groups developed connections through exchange of land; such transactions could signify relationships of kinship, friendship, alliance, subordination, or enmity. Although most documents concerning land relate to the church, they nonetheless show that people of differing economic and social levels participated in these exchanges, which were marked by regional variation.[31] Political and social instability increased the importance of protecting family patrimony, prestige, and memory through donation of land to and membership of kin in religious institutions. Fragmentation characterized landholding in this period, distinguishing the elite from more humble free landowners: the most powerful magnates of the Carolingian era had extensive but scattered holdings. Thus, the Carolingian Empire on one level consisted of overlapping areas of aristocratic influence, from localities to entire regions. Women must have operated powerfully within and among these small worlds, though documenting it satisfactorily is impossible.[32] The actions that aristocratic women took to preserve their families' memories and patrimonies resemble those of queens, but they also reflect non-royal aristocratic concerns and conditions. Distinguishing

---

28. Wood, *The Proprietary Church in the Medieval West*, 178, 345–46, 737.

29. Innes, "Keeping It in the Family," 17, 27.

30. Le Jan, *FP*, 35–38.

31. Hammer, "Land Sales in Eighth- and Ninth-Century Bavaria," 71–74; Innes, *State and Society in the Early Middle Ages*, 93, 165; Goldberg, *Struggle for Empire*, 187, 222.

32. In her study of small village communities in ninth-century Brittany, Wendy Davies noticed that women, usually aristocrats, could occasionally act rather independently and exert substantial power. Davies, *Small Worlds*, 72–79.

between the memorial activity of men and women, much less between that of lay and religious, seems rather artificial, even if the degree of their participation and the remaining evidence for those acts varies. In donating land, praying for the souls of living and dead relatives, and creating bonds between their families and religious institutions, men and women, both lay and religious, employed knowledge of their ancestors and relatives, basic religious precepts, and liturgical acts.

Carolingian female preservation of familial memory had roots in late antiquity and in the Merovingian and Lombard kingdoms and thereby resulted from a complex network of traditions and beliefs. Merovingian religious women's main duty was prayer, and the liturgy for the dead was central to their daily life. Although no memorial books remain from c. 550–c. 750, other evidence demonstrates that contemporaries believed that female prayer was efficacious, offering protection for those outside the religious community and ensuring the spiritual health of the dead, whom the women commemorated.[33] Lombard families started communities for women and men to help ensure their commemoration and to bolster their own power. Eighth- and ninth-century Carolingian women throughout the empire continued such practices, especially at religious communities such as San Salvatore in Brescia and Remiremont, which had memorial books. Young girls entered the religious life, where they stood between the living and the dead, offering prayers for their families. Evidence for similar commemoration is also relatively rich in Saxon *vitae*. For example, in the *Vita Hathumodae*, Agius notes that included among those who gathered to mourn Hathumoda's passing were people in the community whom she had affected.[34] His account presents both an expression of Hathumoda's perceived sanctity in the local area and an expectation of religious women's role in mourning and commemorating those from their own house, particularly abbesses.

These arguments concerning Carolingian women conform to current scholarly consensus concerning the other ways women cared for the memory of their families. From at least the seventh through eleventh centuries in western Europe, women were sometimes responsible for caring for the sick, preparing the dead for burial, and mourning the dead with lamentations.[35] Warfare, sickness, and accidents, especially as a result of hunting, spelled premature death for many men. Religious women were not at risk of

---

33. Muschiol, *Famula Dei*, 168–91, 312–43.

34. Agius, *Vita Hathumodae*, chap. 25, 174–75.

35. *Beowulf and the Fight at Finnsburg*, 42, lines 1117–18, and 118, lines 3150–55; Geary, *Phantoms of Remembrance*, 52–54; Innes, "Keeping It in the Family," 27; Bonnie Effros, *Caring for Body and Soul: Burial and the Afterlife in the Merovingian World* (University Park, Penn., 2002), 177–80.

dying in childbirth, and their longer life spans meant they may have acquired substantial land and wealth.[36] Though historians once believed that women usually had little charge over such family resources, the relatively frequent interventions of women in donations demonstrate that they sometimes could exert control while their spouses lived. Among the documents from St. Gall between c. 700 and c. 900, a high number of married women made independent donations or transfers, in addition to their joint donations with their husbands.[37]

Although laywomen retained strong bonds to religious houses into the ninth century, aristocratic families less frequently founded female houses in the eighth and ninth centuries than in the seventh century. The Carolingian family gained ever more control over monasteries. Many powerful families sent their daughters to royal monasteries to acquire prestige and to create bonds with the royal family. In this way, the royal family helped aristocrats to maintain their family memories. These royal foundations therefore offer a natural starting point for investigating the ways female preservation of family memory reflected the negotiation between lay and clerical needs as well as between those of magnates and the king.

Remiremont

Remiremont and San Salvatore produced the only two memorial books surviving from female houses, and both books share an emphasis on familial entries over those of confraternity. The wider social, cultural, and political implications of the two female memorial books remain understudied, for the study of memorial books is young. Because only six Carolingian era memorial books survive, the two female ones make up one-third of the corpus, but each *liber memorialis* is unique, making it impossible to write about a specifically female form.[38] Though the vagaries of chance and changing perceptions in the historical value of source types have naturally affected the kind and number of remaining texts, this rather high proportion of memorial books from convents speaks to the prominence of female memorial activity in the Carolingian Empire. Further investigation of the two—from Remiremont

---

36. Leyser, *Rule and Conflict*, 52–62; van Houts, *Memory and Gender*, 149. For evidence of Carolingian lay women's shorter life spans see Dutton, *Charlemagne's Mustache*, 159 and appendix 3, 197–98.

37. Hellmuth, *Frau und Besitz*, 236.

38. Karl Schmid, "Der Codex als Zeugnis der liturgischen und historischen Memoria einer königlichen Frauenabtei," in MGH Libri mem. N.S. 4, ed. Dieter Geuenich and Uwe Ludwig (Hanover, 2000), 3–19, 12–14.

(Biblioteca Angelica MS 10) and San Salvatore in Brescia (Biblioteca Quer-iniana MS G. VI. 7)—provide an opportunity to reflect on women's role in the preservation of memory. Only these two memorial books contain liturgi-cal texts bound into the same volume as the memorial lists.[39] The memorial book from San Salvatore in Brescia contains a partial sacramentary, while the one from the community at Remiremont has three masses.[40] By the ninth cen-tury, when the two books were produced, Remiremont and San Salvatore at Brescia had come under the direct patronage of the Carolingian royal family. Examining these two communities demonstrates that female membership in royal monasteries created mutually beneficial bonds between the royal family and aristocratic families.

Founded in 620, Remiremont was originally a double monastery. It gradu-ally came to be an exclusively female community over the course of the late seventh and eighth centuries. By the early ninth century, its leaders were abbesses, and it became a royal monastery. The patronage of the Carolin-gian family and of powerful magnates helped to make Remiremont's memo-rial activities possible. Under Louis the Pious's rule, Remiremont played a prominent role in Carolingian religious reforms, serving as the model for the changes of 816. Under the tenure of the abbess Imma (d. 818/9), as required by the Aachen Council of 816, the community adopted the *Rule of St. Benedict* to replace the *Rule of Columbanus*.[41] Remiremont was at the center of Carolin-gian political life, acting as a prominent royal meeting place. Louis the Pious and Lothar II sometimes hunted in the rich forests near Remiremont, and Lothar I, Louis the German, and Lothar II used Remiremont as a meeting place.[42] Furthermore, the community was relatively large, with an average of eighty-four members per year in the ninth century.[43] Its many aristocratic

---

39. Arnold Angenendt and Gisela Muschiol, "Die Liturgischen Texte," in MGH Libri mem N.S. 4, 28–55, 28. The Codex Forojuliensis (Museo Archeologico Nazionale Cod. CXXXVIII in Cividale del Friuli), a late fifth- or early sixth-century evangelary, had liturgical instructions added to it in the seventh and eighth centuries and many names entered in the ninth and tenth centuries, but unlike the Remiremont and San Salvatore books, the names and liturgical texts were not entered at roughly the same time. Ludwig, *TB*, 175–236.

40. Angenendt and Muschiol, "Die Liturgischen Texte," 28. The partial sacramentary appears on fol. 62^r-87^r in the San Salvatore manuscript. *Liber Memorialis von Remiremont*, 33. These masses are on fol. 1^v-3^v, 19^v-20^v, 21^v-22^r of the Remiremont manuscript.

41. Hlawitschka, *Studien zur Äbtissenreihe*, 34–35. Columbanus (d. 615?), founder of the monasteries of Luxeuil and Bobbio, wrote two influential monastic rules, the *Regula mona-chorum* and the *Regula coenobialis*. See Stevenson, "The Monastic Rules of Columbanus."

42. *AB*, yr. 836, 19, yr. 864, 112; MGH Ep. 6, 213. Formularies from the first half of the ninth century also mention Remiremont. Hlawitschka, "Herzog Giselbert von Lothringen und das Kloster Remiremont," 425.

43. Hlawitschka, "Beobachtungen," 38–9.

members were well connected. The abbess Theuthild (819/20–c. 862/65) corresponded with Louis the Pious, the empress Judith, and other imperial magnates and advisers. She was related to Adalhard, a cousin of Charlemagne, and had connections to Waldrada, Lothar II's concubine.

Some have ascribed a zeal for reform to Theuthild and noted that the communication between the members of Remiremont and their families and *amici* increased after her death and the death of Remiremont's provost, the priest Theoderic in 865. Like Theuthild, he had promoted strict Benedictine reform. Because of this difference between strict claustration and the community's practice of maintaining strong ties to the outside world, Remiremont provides an excellent example of the tension between clerical and lay values in the ninth century, particularly in its memorial book, which underlined the traditional practice of prayer while emphasizing the need to commemorate kin and donors in the context of mass. Unfortunately, no charters survive from ninth-century Remiremont against which to measure the evidence of the memorial book.[44]

An explanation early on in the memorial book details its dual purposes of everyday liturgical use and memorial commemoration. The opening passage on folio 19[r] relates that the nuns at Remiremont decided, with the agreement of Abbess Theuthild and Provost Theoderic, to celebrate mass regularly for all those who deserved their prayer. These individuals included both the living and the dead: the community's founders and early abbots Romaricus and Amatus, the convent's past and current patrons and *amici*, groups of monks, and deceased and living sisters.[45] Furthermore, Remiremont's members called for annual memorial celebrations and admonished their successors to continue such commemoration. According to that passage, the community decided to create the memorial text in the seventh year of Louis the Pious's reign (28 January 820 to 27 January 821).[46] That decision coincides with the period of reform and claustration at the community. Yet, rather than stifling the women's opportunities to affect the world around them, this formalization of the duties of *memoria* provided an impetus to creating significant social and political relationships with the laity. The memorial book reveals continuity with the Merovingian religious women who offered frequent and regular commemorative prayer, but at the same time it expands upon the Merovingian model through its broader scope. Because Remiremont was a royal convent,

---

44. At the beginning of the tenth century Remiremont suffered a Magyar raid, which may help explain the lack of documents. Hlawitschka, "Herzog Giselbert," 425–26.

45. The name Remiremont comes from *Romarici mons*. Hlawitschka, "Beobachtungen," 32.

46. Hlawitschka, Schmid, and Tellenbach, introduction to MGH Libri mem. 1, xvi.

its members prayed for the living and the dead throughout the Carolingian Empire. Theirs was a memorial commemoration writ large.

The introductory passage's indication that the women at Remiremont themselves chose to institute this commemoration argues for the dynamic and personal nature of their memorial activity. It is hardly probable that the sisters made this decision independently; the abbess and male clerics with responsibilities at Remiremont must have given approval for it. Nevertheless, this plan envisaged an active role for the women in the community. Almost certainly women at Remiremont helped to determine whom the community should commemorate, prayed for those individuals, therefore maintaining a connection to those who had relationships with their community.

Our knowledge of the members' instrumental roles in creating and preserving such bonds would be further strengthened if discerning their precise roles in the collection of names and in the production of the books were possible. The sheer number of scribes who worked on the memorial book—at least 160—makes its genesis a complicated subject.[47] These scribes demonstrated a range of skill, from accomplished writers to beginners.[48] A number of female scribes worked on the Remiremont memorial book, although the names of only two, Lizuidis and Cecelia, are known. Remiremont's many family entries frequently included a member of the community; in some cases it is possible to trace multiple generations of female relatives sent to Remiremont to maintain a continuing bond. Lizuidis, or scribe forty, even recorded her own family.[49] In their lists families also ensured the memory of kin in the religious life. The name of an abbess Richildis (*Rihildis abbatissa*), once thought to be an abbess of Remiremont, appears only in a long list of men and women but not in the lists of abbesses, in the list of ninety members from the tenure of Theuthild, or in any of the three necrologies.[50] Thus, her kin helped to ensure her commemoration at a religious community other than her own. The purposes of the community's memorial book reflected the family relationships its pages preserved. The entries may also reflect political affiliations if Abbess Theuthildis and the nuns at Remiremont purposefully left the name of Lothar II off from an entry of 862/3 to demonstrate their disapproval of his efforts to obtain a divorce from his wife Theutberga.[51]

Examining Remiremont's liturgical texts alongside its memorial entries can enrich our understanding of the community's commemoration. The

---

47. Ibid., xvi–xxi.
48. Hlawitschka, *Studien zur Äbtissenreihe*, 20.
49. Hlawitschka, Schmid, and Tellenbach, introduction to MGH Libri mem. 1, xxv, xxxi.
50. MGH Libri mem. 1, fol. 42ᵛ, 92; Hlawitschka, *Studien zur Äbtissenreihe*, 41.
51. Hlawitschka, *Studien zur Äbtissenreihe*, 36–38; Airlie, "Private Bodies and the Body Politic in the Divorce Case of Lothar II," 37–38.

organization of Remiremont's memorial book appears to be more the result of organic growth than of a unified plan. The entries began during the 820s, and, based on paleographical grounds and on the dates of entry for abbesses' deaths, later entries date to the tenth century. After the tenth century, the memorial entries taper off, with some rather late ones from the eleventh and thirteenth centuries. In comparison to other contemporary memorial books, the Remiremont one has an unusually high number of direct necrology and memorial entries.[52] This feature argues for an emphasis on aristocratic families and *amici*. Recent scholars have explored liturgy's social and political meanings rather than concentrating on textual comparisons and the origins of certain rites.[53] Liturgy was not solely an "official" form of piety; many people participated in liturgical acts, and studying liturgical texts offers an opportunity to examine the meanings those rites may have had for participants.[54] As with any source, liturgy cannot offer a perfect reflection of its contemporary society, but it provides another means of detecting the values of those who produced, used, or heard liturgy. Liturgical sources also convey a sense of the rhythm of everyday life: most celebrations had to be observed either at certain times of the week or year or at transitional moments, such as baptism, consecration to a holy order, or death.

Remiremont's liturgical texts reflect the weight of continuing family bonds and memorial commemoration. Their placement within the overall order of the manuscript is revealing. The mass texts follow on the heels of the explanation offered for the book's production on folios 19^v–20^v and 21^v–22^r, further underlining the planned commemorative actions of the community. Both mass passages and the introduction date to the tenure of the abbess Theutild.[55] Their production at the same time reveals the stress the community placed upon commemoration during mass. The memorial book's three masses relate to care for, burial of, and prayer for the dead, while appropriately emphasizing intercession and prayer for the living. Furthermore, two masses offer prayers for all Christians, particularly those buried nearby.[56] Frequent reference to those listed in the memorial book indicates that the women regularly prayed for their families and the convent's *amici*. One mass had the title "Mass said specially for the living and for the dead of both sexes, whose commemoration

---

52. Hlawitschka, Schmid, and Tellenbach, introduction to MGH Libri mem. 1, xxx.

53. Hen, *Culture and Religion in Merovingian Gaul A.D. 481–751;* idem, *The Royal Patronage of Liturgy;* Palazzo, *Liturgie et société au Moyen Âge;* Hamilton, "'Most illustrious king of kings'"; Muschiol, "Men, Women and Liturgical Practice in the Early Medieval West," 198–216.

54. Boyle, "Popular Piety in the Middle Ages 187–88.

55. MGH Libri mem. 1, xvii, fol. 1^v–5^v and 10^r–26^v.

56. Ibid., 41–42, fol. 19^v and 20^r.

it should contain and whose names are seen written below." Its secret (*secreta*) contained the phrase: "of those they commended with prayers or of those whose names are seen written below in this breviary."[57] In the same mass' introit is the phrase: "or of those names seen below written in this breviary."[58] In both its *infra actionem*, (a prayer that drew its name from the title "infra actionem" [within the canon] that originally was, in texts, placed above this prayer's variations, which were to be included among other prayers on certain feast days) and its secret, the daily mass commemorating the dead sisters in the cemeteries mentions the recording of the sisters' and abbesses' names in the memorial book. Finally, the statement after communion in that mass refers to the sisters listed in the memorial book.[59] The members regularly commemorated the passing of their sisters in a mass whose opening alludes to their records in the memorial book.[60] Such constant repetition of the memorial liturgy and the lists made consideration of the community's memorial book and of those entered in it a daily part of life for the women at Remiremont. Their participation in this liturgy would have made the memorial book a central element of their regular commemorations. Even those who did not read or write in the book would have been aware of it. The liturgical texts' emphasis on the names recorded in the memorial book demonstrates both cohesion between the memorial entries and liturgy and the centrality of commemorating the dead and praying for patrons as well as spiritual and secular kin.

The liturgical texts also emphasize the spiritual worth of gifts. In the two *sequentiae* before the offertory of the mass for the living and the dead, biblical passages underline the benefits of giving up one's earthly treasure. The first is Luke 12:30–34: "Wherever one's treasure is, that is where one's soul is." The second, Mark 12: 41–44, tells of the widow's humble offering to the Temple that was greater than the offerings of others because she was so poor.[61] Such readings served to remind those present of the rich gifts of family and *amici* and perhaps helped to spur the living who worshipped at Remiremont to donate more generously.

The liturgy reveals a rhythm of commemoration that reminded the women regularly of their bonds to the living and the dead, including those to their sisters and brothers in the religious life, the patrons of their houses, and their families. In addition to the annual memorial celebrations, women at Remiremont engaged in nearly constant prayer.[62] The community's emphasis on

---

57. Ibid., 3, fol. 3ʳ.
58. Ibid., 1, fol. 2ʳ.
59. Ibid., 41–42, fol. 19ᵛ–20ᵛ.
60. Ibid., 44–46, fol. 21ᵛ–22ʳ.
61. Ibid., 1, fol. 2ᵛ–3ʳ.
62. Muschiol, *Famula Dei*, 132.

mass as the moment of commemoration necessitated the presence of a priest to carry out the liturgical rites. Throughout late antiquity and the early Middle Ages, abbesses had no priest-like roles. Carolingian church and secular legislation forbade women (and laymen) from approaching the altar.[63] Only in a vision could a nun perform acts involved in the celebration of mass; in the ninth-century version of her *vita*, the abbess Aldegund appeared in a nun's vision breaking mass offerings into a chalice at an altar.[64]

Although the male celebrant accomplished the rites, women presented the dead for commemoration. They prayed for the dead, remembered donors and their spiritual and natural kin, and participated in the production of the memorial book. The manuscript itself was a significant and meaningful object. Some communities kept memorial lists on loose sheets. That Remiremont's memorial lists were bound in the Carolingian era attests to their consequence to the community.[65] The sisters under the rule of abbess Theuthild chose to emphasize memorial acts, and the liturgical texts suggest that the sisters and others expected regular commemoration of the dead to continue over time. The book was not meant to constitute a single instance of remembering but rather was to be the part of an ongoing practice tied to past, present, and future. The recording of the masses furthermore indicates an intention to celebrate them with the memorial book as a central component. Women's celebration of this liturgy and their prayers for the dead gave their families great comfort and bound Remiremont to the royal family, to magnates, and to other religious communities. Female prayer at Remiremont therefore answered the needs of the laity while being performed within the bounds of claustration as clerics of that era wished. The case of Theuthild indicates that some religious women supported claustration or at least worked within its constraints. In fact, enclosure can give a certain freedom to religious women.[66] The case of Remiremont underlines the ways in which women often stood between lay and clerical values, having to answer to both. Theuthild may have enforced claustration, but she and her sisters found the means to satisfy the needs of the lay aristocracy.

---

63. Council of Paris of 829, canon 45, MGH Conc. 2.2, at 639–40; Regino of Prüm, *De synodalibus causis et disciplinis ecclesiastici*, no. 1.105, no. 1.121, no. 1.200, and no. 1.202, 82, 86, and 114.

64. This account emphasized that only a priest could give Aldegund the eucharist. BNF lat. 5275, fol. 50ʳ–50ᵛ; see also Vita Aldegunis, chap. 31, 1046, and *Vita sanctae Aldegundis*, chap. 31, PL 132, col. 874.

65. Schmid, "Der Codex als Zeugnis," 12.

66. Late medieval English women, confined either to the cloister or to certain parts of buildings, may, for example, have found their situations conducive to developing their piety. Gilchrist, *Gender and Material Culture*, 167–69.

San Salvatore

The memorial book of San Salvatore at Brescia displays an emphasis on familial and donor bonds and memorial commemoration similar to Remiremont's memorial book. A richer array of sources than those available for Remiremont, however, permits deeper contextualization of San Salvatore's book and more comprehensive analysis of the Brescian community. Surviving charters from Brescia and elsewhere in northern Italy as well as archaeological evidence from excavations conducted at San Salvatore provide information about the religious house's relationship to the outside community and to the Carolingian royal family. The patronage of first the Lombard and then the Carolingian royal families gave this foundation great prominence in the early medieval West in the eighth and ninth centuries. In addition, San Salvatore's transalpine connections to aristocratic families, royal families, and religious houses during the ninth and tenth centuries were extensive. Much of the work done on the San Salvatore memorial book to this point has stressed the benefits that accrued to men and their families, but attention needs to turn to the community's members.

Before the Carolingian conquest of the Lombard kingdom, San Salvatore had prestigious connections to the ruling family and benefited from that family's and other aristocrats' substantial wealth. Ansa, the wife of Desiderius, founded the community in 753, before they became king and queen of the Lombards, and their daughter Anselperga became its abbess.[67] San Salvatore became an administrative and political center.[68] The community was a showcase for Lombard mechanical and artistic skills. Built on a hill near the site of the old Roman forum and taking advantage of existing infrastructure, San Salvatore used a revamped version of an old aqueduct to supply the convent.[69] The eighth-century structures and courtyard show evidence of technical expertise and demonstrate the resources put into the community.[70] A number of Lombard donors saw potential benefit in creating a bond with the community through a gift of land.[71] Other men and women exchanged land with or took land back in usufruct from San Salvatore, sold land to the convent, or

---

67. Nelson, "Making a Difference," 172–73.

68. Erhart, "*Gens eadem reparat omnia septa gregis*—Mönchtum unter den langobardischen Königen," 407.

69. Both a 761 charter and archaeological evidence confirm this reuse. Brogiolo, "'Flavia Brexia,'" 467–68.

70. Christie, *The Lombards*, 158–60.

71. *CDLang*, no. 47, cols. 89–90; *CDLong*, no. 226, 271–75.

deposited copies of their documents with the community.[72] The royal family continued to support the community through reconfirmation of the community's rights and privileges and gifts of land and goods.[73]

Following Charlemagne's conquest of the Lombard kingdom in 774–76, San Salvatore became a vibrant Carolingian community. Only after the Lombard revolt in the Friuli had died down did Charlemagne grant favors to the convent. During Carolingian rule, for example, San Salvatore's church was expanded into the triple-apsed structure that remains today.[74] Anselperga does not appear in records dated after the Lombard fall, and by 781, Charlemagne had made Radoara abbess.[75] During the ninth century, San Salvatore became a principal support of Carolingian rule in northern Italy and a community where the daughters of the powerful came together and formed bonds among their families. This practice continued into the tenth century, when Berengar I made his daughter Bertha abbess. Probably during his reign in 905 or 906, San Salvatore was renamed Santa Giulia after a saint whose bones had been interred in 760–62 in a crypt that also came to be the resting place of the community's founder, Ansa.[76]

The evidence of the memorial book points to women's personal and active preservation of familial memory and the maintenance of strong connections among families of the members of San Salvatore, including some of the most powerful nobles in upper Italy as well as the Carolingians themselves.[77] Like other Carolingian memorial books, the one from San Salvatore contains lists of the living and the dead, including donors, family, visitors, friends, and royal family members. One of the more revealing aspects of the San Salvatore book is its order of entries. Rather than demonstrating an ad hoc construction, this book seems to have been a planned compilation of already extant lists, probably made around 856. This feature sets it apart from the Remiremont book,

---

72. For exchange of land see *CDLong*, no. 155, 77–84; no. 257, 345–52. For an example of a sale see *CDLong*, no. 228, 277–81. For safeguarding of documents see *CDLong*, no. 137, 29–34. Perhaps the independence of the community made it appealing as a repository. Besides royal guarantees of immunities, see the guarantee of immunity from Sigoaldus, patriarch of Aquileia, *CDLong*, no. 48, 90–92.

73. *CDLang*, no. 20, cols. 40–43; no. 27, cols. 54–55; no. 30, cols. 58–59; no. 47, cols. 89–90.

74. Christie, *The Lombards*, 193–95.

75. Her name appears in an immunity document dated to that year. MGH Dipl. Kar. 1, 135, ed. Engelbert Mühlbacher (Hanover, Germany, 1906), 185–86.

76. Christie, *The Lombards*, 158; Wemple, "S. Salvatore/S. Giulia," 85. Wemple's essay offers useful information concerning the community's Lombard charters, but for a few errors she made, see Nelson, "Making a Difference," 173, note 10.

77. No women from outside the Italian *regnum* appear to have belonged to San Salvatore. Ludwig, *TB*, 17.

whose organization resulted more from organic growth than a single act. The entries for the San Salvatore book were inscribed mainly at one time, and, in comparison to Remiremont's memorial book, fewer scribes worked on it.[78] The book almost certainly retains its original order.[79]

One of San Salvatore's memorial book's chief functions was the commemoration of nuns' kin and *amici*. The manuscript contains numerous family entries, particularly during the mid-ninth century, an especially dynamic period of memorial activity at the community. Having a female relative in San Salvatore was one way for a northern Italian family to mark its status and compete with other families. Following the rule of Berengar (888–924) the number of entries sharply declined: additional family groups only reappeared in the early eleventh century, continuing in relatively small numbers until 1514.[80] In contrast to other memorial books such as Reichenau's, the San Salvatore lists of *amici*, which include the bulk of the family entries, precede the confraternity lists. The *amici* and donor lists, along with the cloister lists of nuns in San Salvatore, make up the core of the book, showing an emphasis on the commemoration of donors.[81] The San Salvatore book differs from Remiremont's because it lacks calendrical and specific necrologies; in fact, it contains no special lists of the dead. Until the death of Louis II, son of Lothar I, in 875, only powerful Carolingians and aristocrats with close associations to San Salvatore were listed, but later entries included groups from outside northern Italy, and the organization of names was no longer by precedence (as in the oblation list).[82] The book therefore eventually helped to bind the empire together, for its prayer group contained entries from West and East Francia as well as Italy. The transalpine connections of San Salvatore, especially to the monasteries of Lake Constance, are extensive, and the memorial book contains entries of pilgrims, most famously Æthelwulf of Wessex, who stopped in Brescia on his way to Rome in 855/6.[83]

These functions, which place San Salvatore at the center of Carolingian political and social relations, make its book similar to those of Remiremont, St. Gall, and Reichenau. Folio 34[v], for example, contains a rather lengthy list of

---

78. Uwe Ludwig, "Die Anlage des 'Liber vitae,'" in MGH Libri mem. N.S. 4, 56–88, 61–64.

79. Jean Vezin, "Beschreibung des Codex und des Einbandes," in MGH Libri mem. N.S. 4, 20–27, at 20.

80. Becher, "Das königliche Frauenkloster San Salvatore/San Giulia in Brescia im Spiegel seiner Memorialüberlieferung," 362–64.

81. Ludwig, "Die Anlage des 'Liber vitae,'" 83.

82. Karl Schmid suggested that a necrological text must have once existed for the San Salvatore community but is now lost. "Der Codex als Zeugnis," 15.

83. Ludwig, *TB*, 13–126.

some of the most powerful magnates in northern Italy, and in the Carolingian Empire. Uwe Ludwig has noted that this list resembles the *pactae* of powerful men that Gerd Althoff identified in the late ninth and early tenth centuries.[84] From at least the ninth to the eleventh centuries, various alliances based on kinship, lordship, and friendship helped to provide security, aid, and rank for their members or allowed the group to accomplish a particular goal. Because these groups often resembled families in structure, it is unsurprising to find memorial entries reflective of such artificial kinship.[85] The entry on folio 34^v demonstrates both the early origins of such groups and yet another way in which women had to aid in the development and maintenance of male bonds.

Among the identified aristocratic families are those of Eberhard of Friuli and his wife, Gisela; either Count Liutfrid I (845–865/6) or Count Liutfrid II (876–884); Count Adelgis of Parma, the father-in-law of Louis II (844/50–875); Count Bernard of Verona; and Adelbert I, margrave of Tuscany.[86] The names of these men, along with about forty-five others who gave their daughters or nieces to the convent, appear in the oblation list, on folios 42^r–44^v sandwiched between various memorial entries and begun with large red majuscule script so that it seems like an interruption. The names of some of the men and women listed here appear elsewhere in the memorial lists, connecting the oblation list with the contents of the memorial book.[87] With the exceptions of two imperial entries, the rest of the men and women in this list appear to have been members of powerful northern Italian aristocratic families, many of whom had close connections to the Carolingians. The list employs a language of donation that presents men as having control over the entry of their relatives into San Salvatore: they handed over (*tradidit*) their daughters or nieces. An example that follows the pattern is: "Riculfus tradidit filiam suam, Teupurgam" (Riculf handed over his daughter, Teupurga).[88] The men brought their female kin to the altar as they would have done in presenting any offering. The act may have been similar to the way modern-day fathers often bring their daughters to the altar for marriage or consecration to the religious life. In fact, only three examples appear in the book of women who were not given by male relatives, and they all joined the convent in the eleventh century.[89] The prominence accorded male kin indicates that the sisters retained the memory of members' natal families; the liturgical evidence

---

84. Ludwig, *TB*, 69; Althoff, *Amicitiae und Pactae*, 8–14, 52–68.
85. Althoff, *Family, Friends, and Followers*, 160–62.
86. Ludwig, *TB*, 29–34.
87. Because more than one person could have the same name, it is uncertain if these names consistently refer to the same individuals in the oblation list.
88. MGH Libri mem. N.S. 4, 183, fol. 43^r.
89. Angenendt and Muschiol, "Die Liturgische Texten," 53–54.

shows that their participation in the commemoration of San Salvatore's *amici* frequently reminded them of that relationship. In sum, though the women at San Salvatore remained cloistered, they nevertheless served the needs of their lay families and had reasons to think of them often.

The liturgical texts reveal that members of San Salvatore actively maintained those bonds with their families and others through their prayer and commemoration of the dead. Although the liturgical texts contain various formularies, their three emphases are the veneration of the saints, brotherhood, and the death liturgy. Prayer, intercession, and commemoration were the principal tasks of the community at Brescia; as at Remiremont, the mass was the main occasion for their memorial activity.[90] Like the book from Remiremont, the San Salvatore manuscript shows clear signs of use; if that wear occurred at least in part during the ninth century, it would help to support the direct participation of members of San Salvatore in the liturgical rites recorded in the book. The intention to celebrate these masses spurred those planning the memorial book to record the liturgical texts. As in the Remiremont masses, the San Salvatore texts indicate at various points that the women are praying for those listed in the memorial book; furthermore they indicate the book's placement on the altar. The opening lines of the "mass for the <salvation> of the living and the dead" are an excellent example: "those who commended themselves unto our prayers, both for those who are alive and those who have paid death's debt, or those whose requested alms we received, and whose names are seen to have been written on your holy altar."[91] Almost the same wording appears in that mass's secret: "and whose names are seen written on your holy altar."[92] Though the sisters could not approach the altar, they nevertheless could participate in the mass, take communion, and envision the book upon the altar, sending their spiritual presence to a place forbidden to them. The women at San Salvatore also prayed more frequently than during mass, because they were meant to keep the monastic offices under the *Rule of St. Benedict*.[93]

Despite similarities the liturgical texts in San Salvatore's memorial book appear to be more recent than those in the Remiremont memorial book. Based on their shared elements, they might have a common early ninth-century

---

90. Ibid., 28, 55.

91. MGH Libri mem. N.S. 4, 215, fol. 74ʳ.

92. Ibid., 215, fol. 74ᵛ.

93. No liturgical texts for the monastic offices per se survive from San Salvatore, but the profession formularies in the liturgical texts point to adherence to the *Rule of St. Benedict*. Angenendt and Muschiol, "Die Liturgische Texten," 55.

model.[94] The prayers of the two books seem to be more closely related to each other, however, than they are to prayers in other liturgical/memorial books. Most of the masses for the dead already existed in earlier sources.[95] Although the nuns may not have heard these masses each day, they surely participated in masses at times, and the memorial book's location on the altar would have reminded them to pray for the dead at other moments. The celebration of the book's liturgy probably punctuated their daily life, which followed the rhythm of more frequent liturgical observances, such as daily offices and Sunday mass. The texts under "On the Virgin's birth," for example, would have been heard annually. Others, such as the "mass for the health of the living and those who are going to die," may have been said quite regularly. Only at appropriate occasions would the sisters have celebrated the mass for a dead person.[96] These three examples suggest how the mass formularies in the book contributed to daily, annual, or other regular liturgical rhythms and emphases in the community.

Blessings for the women's veils in the Brescian liturgical texts indicate the centrality of wearing the veil.[97] They are unique to the San Salvatore memorial book and may have originated there.[98] The veil symbolized the chastity of the consecrated woman.[99] It was also the moment when the family transferred authority over their daughter to the religious community. *Vitae* often contain a section about the veiling of the saint. Agius noted that Hathumoda took the veil with her parents' permission, thereby separating herself from her parents' household: "then from outside the shining roofs of her parents, standing before the fellowship of the handmaids of God, with the consent of her parents, she was consecrated with the holy veil."[100] Because taking the veil signified entrance into the religious life, it stood as an alternative to marriage. According to their late ninth-century *vita*, the abbesses of Aldeneik Herlindis and Renula, for example, welcomed many local aristocratic daughters to their community. "It happened that, on account of the holy virgins' example, many daughters of noble men or in service of the free, disdaining

94. Hlawitschka, Schmid, and Tellenbach, introduction to MGH Libri mem. 1, xxxv. Though both sets of liturgical texts draw from older sacramentaries, their exact relationship to each other has yet to be worked out.

95. Angenendt and Muschiol, "Die Liturgische Texten," 39, 42.

96. MGH Libri mem. N.S. 4, 210, 216, 218.

97. Ibid., 226, fol. 87ᵛ–88ʳ.

98. Angenendt and Muschiol, "Die Liturgischen Texte," 55.

99. Constable, "The Ceremonies and Symbolism of Entering Religious Life and Taking the Monastic Habit," 798.

100. Agius, *Vita Hathumodae*, chap. 3, 167.

the enticing ceremonies of marriage, were veiled on their heads with a black veil and together with the blessed virgins of Christ zealously served only the Lord."[101]

Veiling became more important during the ninth century. Consecrated women in Gaul in the sixth to seventh centuries did not necessarily wear veils, nor were those who did wear veils distinguished from those who did not. A rite upon entrance to a religious community was not yet well developed, although references to a changing of clothing existed from at least the Merovingian era.[102] Thus, the appearance of this blessing marks a development in the practices surrounding religious women. In the 780s, when clerics learned about fourth-century conciliar legislation concerning veiling, they often quoted it but with little effect. Though those councils set the upper age limit for veiling virgins at twenty-five, clerics raised no objections to a bishop consecrating and veiling a younger woman so long as her family requested it.[103] Ninth-century capitularies concerned themselves with the entrance of girls into the religious life and veiling. If a family wished to send a female relative to a convent, a capitulary of 805–6 made clear that the family could not take the girl back later.[104] This evidence suggests that parents indeed tried to reclaim daughters from the religious life.[105] A capitulary for the *missi* (royal inspectors) of 805–6 forbade the veiling of girls "before they might know what they want."[106] The Council of Aachen of 817, which set three days as the waiting period for veiling, shows a continuing concern that women and their families not undertake this choice lightly.[107] The Council of Tribur of 895 stated that:

> If a girl takes the veil of her own free will before the age of twelve, her parents or guardians can immediately make that act void if they wish. But if they will have consented for a year and day letting it pass unnoticed, neither they nor she can change this. For if they impetuously choose to serve God in the adolescent state or as an adolescent, it is not in the power of her parents to prohibit it.[108]

This statement demonstrates not only the continuing importance of veiling but distinguishes it from oblation, which could occur earlier. The clerics who

---

101. *Vita Herlinde et Renulae*, chap. 11, 388.
102. Muschiol, *Famula Dei*, 49–50, 276.
103. de Jong, *In Samuel's Image*, 63.
104. *Capitula ecclesiastica ad Salz data*, chap. 6, MGH Capit. 1, 119.
105. de Jong, *In Samuel's Image*, 65.
106. *Capitulare in Theodonis villa datum*, chap. 14, MGH Capit. 1, 122.
107. Constable, "The Ceremonies and Symbolism of Entering Religious Life," 798.
108. MGH Capit. 2.2, no. 252, chap. 24(b), 227.

wrote this rule, however, were not so much interested in the girls' wishes as in ending arguments between parents and convents about the removal of girls from religious communities.[109] Their allowance that parents may still take away a young girl but not an "adolescent" demonstrates a concession to the needs of the lay elite, who may often have wished to wait before deciding if a daughter should enter the religious life. An advantageous marriage prospect could present itself, or the death of other children could change familial strategy. After a certain age, however, clerics demanded that a woman's kin respect the permanence of vocation that veiling entailed.

The rite of veiling a woman brought together clerics, kin, and possibly members of the local community to witness a woman's entrance to the religious life. Their presence underlines the importance of that moment and of the woman's subsequent vocation. The purposes of this ceremony help to explain why it became more prominent in the ninth century and developed into a more standard form by the tenth century. The blessing of the veil in the Brescia memorial book may be related to the three prayers concerning a virgin's or widow's clothing in the eighth-century Gellone sacramentary, with the exception of one blessing that notes how the virgin's new clothes set her apart from others, and to the two blessings for a virgin's or widow's clothing found in a ninth-century Gregorian sacramentary from Padua.[110] In Hucbald of St. Amand's early tenth-century *Vita Rictrudis*, her adoption of new clothing marks her consecration.[111] The eighth-century Gelasian sacramentary of Angoulême contains the first known prayer to bless solely the handing over of the veil.[112] Prayers in the tenth-century Romano-Germanic Pontifical that bless monastic clothes descend from early medieval blessings of women's habits.[113] A blessing for the consecration of a widow from the Gregorian sacramentary of Padua, for example, also appears in the Romano-Germanic Pontifical as the prayer of benediction before the adoption of the veil.[114] An early ninth-century fragment of a St. Gall manuscript provides some clues as to the rite of veiling. It mentions the white clothing and white veil that the consecrated woman is to take up in her new life.[115] According to the Brescian liturgy and Carolingian secular and ecclesiastical legislation only bishops were to consecrate women, although they could delegate this

109. de Jong, *In Samuel's Image*, 98.

110. Metz, *La consécration des vierges dans l'église romaine*, 174–75.

111. Hucbald, *Vita Rictrudis*, chap. 15, 84–85.

112. Metz, *La consécration des vierges*, 175–77.

113. Constable, "The Ceremonies and Symbolism of Entering Religious Life," 812.

114. Metz, *La consécration des vierges*, 175.

115. Untitled entry, *Archaeological Journal* 31 (1874): 85–86.

responsibility to priests.[116] For example, the *Admonitio generalis* of 789 forbade abbesses to consecrate virgins, and the Council of Paris of 829 repeated that prohibition.[117]

The title of the Brescian consecration rite included its most important elements: the bishop, a virgin (*sanctimonialis virgo*), and her new clothing. A bishop was to celebrate the consecration of a virgin on Epiphany, Easter Monday, or the Feast of the Apostles.[118] The woman first took her clothing (*vestibus*) to the altar where the bishop blessed them, noting that they were the sign of her new vocation and her taking up of the "habit of holy chastity."[119] The others present then responded with requests that God bless the woman and the clothing whose adoption will demonstrate her embracing chastity. The woman then retired to the sacristy (*sacrarium*) to put on her new clothing, with the exception of the veil, which she left with the bishop, and to obtain two lit candles that she carried with her to the altar for the beginning of the mass for the consecration of a virgin.[120] In the margin of folio 51ᵛ, on which these instructions appear, is a note indicating that the blessings for the veil are at the end of the book. It is not entirely clear when the bishop would employ these prayers.[121] After a prayer for the preservation of the woman's virginity and the reading of some appropriate biblical passages, the bishop held the veil above the woman's head and blessed her with these words: "Look favorably, Lord, upon this your servant and her pledge of holy virginity, which inspired by you she accepts; may she be preserved under your guidance."[122] The bishop then blessed her before giving her the veil to wear. She next deposited the candles she had been carrying in order to make an offering before returning to a kneeling position. Later in the mass, the bishop gave her enough consecrated

---

116. Among the earliest church legislation containing this prohibition was the Council of Carthage in 390. Metz, *La consécration des vierges*, 102, 104. Ninth-century legislation repeating this ban includes the Council of Paris in 829, canon 41, MGH Conc. 2.2, 637–38; Council of Pavia in 850, canon 7, MGH Capit. 2.1, ed. Alfred Boretius and Victor Krause (Hanover, Germany, 1890), 118; and the Council of Worms of 868, canon 8, Mansi, vol. 15, col. 871.

117. *Admonitio generalis*, chap. 76, MGH Capit. 2.1, 60; Council of Paris of 829, canon 43, MGH Conc. 2.2, 638.

118. MGH Libri mem. N.S. 4, 199, fol. 51ᵛ.

119. Ibid.

120. Frankish ecclesiastical leaders added some concrete symbols to the consecration ceremony for virgins, including the candles. Their light associated the consecrated woman with the wise virgins who saved the oil for their lamps in the Gospels. The candles also suggested the illumination that came from joining the religious life and reflected their new spouse Christ, the one true light. Vincent, "Le cierge de la consécration des femmes," 359–61.

121. MGH Libri mem. N.S. 4, 226, fol. 87ᵛ–88ʳ.

122. Ibid., 200, fol. 52ʳ.

host that she could partake of it then and over the next eight days.[123] These acts were relatively typical of early medieval consecration liturgy.[124] Only in the late ninth century, however, do consecration texts appear that have similar order and place in the mass to this particular rite.[125]

In addition to their importance in liturgical history, the consecration text and the blessings for the veil underline the moment when a woman ideally left the lay world permanently. In light of the opportunities for marriage alliances her family then gave up, this oblation marked an act of true sacrifice on her family's part. The family bound itself to the community not only through a daughter or niece's membership but also through a gift of land or goods to the convent for her support. Although the consecration text does not state whether family were present or not, the evidence supports an understanding of their centrality to such an act even if they did not literally witness it as Hathumoda's parents did. Legislation indicated that family members needed to approve of a young relative's entrance to the religious life and the oblation list at Brescia records such permission in written form. The rite was equally significant to the woman. Her change of clothes specified in the San Salvatore liturgy, and particularly her adoption of the veil and its blessing by the bishop, concretely established her passage from lay to religious life. The presence of family, religious community, and bishop demonstrates that this event was an occasion for creating bonds, particularly those that resulted in memorial commemoration. The family hoped to benefit from the community's prayer and connections to the other families whose members entered San Salvatore. Clerics expected that the women at San Salvatore would remain cloistered under the *Rule of St. Benedict*, and the consecrated women took up a powerful role in prayer in service to God as well as to their spiritual and natal families. The placement of the oblation list before the liturgical section therefore seems all the more appropriate. The offering of the oblates underlines the lay families' desire that their female relatives enter the religious life to pray for them and to bind them to a religious community engaged in such commemoration. Thus, this liturgy points to ways in which San Salvatore's regular practices responded to the needs and desires of both clerics and lay aristocrats.

For families in northern Italy and Lotharingia, entry of a female relative into San Salvatore and the recording of their kin in the community's book constituted a means of remaining active in the negotiations of aristocratic power. The sheer quantity of aristocratic family names connected to members of San Salvatore underscores the social and political implications of such

---

123. Ibid., 200–201, fol. 89^r.
124. Metz, *La consécration des vierges*, 180–81.
125. Angenendt and Muschiol, "Die Liturgischen Texte," 49–51.

female commemoration. By the 850s, emphasis on family entries waned in memorial books north of the Alps, but in this period San Salvatore's book still contained many.[126] Matching up names in memorial books to identifiable individuals involves quite detailed work and only succeeds, for example, when the person has a title such as abbess or countess to set her apart. Therefore, scholars have only been able to match a limited number of the names to persons. Fortunately, San Salvatore's oblation list contains quite a few identifiable families because names of the powerful men in the oblation list survive in other sources. Among them are the Unruochings, the family of Gisela, daughter of Eberhard of Friuli and his wife Gisela, mentioned at the beginning of this chapter. This family demonstrates the ways in which San Salvatore served to create social, political, and religious bonds within an expansive social network and shows how female memorial activity helped to create a familial identity.

Documents have left a wealth of information concerning Gisela's family. Her parents' will alone demonstrates their considerable ambition. Eberhard worked over his lifetime to increase his power and influence in the Carolingian Empire, and this early medieval "power couple" may have made efforts to establish a dynasty potentially to rival the Carolingians.[127] Although loyal to Lothar, Eberhard acted as an intermediary between Louis the Pious and his sons and later among the sons during their disputes in the 840s. Best known for his campaigns against Slavs and Avars, Eberhard was one of the most well-connected Carolingian aristocrats. Among his clerical friends he counted Hincmar of Rheims, Raban Maur, Sedulius Scottus, Bishop Hartger of Liège, and Anastasius Bibliothecarius, and he had dealings with many of the aristocrats who had family members in San Salvatore.[128] The younger Gisela, therefore, came from an extremely powerful family, and her membership in San Salvatore helped to provide them with further prestige and advantageous connections.

The women of San Salvatore prayed for the Unruochings just as they prayed for the Carolingian family. The names "Gisla, Unroc, Aua, Beringeri, Adelard, Engiltrud, Rodulfus diac(onus), Iudid, Elluic, Ugo, Astat, Liutfrid, Aua, Gisla, Rotruda, Ecchiburc" appear on folio 8^r. A scribe inserted the Unruochings' names among those of magnates associated with Louis II, thereby demonstrating an ongoing connection to San Salvatore as well

---

126. Ludwig, *TB*, 9.

127. Favre, "La famille d'Evrard, marquis de Frioul dans le royaume franc de l'ouest," 157–58.

128. Hlawitschka, *Franken, Alemannen, Bayern und Burgunder in Oberitalien (774–962)*, 56, 59, 169–71.

as the family's prominence and close connections to the royal family. All of the couple's children appear in this list as opposed to the family's entry made c. 840 in the St. Gall memorial book, in which only Unruoch's name appears along with some of the family's *amici*.[129] The difference in entries probably reflects the family's ongoing efforts to retain a strong bond with and indeed to influence the leadership of San Salvatore. Gisela herself doubtless participated in the liturgical commemoration of her family, recalling them in addition to the others listed in the memorial book, as the liturgical texts required. Her membership in San Salvatore helped her parents to establish a competing line of leading women to those appointed abbesses by the royal family.[130] One of Eberhard and Gisela's granddaughters, Unruoch's daughter, also belonged to the convent, further cementing the Unruoching bond with San Salvatore. She may be the Ecchiburc whose name appears in the convent list on folio 5[r] and in the family list above.[131]

Ecchiburc represents the efforts of the Unruochings to carry on the work of Eberhard and Gisela. Their son Unruoch I probably retained a similar level of power when he inherited his father's office and lands in the Friuli after Eberhard's death in 864 or 866. He married Ava, the daughter of another powerful northern Italian aristocrat, Count Liutfrid I of the Etichonid family.[132] Their daughter continued the family connection to San Salvatore. The *Annals of Fulda* record her kidnapping from the convent in 887. The curious passage concerns Liutward, bishop of Vercelli (880–900), who "carried off the daughters of the most noble men in Alemannia and Italy without opposition, and gave them to his relatives in marriage."[133] When he had friends take Unruoch and Ava's daughter, however, the nuns of Brescia prayed to God for revenge. Before Liutward's relative could consummate the marriage, he was struck dead by the hand of God.[134] This particular kidnapping reveals that the Unruoching family maintained connections to San Salvatore into the late ninth century and remained powerful and wealthy enough that Liutward's friends thought an Unruoching daughter worth the risk of abducting a nun.

The continuing prominence of the Unruochings may reveal what Charlemagne feared had his daughters married: Gisela, Louis the Pious's daughter,

129. Le Jan, *FP*, 386.

130. Christina La Rocca and Luigi Provero, "The Dead and Their Gifts," 263.

131. Ludwig, *TB*, 29.

132. Hlawitschka, *Franken, Alemannen*, 276–77.

133. *The Annals of Fulda*, 101.

134. *AF*, yr. 887, 105–6. Liutward was Charles the Fat's archchancellor from 878 and archchaplain from at least 883 until 887. The annalist's hostility toward Liutward probably results from a connection to Liutbert of Mainz who replaced Liutward in 887. See Reuter, *The Annals of Fulda*, 92, note 8, and 102, notes 5–6.

helped to create a rival dynasty to the Carolingians. Eberhard's will states
that Gisela makes these bequests along with her husband, and throughout
the document the continual use of the plural "our" underlines the bilateral
nature of both the will and the family dynasty.[135] Eberhard and Gisela's division of their inheritance among their children is strikingly similar to royal
divisions of the kingdom in its distribution of land and goods, but it does not
mention the donations they must have made to churches or monasteries.[136]
They left land, books, armor, and weapons to two sons in religious orders
and books to Gisela, the member of San Salvatore.[137] They carefully divided
their lands so that their sons would not owe allegiance to more than one king
and required that the sons should revise the division of land should one of the
brothers lose land unjustly through violence.[138] The far-flung locations of the
family's estates in Italy and east, middle, and West Francia were typical of
aristocratic landholdings in the Carolingian Empire. Throughout the strife
among Louis the Pious's sons, when other magnates sometimes lost land in
the kingdom of a brother they had not supported, Eberhard managed to
retain family lands in Alemannia and the lower Rhineland. Through careful
division he hoped to preclude the danger that his sons would lose property
by holding lands under different kings and therefore face the problems of
divided loyalties.[139]

Eberhard and Gisela equipped their lay daughters to maintain the memory
of their natal kin. The bequests of lands to their three lay daughters indicate
that the family wished to perpetuate the bonds among themselves, their sons,
and their daughters.[140] Probably because she had already been consecrated at
San Salvatore the younger Gisela received no land; her family had almost certainly given a donation of land to the convent when she entered the religious
life.[141] Identifying some of the lands the daughters received is difficult. Most
of the sons received properties that had once been royal lands that probably
came to the Unruochings as part of the elder Gisela's dowry.[142] The exception
was Unruoch, who received the bulk of the lands in the Friuli and Alemannia,
because he was the heir. Nevertheless, Eberhard and Gisela left Judith the
possession of Balingham in Württemberg as well as Heliwsheim on the Rhine

---

135. "Ego Evrardus, comes, cum coniuge mea Gisla...." *CAC*, no. 1, 1.
136. La Rocca and Provero, "The Dead and Their Gifts," 242.
137. *CAC*, no. 1, 1, 3–4.
138. Ibid., 2.
139. Hlawitschka, *Franken, Alemannen*, 62 and 65, note 47.
140. *CAC*, no. 1, 2.
141. La Rocca and Provero, "The Dead and Their Gifts," 245, 247.
142. Grierson, "The Identity of the Unnamed Fiscs in the *Brevium exempla ad describendas res ecclesiasticas et fiscales*," 442.

(or lower Meuse).[143] Thus, she had possessions in the vicinity of Unruoch; Gisela and Eberhard even noted in their will that Unruoch was not to receive Balingham, indicating its proximity to his inheritance.[144] Ingeltrud received Ermen and Mareshem which may be two contiguous properties north of Brussels (Herent and Merchtem) or on the right bank of the lower Rhine, near Utrecht (Harmellen and Meersen). Heilwig received land in the family's heartland, near Lille on both banks of the River Scheldt (Ootegen, Luinhue, and Vendegie).[145] Eberhard and Gisela gave their daughters lands in the vicinity of their sons partly because their lands were clustered in a few specific regions (the Friuli, Alemannia, and Flanders), but they may also have been trying to ensure that their daughters retained some connection to the family patrimony and to their brothers. Perhaps they hoped that their daughters' husbands would come to the aid of their sons if future problems arose.

The personal and devotional nature of some of the books the couple bequeathed to their daughters could indicate that they related to the women's roles as bearers of family memory who would pray for the family dead and remember their deeds.[146] The elder Gisela may have prayed for the family's memory and welfare in the family chapel, just as her lay daughters may have prayed for their marital and natal families. With the exception of the laws of the Lombards, the works either discussed Christian virtue or aided in devotions. Caution, however, should prevent reading too much into the selection of particular works for particular children, because others in these individuals' households or religious houses could also have read these books, and they may have been meant to serve purposes other than the edification of the individual who inherited them.

Aside from books, the brothers received items from the chapel, such as vestments and liturgical vessels, as well as objects for personal use, such as weapons and armor. Although none of the daughters received similar articles, their parents made sure that each daughter received "a phylactery of gold from the chapel so that they may not seem to be deprived of a blessing from our chapel."[147] On the one hand, the relics contained in each of these phylacteries suggest that Eberhard and Gisela wished to equip their daughters with a potentially powerful avenue of prayer, that to the particular saint associated with the given relics. On the other hand, such bequests suggest an expression of love for their daughters, ensuring that each one might benefit from

---

143. Harald Krahwinkler, *Friaul im Frühmittelalter* (Vienna, 1992), 90; La Rocca and Provero, "The Dead and Their Gifts," 247.

144. *CAC*, no. 1, 1.

145. La Rocca and Provero, "The Dead and Their Gifts," 247.

146. Ibid., 257.

147. *CAC* no. 1., 3.

the protection of the saints, and the further hope that their daughters, when reminded of these gifts, would remember their parents in their prayers.

San Salvatore was, therefore, not the only focus of the Unruochings' efforts to preserve their memory. In addition to their possible efforts to preserve familial bonds and memory through their daughters in the lay estate, they focused efforts on the monastery of Cysoing in Flanders. Through donations specifically made to guarantee the burial of Eberhard, herself, and her daughter Ingeltrud, and to provide lighting for the community's church and the oratory where they would be buried, Gisela made certain that the family would be remembered at Cysoing.[148] In c. 874, she had listed in the martyrology of Cysoing her own parents and her brother, the emperor Charles the Bald, as well as her eight children: "Hengeltrude, Hunroc, Berengario, Adelardo, Rodulpho, Hellwich, Gilla, Judich."[149] Strangely, Eberhard does not appear in the entry. Gisela's careful arrangements for Eberhard's burial there already guaranteed his commemoration, and she may have taken this occasion to emphasize her imperial connections and to provide for the continued memory of her own line.[150] Gisela pursued a bilateral strategy, commemorating her husband at the same time she ensured that she and her children would be remembered as members of the Carolingian line. The couple had built the monastery in 856 on lands that belonged to Gisela; thus, this religious house reflected the power and connections that she brought to the marriage.

Cysoing continued to be a focus for the family's ambitions. After the death of his brother Adalard, who had inherited Cysoing from his father Eberhard, Rudolf became abbot of the monastery before bequeathing it to Rheims. Hucbald, count of Ostrevent, claimed the abbacy of Cysoing "in the name of his wife" Heilwig, a daughter of Eberhard and Gisela. Hucbald thought he should control the family monastery where his in-laws and their two children were buried.[151] A locus of sacred family power could stabilize and promote those trying to establish power in a given area. Although Heilwig did not make the claim herself, through marriage to her, Hucbald was able to make a claim to Cysoing, demonstrating that this couple retained the memory of and connections to her kin.

Although the information concerning the female Unruochings is unusually extensive, other examples from the memorial book demonstrate the advantages the entry of female kin into San Salvatore brought: commemorative prayer, association with a royal foundation, and connections to the other

---

148. *CAC*, no. 3, 4, and 5, 7–11.
149. Ibid., no. 6, 11.
150. Ibid., no. 5, 10–11.
151. Flodoard, *Historia Ecclesiae Remensis*, 558; *CAC*, no. 4, 5, 8–11.

powerful families of northern Italy. Almost all the nuns' names known from convent and necrology lists may be found elsewhere in the book, demonstrating the strong bonds between the women and the donor community. The nuns never appear together in one list, but in smaller lists scattered throughout the book. Tracing some specific families at San Salvatore is possible. The names Grimald and Ingelfred, which appear in the entry of a family group on folio 37[r], record two magnates known from other early tenth-century sources who had three female family members in San Salvatore.[152] The oblation list records that Rotperga and Regimberga—daughters of Count Grimald, one of the most faithful and powerful followers of Berengar I—entered San Salvatore. Grimald's relative Gumbert had a daughter named Rotpern who joined San Salvatore. Grimald's less influential relative, Ingelfred of Verona, also cultivated ties with San Salvatore. Numerous early tenth-century documents reveal that the two men played prominent roles in the politics of northern Italy.[153] It is difficult to determine if the two memorial book entries for men named Riculf refer to the men of the same name in the donation list. One gave his daughter Cecilia and the other his daughter Teupurga to San Salvatore.[154] During the tenure of Noting as bishop of Brescia, many of his relatives were entered in the book. His relative Astat gave his daughter Suaneberga to San Salvatore.[155] One Radaldus gave seven daughters, recorded together in the oblation list but separately in the list of sisters in order of their entrance into San Salvatore. A significant amount of time could pass between oblations and professions.[156] In recorded oblations and professions at San Salvatore, only rarely did a woman enter the community without mention of her family's involvement; one case involved a widow named Perisinda who made a donation and retired to San Salvatore.[157] Her status as a widow probably helped to allow this seemingly "independent" move.

The nuns' role as conduits of familial memory would be further strengthened if it were possible to discern their role in the collection of names and in the production of the manuscript. Close examination of the liturgical texts in relation to other evidence concerning the community shows that women probably had an active hand in its production, contrary to earlier theories about its creation. Although some scholars have suggested that the book was produced

---

152. Ludwig, *TB*, 96–101.

153. Hlawitschka, *Franken, Alemannen*, 190–92, 209–10.

154. Ludwig, *TB*, 91. MGH Libri mem. N.S. 4, fol. 42[v], 182, and fol. 43[r], 183.

155. Ludwig, *TB*, 86–90.

156. MGH Libri mem. N.S. 4, fol. 43[r] and 183. Ludwig, "Die Anlage des 'Liber vitae,'" 60–61.

157. Her entry and the existence of the charter in her name help to date the book. Ludwig, "Die Anlage des 'Liber vitae,'" 58–59.

mainly through the agency of the bishop of Brescia and his clerks, no evidence survives that clearly indicates this to be true. Karl Schmid believes the question of the influence and participation of the nuns in the production of the book remains open.[158] Rosamond McKitterick is convinced that the nuns produced it themselves.[159] An early tenth-century inventory records items possibly for use in a scriptorium, and it lists missals, Gospels, letters of Paul, a psalter, and various patristic texts that may have been produced in San Salvatore's own scriptorium.[160] The feminine forms of pronouns used throughout the memorial book reveal that those who put it together tailored it for female use and leave an impression of the manuscript as a female work.

San Salvatore held charters and other documents that its members may have produced, or persons mentioned in the charters may have deposited them there in order to preserve these records. In fact, the composition of some quite clearly took place elsewhere according to the scribe who signed them.[161] Their possession of charters, however, reveals that they at least maintained an "archival memory" of some transactions in the Brescia area.[162] Furthermore, female scribes helped to produce the Remiremont memorial book. Chelles's scriptorium produced a number of manuscripts, including the eighth-century Old Gelasian Sacramentary (Vat. Regin. 316).[163] It is, therefore, quite possible that the members of San Salvatore produced the memorial book. Given the relatively ambiguous nature of early medieval Italian manuscripts, proving or disproving direct composition of the memorial book by women will probably remain impossible. Even if the location of production was outside the convent, the emphasis on the nuns and their families highlights the women's unambiguous roles as the bearers of familial memory. Although the sources reveal little of their individuality beyond their names, these women maintained connections with their families and others in a dynamic, not passive, manner.

San Salvatore offers an excellent example of the ways royal foundation of female monasteries and recruitment of members from the aristocracy bound the elite to both the royal family and the wider Frankish church, giving both king and clerics some influence over the actions and wealth of those families.[164] Certainly San Salvatore played a major role in the power of Lothar I in Italy, and it acted as a refuge for his wife Irmingard and daughter Gisela. The lack of entries dated before 830 indicates that the book's compilation began in the

158. Schmid, "Der Codex als Zeugnis," 14.
159. McKitterick, "Women and Literacy," 19–20.
160. *CDLang*, no. 419, cols. 706–27.
161. *CDLong*, no. 137, 29–34; no. 155, 77–84; no. 226, 271–75.
162. Nora, "General Introduction," 9–10.
163. Bischoff, "Die Kölner Nonnenhandschriften," 27–33.
164. Nelson, "Commentary on the Papers of J. Verdon, S.F. Wemple and M. Parisse," 332.

830s and further helps to demonstrate the book's potential associations with Lothar I, who ruled from 840 to 855. It was also in the 830s that Lothar I gave the convent to his wife Irmingard and that a list of Brescian nuns appeared for the first time in Reichenau's memorial book. Reichenau's inclusion of San Salvatore into its confraternity list further underlines the community's imperial connections. The rule of Lothar I over the central part of Charlemagne's empire helped to create strong ties between northern Italy and the Germanic areas just beyond the Alps. Prayer connections between Reichenau and San Salvatore were not independent of political relations between the two parts of the empire. During the reign of Louis II, a strong relationship between San Salvatore and Reichenau is still apparent. Prayer lists of names from Reichenau, dating to the 860s and 870s, made their way into the San Salvatore book. The community at Brescia continued to be a refuge for Louis II and his successors, especially Berengar, son of Eberhard and Gisela, (d. 924).[165]

The many royal charters concerning San Salvatore provide another sign of royal interest in maintaining the prestige of the community. Over the ninth century Carolingian rulers reconfirmed and added to the privileges, rights, and holdings of San Salvatore.[166] They believed that San Salvatore could effectively commemorate the dead and pray for the royal family. In order to provide for the perpetual commemoration of his sister Gisela, the emperor Louis II gave land to San Salvatore in a charter of January 12, 862.[167] During the period in which Bertha, daughter of Berengar I, was abbess (c. 915–c. 942), some royal charters concerning San Salvatore explicitly mention her father's familial relationship to the abbess, emphasizing the community as royal family institution. For example, in a charter of March 4, 915, in which Berengar gave her the right to control a road and construct buildings along it, the charter names the abbess as "Bertha, the very pious abbess of the convent of Santa Giulia and our beloved daughter."[168]

In their donations, other families recognized the status accorded to San Salvatore through its connection to the royal family. Aristocrats and landowners in the local area almost certainly wished to maintain bonds with the religious house, particularly by arranging to obtain usufruct of donated land from San Salvatore. In a charter of November 17, 878, for example, the abbess Ermengard granted one Rotechar and his heirs the right to maintain use of

---

165. Schmid, "Der Codex als Zeugnis," 17.
166. *CDLang*, no. 48, cols. 90–92; no. 194, cols. 325–26; no. 195, cols. 326–27; no. 211, col. 348; no. 212, cols. 348–49; *I Diplomi di Berengario I*, Fonti per la storia d'Italia, vol. 35, ed. Luigi Schiaparelli (Rome, 1903), no. 5, 28–29; no. 110, 281–83.
167. *CDLang*, no. 220, cols. 368–69.
168. *I Diplomi di Berengario I*, no. 96, 253–54.

a *curtis* for twenty years in exchange for payments of money.[169] Payments in kind or money for usufruct of land on an annual or regular basis created a lasting relationship that the parties would have to remember each time payment was made.[170] Landowners may have continued to recognize San Salvatore as a stable and powerful place that could safely hold their documents. If some tenth- and eleventh-century charters are indeed faithful copies of Carolingian-era originals, some individuals placed copies of their documents with the community just as others had done during Lombard rule, allowing these documents to survive.[171] For example, San Salvatore held a charter from one Zacano recording his marriage gift to an Andreverda, dated February 6, 889.[172] Thus, the local community within and surrounding Brescia maintained a relationship of donation, exchange, and deposit with the religious house, and the female community continued to transact business with those beyond their house's walls.

The rich evidence from San Salvatore helps to demonstrate in contrast to earlier views the vibrancy of ninth-century "Italian" monasticism.[173] Many practices were common to royal foundations north of the Alps and San Salvatore, though the need for further work on other Lombard and Carolingian monasteries in northern Italy makes difficult a clear comparison among communities. Differences in surviving sources play no small role in any perceived disparities. Had *vitae* of northern Italian women of the ninth century survived in comparable numbers to those north of the Alps, scholars might know more about female religious life there. Many of the surviving Carolingian female *vitae*, however, are related in some way to the monastery at Fulda.

The Female *Vitae* Related to Fulda

Boniface (c. 680–755) founded Fulda, a male religious community, in 744, and from its inception it benefited from Carolingian patronage. Over time,

---

169. *CDLang*, no. 279, cols. 471–72.

170. See also *CDLang*, no. 96, cols. 178–79.

171. These lands may also have somehow related to the holdings of San Salvatore or may have been of interest to the community itself. Even if these documents are not originally from the Carolingian era, they are nevertheless interesting of their own accord. Unfortunately, some are rather badly damaged. Archivio di Stato e Archivio Storico Civico Brescia, Busta 2, XXIV, XXVI, XXIX, XLIX. *CDLang*, no. 152, cols. 262–64.

172. Archivio di Stato e Archivio Storico Civico Brescia, Busta 3, XLVI. Unfortunately, this potentially fascinating charter is nearly impossible to read in full. It has darkened very badly and has long been damaged: an eighteenth-century catalogue mentions its worn condition. G. Asterazi, *Indice alfabetico-istorico-cronologico-perpetuo dell'Archivio dell'insigne, e real monistero novo di S. Salvatore e Sa.Giulia di Brescia*, Biblioteca Queriniana MS G.I.4, fol. 65.

173. Compare to Wemple, "Female Monasticism in Italy," 295.

local families increasingly attached themselves to Fulda.[174] Many women from powerful families had connections with Fulda through donation, friendship, or relation to a member of the community. In particular, the authors and subjects of many eighth- and ninth-century *vitae* of and mentioning women had some association with Fulda. Because *vitae* had to display some verisimilitude in order to be believable, they reveal much about family life, even though their subjects joined spiritual families. Repetition of certain topoi may reveal possible practices. More compelling, however, is the support found in other sources, especially letters, for the hagiographic evidence. These other texts serve not only to contextualize but also to flesh out the information concerning families in *vitae*.

Eighth-century letters to and from women that passed among members of Boniface's circle reflect the continuity of family bonds beyond religious consecration. Although many of these letter writers were Anglo-Saxon, they provide an earlier context for the later evidence from Remiremont, San Salvatore, and the *vitae* related to Fulda. In a letter to Boniface written shortly after 732, Leoba, abbess of Tauberbischofsheim, asked that he pray for the souls of her deceased parents:

> I ask for your mercy, that you deign to remember the former friendship which you once had long ago with my father, whose name was Dynne, in the western regions who, eight years ago now, has been taken from the light, so that you may not refuse to offer prayers for his soul. Also I commend to you the memory of my mother, who was named Aebbe, who, as you well know, is connected to you through bonds of blood and who still lives, though with hardship, and for a long time has been greatly oppressed by sickness.[175]

A trio of letters from Boniface's circle from the late eighth century reveals concrete reasons for the desire to maintain family bonds beyond religious consecration. Berthgyth complains to her brother Balthard, the possible first abbot of Hersfeld, that he has not maintained sufficient communication with her. In two letters she writes that she has no neighbors or another brother upon whom to rely and that she is lonely and discouraged. The third letter followed after she received news of her brother via messenger. Though she writes that she is less disheartened, she urges him to visit her.[176] Women

---

174. Rösener, "Die Grundherrschaft des Klosters Fulda in karolingischer und ottonischer Zeit."

175. MGH Ep. S 1, no. 29, 52–3. This translation draws from that of Andy Orchard, "Old Sources, New Resources: Finding the Right Formula for Boniface," *Anglo-Saxon England* 30 (2001): 15–38, at 30.

176. MGH Ep. S 1, no. 143, 282; no. 147, 284–85; no. 148, 285–87.

such as Berthgyth did not merely want to maintain contact with relatives; it was a necessity for them. Given that Berthgyth's parents had died, she would have been reliant upon her closest male kin for protection, whether or not she was in a religious community. Balthard was making his own way on the continent, where family bonds may have seemed less immediate. Another of Boniface's circle, Gregory of Utrecht (707/8–775 or 780), though promoted through the agency of his grandmother Addula, did not remain in the same region as she did. Certainly Gregory retained ties to his family, resting great hope on his young relative Albricus, who was in Italy on royal business near the end of Gregory's life.[177] But a man had a greater degree of mobility than a woman; Gregory's *vita* indicates that Albricus traveled widely, just as Gregory had done.

Many of the women of Boniface's circle expressed concern for the maintenance of kinship ties, and they often cultivated spiritual bonds in the absence of or in addition to those of blood. In this period, as the women at Remiremont and San Salvatore later did, women maintained the memory of their sisters in the religious life. An Anglo-Saxon case involving members of Boniface's circle offers a wide context for prayer relationships. In a letter of 729 to c. 744, Abbot Aldhun and the abbesses Cneuburga and Coenburga sent a list of the dead to the abbots Coengilsus of Glastonbury and Ingeldus and to the priest Wiehtberht. Wiehtberht later became active in Boniface's circle during his missionary work on the continent. Cneuberga sent the list of her dead sisters' names with the plea that Wiehtberht spread them among his friends. The first two listed were Cneuberga's sister, Quoengyth, and Aldhun's mother, Edlu.[178] Their case shows the ways that multiple relatives in the religious life promoted a family's influence and ensured its commemoration. Their request that others pray for natal and spiritual kin underlines that natural familial bonds endured beyond religious consecration and that additional spiritual kinship could strengthen those original bonds. This letter also demonstrates the early significance of female commemorative prayer. Just as Reichenau and San Salvatore later did, earlier groups of religious men and women exchanged prayer lists.

Prayer could be a requested and useful gift. Female prayer not only commemorated those who had died but also aided the living. Desire for the protection and advancement such bonds could provide made developing links with other religious people and creating brotherhoods significant to the men doing missionary work as they traveled far from home. Missionaries' desire for security and aid probably helped to spur the men and women associated

---

177. Liudger, *Vita Gregorii*, chap. 1, 67–68; chap. 15, 79.
178. MGH Ep. S 1, no. 55, 97–98.

with Boniface's missionary circle to urge others to pray for them. Requests for prayer were a common component of early medieval letters, and some women received them from men active in missionary work. In two letters of 742–43 and 742–46, Boniface asked Eadburg of Thanet and an unnamed religious woman to pray for him and his followers. Writing to Leoba, Thecla, and Cynehild in 742–46, Boniface solicited their prayers and those of the sisters living in their houses. Lull, archbishop of Mainz (d. 786), asked Eadburg to pray for him in a letter of 745–46, and sometime between 746 and 785, he made the same request of an unnamed woman.[179]

Women helped to consolidate the conversion work of these male missionaries. For example, Boniface invited his Anglo-Saxon relative, Leoba, to be abbess of Tauberbischofsheim. In his *Vita Leobae*, Rudolf wrote that "Many nobles and powerful men gave their daughters to God to remain in the convent in perpetual chastity; many matrons (*matronae*) also chose the monastic life, abandoning secular life, and made vows of chastity, taking up the holy veil."[180] Leoba herself maintained contact with the royal family.[181] The *Vita Leobae* fits with the evidence from Remiremont and San Salvatore indicating the lasting bonds between religious women and their families. Rudolf wrote this *vita* in the 830s, the same time when the compilation of the San Salvatore memorial book began and only a decade after the decision of the abbess and sisters at Remiremont to compile their memorial book. Rudolf, a monk at Fulda surely knew about ninth-century religious reforms concerning monasticism and gender, and these ideals doubtless affected his presentation of Leoba's life. Though Rudolf reported that Leoba traveled among monasteries, to the court, and to Fulda, he was careful to show that Leoba experienced and maintained relatively strict claustration.[182] Yet similarly to the evidence from Remiremont and San Salvatore, Rudolf's *vita* allowed for forms of continued familial contact and remembrance for the members of Tauberbischofsheim. Maintaining ties with daughters and nieces in the religious life was necessary, and many *vitae* reveal this practice despite its tangential relationship to the main purposes of the texts.

Two cases from Leoba's *vita* show that membership in a convent did not cut religious women off from the bonds of kinship. The first concerns the time when the local community accused Leoba and her nuns of being unchaste after a dead infant was found in a pool and one of the nuns was missing. A local

---

179. Ibid., no. 65–76, 137–40; no. 70, 143; no. 140, 279–80.
180. Rudolf, *Vita Leobae*, chap. 16, 129.
181. For Leoba's friendship with Hildegard, the wife of Charlemagne, see ibid., chap. 20, 130.
182. Ibid., chap. 5, 124, and chap. 12, 126–27.

woman had given birth to an illegitimate baby and then drowned it. The nun, Agatha, "had gone with permission to her parents' house having been summoned there on urgent business."[183] Her temporary absence contrasts with the ideal of strict claustration. The other instance of a sister leaving the community is mentioned in Leoba's *vita*. When the nun Williswind became so ill that the others could not stand her stench, she was taken to her parents' nearby home with full permission.[184] This episode demonstrates that Williswind must have retained contact with her family and that her parents lived close enough that their sick daughter could have been transported safely to their home. Thus, similarly to Remiremont and San Salvatore, Tauberbischofsheim probably served as a site of localized aristocratic relations while providing access to the royal family.

Rudolf's attempts to show the primacy of the spiritual kinship of Leoba and Boniface over their familial kinship creates a tension in the *vita*. According to Rudolf, Boniface had hoped that Leoba's connections to him and the community at Fulda would extend beyond her death: he had recommended Leoba to the senior monks at Fulda, who then allowed her to pray there, an extraordinary privilege for a woman because Fulda had been off limits to women since its foundation. Boniface also wanted Leoba to be buried in his tomb at Fulda.[185] Rudolf's *vita*, the principal source for Leoba's life and influence, is the only text to mention this wish. Perhaps Rudolf wanted to highlight her contemporaries' recognition of Leoba's extraordinary holiness by stating that Boniface had made a highly unusual request at odds with the widespread concern that women not enter male communities. Yet Rudolf had many other conventional means of demonstrating Leoba's holiness, not least her miracles, that the request seems odd enough to suggest it was genuine, or at least Rudolf's contemporaries accepted it as such. Leoba's remains rested at Fulda, and their presence may have helped spur Rudolf to write about her. Leoba was, however, to be buried and reburied three times, not once in Boniface's tomb and each time successively farther away from him. The confluence of Rudolf's composition of her *vita* and the second removal of her relics to a church built by Raban Maur occurred in the 830s, at a time when sexual division of monasteries was to be enforced more effectively.[186] Rudolf frequently underlines the need for female claustration, for example describing the strict segregation in force at Leoba's first community, Wimborne.[187]

---

183. Ibid., chap. 12, 127.
184. Ibid., chap. 15, 128.
185. Ibid., chap. 19, 129–30.
186. Lees and Overing, *Double Agents*, 170.
187. Rudolf, *Vita Leobae*, chap. 2, 123.

Carolingian reformers may have increasingly defined the purview of religious women in an effort to channel the prayers of institutions such as Remiremont and San Salvatore to ecclesiastical, not lay, matters. When Rudolf explained the presence of Leoba's relics at Fulda at the time of their translation to a less prominent position, he revealed much about perceptions of women's influence at that time. St. Peter's Church, where her relics still rest, is now a fifteen-minute bus ride from the center of Fulda; in the ninth century, that distance was much more substantial. By placing her relics so far from Boniface's, Raban Maur may have been trying to demonstrate the necessity for the separation of the sexes in the religious life, even after death, but he also reduced Leoba's prominence. Had women's activities not been important, prominent men such as Raban Maur would have had no reason to circumscribe women's activities.

Although Saxon families around the time of conversion participated little in donation, later lay aristocratic families developed lasting bonds with the community at Fulda.[188] The family of Raban Maur, for example, gave him as an oblate to Fulda and made donations that furthered his career, and Gottschalk (d. 866/870) entered Fulda as part of a donation his mother made in memory of his recently deceased father.[189] Though they did not place any oblates at Fulda, the family of Gisla and Bernard, patrons of the holy woman Liutberga, had connections to the monastery. In fact, a record survives of a donation that Liutberga herself almost certainly made to Fulda.[190] Memorial activity did not comprise one of the main themes of the anonymous *Vita Liutbirgae virginis*, composed sometime prior to 876, but its references to prayer and commemoration support the existence of continuing family bonds to religious institutions and to consecrated family members. Liutberga urged many to pray, but specifically told the aristocratic woman Pia to pray for her mother's soul.[191] Gisla's foundation of churches and her daughters' foundations of a convent each further testifies to the magnitude of families' links to religious institutions through female family members.[192] Bernard helped to establish Liutberga as a recluse at his sister's foundation of Windenhausen and was involved in the foundation of Corvey.[193] Because this *vita* was associated with Fulda, it unsurprisingly draws on similar themes and topoi as other *vitae* related to Fulda, like Rudolf's earlier *vita* of Leoba. The author of Liutberga's *vita* depicts at least one woman in the religious life, Liutberga, urging a laywoman

188. Carroll, "The Bishoprics of Saxony in the First Century after Christianization," 224.
189. de Jong, *In Samuel's Image*, 76–91.
190. Stengel, *Urkundenbuch des Klosters Fulda*, 410.
191. *Vita Liutbirgae*, chap. 35, 41–42.
192. Ibid., chap. 2, 11.
193. Ibid., chap. 14, 20; Carroll, "The Bishoprics of Saxony," 226.

to commemorate her own kin and another maintaining a link with her natal family—Bernard's sister who welcomed Liutberga at her community. A single family could found its own communities, thereby creating opportunities over generations to preserve the family's memory and patrimony.

A later *vita*, Agius's life of Hathumoda, shows continuing familial bonds in Saxony. Hathumoda's family had strong relations with Corvey, and they founded a convent for her.[194] Her parents, Liudolf and Oda, went on pilgrimage to Rome and there received the pope's blessing and permission to transfer relics of the popes Anastasius and Innocent to the convent they founded for Hathumoda.[195] They established it first at Brunshausen in 852 and moved it to Gandersheim in 856, where Hathumoda became its first abbess.[196] Those living at Gandersheim retained relatively frequent contact with their families and certainly had flexibility concerning the land they held.

> None of the sisters could either eat or speak with their parents or any guests without permission. None could leave the monastery to go to anyone, because it is customary for most *sanctimoniales* and those who have left the world, either to parents or to neighboring holdings. No one has permission to eat outside the common meal and house and hour except if sickness afflicts someone.[197]

Though this passage seems quite restrictive, it allowed women to have contact with visitors and family members so long as it was done under supervision of the abbess. It is telling that the passage implies that land holdings and families are nearby. It indicates that women were able to maintain contact with their kin despite the restrictions of the religious life. Hathumoda's *vita* could provide an image of life under either the *Institutio sanctimonialium* or the *Rule of St. Benedict*. The flexibility to take care of family and land-related matters may argue for the *Institutio sanctimonialium*, but in no way would the *Rule of St. Benedict* have prevented the women of Gandersheim from acting as they did.[198]

In its passages concerning the burial of Hathumoda following her death from a plague, the *Vita Hathumodae* offers evidence for connections between Gandersheim's inhabitants and their neighbors. Not only did her sisters

---

194. Hans Jürgen Warnecke, "Sächsische Adelsfamilien in der Karolingerzeit," in *Kunst*, 354.
195. Agius, *Vita Hathumodae*, chap. 4, 168.
196. Berschin, *Biographie und Epochenstil im lateinischen Mittelalter*, 353.
197. Agius, *Vita Hathumodae*, chap. 5, 168.
198. Schilp, *NW*, 147–48.

mourn Hathumoda's death and commend her soul, but many others from the area came to the community's church on the day of her burial:

> When throngs of men and women gathered, they wore the clothes which they had received from her; they presented other gifts gathered for her kindness. Meanwhile, a crowd of great number assembled through the whole night and day up to the hour of her burial.[199]

Those living around Gandersheim knew who Hathumoda was, and many benefited from her gifts. Discussion of the early development of a cult for Hathumoda should come as no surprise in her *vita*; however, this passage argues that women in religious communities maintained contacts with the world even when they lived under claustration as strict as that reportedly in force at Gandersheim.

Aristocratic religious women were not as shut off from the outside world as some Carolingian reformers would have thought ideal, but such clerics may have recognized the need to compromise with the desires of the lay elite. Though nuns' outside contact was limited, they offered benefits to their families as members of religious communities that helped maintain kinship ties beyond religious consecration. Being able to pursue a family strategy rested upon possession of land. A family could protect the integrity of land given in the name of the dead. Giving a portion of the family patrimony to a female house could give men a means to protect that land while looking after it from close proximity. As mentioned above, religious men also retained family bonds, but they could stray much farther from their families than women. Huneberc of Heidenheim, for example, related that Willibald, future bishop of Eichstätt and another relative of Boniface, invited his father to accompany him on his pilgrimage to the Holy Land and that he traveled there with his brother, thus demonstrating a continued attachment to family after his consecration as a monk.[200]

Other Cases

Further evidence from smaller foundations and other, scattered cases suggests that the memorial activities and familial bonds of large religious houses reflected widespread practices. Throughout the ninth century evidence points

---

199. Agius, *Vita Hathumodae*, chap. 25, 175.

200. Huneberc, *Vita Willibaldi*, chap. 3, 90–92. See also Noble and Head, *Soldiers of Christ*, 148, note 4.

to increasing memorial commemoration among laywomen who maintained the memories and lands of their families, both natal and marital, by donating land, praying, and teaching their children to care for their family's memory. In so doing, they followed the lead of religious women; as the ninth century progressed, queens especially developed stronger associations with religious communities, in part to protect themselves against the increasingly common accusations of immorality, adultery, and witchcraft.[201] Other aristocratic women may have cultivated the appearance of virtue or genuinely pursued it through the action of commemorating their relatives. By doing so they promoted the well-being and prosperity of their families through actions they could carry out at home, just as their sisters in the religious life were able to pursue memorial commemoration precisely because claustration may have enhanced its efficacy in the eyes of others. At smaller houses that have left few if any records, religious women probably also preserved the memories of their families, friends, and sisters.

From an early date, control over religious houses became a primary means to bolster the power of an early medieval family. The convent of St. Stephen in Strasbourg offers a good case study of typical changes from the early eighth to the late ninth century. The Alsatian duke Adalbert (d. 722) from the Etichnonen family founded St. Stephen. His daughter Attala was its first abbess; since the tenth century, she has been honored as a saint. Both of Adalbert's wives, Gerlindis and Bathildis, were buried in the community's choir. This foundation, therefore, became a focus of family memory and both a means and reflection of Etichnonen power. In the ninth century, lists of nuns from this community were recorded in both the Reichenau and St. Gall memorial books. Because the second woman in the Reichenau list, Onhilt, has the designation *praeposita*—an office described in the *Institutio sanctimonialium* as second only to the abbess—by this point the community probably followed this early-ninth-century rule. This adoption suggests that this rule was more attractive to family foundations, whose members may have wished to keep control over family lands and to remain in closer contact with family members. The Reichenau and St. Gall lists indicate that sometime during the mid-ninth century, control of St. Stephen in Strasbourg shifted to the Erchanger family, who had been rivals of the Etichnonens in the early part of the ninth century. Following the marriage in 861 or 862 of Charles the Fat to Richardis, her family, the Erchangers, rose to greater power in the Alsace.[202] Richardis had been abbess of St. Stephen for a short time prior to her marriage to Charles the Fat,

---

201. MacLean, "Queenship, Nunneries and Royal Widowhood in Carolingian Europe," 1–38.

202. Geuenich, "Richkart, *ancilla dei de caenobio Sancti Stephani*," 97–109.

and her patronage linked St. Stephen to other houses under royal patronage.[203]
The convent's associations with the royal family help to explain the inclusion of St. Stephen's in the memorial lists of Reichenau and St. Gall, two of the most prominent monasteries of the Carolingian Empire. The abbesses of St. Stephen who came from the Erchanger family and that community's changing profile demonstrate the ways in which control over a female religious community could help both to develop and reflect changes in regional and imperial power. Proprietary religious houses were also locations for the preservation of familial memory, sometimes remaining under a family for generations. In 936, the Ottonian empress Mathilda took over Windenhausen, the house that Gisla had founded for her daughter, probably because the empress was related to Gisla and Bernard's family.[204] The later female foundations important in Ottonian Saxony had their roots in the ninth century.

Sometimes religious women made donations that demonstrated their continuing management of land, presumably from their families or deceased husbands. The charters of St. Gall offer at least three such cases. The nun Cotaniwi gave land in Lauterbach and Beffendorf and bondsmen (*casatos*) to St. Gall on September 25, 769. On January 23, 786, Gundrada, a nun at Lauterbach, had a precarial charter drawn up, transmitting to Sigimund and his wife Nandila and to the priest Ebrachar usufruct of lands, which they had given to the church at Lauterbach as rent. Another *deo sacrata* (consecrated woman) named Ata donated her possession at Seedorf to St. Gall on November 17, 797. She maintained usufruct of these lands as long as she lived.[205] In these St. Gall charters, women retained control over land after religious consecration. Cotaniwi and Ata disposed of theirs as they pleased. Ata retained usufruct of her donated land, meaning that she either still required the income or that she wished to retain control of the land during her lifetime.

Strong family connections and retention of family lands probably continued at small foundations in the late eighth century and early ninth century. A community that attracted members from local families could help to establish social and political bonds on a smaller scale than the empire-wide bonds developed at royal monasteries like Remiremont and San Salvatore. Such houses had a long history. Since the Merovingian period, families founded monasteries in order to maintain their patrimonies. Surviving evidence reveals glimpses of the small family religious communities that almost certainly existed throughout the Carolingian Empire. San Salvatore at Versilia in Italy offers an example of a convent that enjoyed no royal patronage. The aristocrat Walfred and

---

203. MacLean, *Kingship and Politics in the Late Ninth Century*, 186.
204. Warnecke, "Sächsische Adelsfamilien," 354.
205. *Urkundenbuch der Sanct Gallen*, vol. 1, no. 53, no. 104, no. 150.

his wife decided to lead a religious life, and their sons joined them. In doing so, the couple was far from unusual. Yet the communities they founded, joined, and led, including San Salvatore at Versilia, were remarkable for covering such a vast amount of land and for their independence. Records reveal that San Salvatore at Versilia was an active convent from at least 804 to 806, and seems to have remained autonomous until the eleventh century. The lack of further information about this foundation stems from the fact that it lacked royal protection.[206] San Salvatore at Versilia and similar houses may have functioned in ways comparable to larger, royal foundations. In two late ninth-century *vitae*, parents founded communities where their daughters became abbesses, Hathumoda at Gandersheim and Herlindis and Renula at Aldeneik.[207] That the *vita* of Herlindis and Renula was meant to recall an eighth-century foundation underlines the long history of this practice. Proprietary foundations provided aristocratic families with means to preserve both their memories and lands, but over time, in order to be associated with large houses, women may have increasingly entered convents under royal patronage.

Sometimes families benefitted if their female relatives left the religious life after a time, further helping to explain the desire that these women retain control over land. Richardis offers an example of women who left a religious position—abbess of St. Stephen in Strasbourg—when she married. Naturally, Richardis may have served as little more than a *rectrix* or lay leader of a female community, a common and advantageous strategy among later ninth-century Carolingian rulers and their wives.[208] Often, however, other women in the Carolingian elite may have entered convents for religious instruction, for the connections to that house and the other institutions and families with which it had links, and/or for the protection of their virtue and reputation. All of these advantages made them more attractive marriage partners and explain why their families and they may not have intended that they would stay permanently in the religious life. Some may never have taken vows of consecration. Complaints about this practice first came early in the eighth century and then regularly throughout the Carolingian period.

The benefits of having a female relative leave the religious life helped to spur Carolingian legislation attempting to enforce claustration.[209] Female

---

206. Hasdenteufel-Röding, "Zur Gründung und Organisation des Frauenklosters San Salvatore an der Versilia," 174–85.

207. *Vita Herlinde et Renulae*, chap. 6, 387; Agius, *Vita Hathumodae*, chap. 4, 168.

208. MacLean, "Queenship, Nunneries and Royal Widowhood in Carolingian Europe," 18–20.

209. Capitulary of Herstal of 779, MGH Capit. 1, 47; General Capitulary to the *Missi* of 802, MGH Capit. I, 95; Synods of Reisbach, Freising, and Salzburg, around 800, MGH Conc. 2.1, 210; Synod of Tours, MGH Conc. 2.1, 290.

communities, however, needed to retain some level of communication with non-members. For reasons of pastoral care and worship, a priest ideally should have visited. Abbesses needed to have contact with the outside world in order to administer their communities; the provincial Synod of Chalon-sur-Saône of 813 stated that an abbess could leave her community if she had received an order of the king or permission of the bishop.[210] Such rules indicate that the abbess could shape the degree of enclosure: she could make exceptions to it, give permission to travel, and allow supervised visits.[211] The passage quoted earlier from *Vita Hathumodae*, which generally conformed to ideals of claustration, echoed this legislation. An example from the early tenth-century anonymous *Vita Aldegundis* suggests both continuing family bonds and the protection a convent could afford young women. After Waldetrud had a convent built and entered the religious life, she wanted to shield her younger sister Aldegund from the temptations of lay life. She wrote to their mother Bertilla asking her to send Aldegund on a visit, and Aldegund remained with her sister in the religious life.[212]

In many respects the *Institutio sanctimonialium* served as a compromise between aristocratic families, the king, and clerics, especially on the subjects of the retention of links to natal families and of the permanence of entry to the religious life. The rule was rather vague on these topics, promoting claustration but allowing some exceptions. Although it stated that women were to avoid unnecessary contact with those in the outside world, particularly men, in order to protect their chastity, they could visit with their families under the supervision of one of the older *sanctimoniales*.[213] Although non-noble women were allowed to enter religious houses, women with an illustrious or prominent background almost certainly had priority.[214] The majority of those living under this rule were undoubtedly members of the elite. The rule seems to have left room for women to leave the religious life for marriage, especially if they did not give over their land to the community. Aristocratic families would have appreciated this flexibility and the potential guarantee of their young relatives' virginity.[215] Certainly, if women retained land, as allowed in the *Institutio sanctimonialium* and supported by some charter evidence, they

210. MGH Conc. 2.1, canon 13, 264.

211. Parisse, "Les chanoinesses dans l'empire germanique," 110–11.

212. *Vita Aldegundis*, chap. 8, 1042; *Vita sanctae Aldegundis*, chap. 8, PL 132, col. 863. The tenth-century author gave more detailed information about Aldegund's stay with Waldetrud than the earlier version of the life provided. McNamara and Halborg, *Sainted Women of the Dark Ages*, 245, note 39.

213. *IS*, canon 5, 435; canon 20, 451.

214. *IS*, canon 10, 446. Schilp, *NW*, 177.

215. Schilp, *NW*, 178.

remained desirable marriage pawns for their families and those of their potential spouses.

The selection of abbesses comprised another area of female religious life for which the *Institutio sanctimonialium* offered benefits to elite families. Although the *Rule of St. Benedict* insisted upon the election of abbots and abbesses, in fact they frequently came from the founding families of communities. Conversely, the *Institutio sanctimonialium* did not forbid founding families from ensuring that a relative became abbess.[216] Such a practice was not uncommon according to various *vitae*. In Hucbald of St. Amand's early tenth-century *Vita Rictrudis*, Rictrud called her daughter Eusebia back from the convent of Hamay, which Eusebia's paternal great-grandmother Gertrude had built and where Gertrude had raised her. Following Gertrude's death, Eusebia succeeded her as abbess.[217] Eusebia's relation to the family that founded the community was crucial.

Women under the *Institutio sanctimonialium* had three choices about how to deal with their lands. They could donate it to the community; they could transfer possession of land to the community but retain its usufruct for their lifetimes; or they could have a caretaker, usually a relative or a friend, administer it with the permission of the abbess. In the last case, the land was not meant to end up in the hands of the community. The second and third options allowed women to embrace a life of poverty while retaining financial and material security.[218] Women under the *Institutio sanctimonialium* could transmit land to others outside their community, a fact that substantially set them apart from women under the *Rule of St. Benedict*.[219] In fact, the main differences between the *Rule of St. Benedict* and the *Institutio sanctimonialium* regard continued possession of land and the more luxurious lifestyle of those women under the latter rule.[220] The decreased power of the bishops under this rule probably resulted from increased aristocratic interest in their own churches and monastic foundations. Later eighth-century church councils often put the female communities under a bishop's care, but the *Institutio sanctimonialium* emphasized the independence of the abbess.[221] Through the *Institutio sanctimonialium* clerics mandated the definition and structure of a specific form of religious life for women. Although they certainly wished to enforce stricter claustration, clerics must have recognized that it was an ideal that could not

---

216. Ibid., 180–85.
217. Hucbald, *Vita Rictrudis*, chap. 25, 87.
218. Schilp, *NW*, 93–94.
219. Parisse, "Les chanoinesses dans l'empire germanique," 117–18.
220. Heidebrecht and Nolte, "Leben im Kloster," 108–10.
221. This change did not go unchallenged; later church legislation shows bishops trying again to exert increased control over abbesses. Schilp, *NW*, 169–72.

be attained completely and that compromise was necessary. They appreciated that the health of female houses rested on families' support for them. Most donations stemmed from genuine religious feeling: male kin expected efficacious prayer and commemoration from their female relatives in the religious life, but they understood that this spiritual relationship had repercussions in the material world. Finally, the king could benefit from the same shifts in land and alliance, directly through his own female kin in the religious houses and through the ties to the families of powerful magnates. Such bonds could help a ruler to retain his followers' loyalty and to counter those men who competed with him for power and influence.

Looking after their land, even if through a proxy, required a religious woman to have some contact with the outside world. For example, in 828 a nun named Engilpurc and her mother, Ellanpurc, gave Freising property from their inheritance and had it given back to them as a benefice. Because Engilpurc's cousin, a priest named Wicharius, wanted the property for himself, Engilpurc went before a synod at Eching headed by Bishop Hatto to ask for help. Hatto renewed the benefice for the lifetimes of Engilpurc and Ellanpurc and forbade Wicharius to preach in the church there without the women's permission.[222] In this charter, a religious woman paid rent and donated land in conjunction with her mother, demonstrating a bond between them that lasted beyond religious consecration and whose memory endured beyond the deaths of both women. Furthermore, their cousin's attempt to take the land reveals a connection between kinship and land tenure that equally endured.

Contemporary evidence reveals similar concerns about family memory and the retention of familial bonds by at least the mid ninth century. In a parallel to the increasing evidence of queens' sacral functions throughout the ninth century, other elite laywomen seem to have taken up religious roles that demonstrated the virtue others expected of them and that allowed them to exert influence within their families and beyond. Dhuoda's instructions concerning the commemoration of her son's kin offer an outstanding example. She urged William to pray for his relatives, mainly those on his father's side from whom he inherited land.[223] Dhuoda was therefore responsible for transmitting the memory not only of her kin but also of her husband's kin, becoming the bearer of memory for the conjugal couple.[224] Throughout the handbook, Dhuoda encouraged William to pray, an appropriate offering for William, as a lay aristocrat, to make.[225] His prayer would serve not only to maintain family

222. *Die Traditionen des Hochstifts Freising*, no. 562.
223. Dhuoda, *LM*, 8.14, 204.
224. Le Jan, *FP*, 56.
225. Claussen, "God and Man in Dhuoda's *Liber manualis*," 46.

memory and aid deceased relatives but also to confirm his aristocratic status in his own mind, making him cognizant of his noble heritage and educated in appropriate ways to commemorate worthy ancestors. Their lands helped to make him an aristocrat and made more fitting his commemoration of those from whom he inherited. Dhuoda made choices concerning the individuals for whom William should pray; she paid little attention to relatives too distant to provide him any material or spiritual advantage.[226] Her decisions regarding which family members were worthy of William's prayer reveal the way kin relations could change from generation to generation, adjusting to differing levels of reciprocity and contact. Such adjustments over time underline the ways that adaptable bonds between women and their relatives could help to define and redefine shifting family relationships.

Prayer for family members was only one of the commemorative practices that Dhuoda explained to William; connections to religious institutions could provide another means for William to ensure prayer for his kin. When Dhuoda directed William to pray constantly for his father Bernard, she also wrote that William should have clergy pray for him.[227] She asked William to guarantee for Bernard a form of prayer that is evidenced for other powerful families in Carolingian memorial books: prayer by those in the religious life. In fact, Dhuoda created a memorial list within her handbook, listing William's deceased kin. She wished him to remember those relatives and to add others as they passed away.[228] She therefore not only provided him with a family history but also encouraged him to maintain and continue it. Dhuoda mentioned other forms of commemoration in her handbook: prayer for the clergy, benefactions, participation in mass, and the oral transmission of stories about kin.[229] She did not expect that William's prayers would replace those of the church, but rather would complement them. Showing that she was mindful of his political and social bonds on a spiritual, not merely a material, level, she insisted that he pray for his king and his lord. Dhuoda requested that William offer alms for the good of her soul and pray for her salvation after her death. The advantages she could offer William were far less tangible but as or more valuable than land: her love, her advice, and her prayers. The epitaph that she asked William to provide upon her death demonstrates her concern for her own memory. Her frequent mention of her sins reveals a reason for her concern that William remember her; their repercussions were

---

226. Dhuoda, *LM*, 8.15, 206. See also Claussen, "Fathers of Power and Women of Authority," 807–9.

227. Dhuoda, *LM*, 8.7, 198.

228. Ibid., 10.5, 226–28.

229. Innes, "Keeping It in the Family," 24.

potentially serious for the health of her soul, requiring the prayers of others to aid in her own salvation. She admonished William to ensure that his younger brother pray for her and that they both have masses said for her.[230] Here a mother transmitted the ways in which her sons should commemorate their relatives, demonstrating that mothers could ensure that their children became bearers of familial memory. Gisela and Eberhard of Friuli may have had this female lay role in mind when they left their lay daughters phylacteries about twenty years after the composition of Dhuoda's handbook.

Just as Gisela, Eberhard's wife, gave land to ensure her family's commemoration, charters and wills demonstrate that other women in the mid- and late ninth century gave land for the memory of their souls and that of their families. Widows often made such bequests because they could at least theoretically manage their own property in the Frankish period. The precise legal and social position of widows has been the subject of some debate, but widows definitely had greater freedom to control their resources than either married or unmarried women despite the many constrictions and family demands with which they had to contend.[231] Of course, they still relied heavily upon men for support in carrying out these decisions. Sometimes widows sought the church's protection from relatives vying for their land. Other aristocrats could also help a widow keep her lands as in the case of Erkanfrida, who at an assembly in Luxembourg in 853, ensured that she had male support for the disposition of possessions and land in her will.[232] Because protecting widows was an ideal activity of aristocrats, it could have enhanced the reputations of those men who helped Erkanfrida.

In Carolingian lands, widows hardly comprised a homogenous group in terms of age or status. Many had to deal with profound external pressures either to remarry or to enter a religious community. In one example, according to Hucbald of St. Amand in his *vita* of the aristocratic widow Rictrud, written c. 907, Rictrud had to trick the king, Dagobert, into giving his permission for her to take the veil: he wanted her to marry one of his followers rather than take her riches into a religious community.[233] Besides their interest in their children's welfare, many widows who had to look after lands of which they had usufruct, would necessarily have had contact with relatives concerning their holdings. Thus, their bonds with their families may have been stronger or more flexible than those of the virgins in religious

---

230. Dhuoda, *LM*, 8.5–6, 198; 10.4, 224–26; 10.6, 228–30.
231. Pellaton, "La veuve et ses droits de la Basse-Antiquité au haut Moyen Âge," 94–95; Santinelli, *Des femmes éplorées?* 179, 263–64.
232. Nelson, "The Wary Widow," 108–10.
233. *Vita Rictrudis*, chap. 14, 84.

communities.[234] Some widows who remarried brought great wealth into their new unions. Marriage to a widow was one means for aristocratic men to gain greater wealth and status. Most famously, Baldwin of Flanders wed Judith, the daughter of Charles the Bald and widow of both Æthelwulf of Wessex and his brother Æthelbald of Wessex.

Laywomen, such as Eberhard's wife Gisela, probably helped to maintain family chapels and churches. In his will of 876, the nobleman Eccard of Autun left his chapel treasury to his wife Richildis for her use as long as she lived. It included gold and silver liturgical objects, silk and linen liturgical vestments and cloths, and four manuscripts. Eccard may have hoped that Richildis would pray for his soul and look after his family's spiritual welfare, just as he ensured such commemorative prayer through the donations of his will. Eccard also left lands to Faremoutiers, the convent to which his sister Ada belonged and where a Bertrada was abbess, so that they and their sisters would pray for him, his parents, and his first wife. He gave objects, including liturgical manuscripts, jewelry, and vessels, to Ada, the abbess Bertrada, and Theutberga, widow of Lothar II. The small psalter, book of prayers and psalms, amethyst seal (*sigillum*), and golden girdle he gave to Ada; and an evangelary in Germanic language, the *Life of St. Anthony*, and a beryl seal he gave to Abbess Bertrada were highly suitable gifts.[235] The items reflected the women's vocation, high status, and learning. These bequests indicate that Eccard probably maintained contact with his sister or her community after her consecration. His specific inclusion of Bertrada may recognize the abbess's power to regulate the communication between a member and her family and to ensure commemoration of certain donors and friends.

For some women who suffered from ill treatment, loss of position, accusations of immorality, and/or their husbands' loss of power, a religious house could provide a haven. In 864, Charles the Bald gave Aveney—a convent near Rheims that had been used for some time to endow Carolingian princesses—to Theutberga, Lothar II's estranged wife.[236] His concubine Waldrada eventually entered Remiremont to escape the divorce controversy.[237] After the death of her daughter Gisela in 868, Engelberga, the powerful and ambitious wife and empress of Louis II, became abbess of San Salvatore in Brescia; the community thus continued its role as a house for members of the Carolingian family. She also tried to found a new religious house. On June 3, 870, Louis II granted

---

234. Parisse, "Des veuves au monastère," 256–66.
235. *RCSBL*, no. 25, 62–63, 65.
236. *AB*, 116. See note 33, page 121, in Janet L. Nelson's translation.
237. Hlawitschka, "Herzog Giselbert," 425. See discussion of the divorce controversy in chapter 3.

her the right to handle her property as she saw fit and gave her the convent of St. Peter near Piacenza along with seven manors to support the women at the new convent. In 874, he gave her more land, confirmed her hereditary rights, and granted her permission to have the convent enlarged and to control the aqueduct system of the county of Piacenza and a canal of flowing water. She was not to alienate any of the land, but her daughter Ermengard could later succeed her. Ermengard, however, could only look after the convent; another woman was to serve as abbess, but only Ermengard's daughter could later assume that position. In essence, this house could act as a refuge for the women of this family if they needed it.[238] That function was particularly significant because Louis II and Engelberga had no sons, and the imperial title would pass to Charles the Bald. Richardis, the wife of Charles the Fat, retired to Andlau in 887 after suffering accusations of adultery with Liutward, bishop of Vercelli and her husband's chancellor, when it became clear she was unlikely to conceive and bear an heir.[239] Some of these queens prepared for these possibilities by becoming patronesses and rectresses (*rectrix*) of religious houses; even if they suffered no problems similar to those of Richardis, these associations could bolster their prestige and influence.[240]

Queens and royal daughters could take advantage of the protection and influence that membership in a religious house gave them. Though a tension existed between monasticism and involvement in worldly affairs, the royal family needed the same flexibility concerning claustration that the *Institutio sanctimonialium* granted to aristocratic families. In the ninth century, increasing calls for enclosure resulted in part from the power that all elite families could develop through their kinship to women in the religious life. Claustration helped to ensure female virtue and therefore the efficacy of religious women's prayer, but desire for enclosure had to be balanced with continuing family bonds. Although ideally women left the world behind upon entry to a religious community, in practice many of them did not abandon familial concerns.

Various examples from the lands of Carolingian rule have revealed that the ninth century marked a change in women's memorial practices. Family foundations, the desire to have female kin in the religious life, and the donations of women that ensured their own commemoration and that of others had a long history, but in the ninth century as queens increasingly associated themselves with religious institutions, smaller family foundations may have become less important. Families may have rather encouraged their daughters to enter

---

238. Odegaard, "The Empress Engelberge," 80.
239. MacLean, *Kingship and Politics*, 169–73.
240. MacLean, "Queenship, Nunneries, and Royal Widowhood in Carolingian Europe," 12–33.

major houses like San Salvatore in Brescia or Remiremont because it brought association with the royal family and other magnates. Part of the attraction for both women and their families was the tradition of liturgical commemoration that developed in the 830s at those houses; such pious acts stood in sharp contrast to the accusations leveled against queens. These houses gave protection and influence to queens and indeed to all women in the religious life. The virtue that clerical rhetoric demanded they uphold could be a difficult, if not impossible, achievement for women in the lay life. With a spiritual vocation, a woman had greater opportunity to balance successfully the clerical and lay ideals of the virtuous woman against the need to act in their own interests and those of their families.

Female Perpetuation of Bonds and Memory

Familial and clerical expectations of women included preservation of familial memory and care for dead relatives' souls through prayer or guarantee of such prayer through land donation. Evidence indicates that women throughout the late eighth and ninth centuries carried out these duties. Such female actions offered many potential spiritual and material benefits. Through connections to religious institutions, women helped to develop spiritual, social, and political bonds. Their membership in royal monasteries such as Remiremont and San Salvatore in Brescia gave their families relations with the other aristocratic families whose daughters and nieces were members. A similar phenomenon was probably at work in smaller institutions such as San Salvatore at Versilia, which lacked royal patronage. Just as less powerful families imitated the royal family in a variety of ways, they may have enjoyed similar but more localized benefits from the bonds created through female communities.

Female family members could help to create or maintain crucial ties to others either by entering a religious house or through marriage. Because of their dependent status, they maintained close contact and bonds to their natal kin while relying upon their spiritual and marital families. Although scholars have traditionally seen that position as a weakness, their dependency, in a sense, strengthened their own and their families' abilities to negotiate social and political networks, partly explaining why contemporary sources both perpetuated and emphasized female dependency. Women were hardly the only ones, however, whose "individuality" was obscured by bonds; all early medieval people had relationships to greater or lesser degrees with family, kin, groups, and God. Rather than concealing women, their kinship and family ties have, in fact, provided a means of studying them, their latitude for action, and the ways their actions affected others' expectations of them.

The activities of Carolingian aristocratic women in these areas reveal their social competence. Their commemorative and familial connections helped to maintain a common culture that knit together the Carolingian elite socially and politically. Although documentation about the individual actions of women in this regard is far from abundant, except for queens, when taken as a group, this female contribution becomes evident. Inseparable from their kin in many ways, the women preserved their families' memories and patrimonies. Not passive participants in aristocratic culture, their celebration of memorial liturgy, prayer, donation of land, and teaching children to commemorate the dead demonstrate that women helped to maintain and transmit these aspects of Carolingian culture. Just as religious and lay aristocratic women shared many common activities and goals, so too did aristocratic men and women. Into the tenth and eleventh centuries aristocratic women continued to commemorate kin and to help their families maintain and gain power through membership in religious communities. Carolingian female memorial activity, therefore, built upon earlier models and practices and contributed to later ones.

Chapter Three
PRUDENCE
Instruction and Moral Exemplarity

Dhuoda's handbook for her son William, the *Liber manualis*, reveals to modern readers a learned and practical mother who imparted pragmatic wisdom as well as religious teachings to her son in written form:

> I have perceived that most women rejoice that they are with their children in this world, but I, Dhuoda, observe that I am far away from you, my son William. For this reason I am troubled and full of longing to be useful to you. So I am happy to send you this little book written down in my name, that you may read it as a sort of model. And I rejoice that, even if I am apart from you in body, the little book before you will remind you, when you read it, of what you ought to do on my behalf.[1]

One problem in interpreting her work is its singular nature; it is the only long text of a laywoman that survives from the Carolingian era. Without sufficient evidence with which to compare the handbook, it is impossible to know for certain if Dhuoda was exceptional in comparison to her female contemporaries. The *Liber manualis* suggests that mothers bore great responsibility for transmitting moral ideas and practices to their children and wider household. In the above passage, Dhuoda implies both that others expected mothers to provide instruction and act as examples for their children and that some mothers, like herself, did just that.

---

1. Dhuoda, *Handbook for William*, 2. All English quotations from Dhuoda's handbook draw from Pierre Riché's, Carol Neel's and Marcelle Thiébaux's translations. All citations of the handbook refer to the Latin text found in Thiébaux's edition, except in cases, as here, where I quote Neel's translation directly.

Other evidence from a variety of sources from the late eighth century to the early tenth century supports a wider instructional role than scholars have yet appreciated for aristocratic women; their contemporaries believed them to be responsible for providing a moral framework and occasional edification to their social inferiors, particularly children and servants. Their male contemporaries wished them to possess a prudence that would allow them to carry out these duties. These expectations grew both because male discourse on female virtue was a means to think about political and social problems and because women needed to perform these duties in order to perpetuate elite culture and to promote the power of their natal and spiritual families. This role underlines the vital part women played in the Carolingian renaissance, particularly laywomen whose efforts have not received the same attention as that of religious women.

The evidence for female instruction demonstrates that it took place not only in religious communities but also in lay households and courts, a further sign of the common experiences of lay and religious women. The duty of aristocratic women to help to shape the behavior of those around them by displaying Christian virtues corresponded to their particular responsibility to instruct young girls. In various clerical texts, men either directly urged Carolingian women to act as a model to those around them—male and female, young and old, or provided examples of women, usually saints, who acted in a Christian manner, gave alms, looked after the sick, and prayed. Conversely, the disreputable acts of women could bring great shame to their families and communities as well as disrupt the social order. Production of legitimate heirs required wifely fidelity, and entering the religious life equally demanded continence. Therefore, contemporary men expected aristocratic women to be especially virtuous. Churchmen exhorted lay and religious men to model Christian behavior as well, but they recognized the duties and activities of both male and female lay aristocrats and fashioned their prescriptions to those exigencies accordingly.[2] They saw the specific ways in which women could help to propagate some of the practices and beliefs related to Carolingian religious reform. Frequently these texts reveal consonance between lay and clerical ideals. The Christian behavior ecclesiastical leaders urged upon laywomen could help them to establish virtuous households that reflected well upon their husbands and themselves. From late antiquity, women had often served as the moral centers of their households, thereby helping to maintain male prestige.

---

2. Specific examples of exhortations to fathers and heads of households to act as models include: Paulinus, *LE*, 29, cols. 225–26; *Capitulare missorum Aquisgranense primum*, chap. 7 and 17, MGH Capit. 1, 153; *Capitulare missorum Aquisgranense secundum*, chap. 5, MGH Capit. 1, 154; *Missi cuiusdam admonitio* of 801–12, MGH Capit. 1, 239–40.

Carolingian sources, however, gave this role a reforming emphasis, which allowed women to maintain or increase their authority within the court or family. Indeed, the perception that they could exert substantial influence led to accusations of immorality, witchcraft, and sinfulness against elite women.

Religious women similarly were to be moral exemplars to their peers and outsiders. Hagiography depicted abbesses acting as models for their sisters, and rules for female religious throughout the early Middle Ages exhorted abbesses to do just that. Carolingian abbesses came from noble families, and aristocratic women entered religious houses before and after marriage or without intending to marry. Early medieval convents served, among other things, as places for raising and instructing young girls. Tempting as it is to term such learning an "education," that word implies a more systematic and regular understanding of this sort of instruction than surviving sources can support. Most work on early medieval education has centered on boys because sources concerning them are much more numerous.[3] Some scholars have assumed that nuns received the same instruction as monks or a comparable one.[4] An absence of information about girls' training does not necessarily mean, however, that it was identical to the education boys received from religious institutions.[5]

This chapter gives female learning the attention it deserves for its own sake. Extant sources suggest a female pattern of instruction that paralleled the timing and goals of male instruction but differed in location and some subjects. Carolingian men did not specifically term this learning an "education," nor would churchmen have considered elite women "learned" for they could not take up the formal study that male clerics did. The examined sources demonstrate a relatively informal transmission of practical skills and knowledge that helped elite girls and young women develop the behavior, knowledge, acts, and beliefs expected of them. The actions of women, for example, were sometimes understood as performative means of instruction. Such "unofficial" teaching was not wholly a female activity. Fathers helped their sons to learn hunting, riding, and other masculine pursuits as they grew old enough, while daughters learned feminine skills by following the example of their mothers. Mothers almost certainly had, however, the primary role instructing young children and acting as models for their inferiors because male aristocrats had less opportunity to do so. Women had fewer official duties to occupy them

---

3. Aside from other works cited here, see the bibliography in M. M. Hildebrandt, *The External School in Carolingian Society* (Leiden, 1992).

4. Heinrich, *The Canonesses and Education in the Early Middle Ages*, 125; Riché, *Education and Culture*, 457.

5. de Jong, "Growing up in a Carolingian Monastery," 101.

than did men and are unlikely to have traveled as frequently as their husbands. Besides tasks relating to their offices that took them away from their main residences, men left home regularly to go to war, hunt, attend assemblies, act as judges, and visit the royal court, leaving their wives to look after the administration of their estates. Churchmen recognized an opportunity to have women spread good Christian practice in households and convents, and their exhortations assumed that women acquired the requisite knowledge to transmit such learning and act as models. Though the evidence for this female practice is prescriptive and comes from sources discussing other matters, its consistency across time and space suggests a common expectation that young girls and women receive preparation so that they, too, could become virtuous mothers and nuns who act as moral exemplars.

The importance of female instruction and moral exemplarity is apparent in the continuing pattern from one generation to the next as former pupils became mothers and nuns who continued to teach others. These ideas became central to conceptions of women in the West for centuries to come. Synod, church council, and capitulary legislation indicate that clerics understood the ways in which women could best influence the behavior of those around them, but they also found even such limited authority potentially dangerous. Accusations of immorality, particularly those leveled against royal women in the ninth century, demonstrate the ways men could invert the ideals of female exemplarity in order to incriminate women. These cases further underline the tricky balance between lay and clerical needs as it was often women's inability to live up to lay desires that left them open to attack on religious and moral grounds.

When clerics formulated their prescriptions to women, they took into account traditional roles that women had long fulfilled and the range of possibilities for their female contemporaries. Instructional texts demonstrate the same creativity the Carolingians showed in their theological and moral writings, rather than simply repeating earlier authorities.[6] Most relevant sources show a distinctly Carolingian concern with women acting as models of Christian behavior within the confines of household or cloister and emphasize the didactic role of abbesses, queens, and mistresses of households. Such Carolingian texts drew from late antique ideals. The church father Jerome's writings, for example, influenced Western ideas of female instruction. His correspondence with women encouraged them to live ascetically. In 403, Jerome responded to Laeta who asked for advice on how to educate Paula, her daughter whom she and her husband had dedicated to the religious life upon her

---

6. Marenbon, "Carolingian Thought," 171, 179–80.

birth. Jerome's advice offered a paradigm that others adopted at least in part during the early Middle Ages. He advised that she first learn the Psalms, her letters, and basic writing through instruction at home. She should have only virtuous tutors, nurses, and maids so as not to be led astray by their example. Her parents should only do what they wished to see her imitate. Paula should not wear fine clothes, rich jewelry, and makeup lest it corrupt her good character, and she should not eat meat or drink wine unless for reasons of health.[7] Carolingian churchmen, however, brought ideals meant for religious women, especially abbesses, to bear upon elite laywomen. By expanding reforms to such women, ecclesiastical leaders further blurred the line between lay and religious women.

Though both sons and daughters received early instruction from their mothers, most left home for further experience and lessons. Teaching helped to mold aristocratic children for their future adult roles and was therefore gendered. Despite church legislation to the contrary, parents probably believed instruction necessary for both daughters and sons because they knew their daughters, who would someday run households and thus play significant political roles, needed preparation.[8] Sometime around the age of seven, aristocratic girls could go to religious communities while their brothers went to court, external school, or monastery. Prescriptions against removing girls from the religious life indicate that girls and women may have moved in and out of religious houses, some acquiring training but leaving for a lay life.[9] The instructional line between lay and religious girls was therefore less clear than that between male and female.

Women in Boniface's Circle

The women of the missionary Boniface's circle represent some of the most learned European women of the eighth century of whom we have knowledge, and evidence concerning them provides early and telling information about the highest levels of female learning in the Carolingian world. Boniface corresponded with some abbesses and nuns, and a few of the saints' lives and other letters of his circle reveal much about the instruction these women received and provided. Boniface maintained contact with some women who remained in England and some, including Leoba and Thecla, who came to

---

7. Jerome, "Ad Laetam de institutione filiae," in *Select Letters of St. Jerome*, ed. and trans. F. A. Wright (1933; repr., Cambridge, Mass., 1991), 338–66.
8. Riché, *Ecoles et enseignement dans le haut Moyen Âge*, 294.
9. MGH Capit. 2.2, no. 252, 206–49, 24(b), 227.

Saxony to head religious houses at his behest. Some women, such as Addula, grandmother of Gregory of Utrecht—who was one of Boniface's students—came from families native to the continent. These women obtained instruction both within their own religious houses and, through visits or letters, from individuals belonging to other communities. Boniface wrote warmly to his female correspondents and considered them part of his group of missionaries, but sometimes he expressed sharply disparaging opinions of religious women generally.[10] This disparity between his view of some women and his correspondence with others underscores that only a small fraction of women then and in the future could attain the same level of education as Leoba.

The letters and depictions of these missionary women indicate that they were to support the work of their male counterparts. Rather than trying to convert pagans, they strengthened nascent Christianity by building up monasticism and creating havens for the daughters of local families.[11] Beyond acting as models, they were meant to bring Saxon aristocrats into Christian society, thus demonstrating that the later Carolingian authors of *vitae* and the women themselves, as evidenced in their letters, believed that their instruction and moral exemplarity could extend beyond their convents and into the local community. According to Liudger's *Vita Gregorii*, Boniface first met Gregory of Utrecht on a visit to Pfalzel, where Addula was the abbess. Sitting around a table, Boniface, presumably some of his followers, Addula, and her household (*familia*), which included her grandson Gregory, discussed scripture. When they needed a reader, Addula had Gregory read aloud before their famous guest. Boniface then asked Gregory to explain the passage, but he was unable to do so and instead started to repeat the words. Cutting him off, Boniface again requested an explanation rather than a repetition; Gregory admitted that he could not give one. Nevertheless, Boniface found his eloquence impressive. Gregory's amazement at Boniface's exegesis of the passage he had just read was so great that it caused him to forget both his kin and his land: he soon begged Addula to let him follow Boniface as his student so that he could discuss holy books with him. Because she did not know Boniface well, much less where he was going, she refused. Stubbornly, Gregory retorted that if she refused to give him a horse, he would simply follow Boniface on foot. As Liudger wrote, "In fact this handmaid of God, Addula, because she was a prudent woman, observing the stubborn nature of the boy, gave him servants and horses and sent him with the holy teacher."[12]

---

10. Hollis, *Anglo-Saxon Women and the Church*, 113–50.
11. Wood, *The Missionary Life*, 67.
12. Liudger, *Vita Gregorii*, chap. 2, 67–68.

Liudger then praises Gregory for defying the wishes of his kin and exhorts other young men to follow his example. Given her earlier actions, Addula's protest seems to be a didactic element more than anything else. Medieval hagiographers often wrote about saints overcoming opposition to their entry into the religious life. Though a topos, this particular instance reveals an expectation that women could aid in ensuring instruction and developing bonds for their young family members. By having Gregory, rather than another member of her household, read, Addula promoted her grandson before the famous missionary. She acted as Gregory's mentor in this episode, helping him to make a valuable connection.[13] Liudger depicts Addula as an intelligent woman. Her participation and leadership in a discussion of scripture demonstrate her own learning. Liudger, furthermore, credits her prudence in deciding to let Gregory follow Boniface. Perhaps she had instructed the young Gregory in preparation for his studies at the palace, from which he had just returned when Boniface came.[14]

Addula may have obtained an education at a religious house, as many of Boniface's female correspondents did. The best known of them, his relative Leoba (d. 779), became quite learned as a young girl at the Anglo-Saxon convent of Wimborne. Soon after 732, she wrote a letter to Boniface in which she included verses she had written for practice. She claimed she had only recently learned to compose verse under the instruction of a nun, Eadburg, who herself, Leoba reported, assiduously studied scripture.[15] Andy Orchard has noted both Leoba's grammatical errors (she was still learning) and her rather formulaic allusions to or use of passages here from the Gospel of Matthew, patristic writers, the Anglo-Saxon churchman Aldhelm (d. c. 709), and Boniface's letters.[16] Once Boniface installed Leoba as abbess in Bischofsheim near the Tauber River, she could have taught her sisters verse and letter composition, passing on the skills she had acquired at Wimborne. Some evidence suggests that religious women in the Carolingian world continued to have an interest in poetry, even if it was not necessarily the right sort of poetry. Charlemagne forbade singing profane songs; in particular his implication that religious women ought not to write or send vernacular love poems called *winileodos* indicates that those women had enough learning to read and (re)produce them.[17]

---

13. For commendation and fosterage of boys to clerics see de Jong, *In Samuel's Image*, 214–16.

14. Liudger, *Vita Gregorii*, chap. 2, 67.

15. MGH Ep. S 1, no. 29, 53.

16. Orchard, "Old Sources," 29–32.

17. Nelson, "Women and the Word," 62; *Duplex legationis edictum*, chap. 19, MGH Capit. 1, 3.

According to Rudolf, who wrote the *Vita Leobae* in the 830s, Leoba's education at Wimborne prepared her well to be abbess at Tauberbischofsheim.[18] Always a model of virtuous behavior for the nuns of her own convent, she also traveled to other monasteries and nunneries, where she encouraged the members to pursue perfection. Providing instruction in scripture to her sisters was one of her chief concerns, and her knowledge of it was so profound that the nuns at Tauberbischofsheim used to make mistakes purposely while reading to her in order to see whether she would notice, which she always did. Besides scripture, Leoba had the nuns study the church fathers, council decrees, and ecclesiastical law. Because of the superior instruction they acquired at Tauberbischofsheim, many of her nuns became abbesses at other convents in the region.[19] Another Anglo-Saxon woman Walburga (c. 710–777), the sister of Willibald and Wynnebald, had been educated in England like Leoba and spent time at Tauberbischofsheim before becoming abbess at Heidenheim.[20] Thus, instruction within a religious community prepared some women to bring their learning to other religious houses, either by traveling or by leading new houses. Because the *vita* appeared about a century after Leoba wrote her letters, it reflects the Carolingian religious reforms. Yet it corresponds to earlier letters, helping to indicate the basis for these ideas. The *Vita Leobae* therefore presents a ninth-century model of behavior for abbesses that reflects the practices of eighth-century religious women.

Other talented and educated women whom Boniface chose to help him provided religious instruction for their monastic sisters. Besides placing Leoba at Tauberbischofsheim, he sent his follower Lull's aunt Cynihild and her daughter Berthgyth to Thuringia, and Thecla, another Anglo-Saxon woman of his acquaintance, to Kitzingen.[21] He maintained correspondence with all three women. In one letter addressed to them and the sisters living with them, he urged them to persevere through troubles and to work against heretics, schismatics, and hypocrites.[22] His letter implies that religious women could affect their surrounding community positively. Their ability to correspond with the learned missionary bishop and his expectation that they had sufficient knowledge to work against heresy suggests their relatively high level of learning. From a later letter of Lull to the abbess Suitha, a reverse picture of these virtuous abbesses emerges. As archbishop of Mainz, Boniface's former student and chosen successor wrote a letter of excommunication to Suitha

---

18. Rudolf, *Vita Leobae*, chap. 6–9, 124–25.
19. Ibid., chap. 11, 126; chap. 18, 129.
20. Wolfhard of Eichstätt, *Vita Walburgis virginis*, chap. 1, AASS February 3, 523–42, at 523–24; Ennen, *Frauen im Mittelalter*, 77.
21. Riché, *Education and Culture*, 433, 435.
22. MGH Ep. S 1, no. 67, 139–40.

shortly after 754, accusing her of failing to look after her flock properly. As punishment for their arrogance and enjoyment of lay delights, he ordered the abbess and the sinful nuns in question to live as penitents, on a diet of only bread and water.[23] Failing to act as a model of virtuous behavior and to correct flaws in others could have serious repercussions. In this case, the exhortations to abbesses to look after their flocks found in so many early rules had teeth.

The learned women of Boniface's circle therefore helped set precedents for rhetoric concerning female exemplarity and instruction that lasted into the ninth century. Though their composition means that they almost certainly reflect ninth-century norms and practices, later *vitae* reflect the literary traditions established in this area by Boniface's circle: these models continued to have currency.

Abbesses, Mothers, and the Carolingian Renaissance

With the Carolingian renaissance ideas concerning religious women and secular women came together; elite women shared a set of social expectations regardless of their vocation. These ideas nevertheless drew on earlier models of the behavior of abbesses such as those in Boniface's circle. Clerical prescriptions that laywomen look after the moral and religious instruction of their children and others in their households or courts resemble similar exhortations to abbesses in rules for religious women. Like that of the head of a lay household, an abbess's authority extended beyond setting an example of right behavior to inculcating it in those under her direction. Conventional expectations that abbesses provide spiritual motherhood colored views of natural motherhood.[24] Both abbesses and lay mothers, writers asserted, could provide moral leadership to those around them.

The *Institutio sanctimonialium* of 816 provides prescriptions concerning the instruction of young women that reveal incidental details of the sisters' lives and demonstrate reformers' concern to ensure the virtue of religious women. Canon 10 directs that the *sanctimoniales* occupy themselves with handwork, singing psalms, and listening to sacred readings in order to prevent gossip and to keep from becoming "dulled by leisure." In order to sing the psalms and understand the readings, the *sanctimoniales* required some learning. The *Institutio sanctimonialium* provided for that instruction in canon 22, which stipulated that a teacher (*magistra*) ought to look after the education of the young

---

23. Ibid., no. 128, 265–66.
24. Atkinson, *The Oldest Vocation*, 64–99.

girls in the community.[25] Note that the form of the word is feminine; the reformers at Aachen took for granted that a female, not male, teacher would instruct the religious women. That women taught women is confirmed by the letter of a female pupil in the manuscript Düsseldorf B3. Produced at Essen, the manuscript contains saints' lives, including those of early virgin martyrs, hymns, and biblical and patristic texts with related commentaries, a highly suitable codex for a convent. On the last folio remains the note from a girl to her *magistra* asking for permission to stay up that night. "Lady teacher, give me permission to stay awake tonight with teacher Adalu, and I assure you with both hands and I will refrain from playing through the whole night. And I want to read aloud. And of course to sing our prayer in sequence. Farewell R. So I seek that it be done."[26] Around the text are various practice letters in the same hand. Written around 900, this precious record of a young girl hints at the importance of the teacher-pupil relationship and at the nature of everyday life in a Carolingian religious house.

The *Institutio sanctimonialium* could have reflected and affected practices and titles in convents. Learning psalms and how to sing and pray, as well as studying scripture, comprised the bulk of instruction discussed in canon 14.[27] Because the rule required that they read scripture, the girls must have learned some Latin. Although the woman who held the office of *magistra* had to be expert enough to teach these skills, the deciding qualification for the office was an exemplary character.[28] Like the abbess, as a woman who served in an official capacity, the *magistra* especially needed to model proper behavior. She had responsibility over girls and women who were particularly impressionable because they had just entered the religious life: as their teacher, she had to be careful to set an example of Christian morality.

The *Institutio sanctimonialium* illustrates the increasing concern with women acting as moral exemplars and conduits of religious instruction apparent in other prescriptive evidence from the first half of the ninth century. In the second book of his *De institutione laicali* Jonas of Orléans discussed marriage, and much in that book applies to the roles of women in the household: their moral exemplarity and their instruction of children. Like most Christian theorists, he wrote that procreation was the main reason for marriage.

---

25. *IS*, 445, 552.

26. "Domina magistra felhin date mihi/liceciam. In hac nocte vigilare cum magistra/ 'adalu et ego vobis ambabus manibus confir/mo atque luro ut per totam noctem de dinare. / volo aut legere. Aut prose ni ore nro cantare/Valete R. Ut peto facite." Universitäts- und Landesbibliothek Düsseldorf B3, fol. 308ᵛ. This manuscript is on loan from the city of Düsseldorf to the Universitäts- und Landesbibliothek Düsseldorf.

27. *IS*, 448.

28. Schilp, *NW*, 73, 203.

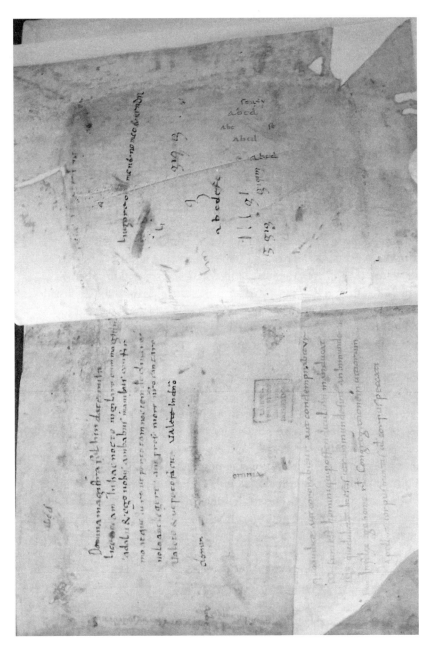

Figure 2. At the end of a manuscript produced at Essen is a remarkable note from a young student to her teacher asking for permission to stay up at night. Note the various practice letters in the same hand that surround the text. Universitäts- und Landesbibliothek Düsseldorf B3, folio 308ᵛ. This manuscript is on loan from the city of Düsseldorf to the Universitäts- und Landesbibliothek Düsseldorf. Photograph by author.

He encouraged men to treat their wives decently, insisting that they not keep concubines, visit harlots, perform illicit sexual acts with their wives, commit adultery, or set their wives aside except if their wives have fornicated. In general, he treats parents equally, often giving advice to both mother and father. Maintaining that "a household of learning is beneficial," Jonas wrote that it was inexcusable if parents and godparents failed to teach children of a "reasonable age" knowledge of scripture, the mystery of baptism, and faith in the holy trinity. Children should learn to love God and their neighbors. Nevertheless Jonas recognized that children could not learn all of Christ's precepts at once. He explained that parents should act as though they are the shepherds of their household. They ought to instill a fear of God in their children and diligently teach them to live chastely and honor their parents, and they must correct wrong or sinful behavior in their sons.[29] Although drawing heavily from Augustine in these passages, Jonas geared his message for a lay couple, expecting that they should encourage moral behavior at home. In this regard, his ideas are consonant with other ninth-century writers who answered to the fear among the male elite that they must atone for the sins they necessarily committed as lay leaders, husbands, and fathers, not least Einhard.[30]

Although he wrote about both parents in these passages, Jonas placed mothers into a familial context where they should act as virtuous models. His prescriptions were to maintain the Carolingian social order and combat sin; his insistence that women care for children provided a perfect counter to the relatively common public accusations against women of infanticide.[31] As a bishop, he had relatively substantial contact with the laity. His understanding of lay life led him to try to shape the behaviors in which women had long engaged in order to promote the practice of Christian virtue among the lay elite. Aristocratic women, for example, could help spread Christian reforms, such as proper recitation of the Lord's Prayer, among those with whom they interacted regularly.[32]

Jonas probably understood that an emotional bond between parent and child meant that mothers were ideally poised to teach their children. The prospect or occasion of children's early deaths appears to have devastated most parents in the Carolingian world. According to Huneberc, Willibald's parents lavished attention upon their little boy and prayed earnestly for his recovery from a childhood illness.[33] Epitaphs for a daughter and a son of Charlemagne

---

29. Jonas, *Institutione*, 1.8, cols. 134–5; 2.1, 3, 4, 6, 7, 8, 10, 12, 13, 14, and 16, cols. 167, 172–83, 186–92, 195, 197.
30. Smith, "Einhard," 64–67.
31. Smith, "Gender and Ideology," 64–67.
32. *Capitulare missorum*, 802–13, chap. 2, MGH Capit. 1, 147.
33. Huneberc, *Vita Willibaldi*, chap. 1–2, 88–89.

and Hildegard each mention parental grief.[34] Sedulius Scottus wrote an epi-taph for a young son of Eberhard of Friuli and his wife Gisela, commenting on the parents' sorrow.[35] Though these poetic references are formulaic, they indicate an expectation of parental mourning. Hucbald of St. Amand offers a vision of a mother's loss that is at turns idealized and believable. Rictrud deeply mourned the loss of her young daughter, Adalsindis, but she waited until an appropriate day, the Feast of the Innocents, before grieving, and even then she withdrew from her sisters so as not to make an inappropriate display of her sorrow.[36] Her heroic effort not to break down immediately, as this *vita* suggests most mothers did at the loss of a child, demonstrated her sanctity. Nevertheless, her sorrow must have seemed credible to Hucbald's audience and perhaps encouraged other mothers to follow her example.[37] Love for their children and a sense of loss at their absence may explain the grief attributed to some parents upon the entrance of their children into the religious life.[38] Though that motif reflects hagiographic traditions and a desire to under-line the ideal separation of the religious from the secular world, such cases also indicate the emotional bond between parents and children. Clerics knew that many parents wanted the best for their children and offered guidance for instilling morality in them.

Jonas's ideas concerning instruction continued to have currency among Carolingian theologians and legislators, including Hincmar of Rheims, Raban Maur, and the bishops who met at the Council of Meaux-Paris in 845 in part to put these ideas into law. The council's legislation urged noble men but especially noble women to look after the moral state of their households, par-ticularly their sexual morality, and to ensure that everyone learned the Lord's Prayer and the Creed and repeated them often.[39] Although those attending the council may have believed that laywomen had a greater obligation to look after the morality of those around them than did their husbands, they more prob-ably recognized that women had increased opportunity to affect household members than their frequently absent husbands. Contemporaries expected that laywomen should act as exemplars through the institutions of marriage and household. This idea became a central conception of the virtuous lay life and its promulgation in the Carolingian world throughout the ninth century.

---

34. MGH Poetae 1, 59, line 8 and 72–73, lines 35–46.

35. Sedulius Scottus, Carmen 37, MGH Poetae 3, 201, lines 7 and 16.

36. Hucbald, *Vita Rictrudis*, chap. 20–21, 85–86.

37. Other mothers probably were part of the intended audience for this *vita*. Smith, "The Hagiography of Hucbald," 526.

38. Eigil, *Vita Sturmi*, chap. 2, MGH SS 2, ed. Georg Heinrich Pertz (Hanover, Ger-many, 1829), 366–77, 366.

39. *Council of Meaux—Paris*, canon 77, MGH Conc. 3, 124.

By their very nature, prescriptive texts mainly provide circumstantial detail concerning female instruction and moral exemplarity. Other texts, especially hagiography and letters but also charters, wills, and Dhuoda's handbook, offer fuller and sometimes more specific information. Saints' lives, possibly the richest sources, can provide hints of actual practices at religious communities or in the lives of their heroines. They even occasionally comment upon the instruction of laywomen, a subject with limited sources.

The Evidence of Hagiography

Herlindis and Renula

The extant evidence concerning Herlindis and Renula, two sisters who became abbesses at Aldeneik, consists mainly of their anonymous *vita*, written around 880. Supplementing this text is the extraordinary Maaseik embroidery, traditionally attributed to the sisters. After the sisters' death in c. 750, their cult started to develop almost immediately. The translation of their relics to a new church at Aldeneik under the abbess Ava on March 22, 860 almost certainly precipitated the *vita*'s composition. Because of its distance from the lifetimes of its subjects, some believe the *vita* to be partly, if not entirely, invented; the anonymous author may well have exaggerated some of their accomplishments.[40] Their *vita* simply does not match the historical record of the early eighth century. It offers evidence, however, about elite women consonant with other ninth-century sources and is therefore a useful source for ninth-century norms concerning women. Because little accurate information concerning these saints may have been available to the author, he could establish them as models by conforming to ninth-century expectations of religious women.

When Herlindis and Renula were young, their parents, Adalhard and Grinuara, employed a tutor to educate them, but then decided to send them to a convent for further instruction. The girls were probably about seven, the age at which social custom and theory stipulated that children were old enough to leave home for an education. Their parents commended Herlindis and Renula to the abbess at Valenciennes, expecting that there they could learn "sacred dogma, practical skills, religious studies, and holy letters." They studied the divine offices and ecclesiastical order. In order to perform the offices properly, they became skilled at reading and singing and mastered the

---

40. Wemple, *WFS*, 153, 176. The manuscript evidence for this *vita* is also problematic. Though the version from the *Acta sanctorum* was based on two manuscripts, one was destroyed in World War II (Münster Universitätsbibliothek 354), while the sole remaining one (Koninklijke Bibliotheek van Belgie MS 3391–3393) dates to c. 1480.

psalms. The sisters also learned to write and paint proficiently. According to their *vita*, they remembered by heart all that they read or heard.[41] These passages suggest that female instruction in religious houses took place both through written and oral means and provided pupils with practical skills for their vocation. Herlindis and Renula thus obtained a relatively advanced level of learning that their parents could not have provided. Their studies prepared them well for the discipline of the religious life, where they needed the skills in writing, painting, reading, and grammar in order to produce manuscripts.

Their *vita* emphasizes both religious education and moral exemplarity among religious women. Having finished their early education, Herlindis and Renula returned to their father's house. Before Adalhard and Grinuara sent them to Valenciennes, they determined that someday they would found a convent for their daughters. When the right time arrived, the parents had the convent at Aldeneik built. The author connects his subjects both to Boniface and Willibrord, writing that the two bishops consecrated Herlindis and Renula as abbesses shortly after the formal establishment of Aldeneik under the Benedictine rule.[42] Twelve other women joined them in the religious life; some may have moved from Valenciennes, while the rest came from prominent local families. In this detail, the *vita* seems to draw from the "missionary ideal" Ian Wood attributed to the women in Boniface's circle, because the author depicts the sisters helping to Christianize the local elite. Equally it reflects the way convents could act as places for a local or regional aristocracy to build bonds through membership of their female kin. The sisters acted as models to those around them. Every day Renula and Herlindis urged the other sisters to live chastely, avoid the snares of sin, and shun leisure. Particularly in need of the abbesses' instruction were the newly Christianized catechumens accepted into Aldeneik, whom Renula and Herlindis educated until they could take full vows.[43] Some of their fellow sisters probably helped instruct the catechumens and each other.

According to their *vita*, during the sisters' lifetimes and afterward, Aldeneik became a prominent cultural center, known for its embroidery and manuscript

---

41. *Vita Herlinde et Renulae*, chap. 3–5, 386–87.

42. Ibid., chap. 6–8, 387; chap. 10–11, 388. Pope Sergius I made Willibrord archbishop of the Frisians in 692. He died in 739. Boniface came to Frisia in 716 and 719, but in 719, Pope Gregory II directed him to bring Christianity to Germany; Boniface then became a missionary in Thuringia and Hesse and later founded Fulda in 744. He returned to Frisia as a missionary in c. 752 and was killed at Dokkum in 754. Thus, the time during which both Willibrord and Boniface lived in or near Frisia was quite limited and too early for them to have consecrated Herlindis and Renula. Furthermore, it is improbable that two women would have been invested as abbesses at the same time.

43. Ibid., chap. 9, 11, 14; 388–89.

production. Their *vita* claims the existence of a scriptorium at Aldeneik, suggesting a high level of learning there. Besides instructing the sisters in these skills, Herlindis and Renula taught them about scripture and helped them with reading. The author of their *vita* credits Herlindis and Renula with the production of a Gospel book and a psalter, among other holy writings. The centrality of prayer, praising God, and psalmody in the daily life of their community meant that such book production had both practical and spiritual uses. When the author of the *vita* attributed scribal activity to them, it would have made sense to most readers because scribal work was in fact done in some female houses.[44] The women who produced codices at the scriptoria at Chelles and Jouarre in Neustria must have learned to write skillfully and perhaps understood the texts they copied, as did the women responsible for the production of some manuscripts now in the Würzburg cathedral treasury. Some texts now in Essen also appear to be the work of women, including the manuscript with the girl's letter to her *magistra*.[45] The nuns of Remiremont produced a memorial book for their community, and members of San Salvatore in Brescia may have composed theirs. The author probably exaggerated the sisters' accomplishments, but his positing the existence of a scriptorium at Aldeneik reveals that ninth-century female manuscript production could figure in contemporary rhetoric concerning women.

Religious women had greater knowledge of texts and their production than laywomen. Those who entered female communities almost always learned to appreciate religious texts, whether they copied or wrote them, heard them read aloud, or read them themselves. Even if some religious women did not acquire literary skills, such as an ability to read and understand Latin, to distinguish among and understand the function of letters of the alphabet, to understand rules of grammar, or to write, they may have at least understood how scribes wrote and had some familiarity with the implements of writing. Because religious women read texts aloud to each other during worship and at meals and because some learned to read at an early age and continued to read throughout their lifetimes, their understanding of religious texts would have increased as they aged.

The instructional pattern of the *vita* of Herlindis and Renula has features strikingly similar to those found among the women of Boniface's circle, an unsurprising circumstance since its author connected the sisters with Boniface and was doubtless familiar with *vitae* associated with him. Nevertheless,

---

44. Ibid., chap. 12, 388.
45. Bischoff, "Die Kölner Nonnenhandschriften," 16–34; McKitterick, "Women and Literacy," 4–8, 15; idem, "Nuns' Scriptoria in England and Francia in the Eighth Century"; Lifshitz, "Demonstrating Gun(t)za."

the common features of subjects studied (psalmody, scripture, reading, divine offices, writing), the emphasis on women of influence acting as examples of right behavior, and the passage of these ideas within and among communities indicate common practices over time at least in the areas where these women lived: Saxony, Thuringia, and near Frisia.

Hathumoda

The *vita* of the Saxon abbess Hathumoda, contemporaneous with that of Herlindis and Renula, further supports the importance and continuity of these forms of instruction for religious women. A monk at Corvey and contemporary of Hathumoda, Agius, wrote the *Vita Hathumodae* and its accompanying elegiac verses, to comfort the nuns at Gandersheim shortly after their abbess's premature death at the age of thirty-four from a plague afflicting the area.[46] Much of what Agius wrote reflects ninth-century Carolingian reforms. His text, like other *vitae*, offered models to women to govern their behavior and actions. Hathumoda was born into a powerful aristocratic family. Her father, Liudolf, descended from an illustrious Saxon family, was a *comes* (count) in East Saxony, while her mother, Oda, a virtuous woman, came from a noble Frankish line. Hathumoda entered a convent, Herford, at a young age and received formative instruction there.[47] In 838, the abbess Tetta founded Herford on the model of her former house, St. Mary of Soissons, from which a number of Herford's abbesses would come. Herford, closely connected to the monastery at Corbie, became quite prominent in Saxony; other Saxon houses, including Herzebrock and Freckenhorst, would be modeled on it.[48] Through Hathumoda, Herford's influence extended to Gandersheim, where the learned Ottonian writer Hrotsvitha later lived and wrote. Hathumoda's *vita* helps demonstrate that the learned atmosphere of tenth-century Saxon nunneries had its origins in the ninth century.

When Liudolf and Oda had the relics of popes Anastasius I and Innocent I transferred to Brunshausen and founded a cloister there in 852, Hathumoda became its first abbess. The community moved to Gandersheim in 856. Her two sisters, Gerberga and Christina, who entered the religious life with her, later succeeded each other as abbess after Hathumoda's death (Gerberga from 874 to 896, and Christina from 896 to 919).[49] Thus, Gandersheim functioned

---

46. Berschin, *Biographie und Epochenstil*, 352, 355. According to the entry of 874 in the *Annals of Fulda*, nearly one-third of those living in Germany and Gaul died from hunger or disease that year.

47. Agius, *Vita Hathumodae*, chap. 2–3, 167–68.

48. Heinrich, *The Canonesses and Education*, 74–75.

49. Berschin, *Biographie und Epochenstil*, 353–54.

as a family institution, and local families whose female kin entered Gander-sheim probably wished to develop bonds with the founders. Upon the convent's relocation, Hathumoda enforced strict enclosure, and she herself lived a particularly ascetic life, acting as a model for the other women there. Agius praised her for doing what she taught and teaching what she did.[50] Her teaching and moral exemplarity are consonant with earlier evidence, and reflect the desired reforms of female religious houses that Carolingian ecclesiastical leaders worked to institute. Her *vita* therefore reflects continuity in male writing on religious women.

Like other saintly Carolingian abbesses, Hathumoda cultivated the study of scripture at her institution, punishing any nuns who neglected their readings and frequently asking them questions to test their understanding of what they had read.[51] Scriptural study almost certainly helped to promote the virtuous behavior Hathumoda hoped to inculcate in others while simultaneously providing her sisters with relatively advanced instruction to allow them better to understand the prayers and liturgy in which they participated daily. Hathumoda and the religious women living under her rule transmitted knowledge to each other. Despite changes in legislation and politics after the Christianization of Saxony, Thuringia, and Hesse, religious women in this area continued the tradition of instruction and moral exemplarity first established by the women of Boniface's circle.

Liutberga

In the previously discussed *vitae*, the authors depicted mothers and fathers as showing profound concern for their daughters' religious instruction. The little-read anonymous text, *Vita Liutbirgae*, written shortly after Liutberga's death, c. 870–76, provides further cases of the instruction of young women.[52] Not only does the *vita* contain references to Liutberga's own early education, but also it mentions her subsequent teaching of girls. Liutberga may offer proof of widespread possibilities for the learning of the Carolingian laity.[53] At the very least Liutberga's *vita* reveals much about the kinds of knowledge elite women were expected to possess.

The *vita* opens with the Saxon noblewoman Gisla's overnight visit to an unnamed religious community.[54] At the convent, one girl caught Gisla's eye

---

50. Agius, *Vita Hathumodae*, chap. 7, 169.
51. Ibid., chap. 9, 169.
52. Garver, "Learned Women?"
53. McKitterick, *The Carolingians and the Written Word*, 219.
54. Walther Grosse thinks the convent lay to the south of Saxony. "Das Kloster Wend-hausen, sein Stiftergeschlecht und seine Klausnerin," 60.

because she "seemed to stand out among the others in beauty and intelligence" and was furthermore capable, deferential, and talented. After determining her origin, family, and status, Gisla urged this girl, Liutberga, to come with her on her journeys. Although, according to the author, Liutberga would already have taken her vows were she not so young, Gisla convinced her to leave the convent to live with her and be "loved as one of her own daughters."[55]

Liutberga's social status is not explicitly stated, and this omission has resulted in some disagreement about her background.[56] The evidence that she was either aristocratic or was recognized as such is, however, compelling. Her entrance into a convent as a child, presumably as an oblate destined to become a nun, suggests that her parents or another sponsor were able to afford an oblation offering. Edmund Stengel believed a charter from Fulda recorded a substantial donation by this Liutberga later in her life.[57] Certainly, once she was living with Gisla, she operated in an elite milieu, interacting with aristocratic women and men, and sometime after their return to Saxony Gisla furnished her with *honores* (rights, properties, privileges, or offices that indicated high rank).[58] Thus, she attained elite markers even if she was not already of high status.

High social standing, however, was probably one reason Gisla thought so well of Liutberga. When they met, Gisla specifically asked about her family background:

> Gisla began to ask who she was and where she came from, about her family and her declaration of situation. When she had answered all these things appropriately, she discussed them in order and said that she had parents in a place called Solazburg and discussed their ancestry and the nature of their rank and explained her whole way of life.[59]

Recognition of high social status may have been necessary for Gisla's establishing a relationship of patronage. The author writes that Liutberga answered prudently (*prudenti*), demonstrating her good judgment and intelligence at an early age, and he implies that her intellectual capacity as well as her beauty caused Gisla to want to bring Liutberga to Saxony. This episode recalls the way Gregory impressed Boniface, perhaps purposefully as Liutberga's and Gregory's *vitae* are both connected to the religious community at Fulda.[60]

---

55. *Vita Liutbirgae*, chap. 3, 12.
56. Garver, "Learned Women?" 125–26.
57. *Urkundenbuch des Klosters Fulda*, 409–10.
58. *Vita Liutbirgae*, chap. 7, 15.
59. Ibid., chap. 3, 12.
60. Wood, *The Missionary Life*, 19; on Gregory 107–15. The episodes recall Jesus' calling of his disciples.

Nevertheless, awareness that such encounters between mentor and student may result from hagiographic convention does not diminish the possibility that great men and women could attract followers as they traveled in Carolingian lands. Strangely, no one protested Liutberga's departure as Addula objected to Gregory's. Neither does anyone become upset in the way that Tetta regretted Leoba's departure from Wimborne.[61] Despite their possible and reasonable objections, Addula and Tetta realized that Gregory and Leoba could attain advancement by leaving; similarly, those in Liutberga's community may have realized the same was true of her.

Liutberga's dramatic effect on Gisla's family is unsurprising because Gisla consciously brought into her household a girl she believed to be of good character. Returning with Gisla to Saxony, she spent her time helping her patron, traveling with her between estates. Although young and just beginning to serve Gisla, Liutberga provided an excellent example for those in the household by giving alms generously; caring for the sick, orphaned, and needy; and acting piously.[62] The author depicts Liutberga as simply following her religious inclinations. Although he may have systematized and exaggerated her early possession of Christian virtues, it is significant that he stressed them. No doubt she perfected them by following Gisla's example. An exemplar of ideal aristocratic female accomplishments, Gisla was pious, performed many good works, led a religious life upon the death of her husband, built churches, gave alms, and provided pilgrims with hospitality. Eventually, Gisla founded convents for her two daughters, where they became abbesses, while Liutberga remained with her.[63] That Gisla's daughters became abbesses and that her son showed great religious devotion indicate that Gisla and/or Liutberga successfully inculcated religious ideals in them.

Upon Gisla's death, maternal authority shifted from Gisla to Liutberga. In addition to aiding Bernard with household matters, she influenced each of his successive wives and helped care for his children.[64] Bernard married his first wife, Reginhild, after Gisla died. Liutberga had a profound effect on Reginhild.

[Reginhild] burned with such love for the venerable Liutberga that she was not easily robbed of her sight for even a short time. With maternal precepts from Liutberga's conversation she adorned her charming demeanor and her

61. Rudolf, *Vita Leobae*, chap. 10, 125–26.
62. *Vita Liutbirgae*, chap. 4, 12–13.
63. Ibid., chap. 2, 11.
64. Ibid., chap. 8–10, 15–16.

honest and upright nature with good morals, and she adorned her family each day with the great contributions of her generosity.[65]

She almost certainly transmitted such religious principles to Gisla's grand-daughters from Bernard's first marriage, providing them with the sort of religious lessons she must have received during her childhood at the convent.

Reginhild's death at a young age may have given Liutberga increased opportunity to look after household matters. Liutberga continued to help supervise Bernard's household after his second marriage to Helmburg. Perhaps Helmburg's six children kept her busy, but possible friction between the two women, a natural event if Helmburg expected to direct domestic activities in her own house, may have led to Liutberga's entry to the religious life. With Liutberga out of the picture Helmburg could take greater responsibility for supervising the household.[66]

When Liutberga told Bernard of her wish to lead a solitary religious life, believing he could not deny her reasonable and devout request, he had a cell built for her at the community of Windenhausen. After gaining the permission and blessing of the local bishop and priests, she was enclosed in the cell, where she spent the next thirty years leading an ascetic life full of prayer and helping others. Among those she aided were beautiful young girls that Archbishop Ansgar of Bremen sent to her "for the accomplishment of the divine work, in which she was continually engaged with great devotion. She educated them in psalmody and in artistic work and freely permitted the educated ones to go either to relatives or wherever they wished."[67] Learning to sing may have helped to pass time and kept the students from impure thoughts; as suggested earlier, it also imparted religious lessons.[68] Liutberga was well equipped to provide such instruction. Like her own students, during her childhood she had presumably received lessons from teachers and role models at her former convent. Though the author's indication that Liutberga frequently cited scripture may say more about him than about her, she, like Dhuoda, probably had some familiarity with the Bible and other religious texts. Given her learning and precocious hope, as the author puts it, that she would enter the monastic life, she may have known some Latin.

Some of Liutberga's students returned to the lay world; the girls could either return to their relatives or go where they wished when their education

---

65. Ibid., chap. 8, 15.
66. Ibid., chap. 8–10, 15–16.
67. Ibid., chap. 14, 35; chap. 19–20, 44.
68. Bruce, *Silence and Sign Language in Medieval Monasticism*, 40.

was complete. These fates suggest that some young students were destined for lay life and some for the religious life, though the exact future of each girl may have been undetermined at the time she entered. Such a possibility has implications for the degree to which the line between religious and lay was blurred. It appears that young aristocratic girls, both lay and religious, not only learned similar moral behavior and many of the same skills and religious principles; but they sometimes learned them in the same places, first in the household, later in a religious institution from which some girls departed to return to the lay world.

Liutberga served as an example to all the women she encountered. Before she entered her cell, neighboring aristocrats, both male and female, greatly admired her, praised her for her abilities, and pursued her friendship.[69] Her care extended into the community in general, as it did for many aristocratic women, both lay and religious. Liutberga made such a profound impression because of her prominent position first as Gisla and Bernard's right-hand woman and then as a recluse attached to a prominent local convent. As a recluse, Liutberga literally had a window to the outside world, through which she continued to have regular contact with a wide variety of women, from sisters at the convent to local aristocratic women, and suggests that these women in turn could easily act as examples to one other. Among those were a girl whom she convinced to abandon her illicit lover, a woman whose babies died before baptism because of her own sin, and the aristocratic woman Pia.[70] Liutberga concerned herself with morality and sexual continence, issues Dhuoda repeatedly took up in the *Liber manualis*. Liutberga went beyond acting as moral exemplar to actively assisting others to achieve more virtuous behavior.

Evidence from the *Vita Liutbirgae* reveals that setting an example and teaching basic religious precepts were important not only in the religious world but also in the lay world. Liutberga's childhood experiences indicate that contemporaries expected that girls bound for the religious life continued to receive the sort of instruction seen in earlier evidence. It suggests that members of the elite believed that women should employ such learning to help others lead virtuous lives. Both she and Gisla were pious exemplars. Like Dhuoda, they instructed children as well as younger women in their household and their peers in moral behavior and basic religious knowledge. Most striking, though, is the clear indication that Liutberga instructed, at a religious house, some girls who were bound for lay life. Just as young boys went to religious houses,

---

69. *Vita Liutbirgae*, chap. 6, 14.
70. Ibid., chap. 30, 31–33; chap. 35, 36–44.

as well as to the court, for learning they could employ in the secular world, lay girls, too, had opportunities to study at religious institutions for a time—or, as in this case, at the window of a recluse's cell. Laywomen and religious women shared many similar expectations of instruction and behavior.

Female Instruction in the Lay World

Laywomen's needs in raising their children and their possible efforts to live up to clerical expectations that they produce virtuous offspring meant learning could be of great benefit for women. In fact, clerics seem to have accounted for these circumstances when molding their prescriptions concerning ideal parenting. Some laywomen achieved a similar level of learning to literate religious women. Dhuoda wrote her handbook for her son, and the letters of Charlemagne's daughters Gisela, Rotrud, and Bertha suggest their knowledge of Latin. These women, however, were members of the most powerful families in the Carolingian Empire and therefore had greater opportunity than other women to achieve such learning. Their families probably owned books, perhaps in sufficient quantity to constitute a library. Because they likely had more servants, they had more time available to them for study. Most aristocratic laywomen needed some basic skills in Latin if only to understand records of their households and estates. Their level of training in writing and grammar may not have been equivalent to that of religious women because most would not have had occasion to continue their early studies in these areas. Lay girls almost certainly required and received instruction to prepare them to teach their children and act as moral exemplars to their households. Many may have also learned through oral means.

Wealthy Carolingian laywomen may have actively sought out religious or philosophical works. Royal and lay aristocratic patrons as well as abbots and priests sought and obtained compilations of works or *florilegia*, sometimes in response to particular questions. A certain Ragyntrudis, the eighth-century daughter of a Frankish nobleman, who carried on a correspondence with Lull of Mainz and was therefore relatively learned, requested a manuscript containing Isidore of Seville's *Synonyma* and the *Epistula Leonis* from Lux-euil, as its subscription indicates: "In honore dni. nostri xri. ego Ragyndrudis ordinavi librum istum" (In honor of our Lord Jesus Christ, I Ragyntrudis ordered this book).[71] That she lived before Dhuoda indicates that earlier aristocratic women had taken an interest in books. Other female correspondents

---

71. Fulda MS (CLA, VIII, 1197); Riché, *Education and Culture*, 440, note 509.

of Boniface's circle mention books.[72] In a mid-ninth–century poem John Scottus Eriugena notes that Ermintrud, wife of Charles the Bald, read books.[73]

Historians have long known that psalters were fundamental to female learning, and religious women in the Carolingian world spent much time studying, reading, reciting, and singing psalms, as did religious men. Psalters also had a central role in the spiritual life of their lay counterparts. Learning to recite or sing psalms could have given any woman a basic familiarity with Latin. Yet only a few Carolingian laywomen definitely owned a psalter. Dhuoda certainly did, as did her near contemporary Gisela.[74] Gisela and Eberhard owned a few psalters, among many other religious books, and their will's book list specifically connected two to Gisela.[75]

Eberhard and Gisela's books comprised a rich inheritance, and the four books inherited by each of their three lay daughters, Heilwig, Judith, and Ingeltrud, seem quite appropriate for the instructional roles they probably played. The elder Gisela could have used her psalter in daily prayer, just as Heilwig could have used her *libellum* of prayers and her book of prayers with psalms, and they may have taught others how to sing or recite psalms. Heilwig's martyrology offered rich examples of virtuous behavior, possibly including accounts of early Christian female martyrs; a number of ninth-century Carolingian manuscripts contain such texts.[76] She and Judith also each received a missal, which may have gone to use in their own family chapels. The further bequest to Judith of Alcuin's advice for Wido suggests that elite women were probably familiar with lay mirrors and virtuous advice for men. Such knowledge could have aided them in raising their sons, and as seen from the discussion of Jonas of Orléans's *De institutione laicali*, women had much to gain from a mirror for men. Similarities between Dhuoda's handbook for William and the three mirrors for lay aristocrats by clerics further imply the circulation of such works in aristocratic circles, male and female alike. Isidore's *Synonyms*, the lives of the fathers, and a book of the doctrine of St. Basil could equally have provided advice to Ingeltrud on virtuous Christian behavior and doctrine. One can imagine that Augustine's sermon on sobriety may have further encouraged Judith to promote and model virtuous behavior, especially in light of the mentions in contemporary sources of the problems drinking to excess could cause. In addition, Judith received the *Laws of the Lombards* and Ingeltrud an Appolonius. As for Gisela, both the *Enchiridion* and *The Book of*

---

72. MGH Ep. S 1, no. 30, no. 35.
73. MGH Poetae 3, 533.
74. Riché, "Les bibliothèques de trois aristocrates laïcs carolingiens," 95, 97.
75. *CAC*, no. 1, 4.
76. For example, Österreichische Nationalbibliothek M7J2.

the Four Virtues demanded learning appropriate for nuns and would have been books of great worth to a convent. Both works addressed central Christian teachings, especially on leading a virtuous life. Although we know little about the Laurentius to whom Augustine addressed the *Enchiridion* in 421, its late antique origin may have made it a more appropriate bequest to a woman in the religious life than in the lay life, for whom Alcuin's more recent and lay-directed text contained more useful advice.[77]

Female possession of or access to books would have allowed them to teach their own children basic reading skills. Even now children must be taught seemingly obvious actions in order to learn to read: which way to hold the book, to turn the pages, to read from left to right. A mother holding a book and simply pointing along with the words provided her children with many skills associated with literacy, even if she did not actually teach them Latin. Lay mothers, like religious women, may have used psalters as tools when instructing children. In her *Liber manualis*, Dhuoda showed particular concern with the psalms, devoting the last book of her manual to them. Not surprising, given the psalter's importance in daily spiritual life and devotional practices, of the roughly 640 references Dhuoda makes to texts, about 200 are to the psalter.[78] By teaching William about the psalms and making frequent reference to them, Dhuoda helped him learn how to pray and demonstrate his piety.

Over the course of their lives, laywomen with access to books could have continued to acquire religious knowledge. In an essay about the libraries of three aristocrats, Pierre Riché reconstructed the collections readily available to Gisela and Dhuoda. Among the works with which Dhuoda was familiar were Isidore of Seville's *Synonyma*, Gregory the Great's *Regula Pastoralis*, Alcuin's *De Psalmorum usu liber*, and the Bible or parts of it. She may also have had access to *florilegia*. From their will, we know that, besides the books mentioned above, Gisela and Eberhard owned liturgical works, patristic writings, books of exegesis, saints' lives (including the *Life of St. Martin* by Sulpicius Severus and two copies of the *Vitae Patrum*), theological and historical works (including the *City of God* and the *Gesta Francorum*), juridical texts, and some secular books (including a bestiary and a medical book).[79] Because Eberhard and Gisela wished these books kept in the family chapel, others in the household almost certainly used them. Although no evidence connects Gisela

---

77. Henry Paolucci, introduction to *The Enchiridion on Faith, Hope and Love*, ed. Henry Paolucci (Chicago, 1961), vii–xviii, vii.

78. Claussen, "Fathers of Power and Women of Authority: Dhuoda and the *Liber manualis*," 788.

79. Riché, "Les bibliothèques de trois aristocrates laïcs carolingiens," 91–5, 97–100.

directly with any of the books other than the two psalters, this library suggests the types of books to which she and her contemporaries had access. Thus, Gisela and Dhuoda at least had some rather learned works available to them.

Some elite women probably took an interest in books and texts, even if they lacked the wealth to obtain books and keep libraries as rich as those of Dhuoda and Gisela and Eberhard. According to a marginal note in a ninth-century schoolbook of a section of the *Ars Maior* of Donatus, possibly used at Ferrières, a mother obtained the grammar text for her son. The *Ars Maior*, either in full or in part, was a well-respected grammar text in the ninth century. Across the top of folios 11ᵛ and 12ʳ of MS Phillipps 16308, a schoolboy at a monastery wrote: "Sadonis iste liber est sua mater dedit illi Magnum onor illa sit qui dedit hunc librum" (This is Sado's book. His mother gave it to him. Great honor to her who gave this book.).[80] As Rosamond McKitterick observes, Sado's grammatical errors reveal his inexperience with Latin composition: "Note that Sado erroneously takes *onor* as neuter, that *illa* is mistakenly written for *illae* in the second line, and that the pronoun should be *quae*, not *qui*."[81] The existence of this text suggests that Sado's mother commissioned or purchased it or passed along a family text to her son. Such mothers may have understood enough about formal instruction to realize the necessity of a grammar text for a son bound for the religious life. Sado's book recalls the oft-repeated story from Asser's *Life of Alfred* in which Alfred's mother showed her sons a book of poetry and offered to give it to the one who could learn it most quickly. Alfred, who eagerly read it before his older brothers, received from his mother not only the book but also a love of knowledge.[82] Other women probably provided their sons and possibly daughters with books for their later education. Rictrud, for example, made sure that her children were educated and established in the religious life, and she looked after the material and spiritual well-being of her granddaughter Eusebia.[83] Of course, this example as well as those of Hathumoda, Herlindis, and Renula reflect a topos of hagiography, the saint's caring parent, but they also suggest that mothers could take action to provide for their offspring's education.

Many laywomen acquired religious knowledge through oral means via sermons and hymns. Decrees from Carolingian councils and synods insisted

---

80. McKitterick, "A Ninth-Century Schoolbook," 225–31.

81. Ibid., note 18.

82. *De Rebus Gestis Aelfredi*, chap. 23–24, 20–21.

83. Hucbald, *Vita Rictrudis*, chap. 10, 25; 83, 87. The cult of Rictrud and her family members developed in tandem as evidenced by the manuscript tradition for their *vitae*, which frequently appear together with notations of their kinship to one another. Douai MS 849 for example, contains not only the *vitae* of Rictrud, Eusebia, and Maurontus but also an illustration of the family on fol. 126ʳ.

upon regular preaching to the laity in a language they could understand. Stressing that priests ought to use sermons to explain passages of scripture and emphasize the Creed and Lord's Prayer, ecclesiastical legislators clearly hoped that sermons would serve basic didactic purposes.[84] Evidence from homiliaries suggests that priests complied with these prescriptions. Sometimes sermons contained excerpts from saints' lives, which priests may have explicated. Men and women read texts aloud at religious houses, and at least three episodes in Carolingian sources point to the reading aloud of texts in secular households or at court. In her handbook, Dhuoda wrote that she had learned from listening to others read.[85] Einhard wrote that Charlemagne enjoyed having books read aloud, including his favorite, *The City of God*.[86] Presumably the king's daughters sometimes heard these texts. In the early tenth-century *Vita Geraldi*, Odo of Cluny wrote that the virtuous late ninth-century lay aristocrat Gerald had the scriptures read aloud to him during dinner even if guests were present. Often he would stop the reader to ask questions or discuss particular passages.[87]

Such female learning aided mothers in the early rearing of children, especially under the age of seven. Carolingian ecclesiastical leaders recognized the necessity of instructing young children in appropriate behavior and Christian beliefs. Parents and other caretakers may have provided part of the impetus for such instruction, exerting pressure upon clerics to provide advice for raising Christian children.[88] Clerics recognized *infantia* (infancy, usually recognized as the period up to age seven) and *pueritia* (childhood, usually understood as the period from age seven to fourteen) as formative periods during which children required special care. Texts concerning the instruction of lay children show the strong influence of monastic ideals, for they emphasize correction and the inculcation of upright behavior.[89] By encouraging punishment

---

84. Amos, "Preaching and the Sermon in the Carolingian World," 45–49.

85. Dhuoda, *LM*, 1.5, 66.

86. Einhard, *VK*, chap. 24, 29.

87. Odo, *Vita Geraldi*, 2.14, col. 678.

88. Janet L. Nelson, "Parents, Children, and the Church in the Earlier Middle Ages," in *The Church and Childhood*, ed. Diana Wood, 81–114, 82–83. Although a difficult contention to prove absolutely, it conforms to other evidence concerning requests for instruction during the early Middle Ages. Aristocratic laymen allegedly asked for the three surviving lay mirrors by clerics: Wido of Brittany asked Alcuin (c. 800); Eric of Friuli asked Paulinus of Aquileia (c. 795); and Matfrid of Orléans asked Jonas of Orléans (c. 840s). To be sure, such "requests" may stem from literary conceit, but Charlemagne's daughters wrote Alcuin a letter requesting an exegesis of the Gospel of John. He accordingly provided them with one. MGH Ep 4, no. 195, 196, 322–25, esp. 324, lines 25–27. Other aristocrats, therefore, may have made similar requests.

89. Garver, "The Influence of Monastic Ideals upon Carolingian Conceptions of Childhood," 84.

and prevention through *correctio* (correction), ecclesiastical leaders tried to prevent young men and women from developing bad habits.[90] Their realistic yet relatively optimistic view of children accounted for youthful propensity to misbehavior, but allowed that children could grow into adults who strove to be virtuous. For example, Hincmar of Rheims wrote that during *infantia* and *pueritia* a child developed demeanor and behavior that would last his whole life.[91] This awareness of the formative nature of childhood reflects Benedict's stipulations that abbots and monks treat children differently than adult members of monastic communities.[92] Female saints are almost invariably depicted as virtuous children who do not fall prey to temptation, but a number of Carolingian texts reveal recognition of boys' need to learn proper conduct.[93] Gerald of Aurillac was described as exceptional in his childhood manners.

> For at an early age, as we often see, children through the incitements of their corrupt nature are accustomed to be angry and envious, and wish to be revenged, or to attempt other things of this sort. But in this boy Gerald a certain sweetness and modesty of mind, which especially dignifies youth, distinguished his childish acts.[94]

Little boys destined for the lay life played games usually involving toys that simulated warfare, hunting, and the skills they required: riding, throwing, running, handling hunting animals, shooting bow and arrows, wielding other weapons, and developing hand-eye coordination.[95] They certainly started acquiring these skills before going to court for further instruction, and mothers may have helped to acquire such toys for their sons, even if they did not actively teach their sons these skills. They may have protected their sons from reckless activity as well. Ermold the Black described, for example, how the mother and tutor of three-year-old Charles the Bald refused to allow him to join his father's hunt.[96]

---

90. Willibald's *Vita Bonifatii* may have been a model for other authors of *vitae* in this regard. Berschin, *Biographie und Epochenstil*, 7, 132.

91. Hincmar, *OP*, Prologue, 34–36.

92. *Regula Benedicti*, chap. 30, 37, 39, *La Régle de Saint Benoît*. Sources Chrétiennes, 181–82, ed. Adalbert de Vogüé and Jean Neufville (Paris, 1972), 554, 572, 576–78.

93. Rudolf, *Vita Leobae*, chap. 7, 124–25; *Vita Herlinde et Renulae*, chap. 4, 387; *Vita Liutbirgae*, chap. 3–5, 11–13, 17–19; Agius, *Vita Hathumodae*, chap. 2, 167; *Vita Aldegundis*, chap. 4–5, 1041.

94. Odo, *Vita Geraldi*, 1.4, cols. 644–45. My translation draws from that of Gerard Sitwell in *Soldiers of Christ*, 299.

95. Ibid., 1.4–5, col. 645.

96. Ermold, *In honorem*, 182, lines 2400–2415.

One can then imagine that elite women had to discipline their children at times. Jonas of Orléans wrote in his *De institutione laicali* of parental responsibility for correcting the sins of children early and effectively.

> Furthermore there are many parents who neglect to correct their sons, while they are at a critical age, with whippings so that they proceed rightly: who, when they reach the age of reason, begin to be subject to wicked deeds, and cannot easily be restrained from evil with parental chastisement; whose sins it is certain will be ascribed to the parents who did not want to chastise them at a young age.[97]

In his episcopal legislation Theodulf of Orléans urged parents to ensure respectful, modest behavior in their children and to beat their sons if they showed a lack of penance for misconduct, because the parents' blows would be better than incurring the wrath of God.[98] His statement suggests parental reluctance to beat sons. Theodulf does not mention striking girls; one wonders how acceptable it was to beat daughters. The laws of King Liutprand outline when it is acceptable for a guardian to strike his female ward: only when she is a child and in need of correction may he strike her as he would his own daughter. Otherwise striking a girl or young woman could result in the guardian's loss of her *mundium* (tutelage).[99]

One of the only episodes of a mother having a child beaten, however, was Rictrud's punishment of her daughter Eusebia. A separate anonymous *vita* of Eusebia, likely from the first half of the tenth century, repeats the same incident with similar details and is probably based upon Hucbald's *Vita Rictrudis*.[100] When Eusebia became abbess of Hamay at the age of twelve upon her grandmother Gertrude's death, Rictrud, fearing that her daughter was too young for such responsibility, enlisted the aid of the king to convince a reluctant Eusebia to move her community to Marchiennes, where they could remain under her mother's watchful eye. Eusebia, however, sneaked out at night to pray and keep vigil at Hamay. Once her mother discovered Eusebia's deception and could not convince her through both persuasion and reprimand to stop these nightly vigils, she turned to her son Maurontus for advice. They agreed that he should beat Eusebia as punishment. Other mothers may have asked a husband or other male relative to beat a child; Rictrud's *vita* suggests that beating

---

97. Jonas, *Institutione*, 2.14, col. 195.

98. Theodulf of Orléans, First Capitulary, chap. 33, MGH Capit. Epis. I, ed. Peter Brommer (Hanover, 1984), 131.

99. *The Lombard Laws*, 197.

100. van der Essen, *Etude critique et littéraire sur les vitae des saints mérovingiens de l'ancienne Belgique*, 265–68.

was not an acceptable role for a woman. Maurontus's blows caused permanent damage to Eusebia's ribs and lungs, but even this beating could not stop her, and eventually Rictrud allowed her daughter and her community to return to Hamay.[101] This episode is rather unusual, and the authors of both *vitae* appear to have recognized its peculiarity. The author of the *Vita Eusebiae* stated that the tale stemmed from rumor and legend.[102] Hucbald, recognizing that his contemporaries might find the beating of a girl reprehensible, took pains to justify this punishment, noting that, as a result of this episode, some might believe that neither Rictrud nor Eusebia were worthy of veneration. In their defense he wrote: "The holy mother Rictrud did not persecute her innocent daughter. Rather, she reflected upon her immature age, knowing that everything has its time and there is a time for every matter."[103] Although Hucbald had to account for this punishment, it nevertheless illustrates idealized and believable motherhood, depicting Rictrud as a mother struggling with a disobedient daughter. Such discipline in every day life ideally comprised not an immediate reaction to misbehavior but rather an attempt to influence positively the long-term demeanor and actions of the child being punished.

Dhuoda

Because Dhuoda stayed at their estate in Uzès while Bernard was on campaign or traveling extensively in the 820s and 830s, William would almost certainly have stayed with her. She would have acted as his primary model and educated him. This led her to write that her connection to William was both of spirit and of flesh, the former because she educated him in spiritual matters and the latter because she gave birth to him. Dhuoda opened the *Liber manualis* by writing that it had three branches of equal importance: rule (*norma*), model (*forma*), and handbook (*manualis*). She noted that she provided the rule, that the model was for her son William, and that the handbook was as much from her as it was for him.[104] This book constituted an ongoing connection between herself and her exiled son: providing the instruction and example of conduct through words that she would have offered were she and her son together. When she prayed that William consult the book frequently, she underlined this desire.[105]

---

101. Hucbald, *Vita Rictrudis*, chap. 25–27, 87; *Vita Eusebiae*, chap. 7–10, 453–54.
102. *Vita Eusebiae*, chap. 9, 454.
103. Hucbald, *Vita Rictrudis*, chap. 28, 30; 87–88.
104. Dhuoda, *LM*, *Epigrama*, 44.
105. Ibid., *Incipit*, 42.

Beyond demonstrating women's participation in the Carolingian renaissance, particularly in its efforts to offer compromise between lay and clerical desires, Dhuoda's handbook offers a woman's interpretation of the discourse concerning women's learning and its transmission. She directly assumed the authority to carry out the exhortations of the clergy. Though she offered the requisite protestations of humility and lack of understanding of any early medieval text, she countered them by declaring herself William's *genetrix*, literally the woman who gave birth to him.[106] Motherhood gave her a right to comment upon the various subjects of the *Liber manualis*. Though she frequently urged William to follow the example of other men, she never mentioned a female model.[107] Rather it appears that mothers may have had a particular duty to explain appropriate behaviors to their sons; they could not instruct other elite men in this manner, but their maternal role gave them say over certain aspects of male life concerning their offspring. Not long before Dhuoda wrote her handbook, Imma, the wife of Einhard, provided advice for her "dearest son" (*fili carissime*) in a letter, though unfortunately the problem about which he had written to her remains vague.[108] As a literate woman imparting advice to her son via the written word, Imma's example demonstrates that Dhuoda was not unique. To comfort Einhard after Imma's death in 836, Lupus of Ferrières sent a letter in which he praised, among other qualities, her prudence (*prudentia*), dignity (*gravitas*), integrity (*honestas*), and wisdom (*sapientia*).[109] This passage suggests the high regard in which her male contemporaries held her, though it may seem formulaic praise of a wife.

Dhuoda may have received instruction at a religious house. She may also have acquired knowledge at the royal court where she was married.[110] Regardless of how she came to be so learned, her knowledge allowed her to produce the *Liber manualis*. Dhuoda was the wife of Bernard of Septimania, who was accused of adultery with the empress Judith in 830. Bernard, caught up in political intrigues during Louis the Pious's reign, fought against Charles the Bald at Fontenoy in 841, an act that resulted in William's presence at Charles's court as a surety for Bernard's support at the time Dhuoda wrote her advice for him. During the conflicts among Louis's three sons following his death in 840, Dhuoda remained at the family's residence in Uzès in the Rhône valley. There she suffered from personal troubles, including separation from both fourteen-year-old William and his infant brother, Bernard

---

106. Ibid., prologue, 46.
107. See, for example, ibid., 4.1, 128–30.
108. The letter dates prior to 836. MGH Ep 5, no. 38, ed. Karl Hampe (Berlin, 1899), 129. On Imma, see Smith, "Einhard," 57–60.
109. *Servati Lupi Epistulae*, no. 4, 8.
110. Dhuoda, *LM*, Preface, 48. Nelson, "Dhuoda," in *LICW*, 118–20.

(born 841 but almost immediately taken away by his father), debt, and illness. William and the elder Bernard came to bad ends, Bernard executed at the order of Charles the Bald and William later killed in an attempt to avenge his father's death. Dhuoda's younger son, Bernard Plantevelue, also plotted against Charles the Bald but was later pardoned; he eventually founded the duchy of Aquitaine and was the father of William the Pious, who founded the monastery of Cluny.[111]

Dhuoda may have written the *Liber manualis* as consolation for her grief and loneliness, and she certainly dwells on her difficult circumstances.[112] Yet the handbook was primarily intended to instruct William and eventually young Bernard in religious and practical matters. In writing it, she was educating her child just as the Carolingian prescriptive sources urged mothers to do, but from a distance. Separated from William, unable to impart her valuable counsel orally, she turned to writing in order to communicate her advice. It is doubtful that she expected her work to remain a "private" family text: a clear distinction between public and private was not a conception Carolingians held.[113] Dhuoda does not appear to have planned to disseminate her work widely, but she did expect that William would share the work with others besides his brother.[114] She therefore anticipated a larger audience than her sons. Hence she provides a written, perhaps idealized version of the instruction mothers normally delivered orally.

With Dhuoda's primary audience—William—in mind, an enumeration of the religious and moral subjects she wished William to understand suggests the matters that concerned other mothers as they instructed their children. Dhuoda wrote that she intended the book to serve the health of William's body and soul and to act as a reminder, in her absence, of what he ought to do.[115] In terms of religious and moral instruction, she had four main concerns: basic religious concepts, requisite religious practices, moral behavior, and etymologies and calculations such as *computus*, the calculation of the dates of Christian holidays based on the lunar calendar, and those associated with numerology. She deeply intertwined all of these subjects within her work;

---

111. Dhuoda's son's identification as Bernard Plantevelue has not gone without question, but the arguments for it are compelling. In the *Liber manualis*, she writes that she does not know what name his father gave him. Bouchard, "Family Structure and Family Consciousness among the Aristocracy in the Ninth to Eleventh Centuries," 641–44, 651–58; Nelson, *Charles the Bald*, 211–12.

112. Dronke, *Women Writers of the Middle Ages*, 36–54.

113. Nelson, "Women and the Word," 77; Janet L. Nelson, "The Problematic in the Private," *Social History* 15, no. 3 (1990): 355–64.

114. Dhuoda, *LM*, 1.1, 58.

115. Ibid., *Incipit*, 42.

understanding that the necessity of particular behaviors and practices to being a good Christian required comprehension of some basic religious ideas. In explaining the purpose of the manual, she noted not only that her text was in three parts but also that it was to be a "destination, perfection and the end."[116] Twice she connects her work to the number three, a reflection of the trinity, which she invokes shortly thereafter and later explains to William. She writes that God provides three gifts: "pure thought, holy speech, and perfect action."[117] These are indeed the three attributes that Dhuoda works to cultivate in William by writing the *Liber manualis*. Numbers therefore served as a means of explaining God's role in the universe and hence had intimate connections to the moral content of her handbook. In elucidating these matters and others, she demonstrated not only a rather sophisticated understanding of Christianity but also pragmatic social knowledge. She knew the behaviors and relationships necessary for William to advance himself at court and in aristocratic society as a whole.

Dhuoda's *Liber manualis* contained a great deal of practical knowledge and wisdom for an elite Christian youth. In terms of fundamental religious instruction, it included certain biblical stories (particularly those concerning Old Testament patriarchs and their sons), explanations of basic orthodox belief and practice, and an explication of virtues and vices. The ideas of clerics concerning maternal instruction and moral exemplarity almost certainly influenced Dhuoda's composition of the *Liber manualis*, but her text demonstrates that women appreciated that teaching children was substantially their responsibility, an area over which they had authority. Throughout, Dhuoda shows a profound concern for her son's future on earth and for the final salvation of his soul. In particular, she explains the social, political, and religious lines of authority that William must understand to succeed in this world and the next.

Among the religious matters she discussed, Dhuoda was very much concerned that William comprehend the nature of God, particularly his power. Explaining that God is "great and sublime" but at the same time humble through Christ's presence in the world, she urged William to remember to honor God, to seek him out and pray to him. She proceeded to explain the Trinity and the three virtues of faith, hope, and charity. Dhuoda made no claim to special understanding concerning these fundamental but complex theological issues; rather, she tried to impart to William a straightforward knowledge of them. As on most matters, she deferred to the wisdom of the church fathers, scripture, and other authorities. In some cases, she defined

116. Ibid., *Incipit*, 40.
117. Ibid., 1.5, 2.1; 64, 72–74.

basic features of the church. For example, Dhuoda explained priests and bishops, both in terms of etymology and function, to demonstrate to William why he ought to respect them.[118]

Like other writers of lay mirrors, Dhuoda urged William to observe proper Christian practices.[119] A chief concern is prayer (*oratio*), which, Dhuoda explains, comes from *oris ratio* (reason of the mouth). In her section on reverence in prayer, she gave him explicit instructions about how one should pray: the proper feelings one ought to have—humility, respect, and spontaneity; the manner in which to pray—silently; when to pray—day and night, keeping the seven canonical hours; the gestures to use in prayer—making the sign of the cross on his forehead and over his bed; and precise suggestions of what to say.[120] For example, after he makes the sign of the cross, Dhuoda urged him to say:

> I adore your cross ✚, my Lord, and I recall your glorious passion: you who deigned to be born, to suffer, to die, and to rise again from the dead, you who are with the Father and the Holy Spirit ✚. May the blessing of God the Father and the Son and the Holy Spirit descend and remain upon me, the least of your servants. Amen.[121]

Later in the book, she urged William to pray for her, his father, his family, his lord, and the clergy, among others. Dhuoda enjoined William to give alms, not just by offering money but by helping the poor in words and deeds. He should offer hospitality and aid to pilgrims, widows, children, and orphans; he should clothe the naked and provide food and drink for those in need. She explained that such good works will receive God's blessing.[122] They should not be empty but rather conscious deeds. In Dhuoda's scheme of salvation, just as these charitable acts indicate high social status, William's prayer, indeed any magnate's prayer, provided a "spiritualized equivalent of aristocratic largesse."[123] Thus, Dhuoda provided William with religious instruction that underscored his elite status. As well as being good works, these actions would mark him as an aristocrat to others, and possibly to himself. Here the compromise between Christian ideals and elite lay obligations is apparent: Dhuoda adopted similar language to other Carolingian reformers.

---

118. Ibid., *Prefatio*, 1.1–3, 1.5, 2.1–2, 3.11; 50, 58–62, 64, 72–76, 116–18.

119. Alcuin, *LVV*, chap. 3, 11–13; Paulinus, *LE*, chap. 3–5, 27–28, 31, 33, 66; Jonas, *Institutione*, books 1 and 2.17–19.

120. Dhuoda, *LM*, 2.3, 76–80.

121. Ibid., 2.3, 78.

122. Ibid., 4.8, 4.9, 8.3–17, 10.4; 150, 152, 158, 162, 196–208, 224.

123. Claussen, "God and Man," 46.

Equally, Dhuoda instructed William in moral behavior. In general, she urged him to lead a just life that would result in the rewards of heaven:

> I wish that you may strive, as you serve on earth among your comrades-in-arms, so that in the end you may be found worthy, along with the servants and soldiers of Christ to be included as a free soul among the free, who serve together and not alone, in that kingdom without end.[124]

Such right behavior included remaining chaste. Dhuoda urged him to shun fornication and prostitutes and after marriage to remain faithful, avoiding illicit intercourse. Unlike Jonas, who explained the characteristics a layman ought to seek in a wife, Dhuoda provided William with no advice on choosing a wife, but this omission fit both her stated purposes and her audience. William was probably too young and in too precarious a social position to take a wife anytime soon; she focused on providing relevant advice for his current life at court. Thus, in relation to women, her principal concern was to exhort William to avoid the sin of fornication. She only hinted at an ideal marriage partner by emphasizing the legitimacy and rightness of marriage. "For learned authors do not refuse sacred rites of marriage to the union of the flesh, but rather try to root out from among us lustful and illicit fornication."[125] By praying for strength to resist them Dhuoda urged William to avoid prostitutes and other carnal temptations and to live either as a virgin or in chaste marriage. She explained virtues and vices to him and offered practical advice about how to deal with the latter. Advising him to set opposite against opposite, she stated that William ought to strive to counter vices with virtues in order to overcome the former.[126] Prayer and chastity, either as a virgin or in faithful marriage, will help him fight the desire to commit sins of the flesh.

Access to sex was a marker of aristocratic men, and young men new to the court might be particularly prone to lust because it constituted a way to exercise their new adult status and because their inexperience might make them more susceptible to the increased temptations they presumably found at court.[127] Dhuoda was all too aware of the accusations against her own husband and Judith. Here again Dhuoda adopts language similar in tone to the clerics who wrote against the immorality of Carolingian queens. Yet she notes that

---

124. Dhuoda, *LM*, 4.4, 134.

125. Ibid., 4.6, 144.

126. Ibid., 4.2, 4.6; 130, 142–44.

127. Issues of sexual continence within and outside marriage concerned clerics offering advice to laymen: Jonas, *Institutione*, 2.2–10, cols. 170–87; 2.13, cols. 191–2. Paulinus, *LE*, chap. 19, cols. 210–2; chap. 25, cols. 220–1; Alcuin, *LVV*, chap. 18, cols. 626–7; chap. 29, cols. 633–4.

William can exercise self-control in order to resist such temptation. Unlike some of her male contemporaries she did not place blame upon women but indicates that men's lust plays a central role in such problems. She tried to curb and shape this need and desire resulting from the realities of lay life by countering it with Christian practice and virtue.

In addition to her exhortations for right behavior at court, Dhuoda provided William with practical advice for social advancement. Should he ever be in a position to offer counsel to the king at an assembly of magnates, he ought to consider how to make worthwhile and useful comments, and he should accept the advice of those who urge him to act "loyally in body and soul."[128] Though common to most mirrors, such advice was extremely valuable, given the volatile period in which Dhuoda was writing and the situation of her husband. Further, she urged William to remain loyal to his lord, Charles the Bald, and his family. Such fidelity was not only right according to the teachings of God; it would also bring him favor at court.[129] By watching some magnates and their counselors, William was to learn humility, charity, chastity, patience, gentleness, modesty, sobriety, and discretion.[130] In writing that William could practice virtue at court, Dhuoda was rather positive about the merits of the male aristocratic lay life in comparison to the other Carolingian authors of lay mirrors. She made an argument for learning through experience, noting the practical knowledge that one could gain through observation of one's own society. Her explanations of the court reveal her social competence, something she hoped to inculcate in her children. She urged William to take advantage of the keen understanding that age had given the older men at court. However, foremost among the objects of his loyalty should be his own father, to whom he should always be respectful. Although he must love and obey God first, he should love and obey his father next. To support this contention, she described some of the early fathers of the Bible, including Noah, Abraham, Isaac, and their obedient sons.[131] In these sections Dhuoda provides a maternal reinforcement of patriarchy, encouraging William to respect conventional lines of authority and loyalty.

Finally, Dhuoda wrote about computations and numerology, particularly in the ninth book of the *Liber manualis*. Dhuoda appears to have been as fascinated with numerology as learned male Carolingians were with it and other studies involving mathematics.[132] The *Liber manualis* suggests that laywomen

128. Dhuoda, *Handbook for William*, 3.5, 27.
129. Dhuoda, *LM*, 3.4, 92–94.
130. See Claussen, "God and Man," 50.
131. Dhuoda, *LM*, 3.1–3, 10; 84–92, 108.
132. Ganz, conclusion, 270–71.

may have paid enough attention to the subject to tell their children about it. Her references indicate that a woman with sufficient knowledge could have sought out further information about numerology especially as it could aid in her virtuous behavior. Numerology provided an organizing or explanatory principle, and numbers sometimes served as mnemonic devices. For example, numbering the seven gifts of the Holy Spirit helped one remember how many there were, and seven had a positive meaning. Numerology, therefore, aided in devotions and right understanding of Christian principles. When discussing the nature of God, Dhuoda notes the numerical value of the Greek letters that spell God in Latin, explaining the meanings of their values. In so doing, she provides William with devices for remembering, which in turn serve to help him comprehend the world around him. For example, she notes that the five letters in *delta*, the Greek letter which begins "God" in Latin, denotes the five senses through which William will apprehend his surroundings. Dhuoda urges him later to observe animals, plants, and trees for the lessons they can provide but to interpret their meanings by reading the texts of learned authorities.[133] Certainly some aristocratic women would have had a basic understanding of numbers. At times an interest in the meaning of numbers came close to functional mathematics. Churchmen needed to know how to practice *computus* (calculation of the dates of moveable feasts in the Christian calendar) in order to calculate the date of Easter accurately. Dhuoda's handbook suggests that laywomen and men may have known far more about numbers than simple arithmetic.

Throughout the *Liber manualis*, the influence of the reforms of the Carolingian renaissance upon Dhuoda is apparent, but she asserts both authority and agency in the ways in which she adopts and interprets those ideas. Her maternal role allowed her to instruct William, to insert her words at court where she could not go, in many matters touching upon his spiritual and secular life. Under more "normal" circumstances, Dhuoda would have imparted her wisdom to William in person, especially by doing just what Jonas suggested all parents do—to act as an example. Ecclesiastical leaders believed women could have profound effects upon others through their outward behavior. When women transgressed social and religious boundaries, clerics and laymen responded negatively, attacking women they perceived as failing to be exemplary. For that reason, although Dhuoda and her peers were expected to inculcate Christian behavior and clarify social norms for their children and inferiors, that very role put them at grave risk of accusations of immorality. Because they were to behave so well, elite women endured

---

133. Dhuoda, *LM*, 1.5, 3.10; 64, 114.

intense scrutiny under which few could have preserved perfect reputations for long. Dhuoda could serve as an excellent example for William precisely because she was away from the temptations and accusations of court.

Moral Exemplarity

Perhaps the best known Carolingian passage concerning women acting as models appears in the *Opus Caroli*. Although referring to the Byzantine empress Irene, who according to the Carolingians transgressed certain gender boundaries, one of its passages defines women's scope for activity in doctrinal and instructional matters. Theodulf of Orléans's words echo those of Paul on women and teaching more generally:

> but she will be permitted prudence and to be an example of living well; but she will not be permitted to speak in a church or in an assembly or in a synod but rather she may only correct privately the moral faults she notices in the household once she has the experience and maturity of long life.[134]

Speaking in any sort of official capacity was inappropriate for women, but those who possessed the wisdom of age could not only provide others with a model of proper behavior but also could offer corrections to those who failed to follow their example. Exhortations to laywomen in other Carolingian texts often advocate their directional role in moral and spiritual matters within the household: ecclesiastical leaders recognized that women could provide performative instruction through outward display of appropriate behavior and demeanor. At the same time, however, this role brought them under suspicion in the ninth century.

The women who most frequently experienced distrust, who suffered accusations of immorality were those at court. Although this impression may simply be a result of the types of sources that survive, royal women had the most prestigious connections and were among the best known women in Carolingian lands, making them primary targets of scrutiny. Carolingian annals and chronicles mention the meeting of magnates at court for assemblies. This collection of men made court a primary place to gain advancement and to develop ties to other aristocrats and families. At the same time, it made the court a relatively dangerous place. In her handbook, Dhuoda offered

---

134. *Opus Caroli*, 3.13, 388–89. This passage echoes 1 Timothy 2.11–12 and 1 Corinthians 14.34–35 and draws from Titus 2.3ff, which Theodulf quotes just prior to the passage quoted above.

advice to William on how to avoid the immoral behavior and temptations, which Dhuoda suspected he would encounter at court.[135] Hincmar of Rheims described the patronage that older men and counselors at court provided to the young men and vassals (*pueris vel vassalis*) at court in his late ninth-century treatise, *On the Governance of the Palace*.[136] Given the shifting alliances and rivalries among the elite in the Carolingian period, navigating this arena took considerable skill and gave a young man practical experience in dealing with these matters. Minimally, contemporaries recognized a young man's time at court as a period of transition into adult aristocratic roles, when he learned norms of conduct.[137] The young men who came to court to advance themselves would have been highly impressionable. Because we have almost no evidence of elite women who were not members of the royal family being at court, it may have meant that the queen and royal daughters were surrounded by men. With few other women at court, others may have regarded queens with some mixture of suspicion, jealousy, and awe.

Just as they once relied upon their mother's exemplarity to provide a kind of moral compass, the young men at court might be expected to rely upon the queen's model. Yet contemporaries sometimes saw the queen's relationship with these young men as morally ambiguous.[138] The king and certain clerics almost certainly hoped the queen would stand as an example of morality, but scant evidence demonstrates this relationship between the queen and others until the ninth century. Neither the successive wives nor the daughters of Charlemagne played any sort of moral role. During the reign of Louis the Pious, however, the king intended to have a more virtuous court than his father. An increased expectation of moral behavior on the part of the queen helps to explain the accusations and difficulties that Judith experienced. The perceived failure of that court to live up to its own reforms probably only exacerbated the pressure put on Carolingian queens after 840. The moral exemplarity that aristocratic women were to demonstrate to others in the Carolingian world suggests that the germs of courtly behavior, that is conduct appropriate in the presence of women, lay in the eighth to ninth centuries or earlier. The recognition that women could set a standard for proper demeanor at court or within the household helps to explain how women became central to ideal courtly behavior even if the development of courtliness rests on more than women's exemplarity in the early Middle Ages and late antiquity. In the

---

135. Dhuoda, *LM*, 3.4–10, 92–116; 4.2, 130; 4.4, 134; 4.6, 142–44.
136. Hincmar, *OP*, chap. 28, 81–82.
137. Innes, "'A Place of Discipline,'" 68–74.
138. Ibid., 67.

Carolingian era, however, female aristocrats could have felt the effects of such ideas concerning virtue, and the men who expected moral exemplarity in a queen could have encouraged similarly virtuous actions among their female kin, putting them in equally difficult situations.

Charlemagne's Daughters

Charlemagne's rather learned daughters came to have a notorious reputation, a combination that helps to explain the emphasis on female moral exemplarity in ninth-century clerical rhetoric concerning women. Evidence from the court of Charlemagne reveals that his daughters received instruction in the liberal arts and probably participated in intellectual exchange, suggesting that they may have received an education equivalent to or better than that of many aristocratic laymen. Although one cannot automatically equate the royal court with aristocratic households, the prominence of Charlemagne's daughters may well have led powerful aristocratic families to imitate such instruction. For example, Eberhard of Friuli cultivated learning at his court as the Carolingian emperors did.[139] In doing so, such aristocrats both emulated and competed with the Carolingian family. The learning of the royal daughters suggests the kind of knowledge women, such as Dhuoda, may have been expected to possess. Perhaps Gisela, wife of Eberhard, obtained a similar education at the court of her father and Charlemagne's son, Louis the Pious. Nevertheless the elite almost certainly did not want young, unmarried female kin to go to court as their young brothers did.

Charlemagne's daughters had opportunities to obtain a rather high level of learning. Einhard explained that Charlemagne ensured that all of his children, male and female, studied the liberal arts.[140] Alcuin's poem *On the Court* contains tantalizing suggestions of that instruction in a passage from the king's point-of-view:

> Idithun has taught the children holy chant,
> so that they sing sweet sounds with sonorous voices.
> Let them learn the feet, numbers and rhythms in which music consists!
> May my daughter at night-time gaze upon the stars in the sky
> and grow accustomed to giving constant praise to mighty God

---

139. On Eberhard of Friuli's intellectual life, see Kershaw, "Eberhard of Friuli, a Lay Intellectual."

140. Einhard, *VK*, chap. 19, 24–25.

who arrayed the heavens with stars and the earth with grass,
and by His word performed all the miracles in the world.[141]

Of the two liberal arts mentioned here, all the children learn music, but
Alcuin connects one of Charlemagne's daughters with an interest in astron-
omy, a subject rarely if ever mentioned in conjunction with other Carolingian
women. Charlemagne's court offered opportunities for his daughters to meet
some of the greatest scholars of their day. Because they remained with their
father until his death, they witnessed the court culture over the course of a
generation and probably learned much indirectly. Bertha, Rotrud, and Gisela
took part in scholarly discourse through their letters with Alcuin. Rotrud
and Gisela displayed their erudition when they referred to Alcuin as their
Jerome.[142] In one letter, Gisela and Rotrud requested that Alcuin produce a
commentary on the Gospel of John because they found Augustine's work on
John to be hard going.[143] Rather than indicating their lack of learning, this
comment places them within learned Carolingian circles. For many of their
contemporaries, understanding the church fathers proved difficult, for their
world was quite different from that of late antiquity, and the need to provide
clarity concerning their works generated some important commentaries.[144]

Rotrud and Gisela left the court for a time to receive instruction at Chelles,
a center of learning and manuscript production under the direction of their
aunt Gisela. When elite families ensured their daughters' instruction for a
short period at a religious house, they may have imitated the royal family.
Charlemagne's daughters' time at Chelles may therefore have influenced the
pattern of female lay instruction. The daughters' very presence at court and
their later notoriety, however, meant that later ninth-century elite men did
not want their daughters to be like them.

The exact nature of the daughters' "misbehavior" is elusive. Einhard was
at pains to explain their continuing presence at court:

> Although his daughters were extremely beautiful women and were deeply
> loved by him, it is strange to have to report that he never wanted to give any
> of them away in marriage to anyone, whether it be to a Frankish noble or to
> a foreigner. Instead he kept them close beside him at home until his death,
> saying that he could not stand to be parted from their company. Although
> he was otherwise happy, this situation [that is, the affairs of his daughters]

---

141. Alcuin, "On the Court," *PCR*, 121. Translation is Godman's.
142. Garrison, "The Social World of Alcuin," 77.
143. MGH Ep. 4, no. 342, 25–27.
144. Contreni, "Learning in the Early Middle Ages," 15.

caused him no end of trouble. But he always acted as if there was no suspicion of any sexual scandal on their part or that any such rumor had already spread far and wide.[145]

Louis the Pious wished to bring a moral "regime" to court; given the emphasis on lasting monogamous marriage in this period and the desire to carry out reforms, Einhard needed to fit Charlemagne's unmarried daughters into the new paradigm. Although Charlemagne had perfectly good reasons to prevent his daughters from marrying—competing heirs—writers from the 820s on perceived them in a new, unflattering manner. These new ideas, as well as the substantial power they could exert at court, help explain why Louis the Pious, upon inheriting the throne from his father, sent his sisters to monasteries.[146] Men writing about Louis's sisters employed a rhetoric of threatened legitimacy and immorality that would be used to discredit other royal women, including Fastrada, Judith, and Theutberga. Ninth-century Carolingian writers expected that prominent women at court should be virtuous virgins or matrons; if they were not, their behavior was disruptive, even dangerous. Court poets praised women at court for their displaying exemplary virtue, implying that a well-ordered court required female morality. I have found no evidence for the regular presence of young unmarried female members of aristocratic families at court though surely they would have made irregular appearances there. Elite families from the 820s on may have been hesitant to send their daughters to court and instead may have preferred to associate their daughters with religious houses such as Remiremont and San Salvatore in Brescia. Louis the Pious also created problems for himself and his heirs with this change because it helped him to allow his daughter Gisela to marry Eberhard. In so doing he opened himself up to the potential succession problems Charlemagne had avoided by not allowing his daughters to marry.

Ninth-Century Queens

Ninth-century emphasis on female exemplarity explains how and why some men perceived that elite women could undermine the reputation of their husbands and stability of their households. The growing conviction that women constituted the moral center of the household, developed from the writings of the 820s, also applied to the queen. Her moral probity maintained

---

145. Einhard, *VK*, chap. 19, 25. Translation from Dutton, *Charlemagne's Courtier*, 29.
146. Nelson, "Women at the Court of Charlemagne," 57–59.

the stability of the kingdom.[147] Queens who committed sexual sins, or were accused of such acts, could disrupt the proper order of society. Charges of wickedness leveled against Charlemagne's queen Fastrada indicate that a queen's lack of Christian virtue could have detrimental repercussions for the realm. After describing the failed uprisings of both Pippin the Hunchback against his father, Charlemagne, in 792, and of Hardrad in 785–86, Einhard blames Fastrada for them:

> But it is [widely] believed that the cruelty of queen Fastrada was the cause and source of these conspiracies, since in both cases these men conspired against the king because it looked as if [Charlemagne] had savagely departed from his usual kind and gentle ways by consenting to the cruel ways of his wife.[148]

Einhard does not enumerate Fastrada's cruelties, but blaming a "wicked" wife, particularly one like Fastrada who produced no children, provided an excuse for acts that could have reflected badly upon Charlemagne, and conformed to the new moral regime at Louis' court. Einhard also blamed the wicked advice of Tassilo's Lombard wife for causing him to start war with Charlemagne: he believed she wanted revenge for the king's conquest of her father's kingdom.[149] Ermold the Black in his poem in honor of Louis portrays the wife of the Breton magnate Murman in a similar, though more sexualized, manner. She used kisses and affection to persuade Murman to continue his fight against the Franks; Ermold wrote that this act was like a forest fire started in winter. Though he initially resisted her advice, telling her to concern herself with women's affairs, he eventually agreed to resume his fight with the Franks. When he died from a Frankish spear, the Bretons blamed it on the fact he listened to a woman's counsel.[150]

The case of the Empress Judith, accused of committing adultery with Bernard of Septimania (among other immoral acts) around the time of the revolt against Louis the Pious in 830, demonstrates this scapegoating quite clearly. Accused of sexual impropriety, she had to contend with allegations that went to the heart of her principal role, reproduction. Refuting crimes of illicit and immoral sexual behavior proved particularly difficult, and frequently accused women had to retire to religious houses. Judith had a hard time proving her

---

147. Sedulius Scottus, *Liber de rectoribus Christianis*, chap. 5, *Sedulius Scottus*, ed. S. Hellmann (Munich, 1906), 34–35.

148. Einhard, *VK*, chap. 20, 26. Translation from Dutton, *Charlemagne's Courtier*, 30.

149. Einhard, *VK*, chap. 11, 14. Her wicked advice also turns Tassilo against Charlemagne in the *Prior Metz Annals* (yr. 787, 75) and the *Royal Frankish Annals* (MGH SRG 6, ed. Friedrich Kurze, yr. 788, 80).

150. Ermold, *In honorem*, 110–32, lines 1418–747.

innocence. The charges resulted from her stepsons' discontent and rebellion against their father; they wanted to cast doubt on the legitimacy of her off-spring, thereby disinheriting the future Charles the Bald to their benefit. Yet the ways these accusations built from the idea of the moral wife and mother help to demonstrate that model's pervasiveness. Raban Maur, abbot of Fulda (822–842), remained loyal to both Louis and Judith during these conflicts, and in the 830s, he dedicated commentaries on the books of Judith and Esther to the empress. In his texts the exemplary Old Testament heroines resemble vir-tuous Carolingian matrons who perform good works while looking after their kingdoms. Thus, his discussion strongly reflects the ideal of the upright wife and mother found in the other Carolingian sources mentioned above, and the commentaries arrived at an appropriate time. Raban may have sent these texts to Judith when she had just returned from exile at the religious house at Poitiers but had not yet been purified.[151] On one level, because he may have equated her with these virtuous matrons, he may have implied that she had already won back her reputation. At the same time, these examples of beleaguered women who triumphed over their troubles presented models of the behavior she would need to exemplify in the ideally moral court of Louis the Pious.

Theutberga, the wife of Lothar II, suffered from similar accusations of immorality, including a charge that she had committed incest with her brother Hubert, lay abbot of St. Maurice-in-Valais. Not only had Theutberga en-gaged in anal intercourse with Hubert, according to her accusers, but also she aborted the fetus she had subsequently conceived. Even one of her sup-porters, Hincmar of Rheims, noted that, if true, such acts rendered her unfit to be a wife.[152] Because Lothar had children, including a possible male heir, Hugh, with his previous partner Waldrada but not with Theutberga, he had a compelling political reason to divorce Theutberga. Although he appears to have genuinely loved Waldrada but not Theutberga, he ultimately failed in his attempt despite spending most of the 860s working to obtain a divorce. The case became an international scandal with everyone from the pope to hum-ble subjects of the Carolingian kingdoms taking an interest in the divorce.[153] Although Theutberga and Lothar had only been married two years, hardly long enough to conclude that she was incapable of bearing a child, this charge was added to the original accusations of sexual immorality and sin.[154] Though cleared in a trial by ordeal of combat in 858, Theutberga confessed to the acts

---

151. de Jong, "Exegesis for an Empress," 80–86.
152. Airlie, "Private Bodies," 13–14.
153. Hincmar, *DLR*, 1, 3, 120, 122, 130; Bishop, "Bishops as Marital Advisors in the Ninth Century," 62–65.
154. Airlie, "Private Bodies," 12.

of which she was accused at a synod in Aachen in 860; she then asked to be allowed to enter a convent. She eventually fled to the court of Lothar's half-brother, Charles the Bald, where the king and his principal adviser Hincmar of Rheims took up her cause.

Because some powerful men supported Theutberga's innocence, she could contest these accusations. Charles the Bald, worked against the divorce because he stood to benefit from the lack of a Lotharingian heir. When Hincmar wrote a tract against the divorce, he may have meant mainly to support his patron, but his work was equally a moral and legal treatment. Though a group of Lotharingian bishops approved the divorce based upon Theutberga's coerced confession of incest, Hincmar argued that Christian principles did not allow a husband to set aside his legitimate wife no matter how expedient a divorce might be. He pointed out that Lothar's bid for the divorce constituted a moral failing, because he should have set a better Christian example as king. If he could not rule his wife, how could he rule his kingdom well?[155] Hincmar echoed Jonas of Orléans's earlier treatment of similar issues in *De institutione laicali*. Jonas states that fornication is the only reason a man can dismiss his wife.[156] Failure to produce children was insufficient grounds. Lothar therefore realized he had to make a "legitimate" charge to gain a divorce; incest constituted a terrible crime according to Jonas.[157] Yet Hincmar noted, even if incest rendered Theutberga unfit to be a wife, the legal proceedings against her were flawed. She had been cleared by combat in 858; at the synod of Aachen the main evidence against Theutberga, her own confession, was inadmissible; and she could not possibly have become pregnant through anal intercourse. Theutberga's case, therefore, became a means for working out ideas of virtue, law, and just rule, demonstrating the centrality of rhetoric concerning female virtue to the political actions and social norms of the Carolingian elite. The role of the queen as a model for other Christian women is especially apparent: Theutberga had not kept the moral order in the royal household for which Sedulius Scottus wrote that the king and the queen were responsible and she had certainly not lived up to the model queen of heaven Mary.[158] Yet it was Lothar who was most responsible for his lack of moral control, and in the end his tactic of laying blame at Theutberga's door cost him his kingdom, which was split apart at his death. Ninth-century writers still believed as the ancient Greeks and Romans had

155. Ibid., 32–33.
156. Jonas, *Institutione*, 2.12, col. 188.
157. Ibid., 2.8, cols. 183–84.
158. Airlie, "Private Bodies," 7–8, 21–23, 26–28.

that women were the weaker vessel and that men needed to exert authority over them. Female failings therefore had repercussions for the men responsible for them.

Concerns with legitimacy and power found expression through discourse on female moral probity. Though the king ought to act as a model of Christian behavior, queens especially had a responsibility to act morally. Through sexual monogamy a queen's virtuous behavior guaranteed the legitimacy of the family line, and hence the right order of the kingdom resulted from steady and legitimate succession. The queen's behavior also provided a model for those at court whether for good or ill. The scandals that resulted from accusations against queens had especially high stakes because of their prominent role. Ninth-century rhetoric concerning female moral exemplarity undoubtedly furthered the idea that the queen should act as a virtuous model. The situation at court clarifies the great interest in female exemplarity in the ninth century. If women could suffer accusations similar to those of Fastrada, Judith, and Theutberga, then it was all the more important to inculcate virtue in them. By maintaining moral households, the elite could set themselves in contrast to the royal court. It gave them another means to compete with the royal family. In part, Dhuoda's authority to advise William and other young men derived from her very absence from court.

The Advantages of Female Prudence

Female learning in Carolingian lands was a means to make women better moral exemplars and mothers, whether natural or spiritual. At the same time that such roles left them open to increased scrutiny and accusations of immorality that could damage them and their families, that situation only strengthened the desire for female virtue because it could offer women protection from such charges. Clergy encouraged Carolingian aristocratic women to provide basic religious instruction to children and other women because they perceived real peril to their souls as well as seeing how their exposure in the lay world endangered them more immediately and materially. Ecclesiastical leaders saw a means to take advantage of conventional female roles in these areas in order to help to promote right Christian conduct. Women had long molded children's behavior to aid them as participants in the aristocratic world. Their actions in these areas had secular goals, but mothers almost certainly also tried to ensure their children's spiritual health, much as Dhuoda did for William. Abbesses and other religious women had similar concerns for the girls in their charge.

Sources written by contemporary women, including letters and Dhuoda's handbook, support the existence of a relatively learned female elite capable of instructing others. The idea that only a minority of aristocratic women were literate and aware of the religious and intellectual discourse around them is plainly open to doubt. Particularly learned women, like Dhuoda or Leoba, may not have been as numerous as those women possessing more basic knowledge of religious and moral matters. Through an informal means of instruction women could transmit social and domestic competence to others, and sometimes even engage with the "high" culture and discourse of male scholars. Just as modern historians have increasingly noted greater variation and flexibility in early medieval status and politics than was previously recognized, so too women's participation in the culture of the Carolingian renaissance was diverse and complex.

Naturally, women had no monopoly over instruction and moral exemplarity. Besides mothers and abbesses, Carolingian law, church council legislation, and mirrors encouraged priests, monks, and godfathers to instruct others to prevent sinful behavior.[159] The more frequent references in sources to mothers in this capacity and the fact that they were usually at home in the presence of their offspring more often than fathers demonstrate the substantial role of mothers in the instruction of children, similar to that of the abbesses and *magistrae* at religious institutions. Though women such as those in Boniface's circle were active in this capacity prior to 800, the increasing ninth-century exhortations that women live up to these roles indicate the importance of instruction in encouraging a certain level of Christian behavior and practice among Carolingian aristocrats. Imitation of the royal family may have promoted learning among elite women, but the new discourse on female morality and the notorious accusations leveled against royal women from the 820s on may have made the elite wary of letting their female kin be too much like royal women. The examples of Dhuoda, Gisela, and the women at the royal court in Aachen supplement the evidence from Saxony, Thuringia, Frisia, Italy and the West Frankish heartlands, and indicate that the practices common to them all could have been widespread throughout the empire.

Contemporary evidence concerning female instruction and moral exemplarity indicates how powerfully the need for virtue in elite women shaped their depiction in texts. Virtuous behavior naturally contributed to female piety, and churchmen had spiritual reasons to encourage it. Equally, however, lay aristocratic families benefited when female members retained a good

---

159. See for example Dhuoda, *LM*, 3.11, 116–18.

reputation, which ensured the legitimacy of children, prevented scandal, and gave prestige to their kin. Women worked to encourage this behavior in other aristocratic girls and women in both households and religious houses. Furthermore, their moral exemplarity helped ensure concord and ideal lines of authority in lay household, convent, and court.

Chapter Four
WEALTH
Hospitality and Domestic Management

Walter, hero of the ninth-century poem *Waltharius*, had been a hostage of the Huns since his childhood. He grew up to become one of their great and trusted warriors. After returning one day victorious from battle, he went to Hildegund, the daughter of a Frankish king and a fellow hostage to whom he had been betrothed before being given to the Huns.

> For [Walter] was weary, and sought out the royal chamber.
> And he found Hildegund there sitting by herself.
> He first embraced and kissed her sweetly, then he said,
> "Bring drink here quickly; I am gasping with exhaustion."
> At once she filled a precious beaker with a strong wine
> And gave it to the man, who, as he took it, crossed
> Himself, and pressed the maiden's hand with his; but she
> Just stood there, silent, staring at her master's face.
> Then Walter drained the cup and gave it back to her.[1]

On the surface, this episode may seem a simple case of a thirsty man asking for a drink, but given both its location in the poem and the meaning of drink in the early medieval world, great significance attaches to Walter's request

---

1. *Waltharius*, 12–15, lines 220–28. The date of this poem has been subject to some controversy although most scholars date it to the ninth or tenth century. Given that it has references to numerous classical and medieval authors but none later than 900, I am persuaded of a ninth-century composition. If the poem was written in the tenth century, it nevertheless continued to reflect older norms. *Waltharius and Ruodlieb*, xiii–xv. All quotations of *Waltharius* come from Kratz's lucid translation.

of wine specifically from Hildegund. Almost immediately after draining the cup, he asked her to flee with him from the Huns and return to their Frankish homeland; thus he wished to persuade her of a dangerous undertaking. As the offering and accepting of a drink often served as a means of opening negotiations, of creating bonds and social ties, and of sealing promises in the early Middle Ages, Walter was asking Hildegund to establish a setting appropriate for negotiation. Her performance of a hospitable, welcoming act created an atmosphere conducive to Walter's request. By asking her for drink, Walter successfully manipulated social norms to further his own cause.

> Hildegund agreed to flee with Walter, and he suggested the following plan:
> Then Walter whispered this into the maiden's ear:
> "Her majesty has made you guardian of goods;
> So therefore hear attentively these words of mine:
> First steal the helmet and three-layered byrnie of
> The king, I mean the corselet which bears the mark
> Of smiths; and then obtain two coffers—fairly large,
> And fill these with so many arm-rings of the Huns
> That you can scarcely lift one just up to your breast.
> Then make me in the usual way, four pairs of shoes—
> Preparing four for you—and place them in boxes.
> And so the coffers may be filled up to the top.
> Moreover, secretly ask fish-hooks from the smiths;
> For as we travel let our food be fish and fowl;
> …
> I will prepare at great expense a festive banquet
> And try with all my guile to bury them in drink
> Until there is none who knows what is going on.
> But meanwhile you partake of wine in moderation,
> And at the table take care just to quench your thirst.
> Then when the rest arise, resume your usual tasks;
> But when the power of the drink undoes them all,
> Let us at once make haste to seek the western parts."[2]

Walter's plan reveals the opportunities women had to act within the male sphere of the household or court, where bonds among aristocratic men were created, maintained, and broken and where male relations of status were worked out. Though historians have long credited early medieval women with

2. *Waltharius*, 14–17, lines 260–86.

household management, none have yet offered much evidence for that role. Through careful readings of texts I explicate Carolingian women's domestic duties and show the substantial scope for action that their control of wealth afforded them. The queen had given Hildegund extensive power over the goods of the Huns' palace, a palace that in a Frankish poem resembled a Frankish palace more than a stronghold of the Huns, with which the poet would not have been familiar.[3] She had access to treasure, arms, and leather and could direct the smiths, reflecting the Frankish expectation that women have substantial supervisory power over the household.

Furthermore, Hildegund played a key role at the feast, drinking and acting normally, thereby helping to lull the guests into a false sense of security. Although the poet writes that Walter organized the feast, surely he relied upon Hildegund's access to the goods of the palace to create the rich atmosphere in which the temptation to overindulge in drink would prove irresistible.

> And he himself, at great expense, arranged the dishes.
> At length extravagance reigned among the tables.
> The king steps in the hall adorned with tapestries;
> With customary greeting the great-hearted hero
> Led him up to the throne, which purple and fine cloth
> Adorned.[4]

Note that the poet says Walter *himself* arranged that certain dishes be created for the feast, as though a man's interest in the selection of food might be unusual.[5] His arrangements reflect his status as the hero of the poem; Walter appropriately orchestrates the escape. Although one might expect that an aristocratic woman such as Hildegund would normally have had far greater control over food and drink within the household than Walter, were she to have arranged their getaway, not only would she detract from Walter's heroism and cunning but also she would seem less virtuous to the reader. Hildegund dutifully aids Walter in his deception, assembling the goods for their journey. Walter plays a tricky role here, shrewdly selecting food and drink to encourage (over)indulgence, demonstrating his wealth to pay for and arrange the banquet and his access to the powerful, at the same time showing his servility and thereby trustworthiness when helping the king to his seat. He relied

---

3. All suggestions as to the author have been monks; the author therefore probably never personally observed the Avars (the people Carolingians called Huns). Kratz, *Waltharius and Ruodlieb*, xiv–xv.

4. *Waltharius*, 16–17, lines 289–94.

5. The original Latin is: "et *ipse* Waltharius magnis instruxit sumptibus escas" (emphasis added).

upon Hildegund to help to create the festive atmosphere of the banquet in order that he might best take advantage of social expectations. No matter the degree of his involvement in physically arranging the feast, the description of it, along with the drink he earlier accepted from Hildegund, demonstrate the ways in which feasts and other instances of drinking and eating were occasions for the working out or fissure of social and political bonds. Even if the exact circumstances it describes are imagined, the poem provides a view into ninth-century aristocratic values and prefigures Ottonian table politics.[6]

Historians have learned less about the everyday life of the ninth century than of the tenth because of the intractable nature of Carolingian sources that touch upon that subject. In particular, though most historians suspect that women played a key role in providing hospitality and looking after their families, texts provide few cases of or expectations concerning such actions. By reading other eighth- and ninth-century sources in a similar manner to the reading of *Waltharius*—with a clear understanding of their context, their audience, and the limits of known contemporary norms—one can discern a great deal about female hospitality in the Carolingian world and the ways it affected social and political bonds among aristocrats. By drawing inferences about women's specific actions from the available evidence it will be possible to see the female contribution to what contemporaries presented as a male realm. Because such readings push the limits of available sources, they demand a disciplined imagination: thinking creatively about the sources and the questions they pose while carefully accounting for their historical context. I open up the vistas where women may have been active and effective although the sources do not allow one to discern with certainty women's actual actions in this area. The nature and authors of the relevant texts mean that much of their information concerning household management and hospitality conforms to ideals of domestic virtue. In nearly every case, women act either in harmony with men or in ways that enhance their own appearance as upstanding women. The conclusions gleaned from such an approach are often speculative and reveal more about expectations than reality, but the question of women's regular domestic roles demands consideration given the centrality of those responsibilities to female virtue in the Carolingian world.

Similarly to the ways in which Walter and Hildegund employed food, drink, and a rich atmosphere, aristocratic women in the Carolingian world looked after household goods, thus affording them opportunities to manipulate the atmosphere in which social negotiation took place. Furthermore, women's responsibilities concerning hospitality shed light on female domestic

---

6. For Ottonian feasting and drinking see Heinrich Fichtenau, *Living in the Tenth Century: Mentalities and social orders*, trans. Patrick J. Geary (Chicago, trans. 1991), 58–64.

management because they provide a rationale for the activities women most probably oversaw in their households, estates, or religious houses. Their access to these goods and responsibility for hospitality also marked their high status. Female supervision of inferiors helps to make clear why clerics were concerned that women set a good example for their servants. These wealthy women further demonstrated their domestic virtue through care for the sick and dying, a task made easier by their supervisory powers though perhaps it also served to humble the female elite. Thus, this episode from *Waltharius* has identified the issues surrounding women's roles in the domestic sphere. Other Carolingian sources support and expand upon the expectations revealed in *Waltharius*, suggesting a great deal about the specific duties of aristocratic women.

The Connection between Hospitality and Domestic Management

The early ninth-century *Capitulare de villis*, concerning the management of royal estates, reveals the expectation that the queen help to manage those royal estates.

> We wish that whatever we or the queen or our officials, the seneschal, and the butler may order the *iudices* [to do] by our instruction or that of the queen, they shall carry out these things in full as they were instructed.[7]

Drawing analogies between queens and aristocrats, their wives, and their estates by means of this capitulary has been common; scholars assume that we can use statements concerning the queen in this capitulary to discuss elite women with supervisory authority over family estates.[8] The mention of the *iudices* in the *Capitulare de villis* shows that men probably had managers to keep their estates running smoothly in their absence, but this passage suggests that the lord's wife had nearly commensurate managerial power over family estates and, in fact, directed the work of the *iudices*.[9] Because aristocratic women often helped to preserve family lands, they had some part in managing

---

7. *CV*, chap. 16, 57.

8. Wemple, *WFS*, 98; Goetz, "Frauenbild und weibliche Lebensgestaltung," 21.

9. *Iudex* was an ambivalent term in the ninth century; it could have a variety of meanings depending upon its context. In translations of the *Capitulare de villis*, *iudex* is often rendered as steward or bailiff, but in order to avoid giving this term too specific a meaning or using a modern word that connotes an office that may be anachronistic for the era, I will use the original term *iudex* throughout.

those lands and households and providing concomitant hospitality. Although the *Capitulare de villis* concerns ideal supervision of royal estates, it reveals much about Carolingian administrative concerns, the agricultural and craft activities of estates, and the early medieval economy. Focusing on women's role in hospitality makes it possible to explicate in detail the areas aristocratic laywomen most probably controlled or helped to run. Furthermore, because hospitality was a duty for religious women, it allows consideration of how religious women managed their communities. Although evidence is scanter for religious women, it reveals that they performed work similar to that of lay aristocratic women in order to sustain their communities.

Women helped to keep the wheels of the Carolingian economy turning by controlling significant aspects of estate management and production. The lack of a sustained investigation of elite women's household supervision, despite its economic, political, and social importance, may be a consequence of seemingly intractable sources.[10] Prescriptive sources provide almost all of the written evidence concerning the nature and responsibilities of women's work. Asides and brief mentions in sources such as hagiography prove equally difficult to untangle because they often relate to the trope of domestic virtue. The difficulty of examining women's work obscures its potential significance. Expert female management was essential to the prosperity of religious houses and beneficial for the lay household, making skills in this area highly desirable to a woman, her family, and her community. Archaeological evidence, which reveals much about the location of certain craft and agricultural activities, helps to contextualize references to women's supervision of these activities in the written record. Furthermore, previous chapters of this study have produced a framework for Carolingian women's lives into which female domestic management fits well.

Aristocratic women's domestic oversight could have profound social, political, and cultural implications because their responsibility for hospitality could help to forge connections among the Carolingian elite, as well as enhance their own virtuous image. Through their arrangement of lavish display in households and their contributions to the rich decoration of churches, which included textiles and other precious objects and treasures, aristocratic women helped to promote the reputation of their families and the religious institutions with which they had ongoing bonds. They also advanced these same

---

10. Neither scholars investigating the early medieval economy nor those studying medieval women's work have provided sustained considerations of early medieval aristocratic women's work. On the early medieval economy see the bibliographies in McCormick, *Origins of the European Economy*, and Wickham, *Framing the Early Middle Ages*. For women's work see Bennett et al., *Sisters and Workers in the Middle Ages*.

institutions by providing hospitality. When given to pilgrims, the poor, and the religious, it primarily reflected their piety; when extended to other aristocrats, it principally afforded opportunities to impress peers with their display of wealth and, perhaps, to affect political relations. No strict division separated these two forms of hospitality, especially because aristocratic pilgrims and bishops were often their guests. In fact, women's hospitality facilitated the development of bonds among elite families and religious institutions. Furthermore, hospitality had two sides, one involving its outward display, nearly in the form of a ritual, and the more private preparations that allowed for such show and provided basic necessities: food, drink, and household furnishings.

An investigation of Carolingian aristocratic female hospitality and domestic management further defines the contours of female life during the eighth and ninth centuries. Aristocratic women's hospitality, like many of their other activities, reflected both intangible ideals and down-to-earth goals. Given the emphasis upon hospitality in Christianity from its beginnings, its expectation in Frankish religious circles is hardly surprising. Women's participation in and supervision of domestic production and probable management of lands helped to make hospitality possible and provided means by which women aided in sustaining and increasing aristocratic wealth. Furthermore, these acts meant that women of different status interacted regularly and that aristocratic women supervised male inferiors. Elite families who held estates or had dominion over villages doubtless developed bonds with the dependents living on those possessions, together forming a community of which sources reveal only glimpses. The subjects discussed here invariably touch on the way of life for the vast majority of people living in the Carolingian Empire. Most studies of female labor in the early Middle Ages have focused upon women of relatively humble origin, especially those whose existence monks recorded in their polyptychs, surveys of estates held by churches or other owners, listing those who held property from the abbey by precarial tenure and individuals owing labor directly to the lord.[11] Discerning the tasks that many women and men carried out proves easier than determining the activities that aristocratic women oversaw. Examining the expected work at estates reveals much about daily life, offering an image of the ways some Carolingian men understood their world and allowing a glimpse at some practices that are not part of the written record upon which most studies concentrate. The complexity of women's daily tasks required a high level of social, economic, and organizational

---

11. Herlihy, *OM*, 25–48; Kuchenbuch, "Trennung und Verbindung," 227–42; idem, "Opus feminile," 139–78; Obermeier, "*Ancilla*;" Jean-Pierre Devroey, "Men and Women in Early Medieval Serfdom: the Ninth-Century North Frankish Evidence," *PP* 166 (2000): 3–30.

competence, indicating that they would have had to acquire these skills in some manner. Almost certainly, women taught other women or girls how to supervise others and perform certain tasks for the economic welfare of their household or religious house.

By domestic management I mean the various activities and duties that involved the supervision and distribution of the large-scale production of goods, food, and drink, including management of workers, land, and money. Large-scale production therefore excludes the individual labors of Carolingian aristocratic women, such as embroidery, and any work that does not produce a physical item. Instruction of children and fellow religious, for example, is not considered part of women's labor. Among the many production activities women oversaw were candlemaking, dairying, gardening, baking, cooking, and textile fabrication. Elite women may have participated in some of these tasks along with the artisans and workers they supervised; they would have required firsthand knowledge about those various products. Men also participated in and helped to supervise some of these activities. For example, the *iudex* of the *Capitulare de villis* had duties overlapping with those of the queen. Monks carried out much of the same work in monasteries that women did elsewhere, and aristocratic men likely attended to their estates and the work done on them in the winter months when they were probably often at home. Women and men thus shared roles in management, but women had certain duties related to hospitality that gave them room for broad supervision even when men were present. The household and estate were male domains, but women functioned relatively independently within them through a particularly female combination of domestic activities and expectations.

Two sources, the *Capitulare de villis* and the *Brevium exempla*, provide much of the evidence concerning women's supervisory role in domestic management. Both are found in a single early ninth-century manuscript at Wolfenbüttel.[12] The manuscript contains neither specific dates nor references to historical events, but most scholars date it to the reign of Charlemagne on stylistic and historical grounds, although some believe it was produced in Aquitaine during the reign of Louis the Pious (793–813).[13] Both sources concern royal estates. The *Capitulare de villis* establishes rules for the administration of the royal estates; the *Brevium exempla* is a more complex document. Its incomplete first part includes an inventory of the monastery at Staffelsee along with extracts from surveys of other possessions of the bishopric of Augsburg. A second section lists benefactions made to the monastery of Wissembourg

12. Cod. Guelf. 254 Helmst. Der Herzog August Bibliothek, Wolfenbüttel.
13. Dopsch, *Die Wirtschaftsentwicklung der Karolingerzeit*, 53–55; Ennas, Il *"Capitulare de villis,"* 15–18.

in Alsace. Part of this portion resembles a polyptych. Most relevant to this chapter, its final section provides an inventory of some royal estates, not all identifiable. Because the *Brevium exempla* discusses *mansi* (small residential units) and workers, not just goods, it reveals both the probable products of Carolingian estates and information about the production that took place both in workshops near the main house and on dependent farms. Thus, a central brewery may have received malt from dependent farms.[14] The section concerning Staffelsee's holdings inventories a dependent homestead (*curtis*), which had 23 *mansi* of its own.[15] If lay aristocrats had similar documents drawn up, they no longer exist, but some archaeological discoveries support the evidence found in these texts; manuscript illustrations and asides in other texts also provide confirmation. The companion eleventh-century Old English texts *Rectitudines singularum personarum* (later translated to Latin) and *Gerefa* most closely resemble the *Capitulare de villis* and the *Brevium exempla*. The former offers an explicit outline of all the persons on an estate and their duties while the latter ostensibly offers advice to a sensible reeve, though it is more probably a "literary exercise."[16] Despite certain parallels, the *Capitulare de villis* offers an ideal while both the *Rectitudines singularum personarum* and the *Brevium exempla* concern individual estates. Furthermore, no textual link connects these Frankish and Anglo-Saxon texts.[17] Thus, these two royal, Frankish documents suggest common practices among the Carolingian elite while possibly reflecting wider early medieval traditions.

Household and Estate Management

Women probably had some role in visiting and supervising family estates, but the sources obscure their actions in comparison to those of their male relatives and *iudices*. While the limitations of these texts do not allow a precise definition of women's purview in this regard, the available evidence convincingly demonstrates the active domestic roles of women. Just as laywomen had greater occasion to act as moral exemplars and religious instructors because they remained on family estates more often than their husbands, so too they aided in the supervision of estates, an activity that undoubtedly expanded in the absence of men, especially as the main agricultural season (spring to fall)

---

14. *BE*, 51.

15. Ibid., 51–2.

16. *Rectitudines singularum personarum* and *Gerefa*, both in *Die Gesetze der Angelsachsen*, ed. F. Liebermann (1902; repr. Aalen, 1960), 444–53 and 453–55, respectively. See also Harvey, "*Rectitudines Singularum Personarum* and *Gerefa*," 9.

17. Harvey, "*Rectitudines Singularum Personarum* and *Gerefa*," 20.

coincided with the hunting seasons (fall and spring) and military campaign season (summer).[18] Carolingian queens did not accompany their husbands to battle as later queens sometimes did.[19] In the absence of their husbands and perhaps even in their presence, female supervision of family lands required keeping track of many activities and people.

Parallel to the supervision of estates was the role women played at court. Women exerted political influence there in various ways—mainly through their husbands and sons but sometimes through other relatives. They also had administrative means at their disposal. Merovingian queens sometimes had control over the royal treasury, which was kept in the royal bedchamber. Theudechild, widow of King Charibert, for example, offered herself in marriage to her brother-in-law Guntram. In reply, he agreed, asking her to bring "her treasure," but upon her arrival Guntram took most of the treasure and sent her to the convent at Arles. After the death of King Sigibert, King Chilperic not only banished Sigibert's queen Brunhild to Rouen but also seized the treasure she had brought with her when fleeing from Paris. The widowed Fredegund took some of the royal treasure with her to Paris where she took refuge in the cathedral while the treasure she left behind "was confiscated by the treasury officials."[20] Clearly the queen did not exert sole control, but her ability to take treasure at times of transition demonstrates that she had access to it. The wives of some Carolingian rulers appear to have continued this practice. After the death of her husband, Pippin II in 714, Plectrud had charge of a considerable treasure until her stepson Charles Martel took it from her in 716.[21] Chapter 25 of Hincmar of Rheims's *De ordine palatii* indicates continuing female access to the treasury. It stipulated that queens shared, with the chamberlain, the duty of dealing with gifts; presumably they had to draw upon the treasury in order to provide gifts.[22] Frankish queens' access to the royal treasure following the deaths of their husbands sometimes gave them power at a moment when their influence often began to diminish.[23] In 877, for example, Charles the Bald called his childless second wife back to him when he lay on his deathbed. Just before he died, he entrusted to Richildis the royal regalia, including a sword with which she was to invest

---

18. Hennebicque, "Espaces sauvages et chasses royales dans le nord de la Francie viième-ixème siècles," 45–51.

19. Stafford, *QCD*, 118–19.

20. Gregory of Tours, *Decem libri historiarum*, 4.26, 5.1, and 7.4, MGH SRM 1.1, ed. Bruno Krusch and Wilhelm Levison (Hanover, 1951), 159, 194–95, 328.

21. *Continuationes Fredegarii Chronica*, chap. 10, ed. and trans. J. M. Wallace-Hadrill (London, 1960), 89; Fouracre and Gerberding, *Late Merovingian France*, 86.

22. Hincmar, *OP*, chap. 22, 72–74.

23. Stafford, *QCD*, 104–6; Wemple, *WFS*, 63–69.

Louis the Stammerer with his father's realm as well as a robe, crown, and scepter. After a delay because of negotiations between Louis the Stammerer and Richildis, she transferred these items to Louis.[24] The control she exerted over the delivery of the regalia to her stepson demonstrates the influence she had over the transmission of royal authority. Another Richildis, wife of the magnate Eccard of Autun, retained use of her husband's chapel treasury and could thereby benefit from her custody of these items, similarly to queens' direction of royal wealth.[25]

At court, the domestic organization or "women's sphere" took on political and religious meanings. Merovingian queens such as Balthild and Brunhild, distributed food, clothing, and charity, activities that may have given them influence in the space where the king exhibited his power.[26] According to hagiographical accounts, some queens, such as Radegund and Balthild, transferred these domestic duties to the cloister, where they became appropriately virtuous activities that demonstrated the women's sanctity.[27] Both Merovingian and Anglo-Saxon queens, as well as later Ottonian and Capetian queens, carried out a range of domestic duties within the court, generally looking after the appearance of those at court, gifts, and household goods; the authority of Carolingian queens was similar.[28] In the Carolingian period women gained administrative authority at court and sometimes pushed the boundaries of that power.[29] These activities enhanced their influence. Economic management and control of resources show how potentially expansive female power was among the elite, though its possible, particular managerial mechanisms remain vague.

In the case of non-royal women, the problem of specificity of powers and degree of authority is at least as acute as that for queens. By analogy and in light of the evidence, female aristocrats almost certainly wielded considerable influence in areas of domestic management, and in the absence of their male

---

24. Richildis had accompanied Charles to Italy, where, at Tortona, Pope John had consecrated her empress. Upon finding out that Karlmann, son of Louis the German, was about to attack them, Richildis had fled north taking the rich treasure the royal couple had brought with them across the Alps. Charles was able to frighten Karlmann off, but shortly thereafter he caught the fever that caused him to ask Richildis to return to the south and brought about his death. Richildis then traveled with Charles's body north to the area around Lyon, and not long after his burial, her negotiations with Louis the Stammerer began. *AB*, 877, 214–16, 218–19.

25. *RCSBL*, no. 25, 65.

26. Nelson, "Queens as Jezebels," 74.

27. Coon, *SF*, 126–41.

28. Stafford, *QCD*, 99–110.

29. Nelson, "Women at the Court of Charlemagne," 50.

kin, they probably had the opportunity to exert more individual power than royal women, though obviously not on as influential a scale. Aristocratic families imitated the royal family during the Carolingian era, but it is important to remember that the Carolingians had once been one aristocratic family among many. The role of the Carolingian queen helped to mold expectations among the female aristocracy, and the conventional role of domestic management among the female aristocracy doubtless influenced the expected duties and responsibilities of the Carolingian queen.

Looking after their households and estates required astute organization and oversight. The most powerful and best-documented Carolingian families held estates that were often scattered throughout the empire: overseeing far-flung holdings involved potential logistical nightmares.[30] Ninth-century polyptychs indicate that some estates were immense, making it difficult to focus upon their myriad small details.[31] The varied craft and agricultural production involved the labor and supervision of many workers under at least the nominal direction of the estates' lord. Successful management to any degree demanded an ability to deal with complex problems. Women could not have been involved in all areas of estate oversight; they were probably not responsible for some matters. In *On the Governance of the Palace*, Hincmar of Rheims wrote that five male officers, four hunters and a falconer, should make the arrangements for hunts on royal estates.[32] Although women were sometimes present at hunts, they did not run them. A male-controlled domain, hunting provided not merely meat but martial practice and a chance to develop social and political bonds.[33] Responsibility for other aspects of management was not so clearly designated.

Although families somehow oversaw their far-flung estates, it proves difficult to determine which family members consistently performed this task or if appointed *iudices* were mainly responsible. Delegation of such duties depended upon the size of the family and how much land it held, but women undoubtedly shared in this management. As the passage from the *Capitulare de villis* quoted earlier demonstrates, royal women were assigned considerable supervisory power over estates. The queen also ideally wielded substantial authority over the court. In his treatise on the court, after describing the

---

30. For literature concerning estates and land holding see relevant bibliography in Innes, *State and Society*.

31. Elisabeth Magnou-Nortier, "Le grand domaine. Des maîtres, des doctrines, des questions," *Francia* 15 (1987), 659–700, at 659, 682; see also the works of Jean-Pierre Devroey cited throughout this book.

32. Hincmar, *OP*, chap. 24, 76.

33. Hennebicque, "Espaces sauvages," 49–52.

court's two highest officers, the count of the palace and the court chaplain (*apocrisiarius*) Hincmar added:

> Each of these officials of whom we have spoken held chief authority over his office. He was responsible to no one and acted for no one, unless it was for the king alone or, in some instances for the queen and for the king's glorious family.[34]

Because "the king's glorious family" presumably included his daughters, this passage may also reflect or help to explain the influence of Charlemagne's daughters at court.

Aristocratic and royal women had frequent opportunities to exert managerial control over household, court, and estates. The degree to which men were absent from their lands for military service has been subject to debate, but many were away during the summer campaign seasons.[35] The *Capitulare missorum de exercitu promovendo* of 808 stated that a lord called to war could leave behind only four men, two to look after his possessions and two to stay with his wife, presumably for protection.[36] If most armed men left estates in times of war, women could take on male roles, even if they may not otherwise have performed some of those tasks. Nothing suggests, however, that they ever armed themselves—hence the need for men to defend wife and land. During the civil war following the death of their father, Louis the Pious, Hildegard challenged her half-brother Charles the Bald by taking one of his men prisoner in Laon where she was abbess at St. Mary's, but when Charles arrived at Laon with a large force, both Hildegard and the townspeople surrendered immediately.[37] Hildegard used her authority to direct others to seize and hold the prisoner, but she did not take up arms herself.

An absent lord or a busy king necessitated the use of *iudices* and other officers or high-level servants, but the *iudex* had frequent occasion to be absent himself. Chapter 16 of the *Capitulare de villis* gives reasons he might leave his post: "And if a *iudex* is in the army, or on guard duty, or on an errand, or is away elsewhere, and gives an order to his subordinates and they do not carry it out, let them come by foot to the palace."[38] There the queen or king would

---

34. Hincmar, *OP*, chap. 19, 68.

35. Innes, *State and Society*, 151–55; Bernard Bachrach, *Early Carolingian Warfare: Prelude to an Empire* (Philadelphia, 2001), 202–43; Halsall, *Warfare and Society in the Barbarian West*, 55, 93–95, 145.

36. MGH Capit. 2,1, no. 235, 137.

37. Nithard, *Historia*, 3.4, *Nithard: Histoire des fils de Louis le Pieux*, ed. and trans. P. Lauer, Les classiques de l'histoire de France au moyen âge 7, (Paris, 1926), 96–98.

38. *CV*, chap. 16, 57.

decide on a punishment. The chapter goes on to indicate that the queen could direct the *iudices* and other officers of the estate. Even when a *iudex* may have had supervisory authority commensurate with the female head of the family, his absence may have necessitated her stepping into roles she did not regularly fulfill. Chapter 20 explains the duty of the *iudex* to keep the court well supplied with food throughout the year. In order to accomplish this task, he ought to visit the court three-to-four times per year.[39] As an officer of the king, the *iudex* had other duties besides the supervision of royal estates. Chapter 5 suggests what the *iudex* might have done when he was away:

> If a *iudex* is not in his district, or cannot come to a particular place, let him send a good messenger from among our dependents, or some other very trustworthy man, to look after our affairs and settle them effectively; and the *iudex* shall scrupulously see to it to send a reliable man to look after this matter.[40]

Iudices appointed at aristocratic estates probably had obligations that called them away or required that they travel. In the absence of male officers, the managerial oversight of the female head of household may have expanded to areas with which she did not normally concern herself, such as the stables. Moreover, women may have done some of the traveling that *iudices* were expected to do.

The ninth-century *Vita Liutbirgae virginis* describes aristocratic women visiting family estates. Liutberga's patroness Gisla had to visit her estates because she was a widow, and she alone had inherited her father Hessi's lands after the premature death of her brother. She had been traveling on business to inspect her many lands when she stopped at Liutberga's community for the night. Later she took Liutberga with her on these journeys between estates. At Gisla's deathbed Bernard swore to care for Liutberga just as his mother had. Gisla urged Bernard to let Liutberga look after household matters for him and to heed her advice "because she was always trustworthy in all things for me." Bernard followed his mother's advice, and Liutberga became one of his most trusted and indispensable servants.[41] These references to female management of family estates are frustratingly vague. Liutberga's singular supervisory role is quite mysterious.[42] Although a foreigner

---

39. Ibid., chap. 20, 57; chap. 5, 56
40. Ibid., chap. 5, 56.
41. *Vita Liutbirgae*, chap. 3, 4, 7, and 8–10, pp. 11, 13, 15–16.
42. No other such female aides appear in extant evidence making it impossible to tell if Liutberga was exceptional in this regard.

in Saxony and a woman, she had a great deal of power over Gisla's, and later Bernard's, estates. Though less puzzling, Gisla's case raises the issue of whether she would have overseen her estates had she not been widowed and without brothers. If ever a situation demanded a *iudex*, it was Gisla's lack of grown male relatives. Her personal supervision supports the evidence of the *Capitulare de villis* and *On the Governance of the Palace* concerning female oversight of estate and domestic matters, and her practice of traveling widely may reflect the limitations of what officers could accomplish for a family, especially one in which the lord had died. Elite women with living husbands, brothers, or fathers may nevertheless have exerted similar control to Gisla over their estates given that aristocratic courts probably had fewer members than royal courts.

Women's control over and donation of land in charters reveals not only their preservation of familial memory and bonds but also their ability to manage those lands. For example, following the death of Eberhard of Friuli, his widow Gisela made donations to the monastery at Cysoing.[43] Her ability to transfer these lands demonstrates her supervisory power over them. The other charters discussed in chapter 2 similarly indicate women's roles in managing lands. Imma, the wife of Einhard, offers another example of a woman who had substantial power over land. In 815, Louis the Pious named her and her estates in eastern Francia, Michelstadt, and Mulinheim, in a grant to Einhard, and like Gisela, Imma was a co-testator with Einhard, leaving their estate at Michelstadt to Lorsch.[44] One letter from Imma involved her supervision of the lands that she and Einhard held; Julia Smith has argued both that Imma, in this regard among others, was a typical aristocratic women of her era and that she was Einhard's "partner" in "religious devotions and managerial responsibilities."[45]

Women probably learned the requisite skills for dealing with the everyday affairs of the family lands as Liutberga did—from helping and watching her mistress. In many ways this is the most logical way in which such skills could have been handed on from mother to daughter. Gisla, however, probably took Liutberga along with her because she seemed already well prepared for such work. Thus, girls may have learned requisite skills for women's work in religious houses as well. Because the girls sent to Liutberga by Ansgar, once educated in basic religious matters and household arts, were allowed to go to relatives or to wherever they wished, it seems probable that she prepared

---

43. *CAC*, no. 3–6, 7–11.

44. *Codex Lauresbamensis* no. 19 and 20, ed. Karl Glöckner, vol. 1, (Darmstadt, 1929), 299–300 and 301–2; Smith, "Einhard," 57–58.

45. MGH Ep. 5, no. 37, 128; Smith, "Einhard," 58, 70.

them for work in domestic settings.[46] As in the cases of religious instruction, embroidery, and fine display, the skills related to women's work were passed on in various settings. Given the many similarities in responsibilities among Carolingian lay and religious women, this transmission makes sense.

Religious women required the same skills in women's work as their lay counterparts. Evidence concerning religious women's management of their communities and transmission of related skills reveals comparable female supervision of others and concern with tasks essential to the economic and social welfare of a community. Much like Gisla visiting her estates, Leoba traveled to different female communities to urge their members to live more perfectly.[47] In the early tenth-century *Vita Aldegundis* the abbess and senior nuns ran their religious house smoothly. When describing the miraculous opening of a church gate, the author wrote: "Not very much later, when the same beloved sisters [in Christ] gathered together, they administered the care of the flock."[48] This passage refers both to pastoral care and to the necessary administrative duties of the various officers of a religious community. Some Carolingian widows entered religious houses, where they brought to bear their experiences running households to improve the administration of their new communities.[49] The social competence that they learned in the secular world served them well in the religious life.

Older sisters usually held the offices in a convent. The early anonymous version of the *Vita Aldegundis* survives in a ninth-century Carolingian manuscript (BNF lat. 05275) among others; in that particular version the author mentions that the abbess Aldegund instructed the older sisters (*seniores germanas*), who usually carried out the administrative tasks for the community.[50] Curiously, the manuscripts that contain the early tenth-century version of her *vita*, once erroneously ascribed to Hucbald of St. Amand, consistently leave out the part about these sisters being senior.[51] Perhaps the author assumed his readers would understand that these women had reached a mature age and simply left off what seemed a superfluous detail, or he may have wanted

---

46. *Vita Liutbirgae*, chap. 35, 44.
47. Rudolf, *Vita Leobae*, chap. 18, 129.
48. *Vita Aldegundis*, chap. 19, 1044.
49. Santinelli, *Des femmes éplorées?*, 183–87.
50. BNF lat. 5275, fol. 49ᵛ. See also *Vita Aldegundis*, chap. 19, 1038; in this edition the characteristic of "senior" is absent: "Nec multu post tempore dum ambae sorores curam sibi commissi gregis gererent."
51. The passage appears in BNF lat. 5371, fol. 150ᵛ, 1st column; BNF lat. 11108, fol. 60ᵗ; Bibliothèque Municipale de Saint-Omer 724, fol. 163ᵛ, first column; Bibliothèque Municipale, Arras 567, fol. 59ᵛ, second column; Bibliothèque Municipale, Arras 569 fol. 56ᵛ first column. See also *Vita Aldegundis*, chap. 19, 1044 and *Vita sanctae Aldegundis*, chap. 19, PL 132, col. 869.

to underline that virtue, not age, should dictate who held monastic offices. That same tenth-century author, however, emphasizes the age of a nun who saw a vision. In both the ninth- and tenth-century versions of her *vita*, the abbess Aldegund appeared, breaking mass offerings into a chalice at an altar. Aldegund told the nun that because she herself was ill, the nun must tell the priest to give Aldegund communion. The early tenth-century writer provides an additional detail missing in the ninth-century manuscript version: he notes that this woman was "one of the mature nuns."[52] The surprising scene of a woman performing the actions of a priest at the altar may have called the reliability of the witness into question. By emphasizing her mature age, the author hoped to demonstrate the veracity of the tale. These examples from the *Vita Aldegundis* suggest that women in the religious life appreciated the maturity of their older sisters. The *Institutio sanctimonialium* further supports this respect for age because the *praelata*, who aided the abbess in her duties, was meant to be one of the older sisters. When these two officers carried out their responsibilities correctly, they helped to assure the health of the community in a way that complemented their pastoral care.[53] Abbesses and senior nuns, who had many activities to oversee, required organizational skills equal to their lay counterparts.

Some Carolingian widowed queens entered religious houses, but others remained active in secular political life, often as *deo sacrata*. Based on other early medieval queens who acted as powerful regents, one might expect that Carolingian queens also played that role, but Carolingian rulers left behind few young heirs.[54] Despite those circumstances often leaving widowed queens in potentially precarious situations, they played other prominent roles in the political sphere, frequently affecting marriage negotiations, the selection and designation of heirs, and negotiating family influence through control of land. During the early part of Charlemagne's reign, from 768 to 771, when he shared rule with his brother Carloman, Charlemagne's mother Bertha worked to keep peace between her two sons.[55] Arranging the marriage of Charlemagne to an unnamed daughter of the Lombard king Desiderius (757–774) was a means either to retain a balance of power between the two kings or to help Charlemagne to isolate Carloman politically. The marriage alliance also

---

52. "una de maturioribus ancillis." Compare BNF lat. 5275, fol. 50r–50v, to *Vita Aldegundis*, chap. 31, 1046; *Vita sanctae Aldegundis*, chap. 31, PL 132, col. 874.

53. Ibid., canon 7, 442. *Praelata* can simply be rendered as matron, suggesting that the holder of this office was older than many of her sisters.

54. Stafford, *QCD*, 156.

55. Einhard, *VK*, chap. 18, 22.

served to prevent a strong challenge to Charlemagne from his cousin Tassilo of Bavaria, married to another of Desiderius's daughters, Liutperga. When his brother Carloman died on December 6, 771, however, the exigency for the marriage passed, and Charlemagne set aside his Lombard partner.[56] Bertha spent her old age at her son's court, where he treated her with "the greatest respect."[57] When Louis the Stammerer, the great-grandson of Charlemagne, died in 879, his first wife Ansgard, whom he had set aside to marry Adelaide in 876, succeeded in promoting her sons, Louis and Carloman, as his heirs because her powerful family was able to back her claims. Adelaide subsequently fled with her son, the future Charles the Simple, to her own family, who helped her in the 890s to press her son's claims to the throne.[58]

Among the many duties of both abbesses and aristocratic laywomen, handling money and the general economic affairs of religious community and household required at least a rudimentary knowledge of arithmetic and the ability to allocate and organize resources. The extensive interest in numerology that Dhuoda exhibits in the *Liber manualis* demonstrates that women could obtain skill in mathematics. Dhuoda must have employed some math in keeping track of household finances: she asked that William, upon her death, pay her debts to both Jews and Christians, which she had incurred by taking out loans to provide "many necessities" (*multas necessitates*) to protect the interests of her absent husband.[59] The possibility that elite women could take out large loans suggests social recognition of their power over the family purse strings. Increasing evidence for the use of currency has led some scholars to believe that a money economy coexisted with a trade and barter system at this time.[60] Sources concerning aristocratic women support the use of money in the Carolingian world. When young Aldegund no longer had alms to distribute to the poor, she thought that she ought to give away the money that her mother, Bertilla, hid. As a saint, Aldegund resisted this temptation to steal, and learning from her mother's bad example, she later became a generous donor to the poor.[61] The evidence found in hagiography has support in normative texts. Queens often exerted control over the treasury, and they would have reviewed records of financial transactions and production on their estates as outlined in the *Capitulare de villis* and demonstrated in the inventories of royal estates

---

56. Nelson, "Making a Difference," 177–86.
57. Einhard, *VK*, chap. 18, 23.
58. Stafford, *QCD*, 160.
59. Dhuoda, *LM*, 10.4, 226.
60. Blackburn, "Money and Coinage," and Verhulst, "Economic Organisation," McCormick, *Origins of the European Economy*, 319–84.
61. *Vita Aldegundis*, chap. 17, 1044.

in the *Brevium exempla*. The information in the latter document reflects the requirements of chapter 55 of the former:

> We wish that the *iudices* should record, in one document, whatever they have provided or appropriated or set aside for our use, and, in another document, what payments they have made; and they shall notify us by letter of what remains.[62]

In fact, according to this capitulary, *iudices* were to keep quite a few records and make reports to the crown, although it is unclear whether they were to deliver the reports in oral or written form.[63] The king and queen instructed the *iudex* that each year, after he determined the total amount of revenue for that year, he send to them a part of the royal revenue during Lent before Palm Sunday.[64] Such a statement indicates the existence of or at least the desire for careful oral or written reports. Aristocratic women may have inspected similar records for their estates or kept track of reports made to them about supplies and production, if for no other reason than their responsibility for hospitality.

Elite women had a degree of supervisory power over family estates and households. Their control involved keeping track of money and goods, allocating resources, and in some circumstances traveling to inspect estates. The frequent absences of men from family lands argue for a prominent female role in such supervision. Aristocratic women had not only the opportunity to manage people and resources but also the need to ensure sufficient food and drink and adequate household furnishings for their provision of hospitality. Thus, they must have played a major role in management of the domestic sphere.

Hospitality

Like the rich display of women's bodies and their adornment, aristocratic provision of hospitality served male purposes. The actions of women provided prestige and rank to men, and though their duties of hospitality remain in the background of surviving sources, they were essential to the exertion of power by their families. By offering hospitality to those who visited a family's estates or a female religious house, women had opportunities to impress

---

62. *CV,* chap. 55, 61.
63. Ibid., for written records chap. 30 and 62, pp. 58, 61–62; for reports of some kind chap. 13, 25, 29, 31, 66, and 69, pp. 57–58, 62.
64. Ibid., chap. 28, 58.

and thereby influence their guests. Food and drink were central to the development of aristocratic bonds, and feasting and drinking offered opportunities for aristocrats to work out relations of status, friendship, peace, and patronage.[65] Women played powerful roles in these situations. Links between women and food in the later Middle Ages are quite clear because of the rich information late medieval sources provide and the importance of the cult of Corpus Christi.[66] Early medieval women also had close associations with food and especially with providing drink.[67] Although *vitae* from the Carolingian period do not manifest the same quantity or type of food and fasting miracles found in late medieval *vitae*, Carolingian sources reveal an expectation that elite women help to clarify social relations and facilitate the political dealings that occurred over drink and food. Through their supervision of household goods and furnishings, they also may have been responsible for the physical atmosphere of such occasions, thereby affecting social relations. Conspicuous consumption increasingly allowed early medieval aristocrats to demonstrate their rank and "strivers" to raise their social position.[68] Palaces, villas, and estates were critical points of entry into the aristocratic world and the locations where lords carried out their duties.[69] Rituals of supplication and pardon paint a rich picture of elite relations and point out the need for a lord to demonstrate how much he stood apart from any petitioners and from others in his house or court.[70] The arrangement of the goods found in the halls, courtyards, and rooms in which these rituals took place could allow a man to show his high status. Aristocratic women's provision of hospitality, connected mainly to their supervisory place in the economy of the family, had spiritual, political, social, and cultural implications.

Law or religious duty mandated certain kinds of hospitality. Christian beliefs required that religious and secular houses provide pilgrims with food

---

65. Gerd Althoff, "Der frieden-, bündnis-, und gemeinschaftstiftende Charakter des Mahles im frühen Mittelalter," in *Essen und Trinken in Mittelalter und Neuzeit*, eds. Irmgard Bitsch et al. (Sigmaringen, 1987), 13–25; Bullough, *Friends, Neighbors, and Fellow Drinkers;* Michel Rouche, "Les repas de fête à l'époque carolingienne."

66. Bell, *Holy Anorexia;* Bynum, *Holy Feast and Holy Fast;* Rubin, *Corpus Christi.*

67. Nelson, "Family, Gender, and Sexuality," 166; Coon, *SF,* 121; Bonnie Effros, *Creating Community with Food and Drink in Merovingian Gaul* (New York, 2002), 39–54.

68. Fleming, "The New Wealth, the New Rich, and the New Political Style in Late Anglo-Saxon England"; idem, "Lords and Labour," 121–37.

69. Jacobsen, "Herrschaftliches Bauen in der Karolingerzeit," 91. Jacobsen notes that the words referring to royal or aristocratic estates, houses, or palaces (*villa, curtis, castrum, oppidum, civitas, urbs*) have varying connotations depending upon the origin and date of the documents in which they are mentioned. Rather than enter into any discussion of the precise differences among these terms, I consider all locations of aristocratic and royal interaction.

70. Koziol, *Begging Pardon and Favor,* 46–51.

and a place to rest and that they give alms in the form of food, clothing, and sometimes money to the poor, widowed, and orphaned.[71] These occasions provided opportunities to provide hospitality to outsiders, acts that required use of items for whose practical preparation women were responsible. Naturally, such outward hospitality was not solely the duty of women; men, too, were enjoined to provide alms and hospitality.[72] In his *De institutione laicali*, Jonas of Orléans urged men to remember their obligation to provide hospitality to strangers and pilgrims, noting that many were ignoring their responsibilities in this regard. Particularly those with large houses should provide hospitality.[73] Especially because this statement comes from his book concerning marriage and family, Jonas implies that the lord's duty extended to the whole household. In men's frequent absences, women and *iudices* had to provide alms and hospitality; they may even have been the primary providers of these services. Although Jonas, like the *Waltharius* poet, assigns primary responsibility for providing hospitality to men, women almost certainly carried out these activities much, if not most, of the time.

Reception of visitors was a virtuous act. An example from *De institutione laicali* is a quotation from Ambrose's first book about Abraham, which Jonas included in his discussion of how men ought to honor their wives. "In front of the tent [Abraham] watched the arrival of the guests; inside the tent Sarah watched with the shyness of a woman, and she chastely exerted herself in *opera muliebria*."[74] In the Vulgate (Gen. 18:6) she is preparing food for guests, who are in fact a visitation from God that tells the couple that Sarah will conceive. The Bible treats Sarah's work on behalf of the guests as virtuous even before she and Abraham know of the specific importance of these visitors. Welcoming anyone in one's home was potentially an act of piety, and in this instance Sarah's particular task of preparation of food for guests stood as a model to later women to do the same.

Obligations of hospitality like those Jonas wrote about also appeared in capitularies and other legal documents connected with Carolingian religious reform. The General Capitulary for the *missi* of 802 explained that obligations concerning pilgrims extended beyond the wealthy:

> We order that no one in all our kingdom, whether rich or poor, should dare to deny hospitality to pilgrims: that is, no one should refuse roof, hearth,

---

71. Payer, *Von der Gastfreundschaft zum Gasthaus*, 21ff.
72. Jonas, *Institutione*, 3.10, col. 251; Dhuoda, *LM*, 4.8, 150.
73. Jonas, *Institutione*, 2.29, cols. 231–33.
74. Ibid., 2.5, col. 178. In Ambrose's work the original text was in book 1, chap. 5.

and water to any pilgrims who are traveling the land on God's account, or to anyone who is journeying for love of God or for the salvation of his soul.[75]

The same chapter emphasizes the spiritual rewards for those who give such hospitality. Providing shelter and sustenance to visiting religious men and women was also an obligation, and Carolingian sources reveal that these same occasions could become opportunities for advancement.

Hospitality comes up frequently in texts from the period of Anglo-Saxon missionary work in the borderlands of the Frankish realms. Addula, for example, welcomed Boniface to Pfalzel.[76] An Anglo-Saxon abbess, Aelfed of Whitby, wrote to Addula sometime before 713 to request that she receive at Pfalzel another Anglo-Saxon abbess who was traveling on pilgrimage to Rome.[77] Sometime between 739 and 741, Boniface's students Denehard, Lull, and Burchard wrote to the abbess Cuniberga to request her prayer, and in the same letter, Lull asked that she receive at her community two freedmen, Begiloc and Man, whom Boniface and he wanted to travel to Rome. "And if someone should want to keep them from their way without justice, we urge you to deign to defend them."[78] Once a guest entered the host's house, the host became responsible for protecting the guest.[79] Cena, an otherwise unknown female correspondent of Boniface, wrote a letter to him sometime between 723 and 754, sending along gifts and offering her hospitality to any of his followers who might travel into her region.[80]

Providing appropriately for guests of varying status was of great concern to religious women and men. Once when Boniface and Willibrord were reportedly visiting Herlindis and Renula at their community of Aldeneik, the sisters discovered that they had run out of wine, but their prayers miraculously caused wine to overflow from the once nearly empty cask.[81] Certainly this miracle owes much to biblical and earlier hagiographic models, but the expectations it reveals about hospitality conform to examples of female hospitality in other sources.

The *Institutio sanctimonialium* put great emphasis on hospitality and care of the poor. In cases of illness or the need to provide hospitality, the religious

75. *Capitulare missorum generale*, chap. 27, MGH Capit. 1, 96.
76. Liudger, *Vita Gregorii*, chap. 2, 67–68.
77. MGH Ep. S, 1, no. 8, 3.
78. Ibid., no. 49, 80.
79. Goetz, "Social and Military Institutions," 479.
80. MGH Ep. S, 1, no. 97, 217–8.
81. *Vita Herlinde et Renulae*, chap. 13, 389.

women could have food on their own rather than during communal meals.[82] This allowance contrasts with the rule's seemingly strict separation of the religious community from the world. Because of enduring family bonds, many of the frequent visitors and guests were probably related to the *sanctimoniales* or in some way bound to the community through prayer and donation.[83] Other guests doubtless included pilgrims and travelers. The *sanctimoniales* were to set aside a tenth of their donations from the local community for care of the poor. Receiving the poor and pilgrims in female religious houses created occasions of spiritually meaningful gestures as the *sanctimoniales* were meant to wash the feet of widows and the female poor during times of fasting in imitation of Christ's washing of his disciples' feet in John 13:14.[84] Thomas Schilp has suggested that female houses contained areas specifically set aside for administering such care to poor women and possibly allowing them to spend the night. These acts may have helped the *sanctimoniales* in their fight against the sin of greed (*avaritia*).[85] These religious women offered various kinds of hospitality, depending upon the guests. The acts of eating with their families helped to maintain the strength of their familial bonds while providing bodily care to poor women confirmed their membership in a religious community focused on selfless devotion to God and doing good works. Their acts of hospitality made the *sanctimoniales* members of two communities, related because of the women's entrance into the religious life. The authors of the rule, nevertheless, worried that the women would overindulge, perhaps particularly in the presence of their wealthy guests. In the first canon, they quote Jerome on the dangers of excessive drinking and of eating meat, an apt warning considering the elite background of the women in the communities under this rule.[86] Members of Carolingian religious communities were among the key aristocratic players of their day, and the political, religious, and social interactions involved in entertaining visitors could have high stakes.

Similar issues were involved in hospitality extended by laypeople to secular visitors. Sometimes such hospitality had more to do with political exigency than with virtue. According to the *Capitulare de villis*, elite households had

---

82. *IS*, canon 13, 447.

83. In this book, I use the term *sanctimoniales* to refer specifically to women living under the rule of the *Institutio sanctimonialium* in order to differentiate them from religious women living under the *Rule of St. Benedict* and from *deo sacratae*, other women consecrated to God. Variation in use of Latin terms for religious women and variation in their practices complicates making clear divisions among early medieval women who followed religious vocations. Post-medieval changes in church practice also make finding appropriate modern English equivalents difficult; thus I also use the word "nun" rather broadly.

84. Ibid., canon 28.

85. Schilp, *NW,* 97.

86. *IS*, canon 1; Schilp, *NW,* 80.

political and legal obligations to provide hospitality to *missi* and other passing officers of the king:

> And the count in his district, or the men whose traditional custom it has been to provide for our *missi* and their retinues, shall continue in this manner henceforward to provide them with pack-horses and all other necessities, so that they can travel to and from the palace suitably with dignity.[87]

The same chapter of this capitulary states that those same *missi* and their retinues are under no circumstances to stay in royal houses. The king seems to shift financial and protective responsibility for the *missi* to the aristocracy. The Capitulary of Herstal of 779 makes one form of obligatory hospitality a sort of incentive or punishment. Counts who did not dispense justice in their districts were to provide for a *missus* in their own households until justice could be administered. If a vassal did not mete out justice, then both count and *missus* were to stay at the vassal's house, living at his expense until justice was done.[88] Because one had to provide for his retinue, having a *missus* in one's house was expensive. The actual repercussions of a poor report from a *missus* are nearly impossible to measure, but one can at least imagine that the family would not have wanted to make a poor impression. The family may also have wanted to show off its wealth and power to a *missus* or other guest, and may have taken the opportunity to persuade its guests to agree with or support certain political goals. Creating a bond with a guest could offer a family an opportunity to further its members' own interests. For that reason, families had to make careful choices regarding hospitality.

A concern with the quality of food and drink is clear throughout the *Capitulare de villis* but especially in chapter 24. "Every *iudex* ought to take pains so that anything he has to provide for our table is good and of the best quality, and everything he supplies be as carefully and cleanly prepared as possible."[89] Here the *iudex* only provides food, and presumably the queen or a high-ranking servant made choices about what exactly to serve prominent guests. On an aristocratic estate or in a religious house, these decisions fell to those with supervisory power over food and drink, almost certainly to the mistress or abbess, even if they only discussed them with the cook or other servants. An anecdote from Notker's *Gesta Karoli* indicates that men were sometimes also concerned about these issues. A bishop unexpectedly had to provide hospitality to Charlemagne on a day the king could eat no meat, but without advance

---

87. CV, chap. 27, 58.
88. *Capitulare Haristallense*, chap. 21, MGH Capit. 2.1, 51.
89. *CV*, chap. 24, 58.

warning, the bishop was unable to serve fish. The embarrassed bishop instead provided Charlemagne with fine cheese for his meal. When the bishop noticed that the king tossed aside the rind, the best part of that cheese, he pointed it out to Charlemagne. The king enjoyed the cheese so much that he asked the bishop to send two cartloads of it to Aachen each year. The bishop then worried he would not be able to send cheeses of the same quality, but the wise king offered the sage advice of cutting open each cheese to check before sending it on.[90] This tale naturally is meant to convey the wisdom of a good king, but it indicates that the elite in the Carolingian world cared about the quality of food provided on hospitable occasions. Hosts especially wished to ensure that meals pleased important guests.

Much as Walter used expectations concerning feasting and drinking in order to make his escape, women could use their supervisory authority over servants and goods to subvert social norms in order to gain something. Hucbald of Amand's *Vita Rictrudis* offers a rich example of using hospitality as the means to a personal end. According to Hucbald he wrote this *vita* with no earlier version to consult.[91] Though he borrowed episodes from a number of other *vitae*, he almost certainly relied on his own expectations of the way events might have unfolded in order to write parts of the *vita*, particularly a feast Rictrud held.[92]

After the death of her husband Rictrud decided to take the veil, but King Dagobert initially refused, urging her to marry another magnate.[93] In order to get her way, Rictrud invited the king to a feast at her villa.

> She encouraged the king to imagine that she wanted to yield to his will and arranged a banquet of sumptuous splendor suitable for a king at her estate in the villa called Baireius. She invited the king and his optimates and, with the salty seasoning of the banquet, they all enjoyed the sweetness of her talk.[94]

This passage suggests that abundant and tasty food could render discussion easier, sweeter. The food makes Rictrud's speech all the more palatable. Furthermore, the passage reveals that the atmosphere, created by the people

---

90. Notker, *GK*, 1.15, 18–19.

91. Hucbald, *Vita Rictrudis*, chap. 1, 81; L. van der Essen, "Hucbald de saint Amand (c. 840–930) et sa place dans le mouvement hagiographique médiéval," *Revue d'histoire ecclésiastique* 19 (1923): 333–51, at 342.

92. van der Essen, *Etude critique et littéraire sur les vitae des saints mérovingiens de l'ancienne Belgique*, 262–64; Platelle, "Le thème," 515; Smith, "The Hagiography of Hucbald," 538–40.

93. Hucbald, *Vita Rictrudis*, chap. 13, 84.

94. Ibid., chap. 14, 84.

present and the fine food and possibly by a "magnificence" produced by her hall's furnishings, made a difference to the degree to which she could convince the king of her supposedly good intentions. Drink also aided her in making the king believe that she would abide by his demand.

> First, she asked the king to allow her to do what she wanted in her own house and to use that power freely in his presence. He then agreed quickly, thinking that, with her raised cup, she would command him to drink, as is the custom with many; that she would please him and his companions.[95]

By presenting wine, beer, or mead to others in a particular order, a woman could indicate the status of those present, make peace among those quarreling, and direct attention to her own petitions. Hucbald refers to her command to Dagobert to drink as "the custom with many."

Similar female actions occur in other early medieval sources, most famously Queen Wealhtheow's actions in the mead hall in *Beowulf*.[96] These occurrences constitute a trope in early medieval literature, but they clearly had great meaning to audiences, who either personally experienced similar situations or understood these conventional female actions. In his *Historia Langobardorum* of the 790s, Paul the Deacon wrote that Theudelinda, daughter of the Bavarian king Garibald, offered a Lombard king Autheri a drink, unaware that he was testing her to determine her suitability as a wife. He wished to receive wine from her because she would be serving him in the future as his queen.[97] In his poem in honor of Louis the Pious, Ermold the Black described Judith preparing a picnic in the woods for her husband's hunting party. While the men hunted, she built a sort of arbor using cloths and the available branches. After the hunt, the men joined her for food and drink.[98] This motif reveals much about the understanding of social relations among the early medieval elite and reflects women's responsibility for hospitality. Feasting together could signify a common goal or mind-set, and words spoken over a toast could convey deeper social and political meanings. Rictrud took advantage of the expectations surrounding this custom to influence the king's expectations

---

95. Ibid.

96. Wealtheow offered drink to Beowulf, honoring him with a speech and creating an optimal situation for him to make a speech after drinking from the cup. Later she offered her husband Hrothgar a drink and then immediately urged him to leave Heorot to his kin, particularly to his young sons, implying that Beowulf ought not become his heir. *Beowulf*, 23–24, lines 607–41, and 44–5, lines 1168–91. See also Enright, *Lady with a Mead Cup*, 4–12.

97. Paul the Deacon, *Historia Langobardorum*, 134.

98. Ermold, *In honorem*, 184, lines 2418–37.

of her actions. After receiving the king's permission to do as she liked, she had the prelate Amand come out, and she took the veil immediately. The angry king "left the feast, abandoning the disagreeable food."[99] Rictrud's formerly pleasing food became unwelcome once she disrupted the feast's expected course. Depicting a woman using hospitality to foil a man's plans, this episode indicates that female hospitality could be a powerful means for women to gain their own ends or those of their families.

Sharing food and drink was a sign of peace and a recognition of relationships among those at a table. Even if negotiation of power and status took place during them, feasts were meant to be peaceful, hence the ongoing concern in early medieval texts with preventing violence among men who were drinking or eating. In 870, after Zwentibald, the nephew of Rastiz, duke of Moravia, commended himself and his kingdom to Carloman, his uncle plotted to strangle him at a banquet "when he was not expecting any attack."[100] Inviting people to dinner only to kill them, or trick them as in the cases of Rictrud and Walter, was a trope of early medieval literature; its power as an image resulted from the subversion of the norms of hospitality. Those attending feasts probably did not regularly anticipate violence, but Carolingian texts addressed the dangers of excessive drink. Lay mirrors warned men of the dangers of overindulgence in food and drink, particularly as such excess revealed the sin of gluttony.[101] Paulinus of Aquileia in his *Liber exhortationis* warned that excessive drink could result in foolish behavior, fornication, and murder.[102] Jonas of Orléans noted that drink could cause one to give false testimony.[103] Overindulgence in food, drink, sumptuous display, and music marked a bishop's feast in Notker's *Vita Karoli*. This bishop was trying to cover for the fact that he had given a terrible sermon before two of Charlemagne's courtiers; he wished to impress them with magnificence so that they would give the king a good report. Though he regretted these actions the next day upon becoming sober, he managed to impress the king's men sufficiently that they gave a glowing account.[104] Notker's tale functioned as a warning against immoderation. Just as some religious women learned of the dangers of drinking from the *Institutio sanctimonialium*, laywomen read or heard prescriptive and literary works warning of those dangers, especially pertinent to their role in the provision of drink. Eberhard of Friuli and his wife Gisela left a text on

---

99. Hucbald, *Vita Rictrudis*, chap. 14, 84.

100. *AF*, p. 70.

101. Alcuin, *LVV*, chap. 28, col. 633; Paulinus, *LE*, chap. 36, cols. 234–35; Jonas, *Institutione*, 3.6, col. 244.

102. Paulinus, *LE*, chap. 37, cols. 236–39.

103. Jonas, *Institutione*, 2.26, col. 225.

104. Notker, *GK*, 1.18, 22–52.

sobriety to their daughter Judith.[105] Such a work may have aided her in setting standards of behavior in her own house. This bequest indicates that others expected women to enforce certain norms of behavior, to encourage virtue among those around them. Walter expected that Hildegund, for example, would remain sober while others drank around her at the Hun's palace; she was capable of participating in his deception. Rictrud's case demonstrates an expectation that women could similarly take advantage of such opportunities to attain their desires. They could use domestic virtue to gain a desideratum; in *vitae* such female desires naturally further promoted virtuous behavior. Similarly, Addula's commendation of Gregory during Boniface's visit shows that women could use hospitality to advance the interests of their families. Women could be as active as men in gaining what they wanted through negotiation; they did so, however, through their expected roles as providers of food and drink in an atmosphere conducive to the negotiation of bonds, status, and familial goals.

A richly decorated hall or court could help to provide an appropriate atmosphere for the creation of aristocratic bonds. Excavations at the monastery of San Vincenzo al Volturno, about 200 kilometers southeast of Rome, revealed a richly decorated complex of buildings for housing and entertaining guests; their construction mainly took place in the first half of the ninth century. John Mitchell has suggested that the monks set out purposely to impress important visitors through their choices of building construction and decoration in order to encourage donations to their house.[106] The lay elite in the Carolingian Empire may have made comparable choices with the goals of pleasing others and developing bonds. Women probably made decisions about the placement of items in a house and supervised their care as well as selecting and keeping track of them. Many household goods appear in written sources. The illustrations of manuscripts and archaeological evidence provide further evidence for the furnishings of early medieval homes, particularly the areas where hospitality was offered: the court or hall, courtyards, and bedrooms.

Though not the most obvious site, the bedroom was a potential locus of hospitality given possible overnight guests. The various *missi*, visitors, and pilgrims who stayed the night suggest the need for the elite to have been well-equipped with bed furnishings. Furthermore, regardless of the number of guests a particular family received, having rich household furnishings served as a marker of aristocratic status. Even if the objects never actually served to inform others of the family's wealth and status, they would have contributed to the family's own self-awareness (*Selbstbewusstsein*) of its aristocratic power.

---

105. *CAC*, no. 1, 4.
106. Mitchell, "Monastic Guest Quarters and Workshops," 131–43.

The *Capitulare de villis* includes beds, mattresses, pillows, and bed linen among the items that each estate should keep in its storeroom.[107] The inventories of the royal estates in the *Brevium exempla* each list a set of bedding. The third (unnamed) royal estate also had a pillow, a mattress, and two linen sheets; the set of bedding at the estate at Treola included a mattress, a pillow, a bed, and a blanket.[108] These inventories probably exclude bedding already in regular use or more would have been listed. Instead, they seem to indicate that the estates stood ready for the arrival of guests by having spare bed linen at hand, although some aristocrats may have brought their own linen with them.[109] Although the inventories give little indication of the bedding's quality, its possible use by prominent guests suggests fine materials. It may have been as rich as the decorations of aristocratic halls and equally instrumental in impressing guests.

Heiric of Auxerre's poem "St. Germanus' Bed," composed in 875–77, provides an antithetical image of the sort of bedclothes an aristocrat may have expected in the early Middle Ages. This poem, a versification of Constantius of Lyons's late fifth-century *Vita Sancti Germani*, that borrows heavily from Virgil, provides an image of a humble, though obviously idealized, bed.[110]

> His bed was a simple affair, made up of planks joined in a square,
> Filled up to the edges with a scattering of hard ash left by the flames,
> For as he lay there the dead cinders had gradually grown firm
> Under his weight, supporting his back on their unyielding surface,
> While hard bristles provided a bed-spread
> Under a flimsy cloak; where most of his neck
> Rose up to the crown of his noble head
> Nothing ever lifted or supported it.[111]

If the ashes and hard bristles—signs of sanctity and penance—are disregarded, the bed seems the simple sort that may have endured for centuries, from before Constantius's composition of the original *vita* and well into the Carolingian period during which Heiric wrote his poetic version. The image of a lack of head support and the uncomfortable bedclothes suggests that

---

107. *CV,* chap. 42, 59.

108. *BE,* 52–55.

109. Pierre Riché has suggested that aristocrats carried portable beds and bedding, tents, drapes (*cortinae*), and tapestries (*tapetia*) in their baggage when traveling because Gerald of Aurillac appears to have done just that. Riché, *Daily Life in the World of Charlemagne,* 160. Odo, *Vita Geraldi,* 1.26, col. 657.

110. See Godman's notes in *PCR,* 306–9.

111. Heiric of Auxerre, in *PCR,* 306–7, lines 113–20. Translation is Godman's.

aristocrats probably desired just the opposite in their beds—soft pillows and covers. The five wooden bed frames that survived in the Gokstad ship burial give an indication of the appearance of beds for the early medieval elite. The low four-postered frames had wooden slats across the bottom. Wooden pins and interlocking pieces held the structure together.[112]

Manuscript illustrations of beds may confirm this image from Heiric's poem. Such depictions provide some indication of household furnishings, although they necessitate great caution because some were directly copied from antique manuscripts. In its most simple form, a bed consisted of a feather mattress set on the ground or more frequently on a wooden plank bed. The wood was rarely painted. Bedclothes in manuscript illuminations were richer than the description of Germanus's bed. They usually consisted of monochromatic sheets, feather bed, and cushions. The gamut of colors was limited to beige or white and mauve or purple. An exceptionally lavish illustration in the Bible of Charles the Bald depicts a red feather bed with a motif of ocelli around points forming a solar motif. One or two cushions, usually in the same colors as the feather bed, support the sleeper's head.[113] The Stuttgart Psalter has a similar image of an elaborate bed, which may reflect actual aristocratic beds.[114]

Rich bedclothes figure into descriptions of other opulent household furnishings found in Carolingian sources. In his sixth-century *Regula sanctarum virginum* Caesarius of Arles expressly forbade religious women from having the luxuries of colored carpets, decorated bedspreads, silver pieces (for purposes other than holy service), curtains, and jewelry.[115] Such concerns continued in Frankish lands. Among the personal items that Aldegund gave to the poor and for church decoration upon entering the religious life may have been some household goods.[116] The *Capitulare de villis* listed tablecloths and seat covers.[117] The inventories of the *Brevium exempla* included tablecloths and napkins, one generic cloth from an unnamed royal estate, and a seat cover at Treola.[118] These items could have created a rich, comfortable atmosphere in the house. Depictions of napkins for dining are quite rare. Tables, though also uncommon, appear in various forms: round and square, high and low.[119] Some have feet in the shape of lion's heads and claws, as does the late eighth-century

112. Nicolaysen, *The Viking-Ship Discovered at Gokstad in Norway*, plate VII, figures 1 and 2.
113. Danièle Alexandre-Bidon and Perrine Mane, "Le vie quotidienne à travers les enluminures carolingiennes," in *Un village*, 340–53, esp. 344.
114. Fol. 30ᵛ.
115. Heidebrecht and Nolte, "Leben im Kloster," 84, 87.
116. *Vita Aldegundis*, chap. 20, 1044.
117. *CV*, chap. 42, 59.
118. *BE*, 52–55.
119. Alexandre-Bidon and Mane, "Le vie quotidienne," 343.

Dagobert throne; both throne and manuscript depictions draw on classical forms. In Charlemagne's will, among his possessions were one gold and three silver tables. The silver ones had elaborate decorations; the two with outlines of Constantinople and Rome were sent to the Church of St. Peter in Rome and Ravenna's episcopal seat, respectively. The third, which had a depiction of the universe, and the gold one were to be sold to increase the lot of his wealth that he had set aside for charity.[120] Such highly decorated tables were probably uncommon, but they indicate that some tables were plated or decorated with fine metal. Seating in illustrations varied considerably: benches, thrones, stools, and x-chairs. Images of thrones indicated majesty, but other forms of seating were used for dining, sewing, and writing. Seats often appear with decorated footrests and large cushions. Images of textile furnishings, curtains, and hanging cloths are also rare. Often decorated with ocelli or a large stripe edged with a border of contrasting color, they could hang in front of a door, around a bed, or over a pulpit on a dais. The walls in illuminations were furnished with miniatures, murals, and tapestries; the floors with woven wicker mats.[121]

Although the layout of Carolingian palaces remains rather mysterious, something is known about the decoration of the *aula regia*, the location of various imperial gatherings and celebrations. At Aachen and Ingelheim, these rooms had beautiful frescoes on the wall.[122] In his 828 description of the court following Harold the Dane's baptism in 826, Ermold the Black provided an impression of its opulence that highlighted its function as a place conducive to the creation of bonds, a locus for gift exchange, and for the meeting of the most important people in the Carolingian world. Following the baptism, the Danish couple admired much that they saw but especially the wealth of the king. Drawing from that treasure Louis then gave a lavish feast with various kinds of food and wine, some served on gold vessels. Ermold then carefully describes how everyone was seated.[123] Though this scene draws heavily upon classical motifs, it reveals an expectation of feasting and drinking upon such an important occasion, even if the details result from literary borrowing, rather than contemporary observation. One can understand the feast as a means of guaranteeing Harold's loyalty both to Louis and to his new faith.

Louis continued to show his hospitality by inviting Harold to hunt with him. After Ermold described all the men mounting their horses and preparing

---

120. Einhard, *VK*, chap. 33, 40.

121. Alexandre-Bidon and Mane, "Le vie quotidienne," 344–45.

122. Ermold, *In honorem*, 162–64, lines 2124–63; Jacobsen, "Herrschaftliches Bauen in der Karolingerzeit," 93.

123. Ermold, *In honorem*, 172–73 and 178–80, lines 2322–55.

for the chase, he noted that Judith and Charles the Bald, then a little boy, rode out with them. Upon reaching the woods, little Charles called out for arms so that he could join his father in the hunt. Both his mother and his tutor refused to give him their permission, but some men captured a deer for him to kill on foot.[124] This scene draws heavily upon the fourth book of Virgil's *Aeneid*, but similar to the description of the lavish feast, it indicates that hunting could be a means of providing hospitality. Not only did it provide a diversion for Harold, but also it helped to seal the new relationship between Louis and Harold. Hunting was highly dangerous, making it unsurprising that young Charles was not allowed to participate. The possible risks and the fact that men who hunted were armed meant participation constituted a bond of trust among the hunters. Furthermore, descriptions of such large hunting parties are unusual in Carolingian sources; such an undertaking, even if it did not transpire so closely to the events of the *Aeneid*, marked the importance of the occasion. A similar description is in the anonymous *Karolus Magnus et Leo papa*, in which Charlemagne and his family line up on horseback in preparation for a hunt.[125] As the discussion of much of this passage in the first chapter demonstrated, these descriptions—drawn just as heavily from Virgil as those in Ermold's poem—showed off the wealth of the king. His daughters allowed Charlemagne another means to flaunt his good fortune, and their presence marks the importance of this event. In both the scenes from *Karolus Magnus et Leo papa* and *In Honor of Louis*, the authors lay the emphasis not on the hunting itself but rather on the preparations and pageantry of the occasion. These scenes therefore clearly indicate the great importance of appearances and hospitality among the Carolingian aristocracy.

While the men were away hunting, Judith prepared the repast described above, which she served under her improvised shelter. After the hunt the men, including Louis and Harold, joined her there for food and wine. Only after refreshing themselves did the party return to the palace with the trophies of the hunt. This section of the poem does not appear to draw much on antique sources and may therefore resemble actual practice among the Carolingian elite.[126] A chance to recover from the physical exertion and danger of the hunt through eating and drinking eased the transition from the forest back to the palace. In this case a woman arranged this event, which suggests a nascent form of courtliness. The move from the masculine, physical arena of the hunt back to the confines of the court occurs under female direction. Her provision of food and drink returns the men to that social atmosphere while again

---

124. Ibid., 182–84, lines 2378–81, 2394–415.
125. *Karolus Magnus*, 72–78, lines 182–267.
126. Ermold, *In honorem*, 184–85, n. 1; 186, line 2438.

serving to show off Louis's wealth and his ability to muster resources. Serving this picnic out in the woods required the help of servants and advance planning. Royal hospitality, therefore, involved both lavish display and the provision of much food and drink.

The fine, comfortable furnishings of palaces and estates contributed to hospitality by positively influencing guests. Aristocratic women's responsibility for such items gave them crucial roles in the development of social and political bonds. By displaying their family's wealth and power and creating a comfortable and peaceful atmosphere, perhaps similarly to Judith's provision of shelter, food, and drink in the forest, they could help realize their own goals as well as those of their families. Extending hospitality also contributed to the maintenance of bonds among aristocrats, much as the hospitality Louis the Pious provided to Harold sealed their new relationship. As elite markers, rich furnishings could impress others, as Louis's wealth amazed Harold and his wife, and even if no guests ever used a family's store of such items, the knowledge among family members that they possessed such wealth contributed to their own awareness of their status and power. The importance of food and drink in Louis's and Judith's hospitality indicates another area over which elite women had authority. Aristocratic women probably ensured that production on their estates could support their hospitality and their household's daily needs in terms of food, drink, lighting, and clothing. Although *iudices* and other higher-level workers oversaw much work on estates, women were almost certainly active in some areas because of their responsibility for hospitality and management. Thus, hospitality can act as a guide in determining the areas of estate production in which women were most active.

Production of Goods, Food, and Drink

Hospitality and management duties helped to give aristocratic women control over human resources as well as craft and agricultural output. Naturally, the lower a woman's status, the more involved she would have been in actual production. As mentioned earlier, men had primary supervision of some activities, such as hunting. Others may have been specifically female; according to Carolingian evidence, however, textile production was the only certainly female craft. Other areas probably fell under the supervision of both men and women. Consideration of these possible responsibilities makes clear the complexity of managing a Carolingian estate. When read with female responsibility for hospitality as a guiding principle, the evidence of the *Capitulare de villis* and the *Brevium exempla* can yield much information about the work of women on estates and in households. Of course, not every estate featured every activity discussed here, some of which were seasonal. Together, however, these activities present an image of early medieval life on an estate and clear indications of the way aspects of the early medieval economy functioned on the ground.

Care of horses, dogs, and falcons was probably not a primarily female responsibility given these animals' close associations with hunting. Because the main means of transportation in the Carolingian world, after walking, was riding horses, most estates must have had stables. Aristocratic men rode horses in hunting and warfare, two male domains. Not surprising, Carolingian sources almost never associate women with the care of horses. The poet of *Karolus Magnus et Leo papa* described Charlemagne's daughters riding horses, but they did not go on the actual hunt.[127] The *Capitulare de villis* mentions that the king or the queen could send commands to hunters and falconers directly or through the butler or seneschal.[128] The authority of the queen to give such orders, especially through these two officers, probably derived from her responsibility for the provision of hospitality; her interests extended both to entertaining guests while appropriately displaying the wealth of the family and to providing meat for gatherings of aristocrats. Here the hunts in questions were probably not the lavish affairs described in court poetry but rather more similar to the relatively frequent royal hunts mentioned in annals, chronicles, and other sources.[129] These hunts probably provided meat and valuable practice for battle and were not appropriate events for women. The detail concerning the care of horses in the *Capitulare de villis*, nevertheless, demonstrates an emphasis among the elite upon maintaining a healthy stable of horses.[130] Presumably riders, male and female alike, took interest in the care of their own mounts, but the stables' centrality to male pursuits meant that running them was a prestigious position for a man.[131] Similarly, care of dogs and falcons seems to have fallen almost entirely to men. Almost no Carolingian documents associate women with the care of dogs, which were mainly work animals used for hunting and shepherding.[132] When Dhuoda mentioned the way puppies eat the crumbs that fall from their master's table, she provided an image readily understandable to a male youth like William.[133] Men seem

---

127. *Karolus Magnus*, 74, lines 212–14.
128. *CV*, chap. 47, 60; see also chap. 36, 59.
129. Hennebicque, "Espaces sauvages," 47–52.
130. *CV*, chap. 13–15, 57; 50, 60.
131. The count of the stable or constable became one of the most powerful offices in the kingdoms that were heirs to the Carolingian Empire.
132. Chapter 69 urges finding and killing wolf puppies in May with poison, hooks, pits, and dogs. *CV*, 62.
133. She drew upon Mark 7:28 and Matthew 15:27. Dhuoda, *LM*, 1.2, 60.

often to have developed strong attachments to their dogs, no doubt because of their hunting skills and companionship.[134] Although reformers railed against male clerics for keeping hunting dogs, they offered no similar condemnations of women bringing animals with them into religious communities, and contemporary sources never discuss religious women having pets.[135] Connections between women and dogs in Carolingian sources mainly relate to the broader female administration of estates. Chapter 58 of the *Capitulare de villis* states that the *iudices* are to look after the puppies, feed them at their own expense with the contingency that the king or queen may wish to feed some pups from royal resources.[136]

Aristocratic women, however, supervised the care of other domestic animals, especially those related to the provision of food. According to the *Capitulare de villis*, geese and chickens were common domestic fowl on estates; ducks were also listed in the *Brevium exempla*.[137] Eggs had to be collected and extra ones could be sold.[138] Although it seems doubtful that aristocratic women themselves collected eggs or fed fowl, they could have made sure other women carried out such chores and kept track of eggs and birds coming in from dependent farms.[139] Similarly, although they probably performed little or none of the physical labor related to the raising of farm animals and crops that peasants did, they must have been concerned with the output of that work, particularly the part destined for the household or any surplus.[140]

Women probably helped to look after some other estate animals kept for decoration and possibly for food. One of the more curious chapters in the *Capitulare de villis* states: "That every *iudex*, on each of our estates, shall always have wild sows, peacocks, pheasants, pigeons, partridges, and turtle doves, for the sake of dignity."[141] All of these animals could be eaten, and peacocks are listed in inventories of two of the royal estates in the *Brevium exempla* along with the chickens, geese, and ducks.[142] In a striking parallel to aristocrats of

---

134. *CV*, chap. 11, 57.

135. Jonas of Orléans chided men whose love of hunting and dogs caused them to neglect the poor. *Institutione*, 2.23, col. 215.

136. *CV*, chap. 58, 61. Perhaps these puppies were the offspring of particularly prized hunting dogs.

137. *CV*, chap. 18–19, 57; chap. 38, 59. *BE*, 50, 53–55.

138. *CV*, chap. 39, 59.

139. Included in polyptychs' lists of tasks for women was care of poultry. Devroey, "Femmes au miroir," 233.

140. *CV*, chap. 23, 25, 32–33, 36 (for fattening pigs in the forest), 51, 62, and 66, pp. 57–62. For lists of crops and livestock in the *BE* see 52–55.

141. *CV*, chap. 40, 59.

142. *BE*, 53–54. Peacocks are not very plentiful at either of them. At Anappes there were 30 geese, 80 chickens, and 22 peacocks; at the next royal estate 40 geese, 6 ducks, 100 chickens, and 8 peacocks.

earlier and later centuries, Carolingians may have populated the grounds of their estates with decorative birds. Large elite estates may have included gardens in which these birds roamed. Both the *Capitulare de villis* and the *Brevium exempla* contain extensive lists of plants and trees.[143] Furthermore, walled parks or *brogili* may have contained these birds as well as the horses that usually grazed there.[144] The *brogili* and the gardens probably served decorative and symbolic functions, not purely practical ones. An ideal garden and/or menagerie of animals recalled Paradise and could act as a symbolic effort to achieve the heavenly order on earth. Charlemagne may have wanted to fill his gardens with exotic birds and animals, including Harun al-Rashid's gift of an elephant, because such a garden evoked the Garden of Eden, where Adam named the animals and demonstrated man's control over nature.[145] Walafrid Strabo used gardens as metaphors for paradise and for political commentary in his *De imagine tetrici* and the *Hortulus*.[146]

Actual gardens and courtyards and the animals in them were probably not as orderly as remaining textual sources indicate. Nevertheless, the visions of poetry and the capitularies indicate an interest in gardens in Carolingian lands. Even if they did not live up to their idealized purposes, they probably served some practical functions. The smaller courtyard at Anappes, "enclosed with a palisade, well ordered and planted with various kinds of trees," may have provided a possible, impressive outdoor meeting place.[147] A ninth-century garden court, discovered in excavations of the complex of buildings for housing and entertaining guests at the monastery of San Vincenzo al Volturno, suggests the possible appearance of such gardens in Carolingian lands. The columned court contained an "elegant" garden that included sculptural decoration.[148] The inventories of the village of Grisio and another village each list a courtyard with a hedge, which may have served grazing purposes like a *brogilus*. More curious is the "secure courtyard with a hedge and two wooden gates with galleries above" in the inventory of an unknown royal estate. Some courtyards had palisades or stone walls and some other buildings or structures within them, implying possible defensive

---

143. *CV,* chap. 70, 63; *BE,* 53–55.

144. *CV,* chap. 46, 60; *Capitulare missorum* a. 808, chap. 10, MGH Capit. 1, 140; *Capitula de functionibus publicis* a. 820, chap. 4, MGH Capit. I, 295; *AB,* yr. 864, 114; *PAI,* vol. 2, 22.1, 227. Percy Ernst Schramm and Florentine Mütherich, *Denkmale der deutschen Könige und Kaiser. Ein Beitrag zur Herrschergeschichte von Karl dem Großen bis Friedriech II. 768–1250* (Munich, 1962), 72.

145. Dutton, *Charlemagne's Mustache,* 52–60.

146. Strabo, *De imagine tetrici,* 373–74, lines 107–27, and *De cultura hortorum,* 335–50.

147. *BE,* 52. Translation from *The Reign of Charlemagne: Documents on Carolingian Government and Administration,* ed. H. R. Loyn and John Percival (New York, 1976), 102.

148. Mitchell, "Monastic Guest Quarters," 137–39.

or production purposes, not all courtyards would necessarily have served the same functions.[149]

Just as the rich display that women produced inside their estate buildings could serve to impress others and provide a suitable background for meetings among the powerful and rich, so too they may have looked after an outdoor show of various plants and decorative fowl. Women may have supervised garden cultivation, selecting the plants and planning their layout for ornamental as well as practical purposes of food and medical care. Fishponds, for example, may have been decorative, but they also supplied food; both the *Capitulare de villis* and the *Brevium exempla* reveal a concern with keeping the pond well stocked with fish.[150] Fish in excess of the household's needs could be sold at market, and the garum mentioned elsewhere may have been a product of the fishponds.[151]

Aristocratic women needed gardens. Many, if not all, of the plants and trees listed in the *Capitulare de villis* and the *Brevium exempla* had practical uses, providing fruit, herbs, dyes, and medicine. Fruit and herbs naturally were welcome additions to any kitchen. Women's responsibility for textile work necessitated obtaining dyes. As primary care givers to the sick, they required growing plants and trees whose parts had medicinal value. Oversight of the garden and decisions about the use of herbs, fruit, and other plant products most likely fell to the mistress or the abbess. The chapter of the *Capitulare de villis* concerning the garden never mentions anyone in charge of gardening. Though this absence may reflect the section's possible late addition to the text (it does not follow the formula of the earlier chapters), evidence from religious texts supports the idea that women looked after gardens. Religious women, too, wanted to obtain food, medicines, and dyes. If the climate permitted, the *Institutio sanctimonialium* stated, communities should try to cultivate vines and olives. According to the rule, the *cellararia* was in charge of food; she may therefore have been in charge of looking after the garden.[152] Note that the grammatical form of this officer is feminine. The authors of this rule assumed that women could serve in such practical capacities within religious communities. A further indication of garden work is a late eighth- or early ninth-century watering can found in the excavation of the female community at Herford.[153] Given the great variety of plants and trees named, the gardens of the *Capitulare de villis* are probably generic, not actual, and

---

149. *BE*, 53–55.
150. *CV*, chap. 21 and 62, pp. 57, 59; *BE*, 53, 55. On management of fishponds see Squatriti, *Water and Society in Early Medieval Italy*, 104–9, 116–19.
151. *CV*, chap. 34 and 65, pp. 59, 62.
152. *IS*, canons 13 and 25, 447, 454.
153. *Kunst*, 369–70.

the *Brevium exempla*, which concerns actual estates, may be closer to "reality." The *Institutio sanctimonialium* is also a prescriptive text. The consistent connection in all of them between the products of gardens and women's concerns, however, strongly suggests that aristocratic women were involved in the care of gardens, if not in charge of their cultivation.

Aside from the raising of animals and agriculture, both the *Capitulare de villis* and the *Brevium exempla* reveal much about craft production on Carolingian estates. Evidence from other written and archaeological sources will help to identify many of these activities and their possible specific locations in the Carolingian world. Craft production was not confined to lay estates; many forms of production were carried out on monastic estates and in female religious communities. Women performed some work entirely on their own, especially textile work, and they helped supervise many crafts. Men also performed such work in situations outside households and female religious communities.[154] Merchants and craftsmen were usually dependent upon kings, bishops, or other magnates. They were either bound to the landed aristocracy's estate organization or worked in trade centers such as those found on the kings' farms at Huy in Belgium and at Karlburg am Main in Bavaria.[155] Monasteries were prominent, expansive economic centers. Among those monasteries yielding either archaeological or textual craft evidence are San Vincenzo al Volturno, St. Riquier, and Farfa.[156] The plan for the monastery of St. Gall allocated space for various crafts.[157] Artisans were concentrated around church centers in newly conquered areas, such as Hildesheim and Paderborn.[158] Other large trade centers with concurrent craft production included Dorestad, Birka, and Hedeby.[159] Small conglomerations of villages and sometimes large villages were centers of local economies.[160] The variety of locations and conditions for Carolingian craft production and regional differences make comparison difficult. Also, because continual habitation

---

154. I use the word craft because the terms trade or profession would indicate their continuous practice by specialists. Discerning which crafts at estates involved professional specialists is difficult given the lack of relevant archaeological evidence, and many of these crafts may have been performed seasonally or irregularly or regularly by people who also did other types of work.

155. Both these locations have many *Grubenhäusern* or sunken huts, workshops, and evidence of production in the form of jewelry pieces, half fabricated items, casting forms, and craft-related trash.

156. Capelle, "Handwerk in der Karolingerzeit," 424–25, and Steuer, "Handel und Wirtschaft in der Karolingerzeit," 413–14.

157. Walter Horn and Ernest Born, eds., *The Plan of St. Gall: A Study of the Architecture and Economy of, and Life in a Paradigmatic Carolingian Monastery*, vol. 2 (Berkeley, 1979), 189–99.

158. Capelle, "Handwerk in der Karolingerzeit," 426.

159. Hodges, *Towns and Trade in the Age of Charlemagne*, 69–92.

160. Fossier, *La terre et les hommes en Picardie jusqu'à la fin du xiiie siècle*, vol. 1, 199–201.

Figure 3. This late eighth- or early ninth-century watering can was found in the excavation of the female community at Herford. Photograph courtesy of LWL-Archäologie für Westfalen/Brentführer.

destroys old layers, archaeologists have trouble finding the remains of settlements and analyzing their material culture; royal residences and palaces as well as monasteries are better understood archaeologically. Thus, the study of craft production on estates and in dependent villages is archaeologically handicapped. Nevertheless, written sources reveal some crafts that aristocratic women would probably have helped supervise.

Among the workers whom, at least occasionally, Carolingian women may have directed were blacksmiths, gold- and silversmiths, shoemakers, turners, carpenters, shield-makers, fishermen, falconers, brewers, butchers, bakers, cooks, net-makers, textile workers, beekeepers, soap-makers, candle-makers, basket makers, millers, and possibly stone masons.[161] Much of this work was seasonal, and the best time of year for many of these activities was the spring and summer months, when male aristocrats were most likely to be away at war, leaving their female counterparts to oversee such labor. Despite the fact that few estates probably had all of these workers, female supervision of such diverse areas indicates a breadth of knowledge about types of production. Throughout an estate or in a large household, informal structures of power

---

161. *CV,* chap. 18, 34, 35, 42, 43, 45, 59, 61, and 62, pp. 57, 59–62; *BE,* 50, 52–55.

must have been in place. Consultation with various workers and direction from one craftsman to another or to their inferiors probably occurred with little supervision from above. Nevertheless, even if workers were not under her regular direction, at times the mistress may have been consulted by or given directions to these workers. Ensuring adequate production necessitated an understanding of some crafts' techniques and skills, even if they lay beyond the prescribed feminine sphere of the family. In the passages from *Waltharius* at the beginning of this chapter, Hildegund had access to arms that allowed her to obtain a byrnie, a helmet, and a corselet although warfare was meant to have little or no role in female life. Aristocratic women likely knew about the supplies of flour, wine, and arms sent to war, as mentioned in three chapters of the *Capitulare de villis*.[162] Women, therefore, could enter into male spheres, where they may have acted in ways not plainly recorded in Carolingian sources.

The fabric of buildings concerned anyone supervising estates, and aristocratic women may have wanted to know about the work of the carpenters, turners, and stone layers on their estates who built and repaired structures such as houses, mills, barns, stables, granaries, workshops, kitchens, bakeries, wine presses, brew houses, and fences.[163] They could not afford to ignore the "byres, pigsties, sheepfolds, and goat stands" that the carpenters maintained.[164] Women may have been especially active in supervising construction work as it was probably most common in the warm months when men were away. Blacksmiths helped to produce the tools that these other craftsmen and agricultural workers used, as well as other practical items such as barrels, hooks for pots and hunting, cauldrons, cooking pans, lamps, and traps.[165] These items, necessary to the kitchens and the supplying of food, could therefore have concerned an estate's mistress. Similarly, stonemasons may have been active at some estates in building certain structures. The *Brevium exempla* mentions stonework or stonemasons a number of times at the royal estates, and wealthy aristocrats may have invested in stone structures on their estates. Among the stoneworks listed are a house "well built of stone," a house built with a stone exterior and wooden interior, a stone chapel, and stone gateways. Fireplaces could include stone.[166]

Because gold and silver objects contributed to rich display, women probably supervised some of the labor of silver- and goldsmiths working on their

---

162. *CV*, chap. 30, 42, and 64, pp. 58–59, 62.
163. *CV*, chap. 18, 19, 27, 31, and 41, pp. 57–59; *BE*, 50, 52–5.
164. *CV*, chap. 23, 57.
165. *CV*, chap. 42, 68, and 69, pp. 59, 62; *BE*, 50, 52–55.
166. *BE*, 52–5.

estates. They may have purchased such items from markets or had them brought from trade centers, but since evidence of metalworking workshops has been found at excavations at Aachen, it is possible that some aristocratic estates had such workshops.[167] Both the *Capitulare de villis* and the *Brevium exempla* mention fine metalworkers at royal estates. At an unnamed village, the scribe noted that: "We found...no goldsmiths, silversmiths or blacksmiths," implying that these workmen might be expected in dependent villages on royal lands.[168] The list of workmen in the *Capitulare de villis* supports such an expectation. A general reference to smiths may have included bronze workers, and lead working is mentioned specifically.[169] The mentions of the bronze vessels and implements in the inventories of the *Brevium exempla* and in the *Capitulare de villis* suggest that bronze workers were active at some estates.[170] Bronzework may have especially interested women, for some bronze vessels were used for eating, cooking, and baking. At the crown estate of Treola, those taking inventory found a lead plate; lead vessels are also mentioned in the *Capitulare de villis*.[171]

Later medieval literature has left a vision of cheating among millers, who sometimes fooled their customers about the weight of their grain.[172] Though Carolingian literature contains no discussions of millers, a concern over cheating a lord of grain appears in prescriptive sources. Therefore, the *iudex*, the lady, and the lord himself tried to manage the milling of grain carefully. Cheating the lord of his just share of grain and stealing seed grain were crimes: "Every *iudex* is to ensure that crooked men do not hide our seed from us, either under the ground or elsewhere, thereby making the harvest less plentiful."[173] Because the *iudex* was urged to keep account of payments from mills in his records, royal mills must have charged a fee.[174] The mill's income and production were undoubtedly included in the reports of a *iudex*. Because women needed the flour processed at mills for food provision, they probably wanted to ensure that flour arrived regularly in adequate amounts of appropriate quality. Thus, women surely either helped to keep or consulted records. The inventories of the *Brevium exempla* demonstrate Carolingian attention to maintaining detailed accounts concerning mills and the precise

---

167. Capelle, "Handwerk in der Karolingerzeit," 425; Braunfels, *Die Welt der Karolinger und ihre Kunst*, 135.

168. *BE*, 53.

169. *CV*, chap. 45 and 62, pp. 60–62.

170. *BE*, 52–55; *CV*, chap. 42, 59.

171. *BE*, 55; *CV*, chap. 42, 59.

172. For example the miller in Chaucer's Reeve's tale.

173. *CV*, chap. 51, 60.

174. Ibid., chap. 62, 61–62.

measurements of all grain and flour at estates and dependent villages. Particularly revealing is a section on grain from the estate at Anappes, the most detailed of the royal inventories:

> Produce: ninety baskets of old spelt from the previous year, which can be made 450 measures of flour; 100 *modii* of barley. For the present year there were 110 baskets of spelt: of these 60 baskets have been sown, and we found the rest; 100 *modii* of wheat: 60 have been sown and we found the rest. 98 *modii* of rye, all of which has been sown; 1800 *modii* of barley: 1100 has been sown, and we found the rest; 430 *modii* of oats, one *modius* of beans, 12 *modii* of peas. From the five mills, 800 smaller *modii*: 240 *modii* were given to the [estate's] dependents (*prebendariis*), and we found the rest.[175]

This part of the inventory lists both the grain that inspectors found as well as grain left from the year before. It furthermore accounts for sown grain that could not have been counted during the inventory, indicating that someone must have kept track of how grain was used at this estate. Landowners, including women, probably carried out the same practice at other estates. Keeping and understanding such records required a high level of organizational competence and basic numeracy.

Aristocratic women oversaw production of wax, candles, honey, and soap because these products provided light and food and allowed for cleanliness. Beekeeping and the rendering of tallow, therefore, related to hospitality and efficient management. Light must have concerned elite women. Candles, made from wax or tallow gave light, but perhaps more frequently light came from lamps that burned oil or tallow. Remains of glass and ceramic oil lamps survive from excavations at the dependent villages of St. Denis, Villiers-le-Sec, and Baillet-en-France.[176] Oil is mentioned once in the *Capitulare de villis* in reference to keeping track of the income resulting from certain sources.[177] Although oil could be quite expensive and some estates probably obtained it through purchase, this mention indicates that other estates produced it. Oil was the lighting fuel of choice for churches, monasteries, chapels, and aristocratic halls because it produced less smoke and odor than tallow.[178] The olives that the *Institutio sanctimonialium* encouraged communities to raise could have been used to produce oil.[179] Yet tallow was useful and valuable because oil

---

175. *BE*, 52–53.
176. François Gentili, "L'éclairage domestique," 271–75.
177. *CV*, chap. 62, 61–62.
178. Fouracre, "Eternal Light and Earthly Needs," 69–70.
179. *IS*, canon 13, 447.

remained a very expensive, though highly desirable, form of light. The *iudex* was to keep track of the estate's production of tallow, made from fattened sheep, pigs, and oxen.[180]

As for honey and wax production, the *iudex* was to appoint as many men to be beekeepers as there were royal estates.[181] The inventory of one of the unnamed royal estates in the *Brevium exempla* lists fifty beehives; the other estates had none. The same document records that the homestead (*curtis*) attached to the monastery at Staffelsee had seventeen beehives.[182] As commodities in early medieval international trade, wax and honey were prized products. Honey, one of the few sweeteners available to early medieval people, was a key ingredient in mead.[183] Women, as providers of food, therefore needed to keep track of honey production. Because it appears so frequently in the *Capitulare de villis*, wax seems to have been a particularly desirable commodity.[184] Although candles are not mentioned in the *Capitulare de villis*, presumably some of this wax was used for their production. Wax had other uses as well: sealing baskets, casks, or barrels; serving as models for lost wax casting some metals; or coating threads for easier use in textile work. Wax was valuable enough that fragments of it, presumably from candles, could not be wasted. In Aldegund's *vita*, the saint had her niece recycle wax: "The blessed virgin Aldegund sometimes directed her to collect together fragments of wax, anxious that not even the smallest of the monastery's goods be lost. When told, she prepared very quickly, gathered the scattered fragments of wax, lit a fire, and set a copper vessel, that is a basin, full of wax above it."[185] An anecdote concerning Gerald of Aurillac further underlines the relatively high value of wax candles. Gerald insisted that any wax he received as a gift go for use in lighting the altar, not for personal use in his bedchamber, where he employed wooden torches.[186] Because candles and seals for containers related directly to their provision of hospitality, aristocratic women doubtless tracked wax production. Wax's use in sewing also interested them.

Another item made mainly from animal byproducts was soap. Cleanliness was of great concern in the *Capitulare de villis*, and presumably to aristocratic women.

---

180. *CV,* chap. 35 and 62, pp. 59, 61–62.

181. Ibid., chap. 17, 57.

182. *BE,* 50, 54. Beekeeping may have been confined to the best locations, and perhaps the labor-intensive nature of looking after even one hive meant that keeping many together was most efficient.

183. *CV,* chap. 34, 44, and 62, pp. 59–62; *BE,* 53.

184. *CV,* chap. 34, 44, 59, and 62, pp. 59–62.

185. *Vita Aldegundis,* chap. 16, 1044.

186. Odo, *Vita Geraldi,* 1.25, col. 657.

Whatever is produced or made should be looked after with great care—that is lard, ham, sausage, salted meat, wine, vinegar, mulberry wine, boiled wine, garum, mustard, cheese, butter, malt, beer, mead, honey, wax and flour—all should be made or prepared with the greatest attention to cleanliness.[187]

The Carolingians were profoundly concerned with purity in everyday life, and the statutes of this capitulary reflect that.[188] In a third tale from Notker's *Gesta Karoli* concerning a bishop's provision of hospitality, the churchman always took great care to provide for the king's needs, but once Charlemagne arrived without notice. Though upset at the lack of warning, the bishop quickly had every part of the cathedral and its buildings and courtyards swept clean. When Charlemagne noted how tidy everything was, the bishop replied that it was only appropriate.[189] Buildings were to be constructed carefully so that "our servants who work in them can carry out their tasks properly and cleanly."[190] Charlemagne chose Aachen as the site of his court partly because its springs were good for bathing.[191] Soap could help to maintain cleanliness, and mentions of it reveal that soap was desirable at Carolingian estates. Because soap makers are among the craft workers listed in chapter 45, soap was probably produced on aristocratic and royal estates.[192] Having a clean interior and food and drink prepared according to contemporary standards of purity was essential to the hospitality that aristocratic women provided; thus, they surely concerned themselves with cleanliness.

In order to provide proper hospitality aristocratic women had to involve themselves in baking, cooking, brewing, and winemaking. Kitchen, bakery, and wine press were essential to providing household or court with food and drink, and they required supervision of workers. Carolingian estates probably all had stables, bakeries, and kitchens, and some, especially in the south, had wine presses.[193] The estates in the *Brevium exempla* had the first three but lacked wine presses, probably because of their northern location.[194] In the *Capitulare de villis* the *iudex* was instructed to look after the vineyards, wine and vinegar production, and the delivery of these products to the court. In an aristocratic household in the south, the wife probably oversaw this work along with a *iudex* or other senior workers. She, like the royal *iudices*,

---

187. *CV*, chap. 34, 59.
188. Meens, "Religious Instruction in the Frankish Kingdoms," 55.
189. Notker, *GK*, 1.14, 17–18.
190. *CV*, chap. 41, 59.
191. Einhard, *VK*, chap. 22, 27.
192. *CV*, chap. 44, 45, and 62, pp. 60–62.
193. Ibid., chap. 41, 59.
194. *BE*, 52–55.

wanted to make sure that the wine production was progressing smoothly and cleanly.[195]

As for food served on aristocratic tables, butchers rendered livestock raised on estates and possibly game animals killed in hunts into meat. Chapter 23 of the *Capitulare de villis* reveals a concern with proper butchering: "And when [the *iudices*] have to serve meat, let them have lame but healthy oxen, cows or horses which are not mangy, or other healthy animals."[196] Consumption of meat was one mark of an aristocrat, and for this reason, among others, the queen or female head of household would have been particularly concerned that the butcher did not cheat them of meat through theft.[197] She also may have wanted to ensure that the best cuts of meat went to an honored guest and that the butchering was done cleanly.[198] She probably monitored the preservation of bacon, sausage, and smoked and newly salted meat.[199] She needed to keep track of the useful byproducts of butchering—lard, offal, hides, skins, and horns—and may have concerned herself with leather tanning.[200] The *Institutio sanctimonialium* states that, if it is possible in the area in which a community is located, the members ought to raise cattle, presumably both to obtain these useful products and for dairying.[201] The fish from the ponds and the fowl could have provided protein in the Carolingian aristocratic diet, as could the old Roman staple garum.[202] Certainly, aristocratic women oversaw the work done in kitchens and bakehouses to prepare meat and other foods, especially on significant occasions or for prominent guests.

Beer, an essential product on elite estates, provided both drink and nourishment and, along with wine, was necessary to lubricate aristocratic proceedings.[203] Brewing probably involved as much female supervision as winemaking.[204] Brewers also produced cider and perry, products of estate orchards.[205] In order to obtain a high quality product aristocratic women surely wanted to

---

195. *CV*, chap. 8, 22, 34, 44, 48, and 62, pp. 56–57, 59–62.
196. Ibid., 58.
197. Le Jan, *FP*, 66.
198. *CV*, chap. 24, 68.
199. *BE*, 53–55; *CV*, chap. 34, 59.
200. *BE*, 53–5; *CV*, chap. 34, 62, and 66, pp. 59, 61–62.
201. *IS*, canon 13, 447.
202. *CV*, chap. 44, 60.
203. Ibid., chap. 62, 61–62.
204. In the pre-modern era, brewing was traditionally thought of as an occupation for women. The Carolingian sources, however, do not support this. Women may have been involved in brewing, but it was clearly designated as a male occupation (chapter 45). Also, chapter 61 seems to imply that the best brewers would have been men. "That each steward, when he is on service, shall have his malt brought to the palace; and with him shall come master-brewers who can make good beer there." See also Obermeier, "*Ancilla*," 203–5.
205. *CV*, chap. 45 and 70, pp. 60, 63; *BE*, 53, 55.

assure proper brewing methods and helped to oversee the amount of grain that went to the brewhouses. They may have also supervised dairying and the creation of cheese and other dairy products. Cheese and butter figure into the inventories and the capitulary, and cheese making is a skilled craft.[206]

Religious women were also concerned with many of these activities related to the kitchen because they had to provide for those in their communities and their guests. Certainly, kitchen and household duties occupied much of their time. The *Institutio sanctimonialium* states that the *cellararia*, like the other officers, must have moral integrity above all other qualifications. Appointed by the abbess, she was to "faithfully and humbly administer the food of the *sanctimoniales* on their behalf."[207] This was no small job. Obtaining sufficient wine for a house alone was a considerable task. In wine producing areas, the *sanctimoniales* were encouraged to cultivate vines, but elsewhere wine had to be obtained from outside the community, or perhaps the *sanctimoniales* drank beer. Food and wine also came to the communities from local donations. The abbess and the *praelatae* were involved in these tasks.[208] In particular, the abbess was to take great care to obtain food to go with the staple bread, including meat, fish, legumes, and olives, as well as firewood and other necessities.[209]

Both lay and religious aristocratic women were involved in diverse activities, particularly in supervision and management of various aspects of the production of food, drink, and other goods crucial to the functioning of estates, households, and religious institutions. Elite women helped to supervise both men and women in these tasks and personally managed activities for which men probably were given credit in written sources. Through their supervision they increased the status and reputation of their families and households and thereby helped to strengthen the authority and influence of their husbands and fathers. They may also have marked their own status through their demonstration of domestic virtue, especially through hospitality, while participating in these aspects of Carolingian aristocratic culture.

Childbirth, Illness, and Death

Attending the sick and dying was a domestic duty of the Carolingian female aristocrat. Wealth could not protect the elite from health problems even if

---

206. *BE*, 53–4; *CV*, chap. 34 and 44, pp. 59, 60. Bitel, "Reproduction," 78–80.
207. *IS*, canon 25, 454.
208. See note 53 for an explanation of *praelata*.
209. *IS*, canon 13, 447.

their access to a better diet and easier living and working conditions perhaps helped them to live longer, healthier lives than their lower status counterparts. When illness or old age incapacitated a person, it was probably a woman who provided care; doing so demonstrated her virtue. References to this duty are scattered, and the medical conditions we can learn about are those that concerned ecclesiastical leaders, including the one most likely to affect elite women—childbirth. One might expect more references to this major event in the female lifecycle, especially the ways in which women helped one another through pregnancy and delivery, but what remains instead are the views of clerics. These men left hints of women's part in looking after those giving birth, lying sick, or dying.

Religious men and women took scant interest in the mechanics of childbirth in their texts because it had little bearing on their lives. Women's responsibility to care for the sick meant that midwives and mothers almost certainly taught each other practical skills related to childbirth, though almost no direct evidence points to transmission of this knowledge among aristocratic women in Carolingian lands. Based on the few surviving manuscripts containing obstetric and gynecological material, early medieval medical understanding of childbirth rested upon late antique learning.[210] Such texts point more clearly to the interest of scholars than practitioners.[211] It is difficult to know how much of this knowledge reached elite households. Eberhard and Gisela left a medical book to their son Rudolf, and Eccard of Autun bequeathed a medical book to Theutberga, wife of Lothar II.[212] If more elite families owned such texts, it would support the idea that aristocratic women had greater access to medical learning than other women.[213]

Childbirth was a major difference between those women who spent their whole lives in convents and those who remained in the lay world for at least part of their adult lives. It comprised one of the greatest threats to female health. Evidence from the excavation of the ninth- to eleventh-century cemetery of Münsterhof in Zurich indicates women's life expectancy remained lower than that of men from their teenage years until about sixty when life expectancy for men and women evened out: the dangers of childbirth account for this discrepancy.[214] The mid-fifth- to mid-eighth–century cemetery of Wenigumstadt in Bavaria shows similar results. Using new histological techniques to estimate age, one study determined that earlier assessments had

---

210. Gerhard Baader, "Frauenheilkunde," *FG*, vol. 7, 126, 130–33.
211. Glaze, "The Perforated Wall," 72–101.
212. *CAC*, no. 1, 4; *RCSBL*, no. 25, 66.
213. Smith, *Europe after Rome*, 71.
214. Etter, "Die Bevölkerung von Münsterhof," 188.

underestimated the number of old (over sixty) individuals represented in this cemetery, suggesting a higher number of elderly present in society than expected. Examined on the basis of sex, this evidence indicated a lower life expectancy for women once they reached childbearing age; their life expectancy then improved. At sixty, the life expectancy evened out, with women even having a slight advantage in life expectancy over men.[215] Based on other early medieval evidence those figures appear indicative of the typical rates of death throughout the early Middle Ages.[216]

Remaining references to pregnancy and childbirth come mainly from miraculous hagiographic accounts and legal texts. Medieval *vitae* often included signs of the child's future piety, before birth and/or during childhood.[217] According to Alcuin's *Vita Willibrordi*, while pregnant, Willibrord's mother miraculously saw a vision of growing light in the shape of a moon. The light entered her bosom through her mouth, signifying the light of truth that Willibrord would bring to dark places.[218] Gerald of Aurillac called out to his parents from inside his mother's womb, his cries predicting the greatness of his future actions.[219] These examples from *vitae* about miraculous feelings, voices, and visions reveal spiritual perceptions of pregnancy and birth as well as of the miraculous and holy concerning infants in the womb or in arms. Hagiographic evidence supports the understanding that fertility and virtue were intertwined. Liutberga's insistence that a woman's own sins were causing the deaths of her infants before they could be baptized, and the reproductive miracles associated with the cult of Verena connect parental morality with bearing and raising healthy children.[220]

Legal texts show a long-term male concern with female fertility. The Council of Worms in 829 decreed, in its list of issues that should be announced to all people, that men should refrain from having sex with their pregnant wives because sex was for reproduction, not to satisfy lust.[221] Earlier Germanic law codes placed a higher *wergeld* (the monetary value based on various criteria accorded to individual victims, which determined the fines for different kinds of crimes) upon women of reproductive age, and particularly upon

---

215. Grupe, Cipriano-Bechtle, and Schröter, "Ageing and Life Expectancy in the Early Middle Ages," 268–72.

216. Smith, *Europe after Rome*, 66–68; Fleming, "Bones for Historians," 35–38.

217. McLaughlin, "Survivors and Surrogates," 112.

218. Alcuin, *Vita Willibrordi*, chap. 2, 117.

219. Odo, *Vita Geraldi*, 1.3, cols. 643–44.

220. *Vita Liutbirgae*, chap. 31–33, 37–40; *Ex miraculis sanctae Verenae*, in *Die Heilige Verena von Zurzach. Legende, Kult, Denkmäler*, ed. Adolf Reinle (Basel, Switzerland, 1948), chap. 10, 18, and 21; 49–61.

221. *Constitutiones Wormatienses*, chap. 23, MGH Capit. 1, 345.

pregnant women, than on girls and post menopausal women indicating their great worth to society as a whole.[222] Salic law stipulated that the *wergeld* for a fertile woman be three times higher than that for a woman past her childbearing years or past sixty.[223] Infertile women, especially older ones, could lose social and legal status as a result of their inability to bear children. Visigothic law forbade older women (*maiores femine*) from marrying young men (*viri minori*). Not only were such unions unlikely to produce healthy children, but also they inverted the natural order by enabling such women to command their young husbands.[224] Churchmen argued that infertility, however, was not cause to end a marriage. According to the late eighth-century Vienna Penitential B, which drew from the penitential of Finnean, one reason that men ought not be allowed to set aside sterile wives was the possibility that they might eventually conceive: Sarah, Rebecca, Anna, and Elizabeth had all conceived and borne their children late in life, demonstrating biblical precedent for such events.[225] Nevertheless, the births of Isaac, Jacob and Esau, Samuel, and John the Baptist seem miraculous for being so unlikely.

The fact that many knew rather little about gynecological and obstetrical practices highlights the importance of prayers concerning fertility to the Carolingian elite. The *ordo* (ceremony) for the marriage of Charles the Bald's daughter Judith in 856 asked to bless her womb and make the couple fruitful; and the blessings for Ermentrude, Charles the Bald's wife, in 862 upon the anniversary of their wedding, and again in 866 at Ermentrude's consecration as queen at Soissons were meant to recall women like Sarah who bore a son at an advanced age.[226] As Janet Nelson has argued, such blessings had political resonance, commenting upon the public roles of the queen. At the same time they underline the degree of helplessness medieval people felt in light of their own inability to help in reproduction and birth when these processes failed to progress smoothly.[227] Carolingian sources offer little concrete information about birth and the care of infants. The dangers of childbirth would have meant that Carolingian women experienced great relief upon a safe delivery, and the

222. Bitel, *Women in Early Medieval Europe*, 67–73.

223. *Pactus legis Salicae*, 24.8–9; 41.15, 17, and 19; 65e.1–4 in *The Laws of the Salian Franks*, trans. and ed. Katherine Fischer Drew (Philadelphia, 1991); see also 45.

224. *Leges Visigothorum antiquiores*, 3.1.4, ed. Karl Zeumer. MGH Fontes, 5 (Hanover, 1894), 88.

225. Cod. lat. 2233, fol 1ʳ–82ʳ, was produced at Salzburg. *Paenetentiale Vindobonense B*, in Meens, *Het Tripartite Boeteboek*, 388; see also 105–14. Hubertus Lutterbach, *Sexualität im Mittelalter. Eine Kulturstudie anhand von Bußbüchern des 6. bis 12. Jahrhunderts* (Cologne, 1999), 125–27.

226. *Ordine Coronationis Franciae*, ed. Richard A. Jackson (Philadelphia, 1995), 77, 82–86.

227. Nelson, "Early Medieval Rites of Queen-Making and the Shaping of Medieval Queenship," 308.

birth of sons into an aristocratic family helped to ensure its continuity. Dhuoda wrote that she was thankful for and pleased at the birth of both her children. She referred to William as her "much-desired firstborn son."[228] For centuries, clerics had enjoined mothers to nurse their own babies, but those exhortations cannot prove that most women either did or did not do so. Augustine of Hippo thought that mothers who nursed their own children benefited their households.[229] In a letter to Augustine of Canterbury, Gregory the Great railed against the "evil custom" of wet nursing, directing his ire toward the perceived lack of sexual continence that this practice implied in the mothers who employed it.[230] Early medieval people knew what modern science later proved: that a woman who continued to nurse could not conceive as easily as a woman who stopped or never started doing so. Aristocratic mothers may have nursed their own children. At least in hagiographic texts, the mothers of saints nursed their babies, but other texts offer little confirmation of this practice.[231]

A text rich in information on female fertility, conception, and childbirth is Hincmar of Rheims's tract on the divorce of Lothar II. The monstrous nature of the charge (that Theutberga had conceived a child with her brother through anal intercourse and later aborted the fetus) made it immediately suspicious. Hincmar noted that no woman except Mary had ever conceived a child except through coitus.[232] He and his contemporaries knew such a pregnancy to be impossible. Hincmar also suggested widespread understanding of the hymen, noting that bishops ought to ensure women be checked physically for their virginity and thereby for virtuous behavior.[233] As mentioned earlier, Theutberga may well have been capable of having children, though the rhetoric of the late 860s paints her as being incapable of biological motherhood. Pope Nicholas I in fact suggested that it was Lothar who was at fault for the couple's infertility, writing in 867 that "sterility does not come from the infertility of the body but from the wickedness of the husband."[234] This text displays an interest in the spiritual, not biological, causes of infertility.

Hucbald's *Vita Rictrudis* comments on sterility through its discussion of the Merovingian King Dagobert's problems in producing an heir. According to

228. Dhuoda, *LM*, prologue, 48.
229. Shaw, "The Family in Late Antiquity," 42.
230. Bede, *Historia ecclesiastica gentis Anglorum*, 1.27, 90.
231. Positive biblical references to nursing may explain this act, mentioned in a few Carolingian-era *vitae*. Willibald, *Vita Bonifatii*, chap. 1, 4; Odo, *Vita Geraldi*, 1.4, col. 644.
232. Hincmar, *DLR*, 182.
233. Ibid. See Stuart Airlie's comments on this passage in "Private Bodies," 23, note 66.
234. Nicholas I, MGH Ep. 6, ed. Ernst Perels (Berlin, 1925), no. 45–46, 320, 324. The translation is Airlie's "Private Bodies," 31, see his note 94.

Hucbald, Dagobert set aside his first wife for her sterility, only to find that his second wife was also sterile. His third union succeeded in producing the male heir he desired.[235] No Merovingian evidence, however, indicates that sterility caused Dagobert to set aside his first two partners. Although Hucbald's relation of Dagobert's claim of sterility results from the increasing emphasis Carolingian clerics placed upon lasting monogamous marriage in the ninth century, it additionally reflects the problems that the Carolingians experienced starting in the 880s in producing legitimate male heirs who lived long enough to have sons of their own.[236] For example, Richildis's sons did not survive infancy; her stepson Louis the Stammerer's two sons both died in accidents at young ages; and Charles the Fat and his wife Richardis had no children.[237] An early tenth-century audience, especially one that remembered that Lothar II had tried to divorce Theutberga for similar reasons and more recently that Charles the Fat had set aside Richardis, almost certainly appreciated sterility as a motivation for repudiation. The reasons that motherhood figured as a central form of identity for women in the Carolingian world, especially by the late ninth century, related not only to biological and social expectations of women but also to specific problems of the last decades. Political and spiritual interests therefore guided clerics, not a desire to provide information about specific care related to childbirth.

The evidence is clearer that women often attended the sick and dying, particular those in their natural and spiritual families, than that they helped in childbirth, because such care demonstrated domestic virtue. The *Institutio sanctimonialium* included the sick and the old, which stipulated that the sisters look after the infirm and feeble with compassion. The rule required that all the sisters should visit these women often, reading scripture with them.[238] According to Rudolf's *vita* of Leoba, when the nun Williswind became so ill that the others could not stand her stench, she was taken to her parents' nearby home.[239] This case suggests not only the lasting bonds between religious women and their natal families but also the care that sisters in the religious life were ideally to provide the sick. The fact that Williswind's parents could tend her implies that she may have been quite young. Her situation suggests that, in their later years, parents may sometimes have looked after ailing adult children. Abbess Hathumoda attended the sick in her community, especially during the epidemic that eventually brought about her death. Her

---

235. Hucbald, *Vita Rictrudis*, chap. 6–7, 82–3.

236. For the former argument see McNamara and Halbord, *Sainted Women of the Dark Ages*, 201, note 21.

237. MacLean, *Kingship and Politics*, 81–121.

238. *IS*, canon 23, 454.

239. Rudolf, *Vita Leobae*, chap. 15, 128.

natural and spiritual sisters at Gandersheim then cared for her during her final illness. She also looked after her old aunt. "First among all the venerable was her aunt, then very aged and enfeebled with senility, whose great suffering allowed [Hathumoda] to go to her so that she might aid her indefatigably."[240] The most famous examples of women caring for an elderly relative are Charlemagne's daughters who looked after him in his last years.

Given the prevalence of disease, accidents, problems in childbirth, anemia, and relatively hard living conditions, aristocratic women could have died at any point of their lifecycle, though early childhood and the years of childbearing posed the greatest dangers. Hagiography and annals record the deaths of saints and queens, but both offer little information on the women's care in their final years, days, and hours. When Leoba fell ill a few days before her death, she had to take to her bed, but Rudolf mentions nothing about those who cared for her.[241] Similarly, the author of the *Vita Liutbirgae* provides few details about the deaths of Liutberga and her patroness Gisla other than mentioning those present. As Gisla died, she gave her son Bernard advice, and on her deathbed, Liutberga asked the priests and her sisters gathered around her for their forgiveness.[242] The *vita* of Herlindis and Renula provides no particulars concerning the manner of their parents' death or the care their sisters at Aldeneik surely gave them as each became ill and died. The author, however, notes that late in their lives, the knowledge of approaching death never slowed them down.[243] The notices for the deaths of queens in annals, histories, and royal biographies are quite brief and provide few particulars. Thegan notes, for example, that Irmingard, the first wife of Louis the Pious, died of a fever.[244] When Emma, wife of Louis the German, suffered a stroke in 874, the *Annals of Fulda* offered the rare detail that it left her unable to speak. That stroke may have contributed to her death in 876.[245]

In sum, Carolingian sources offer little concrete information about female care for the sick and dying though they imply that such duties were part of women's domestic responsibilities. These matters seem not to have interested the men who wrote the relevant sources. Though churchmen wrote about childbirth, they did so from a desire to examine the spiritual, social, and political repercussions for men of female (in)fertility. In some cases women may have believed that their actions and sins were at fault for their childlessness or the deaths of their children. At times, they employed prayer as a means to

240. Agius, *Vita Hathumodae*, chap. 10, 15, and 20, 170–71, 173.
241. Rudolf, *Vita Leobae*, chap. 21, 130.
242. *Vita Liutbirgae*, chap. 7 and 37, 14–15, 45–46.
243. *Vita Herlinde et Renulae*, chap. 8, 14, and 16–19, 387, 389–90.
244. Thegan, *Gesta*, chap. 25, 214.
245. *AF*, 83, 85.

ameliorate or end the suffering of the sick. Though the sources can be frus tratingly vague, they suggest that elite women faced some of the same difficulties as their lower status counterparts in the early Middle Ages.

Wealth and Female Agency

Women may have found their roles in providing hospitality and looking after their families not only challenging but also rewarding. In a thirteenth-century redaction of the *Vita Waldetrudis* the devil tempts the saint by causing her to recall the authority she once held.

> First, he incited in her the memory of estates, noble family, the protection of a household, love of possessions, the superfluous glory of the world, various delectable foods and other pleasures of the life she had given up.[246]

Because Waldetrud lived in the seventh century, this rather late version of her life, composed at the time of her canonization, may seem to have little to do with Carolingian women. The editors of the English translation of this text believe that some remnants of the stories and beliefs of the original cult survived in the *vita*, although they consider this particular passage rather thirteenth-century in tone because it shows the saint's regret for her past life.[247] Yet it seems to summarize the world of the Carolingian aristocratic laywoman and the sort of responsibilities and luxuries a woman might miss after she took vows. It cannot stand as proof of Carolingian practice, but it conforms to the activities and beliefs discussed in this chapter and connects Carolingian women to their earlier and later peers.

Carolingian women, both lay and religious, had substantial opportunities to exert managerial control over household, estate, and convent. Their gendered duties almost certainly gave them power; they demonstrate how instrumental they were in the development of social and political bonds as well as in contributing to the economy. Women were involved not only in an economy of surplus and wealth but also of display and hospitality, which helped to shape relations among the Carolingian elite. Though domestic management rests behind the scenes in the consulted sources, it was central to Carolingian aristocratic culture.

Inferences concerning women's responsibility for management rest fundamentally upon their duty to provide hospitality, and generally their supervisory

---

246. *Vita Waldetrudis* chap. 9, AASS April 1, 840.
247. McNamara and Halborg, *Sainted Women of the Dark Ages*, 237, 260.

duties conform to the images of Carolingian aristocratic women that have emerged in previous chapters. The ways male contemporaries accounted for the domestic activities of women in written sources left compelling traces of their social and practical competence. Their bonds to their families and religious houses necessitated the performance of such work. Female supervision of workers on estates allowed a mistress to act as a moral exemplar to her inferiors, the very people with whom Carolingian reformers probably had the least contact. Their association with women of relatively low status helps to explain why the stakes may have seemed so high to the Carolingian clerics who urged women to set a virtuous example to all in their households. These men were aware of the great number of Christians—children, servants, and other women—with whom women of high status had relatively frequent dealings.

Because Carolingian churchmen treated households and estates as male domains, women's contributions to these institutions have been obscured. Their actions are usually depicted as demonstrating their virtue, as in their care for the sick and dying, or helping to achieve male goals. Yet the extant sources offer clues to this female labor. The access of aristocratic women to household resources could have allowed them to function relatively independently within a masculine sphere, giving them perhaps the highest degree of agency over "wealth" of the four characteristics Jonas listed. Efficient management, women must have realized, could enhance their families' reputation and their own. Their male contemporaries recognized the influence this position provided them. Carolingian prescriptive texts reveal that women were expected to maintain harmonious and virtuous households in order to augment the status of the men who headed them. Clerics saw in the conventional duties of aristocratic women a means of spreading Christian behaviors to those who may have been beyond their own reach. Therefore, these traditional roles gave women opportunities to exert power.

Chapter Five
TEXTILE WORK

A passage from the *Vita Herlinde et Renulae* suggests the kinds of textile skills that early medieval women of high social status learned. When the future abbesses of Aldeneik received childhood instruction at Valenciennes, they learned both basic tasks such as spinning and weaving and highly specialized ones such as sewing with gold.

> In a similar manner, [Herlindis and Renula] were instructed very properly in every kind of work, which was customarily made by the hands of women with various methods and diverse in composition, namely in spinning and weaving, designing and sewing, in gold and in silk with added pearls; they turned into artisans accomplished in extraordinary methods.[1]

Carolingian sources make abundant references to female production of textiles, but no one has yet appreciated the centrality of this labor to the lives of both lay and religious women and to their male contemporaries. This chapter examines this profoundly important female activity, which exemplified each of Jonas's characteristics. The beauty of elite women's fine textiles rested upon the skills they learned and upon their ability to employ cloth and clothing effectively, thereby demonstrating their prudence. Their wealth allowed them to create opulent textiles, often to advance the interests of their natal, marital, and spiritual families, particularly in creating social and religious bonds.

---

1. *Vita Herlinde et Renulae,* chap. 5, 387.

Textile work paralleled the work of both nuns and monks to copy and decorate fine manuscripts; such objects allowed monastery and church to function, and labor on these objects was an appropriate and expected activity of those in the religious estate. The transmission of such skills took place in convents, at court, and doubtless in the households of lay magnates. Women of every social status participated in textile work of some kind. Evidence indicates that no one in Carolingian lands expected men to perform textile work; it was a female activity. Spinning, weaving, and sewing had long indicated female virtue. In describing a steadfast (*fortis*) wife, the author of Proverbs wrote that: "she has sought wool and flax, and worked with willing hands"; and "she lays her hand to the distaff, and her fingers have taken up the spindle." The steadfast wife wanted flax and wool in order to make garments and coverings.[2] In early portrayals Mary commonly appears with a spindle. In an eighth- or early ninth-century Byzantine or Syrian silk fragment now housed in the Vatican Museum, for example, Mary sits on a pillow upon a decorated throne spinning during the Annunciation.[3] By depicting his subjects participating in textile work, the author of the *Vita Herlinde et Renulae* conveyed the virtue and piety of the girls, recalled female biblical models, and underlined the propriety of such domestic work to his probable female audience who almost certainly engaged in textile work.

Sewing not only bore implications of virtue; it provided material and spiritual benefits. Religious women at convents, including Valenciennes and Aldeneik, required clothing, bedclothes, bath and kitchen linens for everyday use, and fine liturgical textiles—probably of rich materials—for use during mass and to decorate and equip their churches. They may also have donated finished textiles to outside churches or male monasteries, pious acts encouraged by Carolingian clerics. Spinning and weaving enabled Herlindis, Renula, and their sisters to provide for their convent's basic needs, and the skills of working with silk, pearls, and gold allowed them to produce elaborately decorated cloths of rich materials for liturgical use. As gifts, such ornate textiles comprised substantial donations that reflected well upon maker and donor as well as provided prestige to the religious houses from which many such pieces originated. Working on cloth indicated female morality; giving a textile to a religious institution helped to make others aware of a woman's virtue.

Although few textiles of this era remain, descriptions of cloths in written sources, especially church and monastic inventories, provide indications of the prominence and high economic value of these items. In a few cases, an extant textile can be connected to a specific woman. For example, Louis the

---

2. Proverbs 31:13, 19, 22–24.
3. Museo Vaticano no. 61231.

Figure 4. This eighth- or early ninth-century Byzantine or Syrian silk fragment now housed in the Vatican Museum shows Mary spinning during the Annunciation. Museo Vaticano no. 61231, Rome. Reproduced by permission from Scala/Art Resource, New York.

German's wife Emma gave a silk and gold belt to Witgar, bishop of Augsburg, sometime between 860 and 876; the inscription woven into the belt names her as donor. The belt, a principal means of marking male rank, reminded those who saw it, especially Witgar, of Emma and her rich gift.[4] Emma probably made the belt herself as its construction technique is not difficult; she certainly took responsibility for its donation. The quality of the belt's materials, construction, and design mattered, as did the appearance of other liturgical textiles.[5] As discussed earlier, Carolingians commented upon the function and appearance of liturgical objects as part of the image controversy of the eighth and ninth centuries. Some theologians believed that an object's beauty could

---

4. Diözesanmuseum St. Afra 5001. Sigrid Müller-Christensen, *Sakrale Gewänder des Mittelalters* (Munich, 1955), 14.

5. The importance of religious textiles, the wealth they represented, and the bonds they created among lay and religious is quite clear in eleventh-century Anglo-Scandinavian sources. Mary Frances Smith, Robin Fleming, and Patricia Halpin, "Court and Piety in Late Anglo-Saxon England," *The Catholic Historical Review* 87, no. 4 (2001): 569–602.

affect those who saw it or that objects could instruct or inspire the illiterate. Textile decorations of a church or monastery were visible to those attending mass or visiting to pray. Women therefore produced textiles expected to influence the viewer; ecclesiastical and monastic leaders used some of those cloths in places that women could not enter, especially altars and cloisters. Textile donations would have helped to create or strengthen a bond between the church and the women's family or convent, especially as Carolingians thought of some fine textiles as treasures and even basic textiles as functionally valuable. Perhaps other textiles were marked with the maker's or donor's name, as Witgar's belt was, to commemorate such relationships. Costly gifts of textiles may have reminded those using or seeing them of their fabricators and donors.

Textiles helped to advance male interests at court and in the households of great magnates. These objects played a principal role in Carolingian aristocratic culture, providing decoration that contributed to an atmosphere of wealth and power that helped the Carolingian family to indicate its royal status and impress magnates at court. The palace at Aachen, for example, had lavish textile wall hangings, perhaps similar to the richness of the famous frescos at Ingelheim. Illuminations in the early ninth-century Stuttgart Psalter depict cloth hangings in a church.[6] Given the value men placed upon female virtue, laymen wanted others to associate their wives, daughters, and female kin with the domestic virtue of textile work. It comprised a means of sexual control; women busy with their sewing lacked the time for sexual indiscretion. Cloth decorations could also indicate the virtue of the women in the household, who were almost certainly responsible for their placement. At the same time, textiles provided women an indirect means of influence over relations of power.

Textile work comprised a substantial economic activity carried out and quite possibly directed by women. Women of low and servile status performed the bulk of textile work in the Carolingian world, and women of high social status almost certainly directed much of that work. In some respects Carolingian textile fabrication and use conformed to long-term Western patterns. Men have often exerted greater control over the passage of finished textiles than women, but women were more often connected with work on and organization of textiles.[7] Carolingian textile production, however, occurred mainly

---

6. Fol. 35^r and 65^r.

7. For example, although the *Odyssey* contains perhaps the most famous example of a woman performing textile work—Penelope weaving and unraveling a shroud for Odysseus (book 2, lines 93–102; book 19, lines 139–56; book 24, lines 128–46), it is mainly men who give textiles in both the *Odyssey* (book 13, lines 10–12; book 19, lines 225–43) and the *Iliad* (book 9, lines 150–56; book 24, lines 272–75). Although Arete gave Odysseus a cloak

on estates in textile workshops staffed by women (in Latin either *gynaecea* or *piseles*), or on dependent farms where women were responsible for a quota of textiles each year as payment to the estate holder. This period was unusual in Western history because men at other times almost always controlled general textile production though women worked in their fabrication.[8] Throughout the Roman era and the central and late Middle Ages, women continued to produce textiles, but much of that work occurred in towns and cities under the direction of men. Carolingian women could play this significant economic role because of the decentralized nature of the economy and the frequent absence of lords from estates.

Through their association with cloth women could advance the interests of their families and convents, demonstrate their virtue, and play a vital economic role. The necessity for textiles encouraged clerics to urge women's participation in textile work as did the long-established model of a virtuous woman working on her spinning. Traditional ideas put forward by male clerics and female work on cloth built upon each other to give textiles crucial roles in Carolingian aristocratic culture.

Transmission of Textile Skills

Producing textiles and supervising textile workers required knowledge of specific skills and materials. Knowing how to arrange and use cloths in an aristocratic house and determining when, where, and how to present gifts of textiles demonstrated female competence, although evidence for these particular activities is sparse. Women almost certainly gained such expertise from other women. The instruction in textile skills Herlindis and Renula received at Valenciennes may have been typical. Various ninth-century Carolingian sources, especially hagiographical texts, contain tantalizing references to the textile work of aristocratic women, both lay and religious, and their transmission of its attendant skills. These descriptions and allusions underline the virtue inherent in textile work, because they often supported a woman's sanctity. At the same time they indicate the wide range of skills that well-born women may have learned. Mentions of rich materials emphasized the wealth to which some of these women had access. Most important, they reveal an expectation

---

and tunic (book 13, lines 66–67), she did so as part of her husband's gifts, and one expects a virtuous wife to give her husband clothing, such as the spectacular cloak Penelope presented to Odysseus (book 19, lines 253–58). Female slaves also wove: Agamemnon expected that Chryseis would work at a loom in his home in Argos (book 1, lines 35–36).

8. Herlihy, *OM*, 185–86.

that aristocratic women perform some textile work, not simply leave it to servants.

Although textual evidence rarely provides any specific details about the techniques and materials that well-born women employed, they probably embroidered or worked with rather expensive materials, because they had the luxuries of time and wealth. However, they also engaged in the basic tasks of spinning and sewing, often to demonstrate their virtue. According to Einhard, Charlemagne insisted that his daughters learn to spin and weave.[9] In part, Einhard wanted to depict Charlemagne instilling traditional female virtues in his daughters; at the same time it is another example of Charlemagne's pragmatic attitude. Mary frequently appeared with a spindle in hand or nearby in mosaics, paintings, and illuminations from late antiquity through the early Renaissance.[10] The Stuttgart Psalter depicts Mary spinning (folio 83ᵛ), and the Vienna Genesis (sixth century) shows the wife of Potiphar spinning (folio 31), a curious example of a wicked woman shown in virtuous activity, perhaps stressing that appearances are not always what they seem. The stipulation that forbade women from working on Sundays in the *Admonitio generalis* of March 23, 789 indicates many of the basic tasks women performed. "Moreover the textile work of women may not be done; they may neither cut out nor stitch clothing and do needlework; nor is it permitted to card wool or to beat linen or to wash clothes in public or to grind herbs so that in every way the honor and quiet of the Sabbath is preserved."[11] Oddly, weaving does not appear in this list, and overall descriptions or depictions of weaving are scarce in other early and central medieval cultures.[12] Other tasks may have indicated higher social rank.

Central and late medieval evidence, as well as early medieval evidence from Ireland and Anglo-Saxon England, indicates that engaging in embroidery and an association with rich textiles marked high status among women.[13] According to fosterage laws, daughters of Irish chieftains had to learn to embroider, and in early medieval Irish accounts, embroidery could indicate high rank and/or raise the status of a woman, because it demonstrated that she had the requisite leisure time and resources to produce luxury goods.[14] Employing self-conscious language in his late seventh-century prose *De virginitate*,

9. Einhard, *VK*, chap. 19, 23.

10. David Linton, "Reading the Virgin Reader," in *The Book and the Magic of Reading in the Middle Ages*, ed. Albrecht Classen (New York, 1998), 253–76, at 254–55.

11. *Admonitio generalis*, chap. 81, MGH Capit. 1, 61.

12. For example, on the scant references to weaving in eleventh- to thirteenth-century Icelandic texts see Jochens, *Women in Old Norse Society*, 141–60.

13. Herlihy, *OM*, 56–58; Parker, *The Subversive Stitch*, 30; Cohen, *The Uta Codex*, 48.

14. Bitel, "Reproduction," 85.

dedicated to the abbess and nuns of Barking, Aldhelm wrote about embroi
dery work and lavish textiles in order to convince the nuns to practice virtues
in addition to their virginity.[15] He used an analogy readily understandable
to well-born women: additional virtues could enhance their beauty just as
purple and varied colors could enhance the beauty of a wall hanging. The
Anglo-Saxon queens Emma (d. 1052) and Edith (d. 1075) both gave textiles to
churches, pious donations that added to their reputations as virtuous queens.[16]
According to the *Domesday Book*, Ælfgyth the Maiden held two hides of land
in Buckinghamshire in return for teaching "gold embroidery work" to the
daughter of Goderic the Sheriff.[17] Such a record indicates that these skills
were desirable in daughters of the elite throughout much of northwestern
Europe. For an aristocratic woman, the spindle could act as an antidote to
the leisure and wealth that embroidery demonstrated, allowing an aristocratic
woman to show her upright nature despite the potential temptations that surrounded her.

Carolingian sources offer evidence that aristocratic women produced
embroideries but none that conclusively demonstrates that lower status women
did, including those working in *gynaecea*. This lack of evidence does not necessarily exclude the possibility that servile or free women of modest means
made fine textiles—those involving a high degree of technical skill, such as
embroideries, tapestries, or appliqué works, and/or constructed with expensive materials, including silk, gold, silver, and expensive dyes. Techniques such
as working with gold, as Herlindis and Renula learned, necessitated significant training. The maker had to hammer gold into a thin sheet to be cut into
narrow strips or "lamella." An embroiderer could then weave those strips into
her work, but more commonly she spun and wound them around a core of
linen, wool, or silk and then sewed them onto the fabric.[18] Women of any
status could have performed such intricate work, which required only careful instruction, practice, and patience. The production of textiles for everyday use by women of lower status and the possible existence of workshops of
skilled artisans explains where some fine works may have been produced.[19] In

---

15. Aldhelm, *De virginitate* (prose), chap. 15, MGH AA 15, ed. Rudolf Ehwald (Berlin,
1919), 226–323, at 244.

16. Stafford, *Queen Emma and Queen Edith*, 143–47. For later medieval female donations of textiles to religious institutions see Mecham, "Recent Research on Women, Spirituality, and the Arts in the Middle Ages," 461–62.

17. *Domesday Book: A Complete Translation*, Buckinghamshire, 20, ed. and trans. Ann
Williams and G. H. Martin (London, 1992), 410 (fol. 149ʳ).

18. Geijer, "The Textile Finds from Birka," 87, 96. The Maaseik embroideries employed
this technique.

19. Budny, "The Byrhtnoth Tapestry," 272; Obermeier, "*Ancilla*," 217–29.

fact, the status of those working in *gynaecea* as "professionals" argues in favor of their ability to perform such work because they surely became practiced in their labors. The rich materials of some objects point to aristocratic interest and commission, if not fabrication, by elite women. Wealthy women also had the leisure to produce fine textiles, a circumstance that helped them to remain socially distinct from women of lower status.

Men commissioned certain textiles and may have provided designs. For example, Eccard of Autun specifically left money in his will of 876 to provide vestments for monks.[20] Heribert, archbishop of Milan (1018–1045), probably commissioned a pallium for the grave of St. Ambrose.[21] However, women almost certainly did the spinning, weaving, dyeing, sewing, and embroidering. Therefore, the many textiles mentioned in the *Liber Pontificalis* are rather puzzling as no evidence indicates women worked at the Lateran. Sources may simply fail to mention the textile work men did, or perhaps women outside the Lateran worked on these cloths. Women were nevertheless much more closely associated with such labor than men: references to men performing textile work in the early medieval period are extremely rare.[22]

The *vita* of Herlindis and Renula presents a description of the training in textile work that girls at convents probably received. Older religious women helped girls to acquire various embroidery and sewing skills. Both basic and fine textile work, such as sewing and embroidery, were part of the education for girls raised in religious communities and an activity for all religious women. When the *Institutio sanctimonialium* stipulated that religious women under this rule were to learn handwork and regularly practice it, the authors were probably referring both to basic production, such as making their own clothing, and fine textile work.[23] Religious women finished, dyed, and embroidered cloth for use in a church, not for their own clothing, which was to be humble. They were forbidden to wear decorated clothing made of silk, a prohibition which echoed earlier rules for women.[24]

The *Vita Liutbirgae virginis* (c. 870–76) provides further examples of practical instruction and activity in textile work. When a demon wanted to

---

20. *RCSBL*, no. 25, 63.

21. Alberto de Capitani d'Arzago and Ferdinando Reggiori, *Antichi Tessuti della Basilica Ambrosiana* (Milan, 1941), 64.

22. I have so far found only one reference to a man in the early medieval world performing textile work: the ninth-century Byzantine monk and saint Blaise wove purple cloth in his hermit's cell at the Greek monastery of St. Caesarius on the Palatine Hill. *Vita Blasii*, chap. 14, AASS November 4, 657–69, 663. See also McCormick, *Origins of the European Economy*, 205.

23. *IS*, canons 10 and 13, 445, 447–48.

24. *IS*, canons 3, 7, and 10, 432, 442, 445; Heidebrecht and Nolte, "Leben im Kloster," 94, 104.

taunt Liutberga with her past sins, he reminded her of a time when, as a small child, she had traded her broken needle for another girl's unbroken one during their communal work. Work with textiles was clearly part of her early education. Even as a recluse, Liutberga practiced textile arts, keeping hot coals and dyes in her cell, presumably to color cloth.[25] Dyeing cloth demanded Liutberga's sacrifice of her personal comfort: it may have been an ascetic practice on her part. The stench of some materials used for dyeing and the mess such work could produce surely made her confined space unpleasant. She passed on this knowledge of textile skills to the young girls whom Archbishop Ansgar of Bremen sent to her for, among other things, instruction "in artistic work."[26] Liutberga probably taught them the same sewing skills she had learned as a child and the dyeing techniques she practiced. Because these girls were allowed to return to their kin or go to another convent or household, they may have later passed on these textile skills to other girls or women.

When women transmitted practical textile skills, they furthered their ability to perform pious acts by creating finished products with an ecclesiastical or monastic destination. Engaging in the work of construction promoted or at least removed obstacles to piety: by minimizing idleness, it kept religious women from gossip, impure thoughts, and the commission of other minor sins.[27] Because the canons of the *Institutio sanctimonialium* and the *vitae* of Liutberga and Herlindis and Renula mention the singing of psalms and reading of divine scripture, one cannot help but think these, in addition to being part of the paraliturgical activities of a convent, may have accompanied textile work to avert idle chatter. Such instruction may have similarly benefited laywomen. Men could use their products in both lay and religious settings. In two mid-ninth–century poems John Scottus Eriugena mentioned robes fabricated by Queens Judith and Ermintrud, mother and wife of Charles the Bald. In one poem, Eriugena praised Ermintrud for her accomplished weaving; she constructed a silk robe woven with gold and covered with gems for her husband.[28] This poem also described her prayer and reading, thereby providing "an essentially domestic portrait" of the queen.[29] According to its dedicatory verses, which Eriugena composed, Ermintrud also finished a robe for donation to a Roman church dedicated to the Apostle Paul during the reign of Pope Nicholas I (858–867). Her mother-in-law Judith had originally

25. *Vita Liutbirgae*, chap. 22 and 28, pp. 26, 32.
26. "in artificiosis operibus," in ibid., chap. 35, 44.
27. *IS*, canon 10, 445; Schilp, *NW*, 83–85.
28. MGH Poetae 3, 533.
29. Dutton, "Eriugena the Royal Poet," 68.

decorated the same robe for Louis the Pious.[30] In letters of 864 and 865, Nicholas thanked Ermintrud for some gifts, noting in one his pleasure with her virtuous labor, implying that she had made the gifts.[31] If the gifts were textiles, they were especially appropriate to her gender, rank, and piety. Queens were not, however, the only women expected to provide textiles for churches. The *Capitula Ecclesiastica* of 810–13(?) contain a chapter reminding priests to urge laywomen to make altar cloths for their churches.[32] Such a general admonition would certainly have applied to aristocratic women. Thus, textile work, part of the female *opus Dei*, seems ideally to have been a virtuous activity of all upright women.

These depictions of women performing textile work are related to a trope of virtuous domesticity that had contemporary resonance given the use and economic value of textiles in Carolingian lands.[33] The well-educated elite who read or heard the texts discussed above would have appreciated the connection between pious women and textile fabrication. Creation and donation of religious textiles constituted a good work, reflecting the virtue of the maker, whether lay or religious. Aristocrats may have provided common women in a workshop with the necessary materials and support to fabricate such pieces, but that possibility hardly explains mentions of elite women performing textile work themselves. Demand for textiles and social expectations could easily have kept both groups of women busy. The various uses and meanings of textiles in Carolingian lands required a relatively abundant supply.

Cultural Implications of Female Textile Work

Both secular and religious textiles served material purposes, but they also had less tangible functions. The spiritual worth of religious textiles and the impression that secular textiles provided in lay courts made them particularly valuable in both economic and cultural terms. Textiles, both basic and rich, were essential in Carolingian aristocratic life, and women's roles in their production and display contributed to the prestige of households and religious institutions, further blurring the line between lay and religious women.

---

30. It may also be the same garment of gold and gems that Charles presented to Nicholas according to the *Liber pontificalis*, vol. 2, chap. 50, 161; MGH Poetae 3, 687–88; Dutton, "The Dubthach Codex and Eriugena," 18–20.

31. MGH Ep. 6, no. 28, 69, ed. E. Perels (Berlin, 1925), 294–95, 387.

32. *Capitula ecclesiastica*, chap. 7, MGH Capit. 1, 178.

33. Lynda Coon described such a literary trope for women extending from New Testament precedent through to Merovingian *vitae*. *SF*, 41–51, 133–38.

The necessity for religious vestments and cloths in Christian worship extended from practices developed in late antiquity. Drawing from references to textiles in the Christian Scriptures and from pre-Christian Roman practices, early Christians began to find meaning in certain textiles and their uses. For example, Paul of Tarsus wrote in 1 Corinthians (11:13–15) that women should cover their heads, and women often wore veils in the late antique world. The Christian idea of the veil as appropriate head covering for lay and religious women therefore resulted from text and practice. Fifth-to seventh-century references to the vestments of priests indicate their liturgical and ceremonial necessity.[34] Some of the earliest mentions of religious and practical textiles, suggesting the value Carolingian and Anglo-Saxon men placed on female textile work, come from the letters of Boniface and his circle. Boniface warmly thanked Bugga, a future abbess, and Abbess Eadburg of Thanet, for the vestments they had sent him.[35] To Eadburg he wrote that her piety, demonstrated by gifts of books and vestments, was a consolation to him.[36] By according two kinds of gifts a similar weight, Boniface reveals the great worth of both. Because some early medieval convents had active scriptoria, it is possible Eadburg or her sisters had a hand in the production of the books she sent. Fabrication of both religious textiles and manuscripts in convents may have served similar purposes: the piety of these activities resulted from both the devotion required for patient construction and the contribution the final products made to the worship and religious observance of others. Missionaries could not have found it easy to procure books, much less clothing or religious textiles,[37] both of which were necessary to their mission and to their spiritual and material well-being. Boniface's gratitude for the gifts is, therefore, natural, but presents of textiles may have been particularly appropriate for his female correspondents given their virtuous implications. In his letter to Bugga, Boniface's language is again somewhat formulaic, but the sentiment is similar as he thanks her for gifts and vestments. "In return for the gifts and garments you have sent me, I offer my grateful prayers to God that he may give you a reward with the angels and archangels in the highest

---

34. Jacques Dubois, "Utilisation religieuse du tissu," in *Tissu et Vêtement. 5000 ans de savoir-faire*, (Guiry-en-Vexin, 1986), 144–52, at 144–47.

35. Sims-Williams has suggested that this Eadburg may be an abbess of Wimbourne instead. "An Unpublished Seventh or Eighth-Century Anglo-Latin Letter in Boulogne-sur-Mer MS 74 (82)," 1–22, at 22, n. 119. This Bugga is probably the Kentish abbess Ethelbert, king of Kent, mentioned in his letter of 748–54 to Boniface. MGH Ep. S 1, no. 105, 229–30.

36. MGH Ep. S 1, no. 35, 60.

37. Ibid., no. 93, 213.

heavens."[38] Rather than including the clothes under the general category of gifts, he singles them out, perhaps an indication of their economic and practical worth.

Conversely, Boniface's female correspondents mention their textile gifts humbly, probably a result of the conventions of composition. Bugga wrote to him in c. 720: "And through this same messenger I am now sending you fifty *solidi* and an altar cloth; the best I can possibly do. But nevertheless they are sent with the greatest love, even if they seem little."[39] Her reference to her best efforts is clearly a statement of humility. She may have meant to suggest the meagerness of her gifts in terms of value or number, but she could equally have been expressing modesty concerning the altar cloth's quality. As in the convention of apologizing for imperfect mastery of Latin in the opening of an early medieval text, Bugga may be claiming to have little talent in producing textiles, and, if this case resembles that literary convention, the fruit of her labor may well have demonstrated great skill. For example, in a letter of 745/6 to Eadburg Lull displayed similar humility when mentioning his "small" gifts of a silver writing instrument, some silken cloth with crosses on it, and cinnamon.[40] These gifts were actually costly, and the silk and cinnamon must have come into Lull's hands through Mediterranean trade. Perhaps Lull's gift of silk indicates one way women such as Eadburg received fine cloth suitable for making ecclesiastical vestments and cloths. An early eleventh-century work, *The Uta Codex*, contains a depiction of an altar covered by a cloth with crosses that may give an indication of such a cloth's appearance.[41] Clearly it would have been an expensive present. Regardless of whether these women in Boniface's circle constructed these textiles themselves, their gifts to missionaries of such costly but necessary items would have demonstrated their virtue.

Men continued to show gratitude for textile gifts from women into the early ninth century. Charlemagne's sister Gisela sent Alcuin a missal and a psalter as well as a cloak, which pleased him greatly.[42] As Bugga had, Gisela combined manuscripts and textiles in a single gift, further indicating the link between women and these forms of religious production. In a number of other letters, Alcuin thanks female correspondents for presents, which probably

---

38. Ibid., no. 27, 48–49. English translation is from Emerton, *The Letters of Saint Boniface*, 57.

39. MGH Ep. S 1, no. 15, 28.

40. Ibid., no. 70, 143.

41. Fol. 4ʳ. Cohen, *The Uta Codex*, 78.

42. MGH Ep. 4, no. 84, 127.

included both textiles and books.[43] Religious men, including Alcuin and Arn of Salzburg, sometimes thanked each other for gifts of textiles. In 800, Arn sent Alcuin a blanket and a canopy.[44] Two years later, Alcuin wrote to Arn:

> I received your agreeable presents with great joy. Though my mind wishes for no gift now other than peace of spirit, still your presents are always delightful to me, especially the clothes, which have always suited me well. I have sent you for the kindness of your blessing two cowls for the two commandments of love and one fine white tunic for the union of eternal peace which should always be the same between us.[45]

The connection of colors and specific meanings is not unusual in Alcuin's letters. Some textile items almost certainly had coded meanings, much as flowers and jewels did. The cloth adorned with crosses sent between Lull and Eadburg of Thanet may well have communicated a meaning beyond its functionality. In letters to and from women, correspondents rarely mention specific colors of textile items. Many women were probably not aware of such meanings. Even for relatively well-educated abbesses the meanings conveyed by a female textile gift may have been more material and practical than symbolic.

When men mentioned vestments or textile items in their letters to each other, they often included them as part of an order for these items or a request to make a purchase on the writer's behalf. In 790 Alcuin made such a request to an Irish pupil:

> Also send our supplies to the coast, and let Odwin, God willing, bring us the five pounds of silver which I sent with you to barter or sell or exchange its equivalent. And send another five of our silver, and three-ply goat-hair garments and wool for the boys' needs, both lay and clerical, and linen for my own needs, and black and red goat-hair hoods, if you happen to find any, and many paints of fine sulfur and pigments for painting.[46]

Alcuin's letter shows a practical focus upon acquiring the appropriate garments or cloths for specific groups of individuals. His request for linen raises the question of whether men were active in textile work, particularly in religious houses, but the context and use of the word *opus* seems to indicate that these cloths were to serve the purposes of the brothers. The other textile or

---

43. Ibid., no. 62, 103, and 300, pp. 105–6, 149–50, 458–59.
44. Ibid., no. 207, 343–35.
45. Ibid., no. 254. 411.
46. Ibid., no. 8, 33. This is a rare letter from Alcuin's time in England.

clothing items mentioned also appear to be finished items. The emphasis on supplies for the scriptorium implies that the monks were engaged in scribal work, not textile production. Certainly monks benefited from the textiles fabricated in workshops on their lands, such as those discovered in excavations at Villiers-le-Sec and Baillet-en-France, Carolingian possessions of St. Denis.[47] Alcuin may have procured the supplies he mentions for use in workshops, in a *gynaeceum*, or by women who helped look after the cleric and his companions, as widows and other consecrated women have helped look after bishops' household needs from late antiquity and the early Middle Ages to the present day. Churchmen's high regard for textiles supports a contemporary expectation and appreciation of women's involvement in these activities.

Another of Alcuin's letters reveals a profound concern with vestments and their proper use among religious men. In 796 he offered advice to his former student, Eanbald: "Never wear the consecrated pallium at divine worship without deacons in attendance....Each office should have its place and vestments."[48] As powerful symbols of the church and of individual offices, vestments required close attention to how, when, and where they were worn. Alcuin reminds Eanbald of the attention necessary to clerics' appearance in an attempt to check male clerical vanity. In the same letter he asserts that: "the clergy should be respectable in dress and sober in expression."[49] Such statements underline the strong impression that dress made. Clothing made the man or, in this case, the office. Alcuin and other clerics wanted to ensure modesty in ecclesiastical dress; a churchman's garb should be appropriate to his station. Clerical gratitude for textile gifts resulted partly from this emphasis on correct vestments; these textiles were necessities. The material maintenance of churches, monasteries, and convents required items such as hoods, habits, and veils so that their inhabitants would be appropriately attired. For example, Louis the Pious gave Harold the Dane various items necessary to celebrate mass including vestments, books, and liturgical vessels after Harold's baptism.[50] Bishop Riculf of Soissons devoted one chapter of his late ninth-century episcopal capitulary legislation to the items priests needed for their duties. Besides listing vestments, altar cloths, and liturgical vessels, he included instructions on the proper wearing of and care for priests' vestments.[51] If women, in addition to fabricating their own clothing, helped to create or supply vestments and textiles to churchmen, they were aiding

---

47. *Un village*, 276.
48. MGH Ep. 4, no. 114, 168.
49. Ibid.
50. Ermold, *In honorem*, 190, lines 2496–99.
51. Riculf of Soissons, *Capitula*, chap. 9, MGH Capit. Ep. 2, 96–111, 104.

those men in fulfilling their offices. In light of the textile skills and religious doctrine that many religious women learned and the relatively frequent celebration of mass at convents, religious women had the requisite knowledge to make vestments and cloths appropriate for liturgical use.

Without textiles religious men and women could not have carried out their liturgical duties. Women's manufacture of items like towels and altar cloths helped make the performance of church rites possible. Such work may have been part of the female "liturgical service" to the early medieval church. Two sixth-century church councils mention the deaconess, *diacona*, who may have offered services similar to those mentioned in fifth-century church legislation.[52] The sixth-century *Vita Genovefae* refers to the lighting that the saint supplied to the church and other examples of the service a *diacona* may have provided.[53] Gregory of Tours mentions a girl taking care of the lighting at the church of St. Martin at Tours.[54] Well into the Carolingian period, decorating, ordering, and cleaning churches probably continued to constitute female activities of great worth to clerics. At the Council of Paris in 829, canon 42 discussed women who took the veil to become guardians or administrators (*excubatrices*) at their parish churches.[55] Their responsibilities may have included taking care of church vestments and cloths, including decorative textiles.[56]

Liturgically appropriate display of textiles within a church contributed to the meaning and function of church rites, and luxurious textiles helped to create an opulent atmosphere for worship. One has only to glance through the papal biographies of the *Liber Pontificalis*, which begin in the early sixth century and end in the late ninth century, to find numerous descriptions of rich church vestments, cloths, and hangings.[57] The texts frequently mention churches hung with colored silk cloths or elaborate altar cloths. Some describe decorative textiles that showed scenes, similar to a tapestry.

> In God's holy mother's basilica *ad praesepe* [Pope Leo III] provided a red crimson cloth with a gold-studded panel in the center representing our Lord Jesus Christ and St. Simeon, when he was presented in the temple, and around it gold-studded edging; and another gold-studded cloth representing

52. Muschiol, *Famula Dei*, 45.

53. *Vita Genovefae virginis Parisiensis*, chap. 20–23, MGH SRM 3, ed. Bruno Krusch (Hanover, Germany, 1896), 215–38, at 223–25. See also Muschiol, *Famula Dei*, 53–54.

54. *Liber in gloria martyrum beatorum*, chap. 14, MGH SRM 1.2, 498.

55. Mansi, vol. 14, 564.

56. Regino of Prüm, *De synodalibus*, no. 1.60 and no. 1.80–81, 66 and 74–75.

57. Osborne, "Textiles and their Painted Imitations in Early Medieval Rome," 309–51; Noble, "Paradoxes and Possibilities in the Sources for Roman Society in the Early Middle Ages," 73–76.

the passing over of God's mother St. Mary, beautifully decorated on a wondrous scale, adorned with precious jewels and pearls, with a gold-studded
fringe and around it gold-studded edging.[58]

Seventh- to eighth-century fragmentary Byzantine silks with scenes of Sam-
son, the Annunciation, and the Nativity now held at the Vatican Museum
indicate the possible appearance of such lavish church furnishings.[59] Determining whether churches in the Carolingian Empire possessed textiles of
similar quality and numbers is difficult. Given the prestige of Rome and the
city's proximity to the main western route of the silk trade through Venice,
the popes undoubtedly possessed and gave some of the best such furnishings
in the West, but these descriptions hint at Carolingian church decoration
that no longer survives, including the hangings from the Stuttgart Psalter
mentioned above. An image of an altar on folio 29^r of the Stuttgart Psalter may
reflect more humble altars than those described in the *Liber Pontificalis*. It shows
a book on top of an altar covered with a cloth; above it hang two censers
and a chalice. The altars on folios 31^v and 51^v, covered in cloths, each with a
book on top, are similarly plain. The altar cloths on folios 130^v and 133^r have
decorated edges, perhaps because the former altar displays the elements of the
Eucharist while the hand of God writes in the book atop the latter.

Rich textiles helped to cement bonds among men in the Carolingian
world. Powerful laymen, especially kings, sent textile gifts to both lay and
religious men. Sometime between 748 and 754, for example, King Ethelbert
sent Boniface two cloaks, among other gifts.[60] Textiles served as worthy presents for auspicious occasions. According to Ermold the Black, Pope Stephen
gave Louis the Pious numerous gifts at his coronation including vestments,
red cloths, white linen cloths, and suitable coverings (*tegmina*).[61]

Perhaps because it was a luxury that Franks could not produce locally, silk
often appears in sources discussing gifts. The now rather mutilated "veil of
Chartres" may have originally come into the Carolingian Empire as a present from the Byzantine emperor to Charles the Bald. According to legend,
the king gave this fragment of a much larger piece of Byzantine silk to the
cathedral at Chartres.[62] Textual evidence suggests a transmission of silks from
eastern emperor to Carolingian ruler and then to church or monastery, which

---

58. *Liber Pontificalis*, vol. 2, chap. 52, 14. Translation from Davis, *The Lives of the Eighth-Century Popes (Liber Pontificalis)*, 203.

59. Museo Vaticano, no. 61247, 61231, and 61258. W. F. Volbach, ed., *I Tessuti del Museo Sacro Vaticano* (Vatican City, 1942), 38–40.

60. MGH Ep. S 1, no. 105, 230.

61. Ermold, *In honorem*, 86, lines 1108 and 1118; 88, lines 1124–25.

62. Delaporte, *Le voile de Notre Dame*, 6–7.

Figure 5. The Stuttgart Psalter, produced at Saint-Germain-des-Prés during the first half of the ninth century, depicts a number of altars decorated with liturgical cloths, including this one on folio 29ʳ. Stuttgart Psalter, folio 29ʳ. Photograph courtesy of Württembergische Landesbibliothek, Cod. bibl. 2° 23, Stuttgart.

may explain many of the surviving Carolingian eighth- and ninth-century silks. Some rich cloths came from the Abbasid caliphate; Harun al-Rashid (786–809) sent rich linen cloths, a tent, and silk robes to Charlemagne.[63] One item among Harun al-Rashid's textile gifts, a robe for Charlemagne, had special meaning. Abbasid caliphs sometimes gave robes to indicate their overlordship. Charlemagne's acceptance of the robe does not necessarily indicate that he acknowledged an inferior position; he probably considered his return gift of Frisian *pallia* in his embassy of 807 a means of sealing a possible alliance with a ruler whose diplomatic interests matched his own.[64] The Carolingians also used cloaks or robes as gifts to individuals they viewed as subordinates.[65] In 798, King Alfonso of Galicia and Asturias sent a tent of "astonishing beauty" as a gift to Charlemagne.[66] Because of its access to the textile trade of Rome and the surrounding area, the papacy was a rich source of textile gifts for the Carolingians.

---

63. *Annales regni Francorum*, yr. 807, 123; Einhard, *VK*, chap. 16, 19.

64. At the time neither Harun al-Rashid nor Charlemagne were on good terms with the Byzantines or the Umayyad Emirate at Cordoba. F. W. Buckler, *Harunu'l-Rashid and Charles the Great* (Cambridge, Mass., 1931), 30–35.

65. Dutton, *Charlemagne's Mustache*, 61–62.

66. *Annales regni Francorum*, yr. 798, 102.

Pope Stephen gave the royal family rich clothing in 816; in return, Louis gave him valuable presents including two cloaks, one purple and one white.[67]

Others could be the recipients of textile gifts. At the Synod of Ponthion in summer of 876, Richildis received a papal gift that included "rich garments."[68] Rulers sometimes shared such presents with the aristocracy. Pippin, Charlemagne's son, gave silks to the magnates who gathered at Regensburg in 793.[69] Those same magnates may themselves have passed textiles on to loyal followers and to their king. In his poem "In Praise of Poetry," "Hibernicus Exul" asks his muse what he can offer the king when others present "vestments gleaming with purple and gold thread."[70] The Old Saxon poetic Gospel, the *Heliand*, composed c. 830, provides an idealized image of female gifts in the passage concerning Mary's present of fine cloths and gems to her son:

> His mother, that most beautiful woman, took Him, wrapped Him in clothes and precious jewels, and then with her two hands laid Him gently, the little man, that child, in a fodder crib, even though He had the power of God, and was the Chieftain of mankind.[71]

In this passage, Mary dresses the holy infant appropriately with rich textiles. Although Mary was meant to stand as an example to women and men, this depiction of her reflects the cultural values of Saxon society in the ninth century, including the strong association among women, textiles, and gems. As a prominent form of gift exchange among the elite, textiles created bonds between giver and receiver that benefited women and their families.

Textiles helped to make a secular household appear rich. As decorations, cloths or curtains were a form of lavish display and a means of insulating a cold room or regulating light. When Hucbald of St. Amand wrote that Rictrud "arranged a banquet of sumptuous splendor suitable for a king at her estate," his note of the "sumptuous splendor" may have reflected both an old concern with the rich furnishing of rooms into which outsiders were admitted and his recollection of decorated aristocratic halls he had seen.[72] As mentioned earlier, Judith prepared a temporary shelter during a royal hunt by draping cloths (*palleolis*, *linteolis*) from branches; beneath it she hosted a picnic following the hunt.[73] The *aulae regiae* of the royal palaces at Aachen and

---

67. Ermold, *In honorem*, 86, lines 1108–19. Compare to Thegan, *Gesta*, chap. 17, 198.
68. AB, yr. 876, 204.
69. *Annales Laurenshamenses*, 35.
70. Hibernicus Exul, "In Praise of Poetry," in *PCR*, 174–75, line 5.
71. *The Heliand*, song 5, 16.
72. Hucbald, *Vita Rictrudis*, chap. 14, 84.
73. Ermold, *In honorem*, 184, lines 2418–36.

Ingelheim displayed not just fresco cycles but also probably ornamented tap-estries.[74] Excavations of the hall used for guests at San Vincenzo al Volturno revealed beautifully painted walls as well as "scattered fragments of drapery" in all of its undercrofts.[75] The inventories of the *villae* and of the palace at Anappes in the *Brevium exempla* list decorative covers and tapestries.[76] Use of textiles in prominent political and social locations meant that many of the most powerful individuals of the Carolingian world viewed them and that some thought doubtless went into the choice of decoration for such rooms. Textiles helped to decorate public spaces conducive to the formation of aristo-cratic bonds, thus serving a crucial function among the Carolingian lay elite. Although it is impossible to know the impression they made, textiles probably conveyed opulence, power, and wealth. Some, however, served humble but common functions that are all but impossible to trace. One of the only extant fragments of textile associated with a secular structure is a bit of fabric embed-ded in a piece of wall from the palace at Paderborn. It appears to have been stuck into a crack prior to the application of some fresh mortar.[77]

Evidence for use of religious textiles is richer than that for secular. Religious textiles turn up in inventories of local parish churches in Bavaria, demonstrat-ing that rather ordinary churches possessed some rich items.[78] If a powerful local aristocratic woman donated fine cloths to a parish church, her gift attests to the workings of elite power at a local level. Because their prestige may have been a principal means for aristocrats to exert influence, rich textile gifts attached to their families would have created a favorable impression among those under their lordship and may have contributed to their ability to affect local politics. Aristocratic women may also have created or donated textiles that caused others to connect them and their families to prominent or royal foundations, thereby influencing social and political relations beyond the local area.

The Use of Costly Religious Textiles

The utility and richness of religious textiles reflected positively on their mak-ers and donors, especially if they came from powerful families. Fabricating

---

74. Ibid., 186, lines 2444–45. Jacobsen, "Herrschaftliches Bauen in der Karolingerzeit," 93. Unfortunately, archaeology is not helpful, for almost no evidence of palaces' decoration remains.

75. Mitchell, "Monastic Guest Quarters," 134–35.

76. *BE*, 52–55.

77. *Kunst*, 143.

78. Hammer, "County Churches, Clerical Inventories, and the Carolingian Renais-sance in Bavaria," 9–13.

such pieces would have been an act of piety, helping to explain why clerics exhorted women to take part in textile work and why female saints were depicted as doing so. Creating a beautiful and opulent object would give glory to God, and many people who came inside churches would have seen and appreciated most of these textiles, particularly those worn by priests or carried in processions, not to mention the banners, curtains, and altar cloths in a church. Like other works of art, a stunning and richly decorated textile may have helped to create a sense of awe and holiness. Both fine and simpler textiles served necessary functions in mass and were therefore useful.

Evidence for the utility of Carolingian religious textiles is far more abundant than for their appearance. Certainly the wealthier religious houses that aristocratic women would have frequented had particularly ornate and numerous pieces so that vestments and decorations could be changed according to the season of the liturgical calendar. Priests and bishops needed the rich vestments that became customary in late antiquity as well as liturgical towels and napkins, and churches were often decorated with hanging cloths, curtains, and altar cloths. Well-born Carolingians probably used their textiles in similar ways to those described in the *Liber Pontificalis*, though on a less lavish scale. Folio 40^r of the Stuttgart Psalter shows a deacon reading at an altar. His clothes may reflect Frankish vestments, especially because vestments are a conservative form of dress, showing little change as a result of shifting fashions. Although Carolingian images of altars or churchmen involved in liturgical activity are rare, some later images help suggest the uses of religious textiles. For example, two late tenth-century ivories from Lotharingia, possibly Metz, depict churchmen in their vestments, and one shows the beginning of the Eucharistic prayer with a priest standing at an altar. A cloth appears to cover the altar. The image in the early eleventh-century *Uta Codex* showing Saint Erhard celebrating mass at the monastery at Regensburg in the late seventh century may also illustrate the appearance of such Carolingian religious textiles. Under an arch with a costly hanging are a small ciborium, a traveling altar, a chalice decorated with precious stones with a paten, and a golden codex. The altar table is covered with a textile bearing a cross design.[79] This image highlights the prominence of the altar in the church interior. Along with sacred vessels, textile decorations and the priest's garments provided visual unity in the area of the altar and focused attention on the mass.[80] Textiles served crucial liturgical functions.

---

79. Fol. 4^r. This is the same illumination that contains the cloth with crosses mentioned above. Because the late ninth-century ciborium survives and accords with this depiction, Victor H. Elbern believes that the illumination may provide a relatively accurate representation of such an altar cover. Elbern, "Liturgisches Gerät und Reliquiare," 696–97. Adam Cohen has called that accuracy into question. Cohen, *The Uta Codex*, 93.

80. Elbern, "Liturgisches Gerät und Reliquiare," 695.

Figure 6. A deacon reading at an altar. This rare depiction of a man in ecclesiastical dress from the Carolingian world appears in the Stuttgart Psalter, folio 40^r. Photograph courtesy of Württembergische Landesbibliothek, Cod. bibl. 2° 23, Stuttgart.

Furthermore, liturgical textiles were costly. In Carolingian church inventories, numerous textiles are listed along with manuscripts and metal items, suggesting their great material and spiritual worth. A number of the textiles were ornamented with precious materials such as pearls, and many were silk or linen. The value of an object used to decorate a holy space was clearly significant to the Carolingians; they took pains to point out the richness of their church decorations in inventories. Precious furnishings could indicate that a place was considered sacred because patrons felt it worthwhile to provide such ornamentation.

We would know more about the relative richness, utility, and beauty of the cloths if we could study surviving ones. However, a catalogue of extant Carolingian textiles would be a slender volume. Certain Carolingian rulers and churches possessed some contemporary Byzantine and Sassanid silks, which came to western Europe either through long distance trade or as diplomatic gifts. In some rare cases, these eighth- and ninth-century textiles survived for centuries inside reliquaries wrapped around relics.[81] The most famous example

81. These include, among others, the Sens textiles, the silk of Calais, the St. Chaffre fragments, the Ottobeuren silk, and most famous, the lion silk at Aachen. Individual studies of such silks are too numerous to cite here but see *Kunst*, 534–36, 654–49 and the encyclopedic, though not always reliable, Francisque-Michel, *Recherches sur le commerce, la*

is the quadriga silk now at Aachen, believed to have been buried with Charlemagne. The early ninth-century Theodulf Bible in the cathedral treasury of Puy-en-Velay held valuable evidence—Carolingian-era textile samples placed between its pages with gold or silver lettering in order to protect the precious decoration from abrasion.[82] In the Vatican Museum reserves are six fragments of an eighth- to ninth-century Byzantine silk decorated with lions that had been glued to the binding of an evangelary from Santa Maria in Via Lata dated to c. 1015.[83] These Roman fragments suggest that the binders of manuscripts sometimes used textiles in their work and may help to explain the presence of the textile pieces from Puy-en-Velay. Because he was a "connoisseur" of art, Theodulf may also have simply admired and therefore collected and preserved these fine samples.[84] Although these cloths were removed from the Theodulf Bible in the nineteenth century for display purposes, forty-three are extant, mostly soft, fine fabrics, the majority of which are silk but include some cotton fabrics.[85] The silk samples, which could not have been of Carolingian origin, must have been imported or come as gifts.

Examples of textiles that Carolingian artisans fabricated are extremely rare, and even then, their exact provenance is usually uncertain. Although an extraordinarily rich and technically superb set of textiles survives at Maaseik, these embroideries may not be Carolingian in origin; they probably came from southern England no later than the late eighth or early ninth century. They have been attributed to Herlindis and Renula because their *vita* contains a description of an embroidery strikingly similar to the Maaseik embroideries.[86] Certainly, the *vita* was written long enough after the embroideries' arrival that an attribution to the local saints seems understandable. Perhaps, the *vita*'s author and his contemporaries thought the embroidery so extraordinary that the saints must have made it. Herlindis and Renula are also credited with the production of an evangelary decorated with gold and rich decorations whose description in their *vita* is similar to the evangelary now at Saint Catherine's Church in Maaseik. Dating from the first half of the eighth century, it was probably made at an Anglo-Saxon influenced religious house on the continent, possibly Echternach.[87] That two items of either great Anglo-Saxon influence or manufacture came to be associated with the saints is no surprise,

fabrication et l'usage des étoffes de soie, d'or et d'argent et autres tissus précieux en occident, principalement en France pendant le Moyen Âge, vol. 1, 6–71.

82. Freeman, "Theodulf of Orléans and the *Libri Carolini*," 698.
83. Museo Vaticano no. 62294. Volbach, *I Tessuti*, 45–6.
84. Freeman, "Theodulf of Orléans and the *Libri Carolini*," 697–98.
85. *Le Puy en Velay 43—Haute Loire (Auvergne)* 2, 4.
86. Tweddle and Budny, "The Maaseik Embroideries," 91–94.
87. Bierbrauer, "Der Einflu insular Handschriften auf die kontinentale Buchmalerei," 470.

given the women's alleged connections with both Willibrord and Boniface. The embroideries' closest artistic parallels are eighth-century Anglo-Saxon manuscripts and metalwork.[88] The embroideries need not, however, be of Anglo-Saxon manufacture and origin. Many continental manuscripts, including the Aldeneik evangelary, and metal works show profound Anglo-Saxon influence, but scholars have determined that some were definitely or probably produced on the continent.[89] By analogy, women on the continent may have produced textiles exhibiting similar Anglo-Saxon influence because of their contact with Anglo-Saxons and with Anglo-Saxon material culture.

The lack of extant embroideries means that it is impossible to determine the prevalence in Carolingian lands of fine textile work of similar quality to the Maaseik embroideries. However, the appearance and the description of those embroideries in the *vita* may give an idea of what finer church textiles may have looked like.

> Whence it happened that the saints made a certain altar cloth, which they had constructed with their own hands, and which with many methods and in diverse arrangements of different skill was decorated with countless ornaments of gold and with pearls, suitable for God and his saints, which they left behind in place after they died.[90]

Their hagiographer was at times prone to hyperbole, but the remarkable consonance between this description and the Maaseik embroideries suggests that, at the time of the *vita*'s composition in the late ninth century, fine textile production by religious women may have been expected. Both description and embroidery suggest the possible technical level, appearance, and richness of Carolingian fine textiles. Of course, not all religious textiles would have been as rich as this altar cloth. The habit of a monk would have been of simple fabric. In their construction, the varieties of religious cloths and vestments would have necessitated a range of quality, material worth, and decoration.

Written texts attest to such a high number of textiles that some surely were Carolingian products. It hardly seems likely that all would have been imported, traded, or received as gifts, as the silk fragments were. In their will of 867, Eberhard of Friuli and his wife Gisela left to their sons both secular and liturgical textiles. The testators listed items for personal use and those

---

88. Budny and Graham-Campbell, "An Eighth-Century Bronze Ornament from Canterbury and Related Works," 13–14.

89. Bierbrauer, "Der Einfluß"; Henderson, "Emulation and Invention in Carolingian Art," 250–56; Wamers, "Insulare Kunst im Reich Karls des Groen," 452–64.

90. *Vita Herlinde et Renulae*, chap. 12, 388.

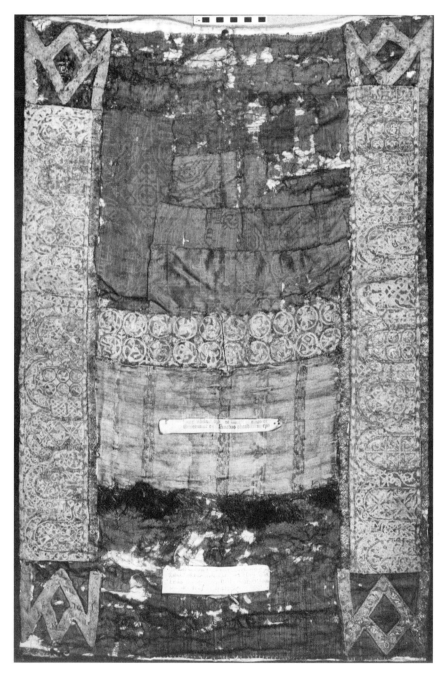

Figure 7. The Maaseik Embroideries, Church of St. Catherine, Maaseik. This extraordinarily rich and technically superb set of textiles includes patterned silk, tablet-woven bands, and elaborate embroidery. Photograph courtesy of and copyright Mildred Budny and Dominic Tweddle.

Figure 8. Detail of the Maaseik embroideries, Arcade I, Piers 4–6. Note the similarities between the passage from the saints' *vita* concerning their sewing and this detail of the embroideries, including the use of gold and silk, the complex patterns, and the aesthetic achievement of this piece. Many of the pearls once attached to this piece are now lost. Photograph courtesy of and copyright Mildred Budny and Dominic Tweddle.

from the chapel separately.[91] Among the personal textile items were a garment and mantle made with gold for their oldest son Unruoch and two richly decorated garments for another son Berengar. Each son also received rich liturgical vestments and cloths.[92] In his will of 876, Eccard of Autun left his chapel treasury to Richildis for her use as long as she lived. In addition to gold and silver liturgical objects and manuscripts, she received silk and linen liturgical vestments and cloths. These items were doubtless for use in his family chapel. To his sister Ada he left a golden girdle among other items.[93] Letters, chronicles, and histories attest to a great many textiles, which usually appear as gifts. Carolingian church inventories indicate the existence of many textiles. The following numbers come only from the twenty-three church inventories dated between 788 and 899 found in Bernhard Bischoff's *Mittelalterliche Schatzverzeichnisse*.[94] The religious institutions represented by these inventories range from small parish churches, with only a few textiles to large monasteries such as Reichenau. Because some inventories did not provide specific numbers for their textiles, these sums are minimums. There were at least 268 altar cloths, forty-seven liturgical cloths, and 294 vestments among a total of at least 761 textile items.[95] These few inventories originate from only a fraction of the total number of institutions that must have possessed textiles. These listings are similar to the descriptions of the church goods Charlemagne left to the poor including curtains, bedspreads, tapestries, and woolen goods.[96] Ermold the Black echoed Einhard's text when he listed vestments and many cloths (*pallia*) among the church goods that Charlemagne left to the poor.[97]

The few surviving religious textiles left to represent the many mentioned in Carolingian texts suggest a range from the economically valuable and technically elaborate to simpler pieces meant for frequent liturgical use. Common textiles in church inventories, *mappae*, were small cloths (usually 30–60 centimeters wide and 50–95 centimeters high).[98] An example survives from one of the Carolingian era sarcophagi in Sant'Apollinare in Classe near Ravenna; others were found in the reliquary treasury of the Lateran chapel Sancta

---

91. *CAC*, no. 1, 2–3.

92. Ibid.

93. *RCSBL*, no. 25, 64–65.

94. Bischoff, *Mittelalterliche Schatzverzeichnisse*, Inventories 1, 12, 13, 15, 19, 27, 28, 33, 34, 49, 56, 65, 66, 80, 82, 85, 89, 97, 107, 110, and 117.

95. Determining the exact form and function of most early medieval textiles is difficult because the Latin terms for textiles usually leave open a variety of possibilities. For more on this problem, see Budny, "The Byrhtnoth Tapestry," 265.

96. Einhard, *VK*, chap. 33, 39.

97. Ermold, *In honorem*, 64, line 814.

98. Only four items in the Bischoff inventories are called *mappae*, but at least seventy-three similar towels, napkins, or other useful small cloths are found in the inventories.

Sanctorum, where they may have served as relic covers or as *brandea*, cloths churchmen used to avoid direct contact with a venerated item. *Mappae* were often decorated with stripes, a cross, or inscriptions of Psalm verses, suggesting their liturgical use, but their precise functions are difficult to determine. In antiquity they were probably napkins or towels used for washing hands and may have been tucked into belts. Carolingian episcopal legislation mentions that priests ought to wash hands prior to mass, necessitating the presence of drying cloths.[99] Sometime in the ninth century the *mappa* developed into the striped liturgical maniple that, until Vatican II, bishops, priests, deacons, and subdeacons wore on their left arm.[100] One from the Sancta Sanctorum chapel in Rome is probably typical.[101] The eighth- or ninth-century linen cloth (62 by 40 centimeters) with wool and silk decorations is thought to have come from either Italy or Egypt, but unfinished cloth or thread could also have been imported into Italy or another part of continental Europe, where the final product could have been fabricated. The twelve rosettes of this *brandeum* may have been embroidered with basic satin stitching, a technique a non-professional could master, although the display conditions of this item prevented examination of its back.[102] Differentiating among raw materials, unfinished cloth, and final products makes it possible that a single piece had multiple "origins."

Such necessary and presumably numerous cloths may have comprised the female donations Carolingian clerics encouraged. As in the example above, surviving cloths indicate that a person could have worked imported cloth or cloth from a local workshop to create a *mappa* or *brandeum* whose completion and donation could indicate that person's virtue. For example, an individual with knowledge of hemming, sewing a satin stitch, and finishing a cloth by creating fringe on one side could easily have finished many of the Vatican *brandea* and other similar cloth fragments, including one with long fringe (61246), another fringed piece with blue crosses as decoration (61277), a yellow silk cloth with an appliquéd red cross (61282), and one with simple red

---

99. Hincmar of Rheims, *Collectio de ecclesiis et capellis*, ed. Martina Stratmann, MGH Fontes 14 (Hanover, Germany, 1990), 107; Riculf of Soissons, *Capitula*, chap. 9, 104.

100. *Kunst*, 825–26.

101. Museo Vaticano no. 61256. In May 2004, I examined many of the Carolingian-era textiles (roughly seventh to tenth centuries) that had once been part of the Vatican Library's Sancta Sanctorum collection, recently transferred to the Vatican Museum. These textiles have been encased between glass panes for roughly the last century; naturally, this preservation method hinders detailed study but nevertheless allowed me to note details not apparent in photographs.

102. Another similar, though discolored, *brandeum* from the Vatican collection could have similar origins (no. 61278).

crosses along with its woven stripes (61280).[103] Women without a great deal of training could have finished some of the relatively plain cloths from the Vatican collection.[104] Much of the hemming and stitching I observed did not appear perfect, nor did it look so difficult that one imagines the sewer having trouble accomplishing the work. However, some remaining textiles probably demanded high levels of expertise. Technically accomplished examples from the Vatican collection include a few seventh- to eighth-century silk cloths embroidered with lozenges, rosettes, and crosses (61279, 61290, 61291, 61310) in similar patterns and techniques to the tenth-century embroidered works found among the relics of Cuthbert in Durham; an accomplished embroiderer finished these pieces.[105] Women with such skills may have numbered among the powerful families of the Carolingian era, or trained women working in *gynaecea* may have produced them.

Among the most amazing surviving religious textiles are vestments from the sarcophagi in Sant'Apollinare in Classe, Ravenna. The three graves were for seventh- to ninth-century bishops, though the attribution is uncertain. These textiles are among the earliest extant Christian vestments. One, a bell chasuble, is a representative example. Made from Italian cloth with decorations of Syrian or Byzantine origin, it probably dates from the late eighth or ninth century based on the order of the burials.[106] In another sarcophagus were the remains of two dalmatics made of patterned silk.[107] Conservation and cleaning recently revealed that some fragments from these graves were in fact a red silk bell chasuble.[108] Numerous relic covers of imported silk survive from western Europe but especially in Rome. In the Vatican collections alone, some ten pieces of patterned silk traced to either Byzantium or the Islamic world from the seventh to tenth centuries survive because they were found with relics.[109] These surviving silk covers further indicate early medieval trade

---

103. I cite the Vatican textiles here with their current five-digit Vatican Museum numbers; upon transfer to the Museum, curatorial staff added a six to the beginning of their former inventory numbers (as listed in Volbach's catalogue). Volbach dates no. 61277 as "medieval," but given its similarity to other early medieval *brandea*, it could well be an early medieval example. Volbach, *I Tessuti*, 16.

104. Examples include no. 61222, 61309, and 61347, whose designs are part of their linen weaves, and possibly no. 61294 though the poor condition of this example could disguise its signs of expert construction.

105. Volbach, *I Tessuti*, 20.

106. *Kunst*, 820–23.

107. Ibid., 823–24.

108. Claudia Kusch, "Liturgical Vestments from Three Archbishops Burials at Sant'Apollinare in Classe, Ravenna," in *Interdisciplinary Approach to the Study and Conservation of Medieval Textiles. Textiles Working Group. Interim Meeting. Palermo 22–24 October 1998*, ed. Rosalia Varoli-Piazza (Palermo, Italy, 1998), 50–53.

109. no. 61231, 61244, 61245, 61247, 61249, 61250, 61251, 61258, 61272, 61275.

in patterned silk for religious and exchange purposes and stand as examples of imported cloth chosen or finished locally, indicating one way in which people in the Carolingian Empire used textiles for prominent purposes.

Given that some religious textiles were almost certainly produced or finished in western continental Europe in the eighth and ninth centuries, women were quite possibly involved in their fabrication. Without doubt, however, Carolingian women and men, donated textiles like these to churches and monasteries.[110] In 796, Alcuin informed Ethelburga, abbess of Faldbury in Worcestershire that "Liutgard, also a noble woman, has sent you the small gift of a garment—regard her as a sister in the love of God."[111] This present from Charlemagne's wife to the Anglo-Saxon abbess may have been a garment for her personal use or a cloth; the term *pallium* used in the letter could mean either. Regardless of its form, the gift created a bond between the queen and Faldbury. If Ethelburga and her sisters were meant to regard Liutgard as a "sister in the love of God," the implication is that Liutgard's gift was a pious act meant to evoke the good will and prayers of these religious women. The dress may have been elaborate, much like "Balthild's dress" that survived at Chelles in a reliquary. The remains of this linen garment, embroidered with colored silk, contain an embroidery imitating the jewels and necklace of the queen who may have donated such treasure to the convent.[112] Unless immediately transformed to serve a wholly new purpose, such a garment unlikely served a liturgical function. If the dress was indeed Balthild's or at least thought to be hers, the embroidery may represent the jewelry Balthild, according to the late eighth-century *Vita Eligii*, gave up when she heard about the vision of a "certain person" at court. Eligius had ordered this person to give the queen a message that she give up her rich jewels.[113] The embroidery would have been a reminder of the queen's humility, and the dress may originally have been one she wore, though it is unlikely it was buried with her, despite the fact that it was preserved in a reliquary associated with her.[114]

Ermold the Black's description of Harold the Dane's baptism demonstrates that textiles could help strengthen religious and political bonds. The empress Judith gave Harold rich clothing: tunic, belt, and cloak made with extremely valuable materials, including gold and gems.[115] Perhaps this gift was meant to

---

110. For comparable late Anglo-Saxon gifts of clothing to churches and use of silk relic covers see Fleming, "Acquiring, Flaunting and Destroying," 142–51.

111. MGH Ep. 4, no. 102, 149.

112. Laporte, "La chasuble de Chelles," 1–15.

113. Audoin of Rouen, *Vita Eligii episcopi Noviomagensis*, 2.41–2, MGH SRM 4, 663–742, 724–25.

114. Laporte, "La chasuble de Chelles," 18–20.

115. Ermold, *In honorem*, 172, lines 2252–65.

help culturally incorporate the Danes into Christendom. Naturally, the same cautions against taking descriptions of garments in panegyric literally apply here. Nevertheless, the idea that clothing constituted a suitable baptismal gift helps flesh out Thegan's more vague statement that after the baptism, Louis "gave [Harold] a large part of Frisia and adorned him with honorable gifts."[116] Similarly, Notker wrote in the *Gesta Karoli* that the sponsors of the Northmen who agreed to be baptized gave each newly baptized person a set of Frankish garments.[117] This episode recalls one in Hucbald of St. Amand's *Vita Rictrudis*, in which Rictrud cast aside secular garb and took up the humbler garments of the religious.[118] Women entering the religious life at San Salvatore in Brescia, as elsewhere, adopted new clothing as part of the entry ritual to their new community. At least rhetorically, a change of clothing implied spiritual transformation, and it probably also provided a visible sign of the transformation both to the recipient of the clothing and to any witnesses.

Gifts of textiles often had religious meaning, particularly those tied to the donation of land. Some of the church inventories mentioned above were recorded as part of land donations, which included a church or chapel along with its related items. For example, in 882 a noble man named Cundbert gave to a parish church in lower Bavaria a chasuble, a linen vestment, and an altar cloth. Similarly, in 899 in Freising, a noble widow named Irmburc gave churches at Murr and Moosburg to Bishop Waldo of Freising, whose treasuries included a silk chasuble, a linen chasuble, a woolen chasuble, a stole, a linen vestment, two handkerchiefs, two belts, four curtains, and four banners.[119] Royal donations were another way churches and monasteries obtained such textiles. For example, in his c. 888 donation to the Benedictine convent at Andlau founded by his wife Richardis, Charles the Fat gave veils, liturgical cloths, altar cloths, and hangings.[120] Gifts of textile items, like donations of land and other goods, may have been a form of *memoria*; in exchange, recipients were expected to pray for donors and their kin.[121] Although presents of ordinary textiles would have been useful to a religious institution, richer textiles would have been all the more worthy. For example, a complex embroidery's material value and requisite fabrication time made it a considerable donation that contributed to the prestige of the donor.

Witgar's belt comprises the most substantial Carolingian evidence for this association. This belt not only contains enough gold thread to give it a

116. Thegan, *Gesta*, chap. 33, 220.
117. Notker, *GK*, 2.19, 90.
118. Hucbald, *Vita Rictrudis*, chap. 15, 85.
119. Bischoff, *Mittelalterliche Schatzverzeichnisse*, no. 15, 26; no. 49, 59.
120. Ibid., no. 117, 119.
121. For an Anglo-Saxon example, see Budny, "The Byrhtnoth Tapestry."

golden appearance but also shows great technical virtuosity with its woven red inscription: "VVITGARIO TRIBVIT SACRO SPIRAMINE PLENVM/ HANC ZONAM REGINA NITENS SANCTISSIMA HEMMA" (Queen Emma, shining and most pious, gave this belt to Witgar, a man filled with the Holy Spirit). Thus, the belt had both substantial economic and artistic value. Furthermore, it served a significant religious function. The apparent shortening of the belt has obscured its use. Now consisting of two end parts joined together, it is only 138 centimeters long (3.8 centimeters wide). Some have suggested that it once displayed a longer inscription or ornamental decoration, while others have speculated that the middle part consisted of less valuable cloth that the bishop's outer vestment would have hidden. Because only the remaining ends would have been visible, only they needed to be rich in appearance. It was definitely a liturgical belt, probably used to tie together the *alba* or priestly undergarment. Belts may not have been mandatory clerical clothing in the Merovingian era, but possible ecclesiastical belts survive from this period, and Peter provided precedent for their use (John 21:18).[122]

The St. Afra treasury contains a band similar to the Witgar belt.[123] Usually dated to the ninth or tenth century, this band is named not for its recipient but for its probable donor, an unknown Ailbecunda. Almost certainly used as a belt, it survives in two fragments of card-woven red silk ornamented with narrow yellow-green borders. The first fragment measures 123.5 centimeters long and 3.8 centimeters wide and consists of two pieces sewn together in the middle where a glass container is attached; the second is 35.5 centimeters long and 3.8 centimeters wide. Both fragments have the same weave and were part of the same belt. They are roughly the same width as the Witgar belt and display a similar majuscule inscription naming their female donor, except that it is the same red as the belt's background, making the script less prominent than on the Witgar belt. The first fragment's inscription reads "IN NOMINE DOMINI AILBECUND[AE] VE...VXPI [*Christi*] IHEV [*Jesu*] NOSTRI IN NOMINE DOME [*domini*]" (in the name of the Lord, Ailbecunda VE...V in the name of our lord Jesus Christ). The second fragment's inscription, "[N]OMINE DOMINI NO[STRI]" (in the name of our Lord), continued from or preceded the inscription of the first. Gold threads decorate the ends of the belt. By the seventeenth century, cathedral documents

---

122. Bonnie Effros, "Appearance and Ideology: Creating Distinctions between Clerics and Laypersons in Early Medieval Gaul," in *Encountering Medieval Textiles and Dress: Objects, Texts, and Images*, ed. Désirée G. Koslin and Janet E. Snyder (New York, 2002), 7–24, 8–9.

123. St. Afra Diözesanmuseum 5002 and 5003. Much of my description of the Ailbecunda belt relies on my own observation and information provided by the museum in June 2004.

Figure 9. Dating to sometime between 860 and 876, this rich belt was a gift from Louis the German's wife, Emma (died 876), to Bishop Witgar of Augsburg (861?–887). Reproduced by permission from Diözesanmuseum St. Afra Augsburg, #5001.

identify it as the belt of Mary because another card-woven band, which I will refer to as the Marian belt, is sewn to the second Ailbecunda fragment.[124] The Marian belt is a narrow, multicolored card-woven band (19 centimeters long, 2.6 centimeters wide), which may be from the twelfth or thirteenth century and of Islamic origin.[125] The second section of the Ailbecunda belt also has a fourteenth-century silver clasp with a depiction of the Annunciation. The first fragment of the Ailbecunda belt has a silver-framed piece of glass containing portions of a multicolored card weaving that match the Marian belt; on the other side of the frame is an unclear seal probably from the fourteenth century. Ailbecunda's anonymity and the belt's later associations with Mary's belt make dating this belt conclusively difficult, but its similarity to the Witgar belt and the appearance of the name Ailbecunda in the *Libri Confraternitum* of St. Gall and Reichenau strongly suggest a southern German origin for the donor.[126]

A few other European collections contain early medieval woven belts. The Vatican Museum has a sixth- to eighth-century belt found with a set of unidentified relics (61292). This belt is card woven in red, yellow, white, and gray with a green border and fringed ends. Its now damaged decoration consists of small white and gray triangles on a red background. At 2.42 meters by 1.8 centimeters it is long and narrow.[127] It may have originally functioned as the belt for churchman. Found in 1962, a bishop's grave at the cathedral of Speyer included another belt that is quite similar to the Witgar and Ailbecunda belts. Dating to the ninth or tenth century, the card-woven, red silk belt survives in three fragments, all 3.6 centimeters wide and 66.2, 11.4, and 54.6 centimeters long. The locations of the three fragments on the body (by the left thigh, the left side, and the right pelvis edge) indicate the pieces were once a single belt. In a 2.4 centimeter central strip are the following inscriptions: "[BENEDIC] TIONEM SICVT ISAC BENEDIXIT JACOB MANU [SUA]" (blessing just as Isaac blessed Jacob [with his own] hand); "S DNI SI" (S Lord SI); "[ANGE] LVM C SVVM CVSTODEM QVI CVSTODIA [TE]" (his heavenly protector [to] watch [over you]). The inscription may be a fragment of a blessing, perhaps "manus domini sit tibi in benedictionem sicut Isaac benedixit Jacob

---

124. The belt, referred to as "unser Lieben Frauen gürttel" among other similar appellations, is mentioned in Augsburg cathedral documents dating to 1622 (Domkapitelsprotokolle/Neuburger Abgabe/Band 5542) and 1719 (Domkapitelsprotokolle/Neuburger Abgabe/Band 5623) now housed in the Staatsarchiv Augsburg.

125. Müller-Christensen, *Sakrale Gewänder des Mittelalters*, 14; *Suevia Sacra. Frühe Kunst in Schwaben* (Augsburg, 1973), 196–97.

126. Heide Werner-Clementschitsch, Denis A. Chevalley, and Martin Mannewitz, *Der Dom zu Augsburg* (Munich, 1995), 390.

127. Volbach, *I Tessuti*, 55.

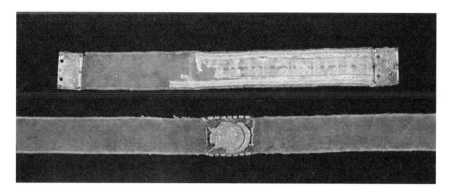

Figure 10. The Ailbecunda belt is another tablet woven band similar to the Witgar belt. It is also housed in the St. Afra treasury. Reproduced by permission from Diözesanmuseum St. Afra Augsburg, #5002–3.

manu sua," "Dominus mittat angelum," or the beginning of a similar blessing. In letter type and technique this belt and the Ailbecunda belt are so similar that they could have come from the same workshop.[128]

Another band with an inscription came to light in 1940 when a chest associated with the relics of Ambrose, packed in 1863 and stored in the Capella del Transito di Sant'Ambrogio in Milan's cathedral, was opened. Inside were many fine but damaged textiles including an eleventh-century band with signs of the cross and an inscription: "✠ SUB HOC PALLIO TEGITUR DALMATICA SCI AMBROSII ✠ SUB QUO EANDEM DALMATICAM TEXIT DOMNUS HERIBERTVS ARCHIEPISCOPVS" (Under this pallium lies covered the dalmatic of Saint Ambrose; under which the lord archbishop Heribert has covered the same dalmatic).[129] In many respects, it is similar to the Witgar, Ailbecunda, and Speyer belts. Made of silk, card-woven, with an inscription, the band survived because of its association with the cult of Ambrose and the archepiscopacy of Heribert. Heribert probably commissioned the band and chose the inscription and design, but he most likely did not make it given the rare instances of male textile work. The Ailbecunda and Witgar belts suggest that a woman may have been responsible for its construction. In light of the other ninth- or tenth-century bands similar in construction, function, and/or donation to the Witgar belt, it seems that such pieces were not unusual. Women may have presented or constructed other belts

128. Hans Erich Kubach and Walter Haas, eds., *Der Dom zu Speyer, Die Kunstdenkmäler von Rheinland-Pfalz* (Munich, 1972), 1016.
129. Reggiori, *Antichi Tessuti*, 15, 62–67.

similar to those now housed in Augsburg in quality and in the designation of the donor's name.[130]

Before becoming bishop of Augsburg, Witgar served in the chancellery of Louis the German and played a major role in the king's diplomatic missions. Emma may have given him the belt on the occasion of his investiture, or she may have given it to him while he was chancellor for her husband between 858 and 860, a period when both Witgar and she were "politically vulnerable."[131] A belt marked the status and office of any male Carolingian aristocrat.[132] Charlemagne always wore a sword belt (*balteus*) of gold or silver.[133] In 791, having reached adolescence, Louis the Pious was belted with a sword at the altar at Regensburg.[134] In their will, Eberhard and Gisela left belts (*baltea*) to all of their sons, even those in the religious life. Presumably these belts went with the swords the sons received, and all except one were described in rich terms, golden and decorated with gems.[135] Two belts (*baltea*) decorated with gems comprised part of the liturgical treasure that Eccard of Autun left his wife Richildis.[136] A belt could serve as a worthy gift for a king: Charlemagne sent Offa a belt along with a Hunnish sword and two silk cloths in 796.[137] Thus, Emma not only congratulated Witgar with her gift but also denoted his status and rank, a queenly duty. Each time Witgar put on the belt, he would have been reminded of Emma and the meanings of her present, and each time he wore it upon the altar, he brought Emma's "presence" to a place where she was never otherwise allowed. Ailbecunda's belt could also have brought her presence into places she could not enter and would have reminded the viewer and wearer of the belt's donor, making it a commemorative object. These two donors probably wove the belts themselves rather than have them made. Although the work is complex, its fabrication technique—card weaving, in existence since the Iron Age—is relatively simple. Given enjoinments to and descriptions of royal and aristocratic women doing textile work, it seems the sort of work that could have been expected of a queen or other wealthy woman.

---

130. Card-woven bands have been found in graves in Germany, England, France, Switzerland, Scandinavia, and Italy. Marie Schuette, "Brettchenweberei," in *Reallexikon zur deutschen Kunstgeschichte*, 2 (Stuttgart, 1948), 1137–49, at 1144.

131. Goldberg, "*Regina nitens*," 81.

132. Leyser, "Early Medieval Canon Law," 51–72; Nelson, "Ninth-Century Knighthood," 264; Régine Le Jan, "Remises d'armes et rituels du pouvoir chez les francs: Continuités et ruptures de l'époque carolingienne," in *Femmes, pouvoir et société dans le Haut Moyen Âge*, ed. Régine Le Jan (Paris, 2001), 171–89, 175.

133. Einhard, *VK*, chap. 23, 28.

134. Astronomer, *Vita Hludowici*, chap. 6, 300.

135. *CAC*, no. 1, 2–3.

136. *RCSBL*, no. 25, 64–65.

137. MGH Ep 4, no. 100, 146.

Women may have selected foreign-made textiles for use in religious settings. Among the rich Byzantine, Persian, and Syrian silks that survived as relic covers is a red silk fragment, (34.5 by 39 centimeters). It depicts the hunt of the Amazons and was made in Byzantium in the late eighth or early ninth century. Now in the museum of Meaux, it came from Faremoutiers (Seine-et-Marne), the convent where Charlemagne's daughter Rotrud was abbess (c. 840–852). During her period in office, the relics of St. Fara, the convent's seventh-century founder, were translated there, and the fragment may have covered the saint's relics. Rotrud would have been familiar with the Amazons from Orosius's *Seven Books of Histories Against the Pagans*. Rotrud and her sisters may have been associated with the Amazons, and the sisters may even have seen the fabric's subjects as role models.[138] The intellectual and political nature of Rotrud's possible selection of fabric design may reflect wider practice. Other prominent religious women, particularly abbesses, may have chosen foreign textiles for use in their religious houses. Laywomen, such as Gisela and Richildis, may also have selected certain rich fabrics to donate to churches or monasteries or provided them for use in their families' chapels. Like Rotrud's fabric, their choices may have reflected their learning and political or familial goals. Perhaps designs may have been meant to recall the donor or her family.

Women who created and donated rich textiles for religious uses performed pious acts associated with female virtue. Although on one level the connection between virtuous women and textile work is a literary trope, Carolingian aristocratic women's connection to textile work had potential social, economic, and political effects for them, their families, and religious institutions. Donations of religious textiles may have enhanced the prestige of their families among groups of both high and low social status, contributing to the family's ability to exert influence. Just as the expectations that women perform textile work, conveyed in written sources, probably influenced their choice of activities, their textile activities in turn affected the image of them in sources as virtuous spinners and embroiderers.

General Textile Production

Women looked after much textile fabrication in the Carolingian world. Although written sources offer examples of fine embroidery work done by aristocratic women, poor women did a great deal more textile work than elite

---

138. Nelson, "Women at the Court of Charlemagne," 46.

women. Working in *gynaecea* on estates, in trade centers, and at dependent villages of religious communities and estates, women produced clothing and other general textile goods. Fortunately, the evidence for textile production is relatively rich in comparison to other areas of craft production. First, the Carolingian reforms sometimes resulted in legislation concerning female textile workers. Second, archaeologists have found postholes of looms in the remains of workshops where textile fabrication took place. The addition of relatively numerous surviving loom weights and spindle whorls makes identification of the loci of textile production possible.

Textiles served essential purposes in the Carolingian world but are frequently missing from scholarly work on the early medieval economy.[139] Women's participation in and supervision of textile work was a key element of Carolingian production, now seemingly absent from the records as so few non-silk textiles have survived. An investigation of general textile production reveals that it was a widespread craft activity and that the demand for textiles meant that *gynaecea* were almost certainly relatively common throughout Carolingian lands. Women on dependent farms also performed textile work as part of their service to estates. Aristocratic women, who themselves received textile training, probably supervised *gynaecea* and kept track of textile production on dependent farms. They needed textiles to provide hospitality, and textile work was considered female work. Their roles as supervisors of these workshops further demonstrate their centrality to family economies and underline the ways in which women helped to produce aristocratic culture.

Under the rubric of general textile production, I include the fabrication of textile goods and the finishing of imported cloth in workshops or on dependent farms. Carding wool, spinning, weaving, beating linen, dyeing, cutting, sewing, and adding final touches such as decoration to textile pieces also fall into this category, but embroidery and other detailed work do not. (The shearing of sheep and harvesting of flax may have been women's work, although the sources are rather unclear about who performed these labors).[140] All these activities would have been done in *gynaecea* or *pisiles*, workshops for women who performed textile work. Although Carolingian and other early medieval sources seem at first glance to use them almost interchangeably, some controversy exists concerning the precise meanings of these terms. In a charter of July 6, 813, for example, Bishop Rotaldus of Verona promised

---

139. Michael McCormick considers silk production and trade but offers no detailed study of other textile fabrication. McCormick, *Origins of the European Economy*, 719–26. Chris Wickham refers to textiles as promising sources but focuses on pottery. Wickham, *Framing the Early Middle Ages*, 699–700.

140. Riché, *Daily Life in the World of Charlemagne*, 163.

his community of canons one-tenth of his estates' produce, including linen. "Of the clothing, which will come from the *pisile* or *ginicro (gynaecea)* [I will give] a tenth."[141] *Pisele* may imply that the room was heated, or it may refer to the status of those working there.[142] In the *Brevium exempla* the writer used the term *pisile* to describe the women's workshops it lists, including eleven at Anappes alone.[143] Regardless of the difference between *pisele* and *gynaecea*, sources from the Gallo-Roman period to well into the ninth century and beyond attest to the operation of these workshops. Their frequent appearance in contemporary sources attests to their widespread existence in the Carolingian period. These *gynaecea* remained the norm until the eleventh and twelfth centuries, when workshops in cities became the primary producers of cloth and textile goods.[144]

Textile work appears mainly in the countryside, where aristocratic women almost certainly helped to supervise the work of women of relatively low status. The requirements in the *Capitulare de villis* for women's quarters conformed to the capitulary's general concern that work be done in an efficient manner, but they also suggest a need to protect the women workers from outsiders or outsiders from the workers.

> That our *genitia* shall be properly arranged—that is, concerning the small houses, *pislis*, covered huts, and cellars; let them have good enclosures all round, and strong doors, so they can do our work well.[145]

The status of women in *gynaecea* has been the subject of some dispute; some have suggested that they were also concubines for the estate's lord or simply women of ill repute.[146] The *Capitulare Olonnense* of 822–23, for example, stated that adulterous women were not to enter *gynaecea* lest they have opportunity to have sex with more men.[147] The Synod of Meaux-Paris of 845 stated that men should not use church tithes to support their dogs or *gynaecea*.[148] Yet, as seen in some other evidence cited here, the sources do not always discuss female textile workers so pejoratively. Based on an assumed ability to mass-produce items of high quality some scholars have thought that the

141. *Italia Sacra sive de Episcopis Italiae*, vol. 5, ed. Ferdinando Ughelli (Venice, 1720), 708.

142. Herlihy, *OM*, 36.

143. *BE*, 52–55.

144. Ennen, *Frauen im Mittelalter*, 89.

145. *CV*, chap. 49, 60.

146. *PAI*, vol. 1, 617–23; Herlihy, *OM*, 36–38.

147. MGH Capit. 2.1, chap. 5, 317.

148. MGH Conc. 3, no. 78, 125.

female textile workers in the *gynaecea* were professionals while others have not.[149] Female textile workers differed from other skilled craftsmen in status and reputation, but most important in gender. The overtones of sexual misconduct in some sources reflect concerns about women not under the direct male supervision.

Monasteries appear to have had little textile work done on location, further suggesting that, although textiles moved through a male world, men, with the exception of felters, rarely produce textiles themselves. By the beginning of the ninth century in the *villae* of the Parisian monasteries, either unfree (*manicipia*) or semi-free women (*lidiles*) wove linen and wool as dues for their monastic lords, as attested in the early ninth-century polyptych of Saint-Germain-des-Prés.[150] The mid-eighth–century St. Gall plan, for example, did not include an area specifically for textile workers in its Great Collective Workshop, though the monastery certainly had many textiles and would have needed them. The plan designates an area for fullers in the annex to the workshop, and the monks may have been meant to finish woven cloth through fulling.[151] In his commentary on the *Rule of St. Benedict*, Hildemar wrote that monks must stop sewing leather and cloth once they hear the bell for prayer, indicating that monks may have done some sewing.[152] Adalhard of Corbie (c. 750–826) mentions a number of handcrafts in his *Statutes*, a text directed to monks, but not textile work. The only references he makes are related to gifts of old clothes to the poor and the tithes of cleaned wool due to the monastery from its dependents. Nowhere do his statutes explain what happens to that wool.[153] At the monastery of San Vincenzo al Volturno archaeologists have found work areas for various crafts, but not for textiles.[154] The evidence points to monastic acquisition of textiles from outside the monastic walls. As Hildemar's commentary indicated, monks may have sewn finished cloth, but weaving was the work of women who could not enter the cloister.

Monasteries obtained textile items through renders from dependents, outside markets and donations, rather than through self-production. Fulda annually received 855 cloaks from its farms in Friesland. *Pallia fresonica*, high

---

149. In favor of professionals is Capelle, "Handwerk in der Karolingerzeit," 425. Pierre Riché did not include them in his list of artisans in *Daily Life in the World of Charlemagne*, 145–46.

150. *PAI*, vol. 1, 723–25; *Un village*, 278.

151. *Mittelalterliche Schatzverzeichnisse*, no. 118, 120–21; Horn and Born, *The Plan of St. Gall*, vol. 2, 189–99; vol. 3, 65–66. Horn and Born suggest with good reason that the *tegmina* in the verse labeling the Great Collective Workshop refers not to clothing specifically but rather generally to all items necessary for the monastic life.

152. Hildemar, *Expositio Regulae*, ed. P. Rupert Mittermüller (Regensburg, 1880), 192.

153. Adalhard of Corbie, *Statutes*, no. 3, 354; no. 10, 376.

154. Mitchell, "Monastic Guest Quarters," 143–53.

quality wool cloths known throughout the Frankish empire in the ninth century, were either manufactured in Frisia or came through there as part of North Sea trade. The monastery at Werden brought in more than a hundred Frisian cloths a year. Monasteries probably acquired this trade product through dependent estates and then bought and sold many of the cloths for a profit.[155] Frisian cloth was not, however, the only textile available to religious houses. Donation charters and polyptychs frequently mention linen fabric (*cam[i]siles*), wool, and flax (*sar[i]ciles*). These cloths were used in manufacturing shirts (*camisiae*). Shirts, coats, and capes of wool (*pallia, saga*) were sometimes made outside the monastery and brought in. Such items were also for sale in markets. Gerald of Aurillac, for example, bought a cloak in Italy at a bargain price compared to what he would have paid in Aquitaine.[156] In Italy, textiles, especially silk, came through Venice.[157]

Women fabricated the textiles from the dependent farms of monasteries. The polyptych of Saint-Germain-des-Prés lists various groups of female textile workers. Because polyptychs display great variety both internally and in comparison to one another, these examples offer some possibilities concerning the cloth fabrication of female dependents in the Carolingian world.[158] In one entry, *ancillae* were responsible for making fabric from linen given to them.[159] In another the female workers were divided in two groups, the *ancillae* (unfree women) and the *lidae* (semi-free women). Of the fourteen *ancillae*, the polyptych states that if they are given linen, they will make *camsilos*; the nineteen *lidae* will also make *camsilos* and pay four *denarii*.[160] Sometimes just a few women worked on cloth; at Cavannas and Lodosa, for example, two *lidae* made four *camsilos* while one ancilla made a wool *sarcilem*.[161] Individual women at certain *manses* had to provide various textiles as part of the dues to the monastery whether *sarciles* or *camsilos*.[162] Every entry concerning *sarciles*

---

155. Lebecq, *Marchands et navigateurs frisons du haut moyen Âge*, vol. 1, 131–34; Olivier Bruand, *Voyageurs et marchandises aux temps carolingiens. Les réseaux de communication entre Loire et Meuse aux viiie et ixe siècles* (Brussels, 2002), 243–44.

156. Odo, *Vita Geraldi*, 1.27, col. 658.

157. McCormick, *Origins of the European Economy*, 680, 726.

158. Devroey, "La démographie du polyptyque de Saint-Remi de Reims," 82.

159. *PAI*, vol. 2, no. 11.13, 121. On these women see Devroey, "Femmes au miroir," 227–49.

160. *PAI*, vol. 2, no. 13.109 and 110, 150. Jean Verdon suspects that the women termed *accolae* in the polyptych of Saint-Remi de Reims worked in *gynaecea* mentioned in the same document. "La femme vers le milieu du ixᵉ siècle d'après le polyptyque de l'abbaye de Saint-Remi de Reims," 111–34. Compare to Devroey's study of the same polyptych, "La démographie," esp. 84, note 10.

161. *PAI*, vol. 2, no. 23.27, 243–44.

162. Ibid., vol. 2, no. 15.70, 76, 78, and 82, 174–76; no. 20.2, 208; no. 20.38–41, 212; no. 25.6, 272; fragment 2.6, 280.

specifies that a woman or women will make them, and one section contains a short series of women listed with no male counterparts whose dues include making a *camisile* of linen.[163] The homestead (*curtis*) attached to the monastery at Staffelsee had a women's workshop with twenty-four women who worked with wool and linen and even made bandages. On the twenty-three *manses* associated with that homestead, the wives were to make one piece of linen and one of woolen cloth as well as prepare malt and bake bread for the monastery once a year.[164] The Constitution of Abbot Ansegis (823–33), recorded in the *Gesta sanctorum patrum Fontanellensis*, lists the goods various dependent areas were to provide to the monastery. Of the twenty-three places listed nine had to provide cloths either to be used as towels or napkins or to be made into clothing. Boulogne and Thérouanne were required to provide sixty finished vestments.[165] The act constituting the "mense conventuelle" under abbot Hilduin of St. Denis on January 22, 832 states that sixteen *villae* situated in the Paris region were to furnish clothing and leather shoes to the monks.[166] In a charter fragment of 833 housed at Chartres, the *comes* Troannus and his wife Bova promised to provide forty-one cloths, among other items, to the monastery of St. Martin each year on Martin's feast day.[167] Louis the German made a donation in 840 to the monastery of Nideraltaich on the Danube that included a *curtis* that listed women who worked in a *gynaeceum* among other workers.[168] An aristocratic household may also have received dues from dependents in the form of textiles.

Monasteries sometimes acquired dependent textile workshops through aristocratic donation. A 735–37 donation by Count Eberhard to the monastery at Murbach, surviving in a fifteenth-century cartulary, discusses women working in a *gynaeceum*.[169] Male monasteries do not appear to have had *gynaecea* attached directly to them. The arrangement of having women on dependent lands provide textile goods to monasteries seems understandable given the sometimes poor reputation of female textile workers and the lack of evidence

---

163. Ibid., vol. 2, no. 20.38–41, 212.

164. *BE*, 50–51.

165. *Gesta sanctorum patrum Fontanellensis Coenobii (Gesta abbatum Fontanellensium)*, ed. F. Lohier and R. P. J. Laporte (Paris, 1936), 118–121.

166. In excavations at the villages Villiers-le-Sec and Baillet-en-France, no elaborate textile fragments were found; women appear to have been creating more basic items. Gentili, "L'éclairage domestique," 275–76.

167. *PAI*, vol. 2, appendix 10, 345.

168. *Monumenta Boica*, vol. 11 (Munich, 1771), no. 7, 108. This donation was reconfirmed in c. 841. Ibid., no. 8, 109.

169. This document is cited in full in Wilhelm Levison, "Kleine Beiträge zu Quellen der fränkischen Geschichte," *Neues Archiv der Gesellschaft für ältere deutsche Geschichtskunde* 27 (1902): 331–408, 387.

indicating that monks had the skill necessary to supervise textile work directly. Clerics wished to avoid the dangers of a female workshop close to a monastery, and monastic rules forbidding women entry prevented female workers within the male cloister.

Religious women were meant to do textile work themselves. The available archaeological and charter evidence indicates that the ideal of Carolingian religious women performing textile work themselves as part of the *opus Dei* was a reality. Although female religious communities could have bought textiles, no records remain of such purchases. Surely the members performed their own textile work, and/or servants within their communities did it for them. Most likely, members divided their textile labor with servants, performing finer, more intricate (and interesting) work themselves, while servants produced more basic items. Ideally textile work contributed to the members' humility: they were meant to do their own sewing, mending, and washing. According to her *vita*, Hathumoda of Gandersheim gave clothes to local men and women—an act of charity resulting from textile work.[170] The allowance for servants under the *Institutio sanctimonialium*, however, suggests that religious women may have maintained an aristocratic lifestyle by supervising their servants in some parts of that labor.[171] Thus, in religious houses as well as on secular estates, wealthy aristocratic women supervised other women in creating basic textiles.

Supervising *gynaecea* may have composed a major duty of some lay aristocratic women. They would have had to help supply the women's workshops in a timely and sufficient manner:

Let them take pains to provide the women's workshops, as instructed, with materials at the appropriate times,—that is, linen, wool, woad, vermilion, madder, wool-combs, teazels, soap, oil, vessels, and other small things that are needed there.[172]

Furthermore, they may have had to buy or arrange for the construction of the vertical two-beam looms used at this time.[173] The sole extant example from this period is the ninth-century loom found in the ship burial at Oseberg, but

---

170. Agius, *Vita Hathumodae*, chap. 25, 175.

171. *IS*, canon 13, 447; Heidebrecht and Nolte, "Leben im Kloster," 108; Schilp, *NW*, 80.

172. *CV*, chap. 43, 59–60.

173. An image in a tenth-century manuscript of Hrabanus Maurus's *De Universo* depicts a two-beam loom. Morisset, "Le tissage," 280. Because this manuscript presumably descends from a Carolingian exemplar, this illustration may be an accurate representation of a Carolingian loom. An image in the Utrecht Psalter, c. 820–30, shows a vertical two-beam loom. Chapelot and Fossier, *The Village and House in the Middle Ages*, 120.

these looms sometimes left telltale posthole remains. At Baillet-en-France postholes remain at intervals of 1.05 meters and 1.42 meters.[174] This width corresponds to the length of *camsiles* of two to three ells—.88 meters and 1.33 meters—to which written sources such as the polyptych of Saint-Germain-des-Prés attest.[175]

No systematic study covering all archaeological remains of textile work in Frankish lands exists, but a sampling of evidence is an excellent guide to the sort of work Carolingian textile workers probably did and that aristocratic women almost certainly supervised. Women spun with two sorts of spindles, long and short shafted.[176] A number of tools and objects associated with textile work were found in the excavations of St. Denis' dependent villages of Villiers-en-Sec, Baillet-en-France, and Belloy. The spindles, shears, combs for carding, stamps made of bone, and many glass linen-smoothers indicate much textile activity.[177] Other examples of Carolingian textile tools abound, but a comprehensive study of these various finds has not been conducted.[178] Dyeing cloth, another task of women in a *gynaeceum*, would have required some expertise on the part of the aristocratic women who supervised it. Because of its mess and smell, they may, however, have avoided direct participation in dyeing. Among the items supplied to the women's workshops were plants and substances for dyeing—"woad, vermilion, madder"—mentioned above in the passage from the *Capitulare de villis*.[179] Some dyes may have been obtained from plants in the estates' gardens.[180] An aristocratic mistress may have coordinated the cultivation and conveyance of such items to the *gynaeceum*. Furthermore, she may have supplied the necessary tools and helped to regulate production so that the requisite numbers of textile pieces were made. Wool and linen were supposed to be included in the annual statement of a royal estate's income.[181] *Gynaecea* at estates probably produced a surplus, allowing for possible donation to a religious institution, sale at market, or gifts to the needy. According to her anonymous *vita*, Aldegund distributed garments that she had inherited, among other items, to the poor and churches.[182] Her act

---

174. Rémy Gaudagnin, "L'habitat," in *Un village*, 150–76, 151–2, and figure 46, 159.

175. Dominique Morisset, "Le tissage," in *Un village*, 278–83, at 279–80. *PAI*, vol. 1, 719–20.

176. Alexandre-Bidon and Mane, "Le vie quotidienne," 351.

177. Gentili, "L'éclairage domestique," 276.

178. Examples of shears, spindle whorls, and loom weights appear in *Kunst*, 239–44, 276–77.

179. On early medieval dyeing, see Colombini, "Teintures attestées de l'Antiquité au Moyen Âge."

180. *CV*, chap. 70, 63; *BE*, 53, 55.

181. *CV*, chap. 62, 61–62.

182. *Vita Aldegundis*, chap. 20, 1044.

demonstrated her humility and her denial of worldly goods, and it was an act of piety that conformed to the Christian duty to look after the poor.

Aristocratic women needed substantial managerial competence in order to keep textile workshops running and to allocate the cloth that may have come from dependent farms. They had both to supervise the women workers and to see to raw materials and finished products. Through participation in these activities elite women developed vertical bonds with their female dependents. Products turned out under their supervision also helped them to create horizontal and vertical bonds with their peers and superiors through providing hospitality, which necessitated (among other things) bed linens. Through their textile work, furthermore, women made a substantial contribution to local, regional, and possibly international commerce. If more was known about the supervision of women's workshops on the dependent farms of monasteries or more generally about who did textile work in trade centers or in Frisia or wherever *pallia fresonica* was made, we would know far more about the relative degree of this female contribution. Women's contribution began at the level of the estate, but as goods produced under their supervision made their way into the European economy, this contribution became a substantial one.

Historians of the early medieval economy recognize the dynamic economic character of the Carolingian estate and its potential to supply products both to markets and to North Sea trade. Scholarly understanding of the extent of Frankish trade with the Mediterranean has recently expanded. Surplus textiles were part of these markets, a fact that gives Carolingian women of every status a much more prominent role in the economy than has heretofore been recognized. Our present historical appreciation for the importance of women's management of household, estate, and religious house in the early Middle Ages must deepen and expand to include a recognition not only of women's competence but also of their crucial contributions to the economy as a whole.

"Made by the Hands of Women"

Textiles "made by the hands of women" comprised essential components of the material culture that marked Carolingian aristocrats. Scholars have long understood that certain items, including horses, arms, and land, indicated high status among powerful men in the Carolingian world. Possession and display of rich decorative textiles and clothing equally indicated wealth and rank. The belts given by Queen Emma and the anonymous Ailbecunda provide compelling examples of the ways in which textiles may have given women an opportunity to denote the status of powerful men. Similarly other textiles conveyed the virtue, wealth, and competence of lay and religious aristocratic women, while also helping aristocratic families to build networks of social bonds with each other and religious households through display and gift giving. More than the other forms of movable wealth mentioned above, many textiles provided material and spiritual benefits to makers and owners alike, similar to those of the fine metalworks, ivories, and manuscripts funded by royal and aristocratic patrons. Because women were closely associated with textiles in the Carolingian world, they were responsible for objects that displayed elite rank to outsiders and reinforced aristocratic self-awareness within families. Women bore and transmitted aristocratic identity through their knowledge of textiles and textile manufacture and decoration, making women and textiles essential to the wider social, political, and religious networks that marked the Carolingian elite.

CONCLUSION
The Lifecycle of Aristocratic Women

In his *De universo* of 842–46, Raban Maur discussed women throughout his explanation of the ages of man, and as the following passage indicates, his beliefs accord with the language of distrust surrounding women, and bear little relationship to the female social practices discussed in the chapters of this book.

> Man and wife, soul and flesh, the work of begetting a son done by both, as in Exodus: Let him serve you with his wife and sons. Likewise man and wife, devil and the city of Babylon, that is, the meeting of all evils. For woman is hindered from learning by weakness (*mollitie*) and transformed, as if softer, so she is named woman (*mulier*).[1]

This rather hostile examination comes from perhaps the only Carolingian text to discuss the female lifecycle directly. Though he lifted the second half of this passage directly from Isidore's *Etymologies*, throughout his own encyclopedia Raban developed original ideas, reflected in his choice and ordering of selections from Isidore and other writers.[2] Here Raban argues that women's inherent weakness prevents them from learning and makes them subordinate to men. In support of this suspicious view of women's ability to reason and control their sexual urges, he quoted many biblical passages.[3] Although Raban

---

1. Raban Maur, *De universo*, 7.1, PL 111, col. 183.
2. Isidore of Seville, *Etymologiarum*, 11.2.18–19; Schipper, "Rabanus Maur and his Sources," 8–13.
3. Maur, *De universo*, 7.1, cols. 179–85.

applied the "ages of man" to women, he believed that women were an inferior embodiment of them. In this regard he is typical of Carolingian churchmen: they used these categories only for men. Although the age of reason or the end of the period of infancy, *infantia*, seems to have applied to girls, other contemporary terms for the stages of men's lives do not transfer well to use for women. Raban's passage therefore underlines the narrow way in which clerics sometimes understood women.

If Carolingian men did not explicate the lifecycle of their female contemporaries, it is now useful to do so both to summarize the findings of this book and to fit them into a broader social picture of the Carolingian world as well as into the history of women and gender in the West. Despite the limitations of the extant sources, the evidence presented in the preceding chapters suggests much about the lifecycle of an elite woman from birth until death. Those possible experiences provide another means to assess the ways in which female social practice affected the rhetoric of reform and to emphasize the many commonalities of lay and religious women. Of course, an "average aristocratic woman" never existed; individual women had different experiences. Many laywomen and women who entered the religious life after marriage had children, while other religious women never experienced childbirth. Queens could play more noticeable roles than other aristocratic women because they were at the center of Carolingian power. Nevertheless, elite women had far more in common with each other than they did with others. Rather than purport to describe the reality of their lives, this sketch presents a range of possibilities for aristocratic women living in the Carolingian Empire during the eighth and ninth centuries, drawing from earlier scholarship but including new aspects of the female experience that I have explicated thus far.

The stages of life for women are relatively clear, though fewer in number than for men. The events that marked a girl's entrance into adulthood were marriage or religious consecration, or at least reaching the age at which either was possible. Women born into powerful families in the Carolingian Empire were generally raised either to be wives and mothers or to enter the monastic life. Naturally the decision of estate often came later than birth. Early instruction could lead to either destination. After infancy and early childhood, girls attained the "age of reason" at seven, from which point they might enter a convent for life or for instruction, or they might remain at home with their mothers. Once they became fertile, marriage was a possibility. Motherhood often marked women's adult years, and once a woman became too old to bear children, others began to consider her old. Though medical history, biology, and demography can help to explain the female lifecycle, cultural conceptions of women and contemporary views of women at different ages provide the clearest picture. One approach to women's (and men's) lives is to trace them through their relations to others and through the various roles they played at different points of their lives.[4] Clear divisions in the Carolingian female lifecycle rested upon women's fertility. By moving through these stages from infancy to death and beyond, it is possible to situate female social actions and the rhetoric concerning women within the context of their everyday lives. This means of summary permits consideration of the broader consequences of the Carolingian era for the history of women and gender in the West.

Infancy and Early Childhood

How did little girls begin their lives in the Carolingian period? Both male and female infants arrived in the world in the same way, and boys and girls usually remained in the family home until they reached the age of seven. Mothers had the responsibility to care for these small children: fathers seem rarely to have taken much interest in the upbringing of infants and toddlers. Though fathers doubtless had certain hopes for their sons and daughters, mothers were meant to start children on the right path. Dhuoda's second son, Bernard, presents one of the few recorded cases in which an infant was taken from his mother. A lack of relevant evidence concerning small children makes it difficult to measure how common such early separation was. Most mothers like Dhuoda had a strong emotional attachment to their babies from their births. Indeed early medieval parents had genuine affection for their children. Motherhood was a learned behavior, not a biological imperative. When Paulinus of Aquileia described hell as a place without a mother's love for her children, this was a vision that any lay aristocrat would easily have understood. Contemporaries considered fondness for one's mother as natural as a mother's love.

Motherhood was a central, perhaps the most important, role of laywomen in the antique and medieval worlds. Both clerical exhortations to mothers to look after their young children and the learned social value placed upon motherhood helped to cause women to develop attachments to their children. Producing heirs was essential, but mothers' concern for their offspring went far beyond birth. Most loved their children, as evidenced by the grief of Carolingian parents—such as Gisela and Eberhard, Hildegard and Charlemagne, and Rictrud—whose children died. Throughout the Middle Ages many aristocratic and royal mothers attempted to further their children's interests and to protect their inheritances. Although such actions often had self-serving purposes, they simultaneously reflected a lifelong bond between

---

4. See for example Stafford, *QCD*, 144–45, and Smith, "Einhard," 55–77.

mother and child. That motherhood has provoked clerical comment from the beginnings of Christianity to the present day demonstrates recognition of its essential place in Western society. Because they deemed virginity a preferable state, the church fathers sometimes commented upon physical motherhood negatively or at least ambivalently. In Merovingian *vitae* mothers generally played positive nurturing roles, a view that carried on into the Carolingian era and beyond.[5] The mothers of Hathumoda, Herlindis and Renula, and Bernard in the *Vita Liutbirgae* all played a crucial part in developing the piety of their children just as Jonas encouraged in his *De institutione laicali*. On the contrary, Aldegund's mother sometimes set a counterexample as when she hid her money so as not to give more alms to the poor. That emphasis on mothering was also an attempt to limit laywomen's possibilities to the domestic sphere. Conversely, spiritual motherhood enjoyed the praise of clerics from late antiquity through the central Middle Ages.[6]

Throughout history many mothers, not least Carolingian ones, cared for infants and toddlers and taught their children essential social mores to help them make their way in society. Nursing was a sign of female virtue in the early Middle Ages, which promoted an emotional and physical bond between mother and child; sources suggest that elite mothers at least sometimes breastfed their babies. Aristocratic mothers also nurtured their offspring through lessons in moral behavior and religious practices. Carolingian ecclesiastical leaders recognized that young children, both male and female, needed particular instruction and urged mothers to take up that task. Though perhaps not as strongly desired as sons, young daughters represented future opportunities to develop ties with other families or with religious houses. Carolingian aristocratic parents looked after the spiritual and material well-being of their small daughters, sometimes sending them to convents and then founding new houses for them as the parents of Herlindis and Renula and Hathumoda did. In the *Vita Liutbirgae*, both natural and spiritual mothers played roles in teaching children to be virtuous.

Elite mothers offered their children a range of instruction including religious practices such as prayer. Dhuoda, Gisela (wife of Eberhard of Friuli), Gisla (mother of Bernard), and Liutberga all stood as models to others. From an early age, by following their mother's example, daughters may have learned domestic management skills and textile work and how to tend the sick and dying. Small boys probably stayed with their mothers, because their fathers frequently traveled or participated in activities too dangerous for small

5. Réal, *Vies de saints, vie de famille*, 413–22.
6. Atkinson, *The Oldest Vocation*, 64–100.

children, such as hunting and warfare. Along with fathers, mothers shared responsibility for appropriate discipline and punishment.

Leaving Home

Little evidence points to young girls going to court, as their brothers did, in order to make valuable contacts with other aristocrats and their families. Young girls gained similar benefits at convents under royal patronage, such as Remiremont and San Salvatore. Certain girls wishing to become nuns— Leoba, Herlindis, Renula, Hathumoda, and Liutberga—set off at an early age in order to study at a religious house. Others may have stayed at religious houses temporarily for instruction, as did the beautiful young girls Archbishop Ansgar of Bremen sent to Liutberga. Learning to read, sing psalms, understand religious concepts, and to fabricate and finish textiles could only have benefited the girls or young women upon their return to lay households as these skills were invaluable for managing estates, acting as moral exemplars, and raising children.

Girls bound for the religious life eventually attained a relatively high level of education, enabling them to produce manuscripts and participate in frequent prayer and liturgical celebrations. They needed and had opportunities to develop their command of Latin further than laywomen. As at Remiremont, Chelles, communities near Würzburg, and possibly Brescia, religious women producing manuscripts needed to write clearly and to know some Latin. Ninth-century *vitae* report that girls and young women studied writing and grammar skills at the houses of Aldeneik and Valenciennes. Presumably some girls learned Latin at Wimborne and Tauberbischofsheim, because Leoba, educated at the former and abbess of the latter, wrote erudite letters. The letters of Gisela, abbess of Chelles, and Leoba demonstrate these religious women's fluency in Latin; the letters of Charlemagne's daughters Rotrud and Bertha, educated both at Chelles and at their father's court, reveal their learning.

Not surprising, women do not appear to have received instruction commensurate with that of the great intellectuals of the Carolingian period. Dhuoda, for example, though quite proficient in Latin, simply did not possess the same level of learning as Theodulf of Orléans, Alcuin, or Raban Maur. Because women could not become priests, composition of certain genres remained off limits to them, including scriptural commentaries, theological treatises, and homiliaries.[7] Nor were even relatively educated women

---

7. Contreni, "The Carolingian Renaissance," 716–17, 720.

ed to produce texts on these subjects. At least since Paul wrote that
were not to speak or teach in public, women would not regularly
en instructed in rhetoric or philosophy. Women did, however, write
histories, letters, and hagiography. Although few texts by women from late
antiquity and the early Middle Ages have survived, elite women, especially
those in the religious life, engaged in creative and learned pursuits.[8] Aristocratic women's need to keep or at least comprehend records concerning their
households and estates required some level of understanding, if not producing, Latin. They also needed some familiarity with numbers, though not
necessarily to the high degree that Dhuoda exhibited in her *Liber manualis*.
Dedications testify to the learning of some Carolingian women. Raban Maur
dedicated his exegetical texts on Judith and Esther to the empress Judith and
later to Irmingard, wife of Lothar I. He therefore expected them to comprehend the texts. Because the two queens almost certainly knew these biblical
tales, they could appreciate why he dedicated those particular commentaries
to them. At the very least, Judith and Irmingard could have understood the
texts if perhaps read aloud to them.

Prime of Life

As women approached adulthood, their lives could diverge in dramatic ways.
At this point families often chose for their daughters entrance to the religious
life or marriage and motherhood in the secular world. Charlemagne's daughters offer an example of women who chose neither path. Especially because
their situation deviated from the later ninth-century social norms that solidi-
fied during the reign of Louis the Pious, Einhard had to account for their
continuing presence at court as single women. They took a path that appears
singular so far as surviving sources allow us to see. How much that decision
actually rested in their hands remains debatable, but family concerns surely
outweighed any specific desires of all but the most determined young women.
Just as it is difficult to measure the lifespan of early medieval women given
the lack of evidence for all but royal women, the same issue applies to age
at marriage. Presumably aristocratic young women married sometime after
menarche. Certainly a number of medieval female saints overcame family
objections to their entrance into the religious life, but this often involved
divine help and/or their particularly strong character and resolve.[9] Most

---

8. Women throughout the Middle Ages wrote intelligent, sometimes erudite texts.
Dronke, *Women Writers of the Middle Ages*; Ferrante, *To the Glory of Her Sex*.
9. For one such an episode see *Vita Aldegundis*, chap. 5, 1041.

Carolingian women probably acquiesced to family desires when profe⟨ religious vows or marrying.

Lay and religious women had to work through the institutions in which they could legitimately exert influence. A woman's relative degree of authority fluctuated depending on the time, place, and conditions as well as her age, children or lack thereof, and family connections. Both marriage and the religious life offered some women—as abbesses, queens, or noble wives— opportunities to direct inferiors of both sexes, influence female peers, and sometimes to affect the actions of powerful men. Stipulations against women speaking in public remained, and women in public gatherings were most often silent. Nevertheless, they had ways to insert their presence on occasions and in spaces where they normally would not be allowed. For example, when Emma gave her belt to Witgar, archbishop of Augsburg, she knew that he would remember her each time he put on the belt in order to perform his liturgical duties. Frequently shifting alliances marked the Carolingian aristocratic world, as did changes in ideology and power emanating from the royal court. The bonds of women to their religious, natal, and marital families made them participants in this sometimes unstable political milieu. With the exception of abbesses, Carolingian women could not hold offices, but they transmitted the good birth necessary to holding office to their sons as well as to daughters who might become abbesses. Abbesses had long played a prominent role in the Frankish world: their image in the Carolingian era drew from the depictions of abbesses in Merovingian *vitae*.[10] Thus, employing flexibility and creativity in a variety of ways gave Carolingian aristocratic women, both lay and religious, some agency within elite society.

Marriage provided women with opportunities to influence a household. In late antiquity and the early Middle Ages, the Christian ideal of virginity did not cause major changes in elite marriage: Carolingian desire for concord and proper behavior in a household is consonant with similar late antique ideals. Clerical writers had attempted to promote religious behavior within lay unions. If one could not remain a virgin, marriage offered an antidote to lust and legitimation for procreation. The ninth century appears to have been a dramatic turning point in the church's ability to exert this sort of influence. An increased adherence to church ideals, such as lasting monogamous marriage, began, and scholars trace marriage's first steps toward becoming a sacrament to this period. This transformation of marriage, however, did not necessarily

---

10. Michèle Gaillard, "Vie quotidienne et culturelle dans les abbayes féminines au travers des récits hagiographiques," in *L'art du haut moyen-âge dans le nord-ouest de la France. Actes du Colloque de St Riquier (22–24 September 1987)*, ed. Dominique Poulain and Michel Perrin (Greifswald, 1993), 13–31, 22–25.

work to the benefit of women. Queen Theutberga's problems, for example, resulted partly from increased insistence on the indissolubility of marriage.

Sexual mores had great consequence for the reputation of elite women, particularly queens. Especially devastating to women's reputations were accusations of sexual misconduct casting in doubt legitimate reproduction. For example, the accusation of adultery against Judith resulted directly from her success in producing a son; to discredit her was to disinherit Charles the Bald. Not only did clerics insist that the sole purpose of sexual intercourse was reproduction; the legitimacy of a child, and thus his ability to pass the land and wealth of his family to heirs, rested upon the fidelity and virtue of a wife. If "irregularly" played, women's reproductive role put them at a social and political disadvantage. If fulfilled "properly," it gave them great influence over kin and an invaluable role in initial instruction of children, both recognized by clerics and others. Reproductive problems could hurt the social standing of women. Theutberga had to endure slander even after she had officially cleared her name. Religious women could also suffer from the accusation of fornication. The incident in Leoba's *vita* when locals accused a sister in the convent of Tauberbischofsheim of drowning an illegitimate baby illustrates the ways such a charge could affect a religious house's standing. When Leoba proved her sister's innocence, she defended the reputation of her community.[11]

Beyond childbirth, women in their prime had similar duties and roles, whether within the household or the religious community. Clerics urged all elite women to act as moral exemplars to those around them, and certainly aristocratic women had contact with a great many people beyond the direct influence of those ecclesiastical leaders. Abbesses, such as Leoba, Addula, Hathumoda, Herlindis, and Renula, stood as examples to those in their houses as well as to individuals in their surrounding communities. Those living near such great monasteries as San Salvatore and Remiremont benefited from their members' prayers, secured by the relationships they forged with the houses through donations of land. Female supervision of estates, households, and religious communities means that women played a central role in the early medieval economy. Through hospitality they maintained their own status and that of their male relatives.

Carolingian clerical writers did not merely "confirm" early medieval woman's role as "mistress of the household"; they recognized the ways in which this role gave women frequent contact with servants, slaves, and other inferiors.[12] Their duties extended to many areas of estate management because few areas of work were completely gendered at this time. Abbesses and other religious

---

11. See discussion of this episode in chapter 2.
12. Quotation from Herlihy, "Land, Family, and Women in Continental Europe," 15.

officers looked after most of the production and work of their communities. Like laywomen, religious women sometimes provided hospitality to important visitors. Boniface visited Pfalzel, Addula's convent, and was believed to have visited Aldeneik, where Herlindis and Renula were abbesses. Carolingian kings regularly hunted near Remiremont, and the memorial book of San Salvatore recorded Æthelwulf of Wessex's stop in Brescia on his way to Rome in 855/6.

Carolingian aristocratic women played a prominent role in the one distinctly female form of work—textile production—making their own fine textiles as well as supervising general textile fabrication, an unusual situation in Western history as men have usually controlled textile work. Both lay and religious women of varying status wove, embroidered, and sewed items necessary to both lay household and religious institution such as clothing, curtains or hangings, altar cloths, liturgical vestments, belts, and bedclothes. Such activity helped them to appear virtuous. For families, female furnishing of rich textiles to religious houses and prelates constituted a means of creating or bolstering bonds. Use of textiles in the settings for elite interaction was a means to display wealth and status during crucial social negotiations. Textile work, therefore, had far more than economic repercussions.

Carolingian women in the prime of their lives played instrumental roles in establishing and designating the rank of elite men. Through their prudence, beauty, wealth, and family they often helped their husbands and other male relatives to maintain aristocratic status and gain increased power and authority. Women enhanced the reputation of family members with their appearance. The textual presentation of aristocratic and royal women in the early Middle Ages emphasized their great beauty, fine clothing, and rich jewelry as well as their virtuous acts. Female beauty comprised two components: innate physical good looks, and the learned employment of dress, adornment, and bearing. Loveliness also implied youth, which in turn suggested fertility. Carolingian texts, including poetry and hagiography, present rather idealized images of female appearance that rely heavily upon late antique and Merovingian models. Whether Charlemagne's daughters ever wore the riches of the Carolingian court is beside the point; that they were described as doing so indicates that women's lavish dress frequently enhanced male status and displayed familial wealth. At the same time poets wrote that virtue should trump any natural beauty or adornments, often praising royal women for upright behavior. Saints were routinely described as both pretty and virtuous. Clerics, including Jonas of Orléans and Hucbald of St. Amand, however, understood beauty's ambivalence: it did not necessarily entail morality. They discussed this matter because they recognized that elite men wanted pretty wives, possibly out of simple desire for an attractive woman but also because the appearance of a wife, or a daughter, could affect the ways in which others perceived an aristocratic man.

Old Age and Death

Jonas's list of characteristics—family, prudence, wealth, and beauty—applied most to women in their prime. As they aged the women who have been our primary subjects lost some of the traits desirable to men. Nevertheless "old" women could play prominent roles in the Carolingian world. Some non-royal widows in the religious life acted as mentors to their grandchildren or provided them with valuable connections. Gertrude, the grandmother of Rictrud's husband Adalbald, for example, raised the couple's daughter Eusebia at her religious house at Hamay where, upon Gertrude's death, Eusebia became abbess. Addula, Gregory's grandmother, helped to promote her grandson to Boniface by having Gregory read aloud before their famous guest. The relative lack of information on grandmothers such as Addula and Gertrude perhaps supports demographic evidence indicating the relatively low life expectancy for women. Einhard noted that Charlemagne's mother Bertha survived long enough to see six of her grandchildren born, but living to their sixties may not have been long enough for some women to play prominent roles in the lives of their grandchildren. Those women who did survive to see their grandchildren reach maturity may have similarly acted as their mentors.

Other old women promoted the well-being of their kin by looking after family lands and ensuring their commemoration following their deaths. The *Vita Liutbirgae* provides an image of the old age of two women, Gisla and Liutberga. Gisla spent her widowhood caring for the interests of her family, particularly looking after her estates and ensuring that her daughters became abbesses and that her son inherited the family lands. Modeling herself upon her patroness, Liutberga then looked after the same family before entering the spiritual life. From her cell she continued to advise and aid the various people who came to her for help. Gisela, the daughter of Louis the Pious and widow of Eberhard of Friuli, must have been a relatively old widow because her children had grown to adulthood before her husband's death. Through donations, Gisela made certain that the family would be remembered at the monastery of Cysoing in Flanders. A responsibility among older women for memorial commemoration may not have been uncommon given that many second wives married much older men, and women may have married at a younger age than men.[13] Queen mothers sometimes meddled in political affairs, and that possibility suggests that old women could still exert influence within their families. Thus, despite the paucity of sources that mention old women, the

---

13. van Houts, *Memory and Gender,* 149; Stafford, *QCD,* 143–45. See also Geary, *Phantoms of Remembrance,* 48–80; Innes, "Keeping It in the Family," 17–35.

difficulty of defining female old age, and the idealized nature of the available information, it is possible to see that old women played important—though sometimes ambiguous—roles in Carolingian elite society. Sometimes sickness meant that old women and old men required care; Carolingian texts suggest that women tended the ill. Carolingian sources, however, offer near silence on the treatment of old or dying women.

Death did not mark the end of a Carolingian aristocratic woman's presence in her society. Rather, members of her religious community continued to commemorate her, or her family ensured that her memory was preserved. She herself could have given land to a religious house so that its members would pray for her and her kin after her death. Numerous charters record women as co-testators with their husbands. The presence of Carolingian aristocratic women also lived on in the practices of their children. Dhuoda exhorted William and young Bernard to remember her in their prayers and to place above her grave an epitaph she had composed. Women kept alive the memory of their family members and others by writing about them. Dhuoda wrote of her own family, while the hagiographer Huneberc of Heidenheim recorded the *vitae* of Wynnebald and Willibald in the mid-eighth century. These conclusions help to explain why writers increasingly accepted the testimony of women in East Frankish lands, from the eighth to ninth centuries on, and abbesses in this area were prominent in their preservation of family memory.[14] Even after their deaths, aristocratic women left traces of themselves; the end of the life of a woman afforded an occasion for her daughters or sons to carry on practices, which she had taught them.

Lasting Expectations

The lifecycle of Carolingian aristocratic women could take a number of different paths, depending especially upon their choice of the lay or religious life, though, regardless of profession, women shared many common experiences. The possibilities presented above cannot represent the lives of all aristocratic women, but they do reflect the available evidence for elite women living in areas of Carolingian rule during the eighth and ninth centuries. In returning to Jonas's list of characteristics, it is possible to see how the stages of life could affect a woman's embodiment of that idea. Jonas referred to a woman who probably had her youthful beauty and fertility. Throughout her life, however, she could employ her connections to her natal kin and develop new bonds on

---

14. Leyser, *Rule and Conflict*, 63–66; van Houts, *Memory and Gender*, 49.

behalf of her marital family. She furthermore aided her natural or spiritual family through instruction and moral exemplarity during the prime of her life, and when women became widows, often later in life, they had the opportunity to have substantial control over wealth. Although women frequently had authority over the goods of a household or convent, widows had more latitude than other women to deal with their property as they wished. Often they could make donations, as did other women, to ensure that they and their relatives would be remembered after their deaths with prayers for their souls. Throughout their lives, their roles and duties had profound implications for their families, their communities, and their peers and inferiors, and Carolingian men acknowledged these responsibilities and actions in their expectations of elite women, revealing to us not only social norms but indications of female social practice.

From a modern standpoint, it has been too easy to see the ways in which Frankish women were constricted, for it was churchmen with an interest in limiting female agency who wrote the sources. Reading those texts from a new vantage means that we must now reassess the Carolingian world both in light of the common experiences of lay and religious women and of the many ways in which they shaped elite culture. Jonas's list of female characteristics is not merely a longstanding list of male desires but clues to the prominent place elite women had in Carolingian-controlled lands from c. 700 to c. 925. He wrote during the 820s, a decade during which evolving Western ideas concerning women stabilized. His list therefore represents the centrality of the Carolingian period to the history of Western women. Not only did women contribute to the transformation and, some might argue development, of European culture through their participation in the Carolingian renaissance, but also their activities and their responses to the reforming rhetoric directed to them helped to shape Western expectations of women's possibilities.

Carolingian sources reveal not only a great deal more about women's cultural contributions than initial narrow readings may indicate but also demonstrate that their authors took account of female activities, status, and spheres of influence when trying to shape the ideal behavior of women. The male lay elite desired that women carry out these duties because they helped to maintain and shape the culture that made individuals cognizant of aristocratic status in others and themselves. Women's unparalleled access to and great responsibility for the members of early medieval households gave them frequent opportunity to help mold the behavior of children, young men, other women, servants and other inferiors, and sometimes their male counterparts. Carolingian aristocratic women were meant to play a substantial role in the religious reforms of the eighth and ninth centuries—a role heretofore underappreciated because it lies in the background of contemporary sources, invisible when scholars do not look for it.

Just as Carolingian women's lives have helped to show how early medieval people remade classical culture north of the Alps and transformed Christian practice, Carolingian rhetoric and female culture shaped the views and actions of later women. This book has outlined changes in women's lives and in the ways others perceived women that underline the centrality of the early Middle Ages and particularly the Carolingian era to the reshaping of antique ideas and the development of lasting social norms. Female hospitality and expectations of domestic virtue, for example, gave women opportunities to affect political relations well into the modern era.[15] Even now the ambivalent views of women among Carolingian churchmen have resonance. Women have made significant steps forward in the West, yet each day they must defend themselves against criticisms based on some of the same traditional norms that Carolingian men used to curb female agency. A beautiful woman must still display acts of virtue in order to achieve social respect; early motherhood remains a frequent obstacle to women's education; and women continue to be subject to sexual double standards. On a more positive note, Carolingian elite women balanced social expectations and boundaries with the pursuit of personal and familial interests, something many Western women have done for centuries. Underlying social norms reflect continuity with the distant past even while women continue to make strides in entering arenas that were once the sole preserves of men.

---

15. See, for example, K. D. Reynolds, *Aristocratic Women and Political Society in Victorian Britain* (Oxford, 1998); Anna Clark, *Scandal: The Sexual Politics of the British Constitution* (Princeton, 2004).

SELECT BIBLIOGRAPHY

Primary Works

Annals and Histories

Annales Fuldenses sive annales regni Francorum orientalis. Ed. Friedrich Kurze. MGH SRG 7. Hanover, Germany, 1891. (English translation: *The Annals of Fulda.* Ed. and trans. Timothy Reuter. Manchester, England, 1992.)

Annales Laureshamenses. Ed. Georg Heinrich Pertz. MGH SS 1, 22–39. Hanover, Germany, 1826.

Annales Mettenses priores. Ed. Bernhard de Simson. MGH SRG 10. Hanover, Germany, 1905.

Annales regni Francorum. Ed. Georg Heinrich Pertz and Friedrich Kurze. MGH SRG 7. Hanover, Germany, 1891.

Annales S. Bertiniani. In *Annales de Saint-Bertin,* ed. Félix Grat, Jeanne Vielliard, and Suzanne Clémencet, with an introduction by Léon Levaillan. Paris, 1964. (English translation: *The Annals of St. Bertin.* Ed. and trans. Janet L. Nelson. Manchester, England, 1991.)

Annales Vedastini. MGH SRG 12. Ed. Bernhard de Simson. Hanover, Germany, 1909.

Astronomer. *Vita Hludowici imperatoris.* Ed. Ernst Tremp. MGH SRG 64, 279–555. Hanover, Germany, 1995.

Bede. *Historia ecclesiastica gentis Anglorum.* Ed. and trans. Bertram Colgrave and R. A. B. Mynors. 1969; repr., Oxford, 1991.

Einhard. *Vita Karoli magni.* Ed. Georg Heinrich Pertz and G. Waitz. MGH SRG 25. Hanover, Germany, 1911. (English translation: Einhard. *The Life of Charlemagne.* In *Charlemagne's Courtier: The Complete Einhard,* ed. and trans. Paul E. Dutton, 15–39. Peterborough, Ontario, 1998.)

Liber Pontificalis. 3 vols. Ed. L. Duchesne (revised C. Vogel). Paris, 1955–1957. (English translations all by Raymond Davis: *The Book of the Pontiffs [Liber Pontificalis]: The Ancient Biographies of the First Ninety Roman Bishops to AD 715.* Liverpool, 1989; *The Lives of the Eighth-Century Popes [Liber Pontificalis]: The Ancient Biographies of Nine Popes from AD 715 to AD 817.* Liverpool, 1992; *The Lives of the Ninth-Century Popes [Liber Pontificalis].* Liverpool, England, 1995).

Notker the Stammerer. *Gesta Karoli.* Ed. Hans F. Haefele. MGH SRG 12. Berlin, 1959.

Paul the Deacon. *Historia Langobardorum*. Ed. G. Waitz. MGH SRG 48. Hanover, Germany, 1878.
De Rebus Gestis Aelfredi. In *Asser's Life of King Alfred*, ed. William Henry Stevenson, 1–96. Oxford, 1998.
Regino of Prüm. *Chronicon*. Ed. Friedrich Kurze. MGH SRG 50. Hanover, Germany, 1890.
Thegan. *Gesta Hludowici imperatoris*. Ed. Ernst Tremp. MGH SRG 64, 167–278. Hanover, Germany, 1995.

Diplomas, Capitularies, and Ecclesiastical Legislation

Capitulare de villis. Cod. Guelf. 254 Helmst. der Herzog August Bibliothek Wolfenbüttel. Ed. Carlrichard Brühl. Stuttgart, Germany, 1971.
Capitula Episcoporum. Ed. Peter Brommer. MGH Capit. Ep. 1. Hanover, Germany, 1984.
Capitula Episcoporum. Ed. Rudolf Pokorny and Martina Stratmann. MGH Capit. Ep. 2. Hanover, Germany, 1995.
Capitularia regum Francorum. Ed. Alfred Boretius. MGH Capit. 1. Hanover, Germany, 1883.
Capitularia regum Francorum. Ed. Alfred Boretius and Victor Krause. MGH Capit. 2.1. Hanover, Germany, 1890.
——. MGH Capit. 2.2. Hanover, Germany, 1893.
Concilia aevi Karolini. Ed. Albert Werminghoff. MGH Conc. 2.1–2. Hanover, Germany, 1908.
Die Konzilien der karolingischen Teilreiche 843–859. Ed. Wilfried Hartmann. MGH Conc. 3. Hanover, Germany, 1984.
I Diplomi di Berengario I. Fonti per la storia d'Italia 35. Ed. Luigi Schiaparelli. Rome, 1903.
Institutio sanctimonialium Aquisgranensis. Ed. Albert Werminghoff. MGH Conc. 2.1, 421–56. Hanover, Germany, 1908.
Mittelalterliche Schatzverzeichnisse. Ed. Bernhard Bischoff. Munich, 1967.
Theodulf of Orléans. *Opus Caroli regis contra synodum*. Ed. Ann Freeman. MGH Conc. 2, supplement 1. Hanover, Germany, 1998.

Exegetical Texts

Alcuin. *Compendium in Canticum Canticorum*. PL 100, cols. 640–64.
Raban Maur. *Expositio in Librum Esther*. PL 109, cols. 635–70.
——. *Expositio in Librum Judith*. PL 109, cols. 542–92.

Hagiography

Agius. *Vita Hathumodae*. Ed. Georg Heinrich Pertz. MGH SS 4, 166–75. Hanover, Germany, 1841.
Alcuin. *Vita Willibrordi, archiepiscopi Traiectensis*. Ed. Wilhelm Levison. MGH SRM 7, 81–141. Hanover, Germany, 1920.
Hucbald of St. Amand. *Vita Sanctae Rictrudis viduae*. AASS May 3, 79–89.
Liudger. *Vita Gregorii abbatis*. Ed. O. Holder-Egger. MGH SS 15.1, 63–79. Hanover, Germany, 1887.
McNamara, Jo Ann, and John E. Halborg, eds. *Sainted Women of the Dark Ages*. Durham, N.C., 1992.
Ex miraculis sanctae Verenae. Ed. G. Waitz. MGH SS 4, 457–60. Hanover, Germany, 1841.

Noble, Thomas F. X., and Thomas Head. *Soldiers of Christ: Saints and Saints' Lives from Late Antiquity and the Early Middle Ages.* University Park, Pa., 1995.

Odo of Cluny. *Vita sancti Geraldi Auriliacensis comitis libri quattuor.* PL 133, cols. 642–703.

Rudolf. *Vita Leobae abbatissae Biscofesheimensis.* Ed. G. Waitz. MGH SS 15.1, 121–31. Hanover, Germany, 1887.

De sanctis virginibus Herlinde et Reinula seu Renilde abbatissis Masaci in Belgio. AASS March 3, 385–92.

Sulpicius Severus. *Vita Martini.* Sources Chrétiennes 133. Paris, 1967.

Venantius Fortunatus. *De vita sanctae Radegundis.* MGH SRM 2, 364–95. Hanover, Germany, 1888.

Vita Aldegundis. AASS January 2, 1040–47.

Vita Liutbirgae virginis. Ed. Ottokar Menzel. MGH Deutsches Mittelalter Kritische Studientexte 3. Leipzig, Germany, 1937.

Vita de Sancta Waldetrude. AASS April 1, 829–42.

Vita sanctae Aldegundis virginis. PL 132, cols. 857–76.

Willibald. *Vita Bonifatii.* Ed. Wilhelm Levison. MGH SRG 57, 1–58. Hanover, Germany, 1905.

Lay Mirrors

Alcuin. *Liber de virtutibus et vitiis.* PL 101, cols. 613–38.

Dhuoda. *Liber manualis. Dhuoda. Manual pour mon fils.* Ed. Pierre Riché. Trans. Bernard de Vregille and Claude Mondésert. Paris, 1975. (English translations: *A Handbook for William: A Carolingian Woman's Counsel for Her Son.* Ed. and trans. Carol Neel. 1991; repr., Washington, D.C., 1999; *Dhuoda, Handbook for Her Warrior Son Liber Manualis.* Ed. and trans. Marcelle Thiébaux. Cambridge, 1998.)

Jonas of Orléans. *De institutione laicali.* PL 106, cols. 121–278.

Paulinus of Aquileia. *Liber exhortationis.* PL 99, cols. 197–282.

Letters

Die Briefe des Heiligen Bonifatius und Lullus. Ed. Michael Tangl. MGH Ep. S 1. Berlin, 1955. (English translation: *The Letters of Saint Boniface.* Ed. and trans. Ephraim Emerton. 1940; repr., New York, 1976.)

Letters of Alcuin in MGH Ep. 4. Ed. Ernst Dümmler. Berlin, 1895. (English translation: *Alcuin of York, c. A.D. 732 to 804—His Life and Letters.* Ed. and trans. Stephen Allott. York, England, 1974.)

Select Letters of St. Jerome. Ed. and trans. F. A. Wright. 1933; repr., Cambridge, Mass., 1991.

Servati Lupi Epistulae. Ed. Peter K. Marshall. Leipzig, Germany, 1984.

Literary Documents

Adalhard of Corbie. "Les Statuts d'Adalhard." Ed. L. Levillain. *Le Moyen Âge,* 13, second series 4 (1900): 233–386.

Agobard of Lyons. *Liber de imaginibus.* PL 104, cols. 199–228.

Dungal. *Responsa contra Claudium: A Controversy on Holy Images.* Ed. Paolo Zanna. Per verba. Testi mediolatini con traduzione 17. Milan, 2002.

Hincmar of Rheims. *De ordine palatii.* Ed. T. Gross and R. Schieffer. MGH Fontes 3. Hanover, Germany, 1980. (English translation: *Carolingian Civilization: A Reader.* Ed. Paul Dutton, 485–99. Peterborough, Ontario, 1996.)

Isidore of Seville. *Etymologiarum sive originum.* Ed. W. M. Lindsay. 2 vols. 1911; repr., Oxford, 1962.
Jonas of Orléans. *De cultu imaginum.* PL 106, cols. 305–588.
Regino of Prüm. *De synodalibus causis et disciplinis ecclesiastici.* Ed. Wilfried Hartmann. Darmstadt, Germany, 2004.
Walafrid Strabo. *Libellus et incrementis quarundam in observationibus ecclesiasticis rerum.* Ed. Alice Harting-Correa. Leiden, The Netherlands, 1996.

Memorial Books

Liber Memorialis von Remiremont. Ed. Eduard Hlawitschka, Karl Schmid, and Gerd Tellenbach. MGH Libri mem. 1. Zurich, 1970.
Der Memorial- und Liturgiecodex von San Salvatore/Santa Giulia in Brescia. Ed. Dieter Geuenich and Uwe Ludwig. MGH Libri mem. N.S. 4. Hanover, Germany, 2000.

Poetry

Beowulf and the Fight at Finnsburg. Ed. Frederick Klaeber. Lexington, Mass., 1950.
Ermold the Black. *In Honorem Hludowici Pii in Ermold le Noir. Poème sur Louis le Pieux et Épitres au roi Pépin.* Ed. Edmond Faral. 1932; repr., Paris, 1964.
The Heliand. Ed and trans. G. Ronald Murphy. Oxford, 1992.
Karolus Magnus et Leo Papa. Ein Paderborner Epos vom Jahre 799. Ed. Helmut Beumann, Franz Brunhölzl, and Wilhelm Winkelmann. Paderborn, Germany, 1966.
Poetry of the Carolingian Renaissance. Ed. and trans. Peter Godman. Norman, Okla., 1985.
Waltharius and Ruodlieb. Ed. and trans. Dennis M. Kratz. New York, 1984.

Polyptychs

Polyptyque de l'abbé Irminon. 2 vols. Ed. Benjamin E. C. Guérard. Paris, 1844.

Monastic Rules

Caesarius of Arles. *Regula Virginum.* In *Césaire d'Arles. Oeuvres monastiques*, ed. Joël Courreau and Adalbert de Vogüé. Sources Chrétiennes 345. Paris, 1988.
Regula Benedicti: La Régle de Saint Benoît. Sources Chrétiennes 181–82. Ed. Adalbert de Vogüé and Jean Neufville. Paris, 1972.

Source Collections

Cartulaire de l'abbaye de Cysoing et de ses dépendences. Ed. I. de Coussemaker. Lille, France, 1886.
Codex diplomaticus Langobardiae. Historiae Patriae Monumenta 13. Ed. Porro Lambertenghi. Turin, Italy, 1873.
Codice diplomatico Longobardo. Fonti per la storia d'Italia 63. Ed. Luigi Schiaparelli. Rome, 1933.
Italia sacra sive de episcopis Italiae, vol. 5. Ed. Ferdinando Ughelli. Venice, 1720.
Recueil des chartes de l'abbaye de Saint-Benoit-sur-Loire. Ed. Maurice Prou and Alexandre Vidier. Paris, 1907.

Sacrorum conciliorum, nova et amplissima collectio. Ed. Giovanni Dominicus Mansi. Graz, Austria, 1767.

Die Traditionen des Hochstifts Freising, 744–926, vol. 1. Ed. Theodor Bitterauf. 1943; repr., Munich, 1967.

Urkundenbuch des Klosters Fulda. Ed. Edmund E. Stengel. Marburg, Germany, 1958.

Urkundenbuch der Sanct Gallen, vol. 1. Ed. Hermann Wartmann. Zurich, 1863.

Unpublished Documents

Archivio di Stato e Archivio Storico Civico Brescia, Busta 2, XXIV, XXV, XXVI, XXIX, XLVI, XLIX.

Düsseldorf MS B3.

Fulda MS (CLA, VIII, 1197).

Secondary Works

Affeldt, Werner and Annette Kuhn, eds. *Frauen in der Geschichte VII. Interdisziplinäre Studien zur Geschichte der Frauen im Frühmittelalter. Methoden—Probleme—Erbebnisse.* Düsseldorf, Germany, 1986.

Affeldt, Werner. "Bemerkungen zum Forschungsstand." In *FG*, vol. 7, 32–42.

——. "Lebensformen für Frauen in Frühmittelalter. Probleme und Perspektiven ihrer Erforschung." In *Weiblichkeit in geschichtlicher Perspektive. Fallstudien und Reflexionen zu Grundproblemen der historischen Frauenforschung*, edited by Ursula A. J. Becher and Jörn Rüsen, 51–78. Frankfurt am Main, Germany, 1988.

Airlie, Stuart. "The Political Behaviour of the Secular Magnates in Francia, 829–879." PhD diss., Oxford University, 1985.

——. "Bonds of Power and Bonds of Association in the Court Circle of Louis the Pious." In *Charlemagne's Heir: New Perspectives on the Reign of Louis the Pious (814–840)*, edited by Peter Godman and Roger Collins, 191–204. Oxford, 1990.

——. "The Aristocracy." In *NCMH* 2, 431–50.

——. "Narratives of Triumph and Rituals of Submission: Charlemagne's Mastering of Bavaria." *TRHS* 9 (1999): 93–119.

——. "Private Bodies and the Body Politic in the Divorce Case of Lothar II." *PP* 161 (1998): 3–38.

Alexandre-Bidon, Danièle and Perrine Mane. "Le vie quotidienne à travers les enluminures carolingiennes." In *Un village*, 340–353.

Althoff, Gerd. "Fest und Bündnis." In *Feste und Feiern im Mittelalter. Paderborner Symposien des Mediävistenverbandes*, edited by Detlef Altenburg, Jörg Jarnut, and Hans-Hugo Steinhoff, 29–38. Sigmaringen, Germany, 1991.

——. *Amicitiae und Pacta. Bündnis, Einung, Politik und Gebetsgedenken im beginnenden 10. Jahrhundert.* MGH Schriften 37. Hanover, Germany, 1992.

——. *Family, Friends and Followers: Political and Social Bonds in Early Medieval Europe.* Trans. Christopher Carroll. Cambridge, 2004.

Amos, Thomas L. "Preaching and the Sermon in the Carolingian World." In *De Ore Domini: Preacher and Word in the Middle Ages*, edited by Thomas L. Amos, Eugene A. Greene, and Beverly Mayne Kienzle, 41–60. Kalamazoo, Mich., 1989.

Ampère, Jean-Jacques. *Histoire littéraire de la France avant le xiie siècle.* 1839; repr., Geneva, 1974.

Anton, H. H. "Beobachtungen zum fränkisch-byzantinischen Verhältnis in karolingischer Zeit." *Beiträge zur Geschichte des Regnum Francorum. Wissenschaftliche Colloquiem zum 75. Geburtstag von E. Ewig*, edited by Rudolf Schieffer, 97–119. Sigmaringen, Germany, 1990.

Atkinson, Clarissa W. *The Oldest Vocation: Christian Motherhood in the Middle Ages.* Ithaca, N.Y., 1991.

Baader, Gerhard. "Frauenheilkunde und Geburtshilfe im Frühmittelalter." In *FG*, vol. 7, 126–35.

Baltrusch-Schneider, Dagmar B. "Klosterleben als Alternative Lebensform zur Ehe?" In *WLFM*, 45–64.

Banniard, Michel. "La réception des *carmina* auliques: Niveaux de latinité et niveaux de réception à la fin du VIIIᵉ siècle." In *Am Vorabend der Kaiser Krönung. Das Epos "Karolus Magnus et Leo papa" und der Papstbesuch in Paderborn 799*, edited by Jörg Jarnut, Peter Godman, and Peter Johanek, 36–49. Berlin, 2002.

Becher, Hartmut. "Das königliche Frauenkloster San Salvatore/Santa Giulia in Brescia im Spiegel seiner Memorialüberlieferung." *FS* 17 (1983): 299–392.

Bell, Rudolph M. *Holy Anorexia.* Chicago, 1985.

Bennett, Judith M., Elizabeth A. Clark, Jean F. O'Barr, B. Anne Vilen, and Sarah Westphal-Wihl. *Sisters and Workers in the Middle Ages.* Chicago, 1989.

Berschin, Walter. "Die Schönheit des Heiligen." In *Schöne Frauen—Schöne Männer. Literarische Schönheitsbeschreibungen. 2 Kolloquiem der Forschungsstelle für europäische Literatur des Mittelalters*, edited by Theo Stemmler, 69–76. Mannheim, Germany, 1988.

——. *Biographie und Epochenstil im lateinischen Mittelalter. Karolingische Biographie 750–920 n.Chr.* Stuttgart, Germany, 1991.

Beumann, Helmut. "*Nomen imperatoris*. Studien zur Kaseridee Karls des Grossen." *Historische Zeitschrift* 185 (1958): 515–49.

Bierbrauer, Katharina. "Der Einfluß insular Handschriften auf die kontinentale Buchmalerei." In *Kunst*, 465–81.

Bischoff, Bernhard. "Die Kölner Nonnenhandschriften und das Skriptorium von Chelles." *Mittelalterliche Studien* 1 (1966): 16–34.

Bishop, Jane. "Bishops as Marital Advisors in the Ninth Century." In *Women of the Medieval World: Essays in Honor of John H. Mundy*, edited by Julius Kirshner and Suzanne Fonay Wemple, 53–84. Oxford, 1985.

Bitel, Lisa M. "Reproduction and Production in Early Ireland." In *Portraits of Medieval and Renaissance Living: Essays in Memory of David Herlihy*, edited by Samuel K. Cohn and Steven A. Epstein, 71–89. Ann Arbor, Mich., 1996.

——. *Women in Early Medieval Europe, 400–1100.* Cambridge, 2002.

Blackburn, Mark. "Money and Coinage." In *NCMH*, 2, 538–59.

Borst, Arno. *Lebensformen im Mittelalter.* Frankfurt am Main, Germany, 1973.

Boshof, Egon. *Erzbischof Agobard von Lyon. Leben und Werk.* Cologne, Germany, 1969.

Bouchard, Constance B. "Family Structure and Family Consciousness among the Aristocracy in the Ninth to Eleventh Centuries." *Francia* 16 (1986): 639–58.

Boyle, Leonard E. "Popular Piety in the Middle Ages: What Is Popular?" *Florilegium* 4 (1982): 184–93.

Braunfels, Wolfgang. *Die Welt der Karolinger und ihre Kunst.* Munich, 1968.

Brogiolo, Gian Pietro. "'Flavia Brexia.'" In *FL*, 467–8. Milan, 2000.

Brubaker, Leslie, and Julia M. H. Smith, eds. *Gender in the Early Medieval World: East and West, 300–900.* Cambridge, 2004.

Bruce, Scott G. *Silence and Sign Language in Medieval Monasticism: The Clunaic Tradition, c. 900–1200.* Cambridge, 2007.

Brundage, James A. *Law, Sex, and Christian Society in Medieval Europe.* Chicago, 1987.

Brunner, Karl. *Oppositionelle Gruppen im Karolingerreich.* Vienna, 1979.

Budny, Mildred, and J. Graham-Campbell. "An Eighth-Century Bronze Ornament from Canterbury and Related Works." *Archaeologia Cantiana* 47 (1982): 7–25.

Budny, Mildred, and Dominic Tweddle. "The Maaseik Embroideries." *Anglo-Saxon England* 13 (1984): 65–96.

Budny, Mildred. "The Byrhtnoth Tapestry or Embroidery." In *The Battle of Maldon AD 991*, edited by Donald Scragg, 263–78. Oxford, 1991.

Bullough, Donald. "Friends, Neighbors, and Fellow Drinkers: Aspects of Community and Conflict in the Early Medieval West." H. M. Chadwick Lectures 1. Cambridge, 1990.

———. *Alcuin: Achievement and Reputation: Being Part of the Ford Lectures Delivered in Oxford in Hilary Term 1980*. Leiden, The Netherlands, 2004.

Bullough, Vern, and Cameron Campbell. "Female Longevity and Diet in the Middle Ages." *Speculum* 55, no. 2 (1980): 317–25.

Bush, M. L., ed. *Social Orders and Social Classes in Europe since 1500: Studies in Social Stratification*. London, 1992.

Bynum, Caroline Walker. *Holy Feast and Holy Fast: The Religious Significance of Food to Medieval Women*. Berkeley, Calif., 1987.

Capelle, Torsten. "Handwerk in der Karolingerzeit." In *Kunst*, 424–9.

Carroll, Christopher. "The Bishoprics of Saxony in the First Century after Christianization." *EME* 8.1 (1999): 219–46.

Carruthers, Mary. *The Book of Memory: A Study of Memory in Medieval Culture*. Cambridge, 1990.

Chapelot, Jean, and Robert Fossier. *The Village and House in the Middle Ages*. Translated by Henry Cleere. Berkeley, Calif., 1985.

Christie, Neil. *The Lombards*. Oxford, 1995.

Cizek, Alexandru. "Das Bild von der idealen Schönheit in der lateinischen Dichtung des Frühmittelalters." *Mittellateinisches Jahrbuch* 26 (1991): 5–35.

Claussen, M. A. "God and Man in Dhuoda's *Liber manualis*." *Studies in Church History* 27 (1990): 43–52.

———. "Fathers of Power and Women of Authority: Dhuoda and the *Liber Manualis*." *French Historical Studies* 19 (1996): 785–809.

Cohen, Adam. *The Uta Codex: Art, Philosophy and Reform in Eleventh-Century Germany*. University Park, Penn., 2000.

Colombini, Alain. "Teintures attestées de l'Antiquité au Moyen Âge." In *Tissu et vêtement. 5000 ans de savoir-faire*, 42–5. Guiry-en-Vexin, France, 1986.

Connerton, Paul. *How Societies Remember*. Cambridge, 1989.

Constable, Giles. "The Ceremonies and Symbolism of Entering Religious Life and Taking the Monastic Habit, from the Fourth to the Twelfth Century." *Settimane* 33, no. 2 (1987): 771–834.

Contreni, John J. "Inharmonious Harmony: Education in the Carolingian World." *Annals of Scholarship* 1, no. 2 (1980): 81–96.

———. "Learning in the Early Middle Ages." In *Carolingian Learning, Masters and Manuscripts*, edited by John J. Contreni, 1–21. Hampshire, England, 1992.

———. "The Carolingian Renaissance: Education and Literary Culture." In *NCMH* 2, 263–78.

Coon, Lynda L. *Sacred Fictions: Holy Women and Hagiography in Late Antiquity*. Philadelphia, 1997.

Cooper, Kate. *The Virgin and the Bride: Idealized Womanhood in Late Antiquity*. Cambridge, Mass., 1996.

Curtius, Ernst Robert. *European Literature and the Latin Middle Ages*. Translated by Willard R. Trask. London, 1953.

Davies, Wendy. *Small Worlds: The Village Community in Early Medieval Brittany*. London, 1988.

Delaporte, Yves. *Le voile de Notre Dame*. Chartres, 1927.

Devroey, Jean-Pierre. "La démographie du polyptyque de Saint-Remi de Reims." In *Compter les Champeois*, edited by Patrick Demouy and Charles Vuilliez, 81–94. Reims, France, 1997.

——. "Femmes au miroir des polyptyques: une approche des rapports du couple dans l'exploitation rurale dépendante entre Seine et Rhin au ixe siècle." In *Femmes et pouvoirs des femmes à Byzance et en occident (vi^e-xie siècles)*, edited by Stéphane Lebecq, Alain Dierkens, Régine Le Jan, and J. Sansterre, 227–49. Lille, France, 1999.

——. "Men and Women in Early Medieval Serfdom: The Ninth-Century North Frankish Evidence." *PP* 166 (2000): 3–30.

Diebold, William J. "The Ruler Portrait of Charles the Bald in the S. Paolo Bible." *The Art Bulletin* 76, no. 1 (1994): 7–18.

Dronke, Peter. *Women Writers of the Middle Ages: A Critical Study of Texts from Perpetua (203) to Marguerite Porete (1310)*. Cambridge, 1984.

Duby, Georges. "Le mariage dans la société du haut Moyen Âge." *Settimane* 24 (1977): 13–39.

Dutton, Paul Edward. "Eriugena the Royal Poet." In *Jean Scot Ecrivain. Actes du IVe Colloque international Montréal, 28 août—2 septembre 1983*, edited by G.-H. Allard, 51–80. Montreal, 1986.

——. "The Dubthach Codex and Eriugena." In *From Athens to Chartres: Neoplatonism and Medieval Thought. Studies in Honour of Edouard Jeauneau*, edited by Haijo Jan Westra, 15–45. Leiden, The Netherlands, 1992.

——. *Charlemagne's Mustache and Other Cultural Clusters of a Dark Age*. New York, 2004.

Eckenstein, Lina. *Women Under Monasticism*. 1896; repr., New York, 1963.

Eco, Umberto. *Art and Beauty in the Middle Ages*. Trans. Hugh Bredin. New Haven, 1986.

Elbern, Victor H. "Liturgisches Gerät und Reliquiare." In *Kunst*, 694–710.

Ennas, Barbara Fois. *Il "Capitulare de villis."* Milan, 1981.

Ennen, Edith. *Frauen im Mittelalter*. 5th ed. Munich, 1994.

Enright, Michael J. *Lady with a Mead Cup: Ritual, Prophecy, and Lordship in the European Warband from La Tène to the Viking Age*. Blackrock, Ireland, 1996.

Erhart, Peter. "*Gens eadem reparat omnia septa gregis*—Mönchtum unter den langobardischen Königen." In *Die Langobarden. Herrschaft und Identität*, edited by Walter Pohl and Peter Erhart, 387–408. Vienna, 2005.

van der Essen, L. *Etude critique et littéraire sur les vitae des saints mérovingiens de l'ancienne Belgique*. Louvain, Belgium, 1907.

Etter, Hansueli. "Die Bevölkerung von Münsterhof." *Der Münsterhof in Zürich: Bericht über die vom städtischen Büro für Archäologie durchgeführten Stadtkernforschungen 1977–78*, vol. 2. Ed. Jürg Schneider, Daniel Gutscher, Hansueli Etter, and Jürg Hanser, 179–212. Freiburg, Germany, 1982.

Favre, Eduoard. "La famille d'Evrard, marquis de Frioul dans le royaume franc de l'ouest." *Etudes d'histoire du Moyen-Âge, dédiées à G. Monod*, 155–62. Paris, 1896.

Fell, Christine with Cecily Clark and Elizabeth Williams. *Women in Anglo-Saxon England*. 1984; repr., London, 1986.

Fentress, James and Chris Wickham. *Social Memory: New Perspectives on the Past*. Oxford, 1992.

Ferrante, Joan M. *To the Glory of Her Sex: Women's Roles in the Composition of Medieval Texts*. Bloomington, Ind., 1997.

Fleming, Robin. "The New Wealth, the New Rich, and the New Political Style in Late Anglo-Saxon England." *Anglo-Norman Studies 23: Proceedings of the Battle Conference*. Edited by John Gillingham, 1–22. Woodbridge, England, 2001.

——. "Lords and Labour." In *From the Vikings to the Normans*, edited by Wendy Davies, 107–37. Oxford, 2003.

——. "Bones for Historians: Putting the Body Back into Biography." In *Writing Medieval Biography 750–1250: Essays in Honour of Professor Frank Barlow*, edited by David Bates, Julia Crick, and Sarah Hamilton, 29–48. Woodbridge, England, 2006.

——. "Acquiring, Flaunting and Destroying Silk in Late Anglo-Saxon England." *EME* 15, no. 2 (2007): 127–58.

Fossier, Robert. *La terre et les hommes en Picardie jusqu'à la fin du xiiie siècle.* Vol. 1. Paris, 1968.

Fouracre, Paul. "Eternal Light and Earthly Needs: Practical Aspects of the Development of Frankish Immunities." In *Property and Power in the Early Middle Ages,* edited by Wendy Davies and Paul Fouracre, 53–31. Cambridge, 1995.

———. "Attitudes Towards Violence in Seventh- and Eighth-Century Francia." In *Violence and Society in the Early Medieval West,* edited by Guy Halsall, 60–75. Woodbridge, England, 1998.

Fouracre, Paul, and Richard A. Gerberding. *Late Merovingian France: History and Hagiography, 640–720.* Manchester, England, 1996.

Francisque-Michel. *Recherches sur le commerce, la fabrication et l'usage des étoffes de soie, d'or et d'argent et autres tissus précieux en occident, principalement en France pendant le Moyen Âge.* 2 vols. 1852; repr., Paris, 2001.

Freeman, Ann. "Theodulf of Orléans and the *Libri Carolini.*" *Speculum* 32 (1957): 663–705.

———. "Scripture and Images in the *Libri Carolini.*" *Testo e immagine nell'alto medioevo: 15–21 aprile 1993. Settimane* 41, no. 1 (1994): 163–95.

Ganz, David. "Conclusion: Visions of Carolingian Education, Past, Present, and Future." In *"The Gentle Voices of Teachers": Aspects of Learning in the Carolingian Age,* edited by Richard E. Sullivan, 261–83. Columbus, Ohio, 1995.

Garrison, Mary Delafield. "Alcuin's World through His Letters and Verse." PhD diss., University of Cambridge, 1995.

———. "The Social World of Alcuin: Nicknames at York and at the Carolingian Court." In *Alcuin of York: Scholar at the Carolingian Court,* edited by L. A. J. R. Houwen and A. A. MacDonald, 59–79. Groningen, The Netherlands, 1998.

Garver, Valerie L. "The Influence of Monastic Ideals upon Carolingian Conceptions of Childhood." In *Childhood in the Middle Ages and Renaissance: The Results of a Paradigm Shift in the History of Mentality,* edited by Albrecht Classen, 67–85. Berlin, 2005.

———. "Learned Women? Liutberga and the Instruction of Carolingian Women." In *LICW,* 121–38.

———. "Old Age and Women in the Carolingian World." In *Old Age in the Middle Ages and Renaissance: Interdisciplinary Approaches to a Neglected Topic,* edited by Albrecht Classen, 121–41. Berlin, 2007.

Geary, Patrick J. "Exchange and Interaction between the Living and the Dead in Early Medieval Society." In *Living with the Dead in the Middle Ages,* edited by Patrick J. Geary, 77–92. Ithaca, N.Y., 1994.

———. *Phantoms of Remembrance: Memory and Oblivion at the End of the First Millennium.* Princeton, N.J., 1994.

Geijer, Agnes. "The Textile Finds from Birka." In *Cloth and Clothing in Medieval Europe: Essays in Memory of Professor E. M. Carus-Wilson,* edited by N. B. Harte and K. G. Ponting, 80–99. London, 1983.

Gentili, François. "L'éclairage domestique." In *Un village,* 271–75.

Geuenich, Dieter. "Richkart, *ancilla dei de caenobio Sancti Stephani.* Zeugnisse zur Geschichte des Straßburger Frauenklosters St. Stephan in der Karolingerzeit." In *Festschrift für Eduard Hlawitschka zum 65. Geburtstag,* edited by Karl Rudolf Schnith and Roland Pauler, 97–109. Munich, 1993.

Gilchrist, Roberta. *Gender and Material Culture: The Archaeology of Religious Women.* London, 1994.

Glaze, Florence Eliza. "The Perforated Wall: The Ownership and Circulation of Medical Books in Medieval Europe, ca. 800–1200." PhD diss., Duke University, 1999.

Goetz, Hans-Werner. "Frauenbild und Weibliche Lebensgestaltung im Fränkischen Reich." In *WLFM,* 7–44.

———. *Frauen im frühen Mittelalter.* Cologne, Germany, 1995.

. "Social and Military Institutions." In *NCMH* 2, 451-80.

Goldberg, Eric J. "*Regina nitens sanctissima Hemma:* Queen Emma (827-876), Bishop Witgar of Augsburg, and the Witgar-Belt." In *Representations of Power in Medieval Germany, 800-1500,* edited by Björn Weiler and Simon MacLean, 57-95. Turnhout, Belgium, 2006.

. *Struggle for Empire: Kingship and Conflict under Louis the German, 817-876.* Ithaca, N.Y., 2006.

Goody, Jack. *The European Family: An Historico-Anthropological Essay.* Oxford, 2000.

Grierson, Philip. "The Identity of the Unnamed Fiscs in the *Brevium exempla ad describendas res ecclesiasticas et fiscales.*" *Revue Belge de philologie et d'histoire* 18 (1939): 437-61.

Grosse, Walther. "Das Kloster Wendhausen, sein Stiftergeschlecht und seine Klausnerin." *Sachsen und Anhalt* 16 (1940): 45-76.

Grupe, G., A. Cipriano-Bechtle, and P. Schröter. "Ageing and Life Expectancy in the Early Middle Ages." *Homo* 46, no. 3 (1996): 267-79.

Hageneier, Lars, Johannes Laudage, and Yvonne Leiverkus. *Die Zeit der Karolinger.* Darmstadt, Germany, 2006.

Halbwachs, Maurice. *The Collective Memory.* Translated by Francis J. Ditter Jr. and Vida Yazdi Ditter. New York, 1980.

Halsall, Guy. "Female Status and Power in Early Merovingian Central Austrasia: The Burial Evidence." *EME* 5, no. 1 (1996): 1-24.

. *Warfare and Society in the Barbarian West, 450-900.* London, 2003.

Hamilton, Sarah. "'Most Illustrious King of Kings': Evidence for Ottonian Kingship in the Otto III Prayerbook (Munich, Bayerische Staatsbibliothek, Clm 30111)." *JMH* 27 (2001): 257-88.

Hammer, Carl I. "County Churches, Clerical Inventories, and the Carolingian Renaissance in Bavaria." *Church History* 49, no. 1 (1980): 5-17.

. "Land Sales in Eighth- and Ninth-Century Bavaria: Legal, Economic, and Social Aspects." *EME* 6, no. 1 (1997): 47-76.

Harrison, Carol. *Beauty and Revelation in the Thought of St. Augustine.* Oxford, 1992.

Harvey, P. D. A. "*Rectitudines Singularum Personarum* and *Gerefa.*" *The English Historical Review* 108, no. 426 (1993): 1-22.

Hasdenteufel-Röding, Maria. "Zur Gründung und Organisation des Frauenklosters San Salvatore an der Versilia." In *Vita Walfredi und Kloster Monteverdi,* edited by Karl Schmid, 174-85. Tübingen, Germany, 1991.

Haupt, Gottfried. *Die Farbensymbolik in der sakralen Kunst des abendländischen Mittelalters.* Dresden, Germany, 1941.

Heene, Katrien. *The Legacy of Paradise: Marriage, Motherhood, and Women in Carolingian Edifying Literature.* Frankfurt am Main, Germany, 1997.

Heidebrecht, Petra, and Cordula Nolte. "Leben im Kloster. Nonnen und Kanonissen. Geistliche Lebensformen im frühen Mittelalter." In *Weiblichkeit in geschichtlicher Perspektive. Fallstudien und Reflexionen zu Grundproblemen der historischen Frauenforschung,* edited by Ursula A. J. Becher and Jörn Rüsen, 79-115. Frankfurt am Main, Germany, 1988.

Heinrich, Mary Pia. *The Canonesses and Education in the Early Middle Ages.* Washington, D.C., 1924.

Hellmuth, Doris. *Frau und Besitz. Zum Handlungsspielraum von Frauen in Alemannien (700-940).* Sigmaringen, Germany, 1998.

Hen, Yitzhak. *Culture and Religion in Merovingian Gaul A.D. 481-751.* Leiden, The Netherlands, 1995.

. *The Royal Patronage of Liturgy in Frankish Gaul to the Death of Charles the Bald (877).* London, 2001.

Henderson, George. "Emulation and Invention in Carolingian Art." In *Carolingian Culture: Emulation and Innovation,* edited by Rosamond McKitterick, 248-73. Cambridge, 1994.

Hennebicque, Régine. "Espaces sauvages et chasses royales dans le nord de la Francie viième-ixème siècles." *Revue du Nord* 62 (1980): 36-57.

Herlihy, David. "Land, Family, and Women in Continental Europe, 701–1200." In *Women in Medieval Society*, edited by Susan Mosher Stuard, 13–45. Philadelphia, 1976.
——. *Opera Muliebria: Women and Work in Medieval Europe*. Philadelphia, 1990.
——. "The Natural History of Medieval Women." In *WFSME*, 57–68.
Hlawitschka, Eduard. *Franken, Alemannen, Bayern und Burgunder in Oberitalien (774–962). Zum Verständnis der Fränkischen Königsherrschaft in Italien*. Freiburg im Breisgau, Germany, 1960.
——. "Herzog Giselbert von Lothringen und das Kloster Remiremont." *Zeitschrift für die Geschichte des Oberrheins* 108 (1960): 422–65.
——. *Studien zur Äbtissenreihe von Remiremont (7.-13. Jh.)*. Saarbrücken, Germany, 1963.
——. "Beobachtungen und Überlegungen zur Konventsstärke im Nonnenkloster Remiremont während des 7.-9. Jahrhunderts." In *Secundum regulam vivere. Festschrift für P. Norbert Backmund O.Praem*, edited by Gert Melville, 31–39. Windberg, Germany, 1978.
Hoffman, Hartmut. *Untersuchung zur karolingischen Annalistik*. Bonner Forschungen 10. Bonn, Germany, 1958.
Hollis, Stephanie. *Anglo-Saxon Women and the Church: Sharing a Common Fate*. Woodbridge, England, 1992.
van Houts, Elisabeth. *Memory and Gender in Medieval Europe, 900–1200*. Basingstoke, England, 1999.
——, ed. *Medieval Memories: Men, Women, and the Past*. Harlow, England, 2001.
Innes, Matthew. "Memory, Orality, and Literacy in an Early Medieval Society." *PP* 158 (1998): 3–36.
——. *State and Society in the Early Middle Ages: The Middle Rhine Valley, 400–1000*. Cambridge, 2000.
——. "Keeping It in the Family: Women and Aristocratic Memory, 700–1200." In *Medieval Memories: Men, Women, and the Past, 700–1300*, edited by Elisabeth van Houts, 17–35. Harlow, England, 2001.
——. "'A Place of Discipline': Carolingian Courts and Aristocratic Youth." In *Court Culture in the Early Middle Ages*, edited by Catherine Cubitt, 59–76. Turnhout, Belgium, 2003.
Jacobsen, Werner. "Herrschaftliches Bauen in der Karolingerzeit. Karolingishe Pfalzen zwischen germanischer Tradition und Antikenrezeption." In *Kunst*, 91–94.
Jaeger, C. Stephen. *The Origins of Courtliness: Civilizing Trends and the Formation of Courtly Ideals, 939–1210*. Philadelphia, 1985.
Janes, Dominic. *God and Gold in Late Antiquity*. Cambridge, 1998.
Jochens, Jenny. *Women in Old Norse Society*. Ithaca, N.Y., 1995.
de Jong, Mayke. "Growing up in a Carolingian Monastery: Magister Hildemar and His Oblates." *JMH* 9 (1983): 99–128.
——. *In Samuel's Image: Child Oblation in the Early Medieval West*. Leiden, The Netherlands, 1996.
——. "The Empire as *ecclesia*: Hrabanus Maurus and the Biblical *historia* for Rulers." In *The Uses of the Past in the Early Middle Ages*, edited by Yitzhak Hen and Matthew Innes, 191–226. Cambridge, 2000.
——. "Exegesis for an Empress." In *Medieval Transformations: Texts, Power, and Gifts in Context*, edited by Esther Cohen and Mayke B. de Jong, 69–100. Leiden, The Netherlands, 2001.
——. "Bride Shows Revisited: The Empress Judith." In *GEMW*, 257–77.
Kantorowicz, Ernst H. "The Carolingian King in the Bible of San Paolo fuori le Mura." In *Late Classical and Mediaeval Studies in Honor of Albert Mathias Friend, Jr*, edited by Kurt Weitzmann, 287–304. Princeton, N.J., 1955.
Kershaw, Paul J. E. "Eberhard of Friuli, a Lay Intellectual." In *LICW*, 77–105.
Kitson, Peter R. "Lapidary Traditions in Anglo-Saxon England: Part II, Bede's *Explanatio Apocalypsis*." *Anglo-Saxon England* 12 (1983): 73–123.

Konecny, Silvia. *Die Frauen des karolingischen Königshauss. Die politische Bedeutung der Ehe und die Stellung der Frau in der fränkischen Herrscherfamilie vom 7. bis zum 10. Jahrhundert.* Vienna, 1976.

Koziol, Geoffrey. *Begging Pardon and Favor: Ritual and Political Order in Early Medieval France.* Ithaca, N.Y., 1992.

Kuchenbuch, Ludolf. "*Opus feminile.* Das Geschlechterverhältnis im Spiegel von Frauenarbeiten im früheren Mittelalter." In *WLFM,* 139–78.

———. "Trennung und Verbindung im bäuerlichen Werken des 9. Jahrhunderts. Eine Auseinandersetzung mit Ivan Ilichs Genus-Konzept." In *FG,* vol. 7, 227–42.

La Rocca, Christina, and Luigi Provero. "The Dead and Their Gifts: The Will of Eberhard, Count of Friuli, and His Wife Gisela, Daughter of Louis the Pious (863–864)." In *Rituals of Power: From Late Antiquity to the Early Middle Ages,* edited by Frans Theuws and Janet L. Nelson, 225–80. Leiden, The Netherlands, 2000.

Ladner, Gerhart B. *God, Cosmos, Humankind: The World of Early Christian Symbolism.* Berkeley, Calif., 1995.

Laistner, M. L. W. *A Hand-List of Bede Manuscripts.* Ithaca, N.Y., 1943.

Laporte, Jean-Pierre. "La chasuble de Chelles." *Bulletin du groupement archéologique de Seine-et-Marne* 23 (1982): 1–29.

Lebecq, Stéphane. *Marchands et navigateurs frisons du haut moyen âge.* 2 vols. Lille, France, 1983.

Lees, Clare A., and Gillian R. Overing. *Double Agents: Women and Clerical Culture in Anglo-Saxon England.* Philadelphia, 2001.

Le Jan-Hennebicque, Régine. "Aux origines du douaire médiéval (vi^e–xe siècles)." In *Veuves et veuvage dans le haut Moyen Âge,* edited by Michel Parisse, 107–22. Paris, 1993.

Le Jan, Régine. *Famille et pouvoir dans le monde France (viie–xe siècle). Essai d'anthropologie sociale.* Paris, 1995.

———, ed. *La Royauté et les élites dans l'Europe carolingienne. Début ixe siècle aux environs de 920.* Paris, 1998.

———. *Femmes, pouvoir et société dans le haut Moyen Âge.* Paris, 2001.

Levison, Wilhelm. "Kleine Beiträge zu Quellen der fränkischen Geschichte." *Neues Archiv der Gesellschaft für ältere deutsche Geschichtskunde* 27 (1902): 331–408.

Leyser, Karl. *Rule and Conflict in an Early Medieval Society.* London, 1979.

———. "Early Medieval Canon Law and the Beginnings of Knighthood." In *Communications and Power in Medieval Europe: The Carolingian and Ottonian Centuries,* edited by Timothy Reuter, 51–72. London, 1994.

Lifshitz, Felice. "Gender and Exemplarity East of the Middle Rhine: Jesus, Mary, and the Saints in Manuscript Context." *EME* 9, no. 3 (2000): 325–43.

———. "Demonstrating Gun(t)za: Women, Manuscripts, and the Question of Historical 'Proof.'" In *Vom Nutzen des Schreibens. Soziales Gedächtnis, Herrschaft und Besitz im Mittelalter,* edited by Walter Pohl and Paul Herold, 67–96. Vienna, 2002.

Ludwig, Uwe. *Transalpine Beziehungen der Karolingerzeit im Spiegel der Memorialüberlieferung. Prosopographische und sozialgeschichtliche Studien unter besoner Berücksichtigung des Liber vitae von San Salvatore in Brescia und des Evageliars von Cividale.* Hanover, Germany, 1999.

MacLean, Simon. *Kingship and Politics in the Late Ninth Century: Charles the Fat and the End of the Carolingian Empire.* Cambridge, 2003.

———. "Queenship, Nunneries, and Royal Widowhood in Carolingian Europe." *PP* 178 (2003): 1–38.

Marenbon, John. "Carolingian Thought." In *Carolingian Culture: Emulation and Innovation,* edited by Rosamond McKitterick, 171–92. Cambridge, 1994.

McCormick, Michael. *Origins of the European Economy: Communications and Commerce, A.D. 300–900.* Cambridge, 2001.

McKitterick, Rosamond. "A Ninth-Century Schoolbook from the Loire Valley: Phillipps MS 16308." *Scriptorium* 30, no. 2 (1976): 225–31.

——. *The Frankish Church and the Carolingian Reforms, 789–895.* London, 1977.

——. *The Carolingians and the Written Word.* Cambridge, 1989.

——, ed. *The Uses of Literacy in Early Mediaeval Europe.* Cambridge, 1990.

——. "Frauen und Schriftlichkeit im Frühmittelalter." In *WLFM*, 65–118.

——. "Nuns' Scriptoria in England and Francia in the Eighth Century." *Francia* 19, no. 1 (1992): 1–35.

——. "Women and Literacy in the Early Middle Ages." In *Books Scribes and Learning in the Frankish Kingdoms, 6th–9th Centuries*, edited by Rosamond McKitterick, 1–43. Cambridge, 1994.

——. *History and Memory in the Carolingian World.* Cambridge, 2004.

McLaughlin, Mary Martin. "Survivors and Surrogates: Children and Parents from the Ninth to the Thirteenth Centuries." *The History of Childhood*, edited by Lloyd de Mause, 101–81. New York, 1983.

McNamara, Jo-Ann, and Suzanne F. Wemple. "Marriage and Divorce in the Frankish Kingdom." In *Women in Medieval Society*, edited by Susan Mosher Stuard, 95–124. Philadelphia, 1976.

McNamara, Jo Ann Kay. *Sisters in Arms: Catholic Nuns through Two Millennia.* Cambridge, Mass., 1996.

McNamara, Jo Ann. "Women and Power through the Family Revisited." In *Gendering the Master Narrative: Women and Power in the Middle Ages*, edited by Mary C. Erler and Maryanne Kowaleski, 17–30. Ithaca, N.Y., 2003.

Mecham, June. "Recent Research on Women, Spirituality, and the Arts in the Middle Ages." *History Compass* 4, no. 3 (2006): 448–80.

Meens, Rob. *Het tripartite boeteboek. Overlevering en betekenis van vroegmiddeleeuwse biechtvoorschriften.* Hilversum, The Netherlands, 1994.

——. "Religious Instruction in the Frankish Kingdoms." In *Medieval Transformations: Texts, Power, and Gifts in Context*, edited by Esther Cohen and Mayke B. de Jong, 51–67. Leiden, The Netherlands, 2001.

Meier, Christel. *Gemma Spiritalis. Methode und Gebrauch der Edelsteinallegorese vom frühen Christentum bis ins 18. Jahrhundert.* Munich, 1977.

Metz, René. *La consécration des vierges dans l'église romaine.* Paris, 1954.

Mitchell, John. "Monastic Guest Quarters and Workshops: The Example of San Vincenzo al Volturno." In *Wohn- und Wirtschaftsbauten frühmittelalterliche Klöster*, edited by Hans Ruldolf Sennhauser, 127–55. Zurich, 1996.

Müller, Mechtild. *Die Kleidung nach Quellen des frühen Mittelalters. Textilien und Mode von Karl dem Großen bis Heinrich III.* Berlin, 2003.

Muschiol, Gisela. *Famula Dei. Zur Liturgie in merowingischen Frauenklöstern.* Münster, Germany, 1994.

——. "Men, Women, and Liturgical Practice in the Early Medieval West." In *GEMW*, 198–216.

Nees, Lawrence. "Art and Architecture." In *NCMH* 2, 809–44.

Nelson, Janet L. "Queens as Jezebels: The Careers of Brunhild and Balthild in Merovingian History." In *Medieval Women.* Studies in Church History 1. Edited by Derek Baker, 31–77. Oxford, 1978.

——. "Les femmes et l'évangélisation au ixe siècle." *Revue du Nord* 68 (1986): 471–85.

——. "Ninth-Century Knighthood: The Evidence of Nithard." In *Studies in Medieval History Presented to R. Allen Brown*, edited by Christopher Harper-Bill, Christopher J. Holdsworth, and Janet L. Nelson, 255–66. Woodbridge, England, 1989.

——. "Commentary on the Papers of J. Verdon, S.F. Wemple, and M. Parisse." In *Frauen in Spätantike und Frühmittelalter. Lebensbedingungen—Lebensnormen—Lebensformen*, edited by Werner Affeldt, 325–32. Sigmaringen, Germany, 1990.

——. "Perceptions du pouvoir chez les historiennes du haut Moyen Âge." In *La femme au Moyen Âge.* Edited by Michel Rouche and Jean Heuclin, 75–85. Paris, 1990.

———. "Women and the Word in the Earlier Middle Ages." In *Women in the Church*, edited by W. J. Sheils and Diana Wood, 53–78. Studies in Church History 27. Oxford, 1990.

———. *Charles the Bald*. London, 1992.

———. "Women at the Court of Charlemagne: A Case of Monstrous Regiment?" In *Medieval Queenship*, edited by John Carmi Parsons, 43–61. New York, 1993.

———. "The Wary Widow." In *Property and Power in the Early Middle Ages*, edited by Wendy Davies and Paul Fouracre, 82–113. Cambridge, 1995.

———. *The Frankish World: 750–900*. London, 1996.

———. "Early Medieval Rites of Queen-Making and the Shaping of Medieval Queenship." In *Queens and Queenship in Medieval Europe*, edited by Anne Duggan, 301–15. Woodbridge, England, 1997.

———. "Family, Gender, and Sexuality in the Middle Ages." In *Companion to Historiography*, edited by M. Bentley, 722–34. London, 1997.

———. "Making a Difference in Eighth-Century Politics: The Daughters of Desiderius." In *After Rome's Fall: Narrators and Sources of Early Medieval History. Essays Presented to Walter Goffart*, edited by Alexander Callander Murray, 171–90. Toronto, 1998.

———. "Violence in the Carolingian World and the Ritualization of Ninth-Century Warfare." In *Violence and Society in the Early Medieval West*, edited by Guy Halsall, 90–107. Woodbridge, England, 1998.

———. "Gender, Memory, and Social Power." *Gender and History* 12, no. 3 (2000): 722–34.

———. "Peers in the Early Middle Ages." In *Law, Laity, and Solidarities: Essays in Honour of Susan Reynolds*, edited by Pauline Stafford, Janet L. Nelson, and Jane Martindale, 27–46. Manchester, England, 2001.

———. "Dhuoda." In *LICW*, 106–20.

Nicolaysen, N. *The Viking-Ship Discovered at Gokstad in Norway*. Oslo, 1882.

Noble, Thomas F. X. "Paradoxes and Possibilities in the Sources for Roman Society in the Early Middle Ages." In *Early Medieval Rome and the Christian West: Essays in Honor of Donald Bullough*, edited by Julia M. H. Smith, 55–83. Leiden, The Netherlands, 2000.

———. *Images, Iconoclasm, and the Carolingians*. Philadelphia, 2009.

Nolte, Cordula. *Conversio und Christianitas. Frauen in der Christianisierung vom 5. bis 8. Jahrhundert*. Stuttgart, Germany, 1995.

Nora, Pierre. "General Introduction: Between Memory and History." In *Realms of Memory: Rethinking the French Past*, 1, edited by Pierre Nora, 1–23. New York, 1992.

Obermeier, Monika. *"Ancilla." Beiträge zur Geschichte der unfreien Frauen im Frühmittelalter*. Pfaffenweiler, Germany, 1996.

Odegaard, Charles E. "The Empress Engelberge." *Speculum* 26, no. 1 (1951): 77–103.

Osborne, John. "Textiles and Their Painted Imitations in Early Medieval Rome." *Papers of the British School at Rome* 60 (1992): 309–51.

Palazzo, Eric. *Liturgie et société au Moyen Âge*. Paris, 2000.

Parisse, Michel. "Les chanoinesses dans l'empire germanique (ixᵉ-xiᵉ siècles)." *Francia* 6 (1978): 107–26.

———. *Les nonnes au Moyen Âge*. Le Puy, France, 1983.

———. "Les femmes au monastère dans le nord de l'Allemagne du ixᵉ au xiᵉ siécle. Conditions sociales et religieuses." In *Frauen in Spätantike und Frühmittelalter. Lebensbedingungen—Lebensnormen—Lebensformen*, edited by Werner Affeldt, 311–24. Sigmaringen, Germany, 1990.

———. "Des veuves au monastère." In *Veuves et veuvage dans le haut Moyen Âge*, edited by Michel Parisse, 255–74. Paris, 1993.

Parker, Rozsika. *The Subversive Stitch*. 1984; repr., London, 1996.

Payer, Hans Conrad. *Von der Gastfreundschaft zum Gasthaus. Studien zur Gastlickkeit im Mittelalter*. Hanover, Germany, 1987.

Select Bibliography

Pellaton, Frantz. "La veuve et ses droits de la Basse-Antiquité au haut Moyen Âge." In *Veuves et veuvage dans le haut Moyen Âge*, edited by Michel Parisse, 51–97. Paris, 1993.

Platelle, Henri. "Le thème de la conversion à travers les oeuvres hagiographiques d'Hucbald de Saint-Amand." *Revue du Nord* 68 (1986): 511–31.

Pohl-Resl, Brigitte. "Vorsorge, Memoria und soziales Ereignis: Frauen als Schenkerinnen in den bayerischen und alemannischen Urkunden des 8. und 9. Jahrhunderts." *Mitteilungen des Instituts für Österreichische Geschichtsforschung* 103 (1995): 265–87.

Portmann, Marie-Louise. *Die Darstellung der Frau in der Geschichtsschreibung des frühen Mittelalters*. Basel, Switzerland, 1958.

Post, J. B. "Ages at Menarche and Menopause: Some Mediaeval Authorities." *Population Studies* 25, no. 1 (1971): 83–7.

Power, Eileen. *Medieval People*. New York, 1924

———. *Medieval Women*, edited by M. M. Postan. Cambridge, 1975.

Le Puy en Velay 43—Haute Loire (Auvergne). Trésor d'art religieux du cloître de la cathédrale. Bible de Théodulph, 9ᵉ siècle. Etude des tissus servant d'intercalaires. Paris, 1994.

Ratkowitsch, Christine. *Karolus Magnus—alter Aeneas, alter Martinus, alter Iustinus. Zu Intention und Datierung des "Aachener Karlesepos."* Vienna, 1997.

Réal, Isabelle. *Vies de saints, vie de famille. Représentation et système de la parenté dans le Royaume mérovingien (481–751) d'après les sources hagiographiques*. Turnhout, 2001.

Reuter, Timothy, ed. *The Medieval Nobility: Studies on the Ruling Classes of France and Germany from the Sixth to the Twelfth century*. Amsterdam, 1978.

Reynolds, Susan. *Fiefs and Vassals: The Medieval Evidence Reinterpreted*. Oxford, 1994.

———. "Carolingian Elopements as a Sidelight on Counts and Vassals." In... *The Man of Many Devices Who Wandered Full Many Ways...*, edited by Balazs Nágy and Marcell Sebök, 340–6. Budapest, 1999.

Riché, Pierre. "Les bibliothèques de trois aristocrates laïcs carolingiens." *Le Moyen Âge*, fourth series 18 or 69 (1963): 87–104.

———. *Education and Culture in the Barbarian West Sixth through Eighth Centuries*. 3d ed. Translated by John J. Contreni. Columbia, S.C., 1976.

———. *Daily Life in the World of Charlemagne*. Translated by Jo Ann McNamara. 1973; repr., Philadelphia, 1978.

———, ed. *Instruction et vie religieuse dans le haut Moyen Âge*. London, 1981.

———. *The Carolingians: A Family Who Forged Europe*. Translated by Michael Idomir Allen. Philadelphia, 1993.

———. *Ecoles et enseignement dans le haut Moyen Âge. Fin du vᵉ siècle—milieu du xiᵉ siècle*. 2nd ed. Paris, 1989.

Rio, Alice. "Freedom and Unfreedom in Early Medieval Francia: The Evidence of the Legal *formulae*." *PP* 193 (2006): 7–40.

Rösener, Werner. "Die Grundherrschaft des Klosters Fulda in karolingischer und ottonischer Zeit." In *Kloster Fulda in der Welt der Karolinger und Ottonen*, edited by Gangolf Schrimpf, 210–24. Frankfurt am Main, Germany, 1996.

Rosenwein, Barbara H. *To Be the Neighbor of St. Peter: The Social Meaning of Cluny's Property, 909–1049*. Ithaca, N.Y., 1989.

Rouche, Michel. "Les repas de fête à l'époque carolingienne." In *Manger et boire au Moyen Âge* 1, edited by Denis Menjot, 265–96. Paris, 1984.

Rubin, Miri. *Corpus Christi: The Eucharist in Late Medieval Culture*. Cambridge, 1991.

———. "A Decade of Studying Medieval Women, 1987–1997." *History Workshop Journal* 46 (1998): 213–39.

Santinelli, Emmanuelle. *Des femmes éplorées? Les veuves dans la société aristocratique du haut Moyen Âge*. Villeneuve-d'Ascq, 2003.

Schilp, Thomas. *Norm und Wirklichkeit religiöser Frauengemeinschaften im Frühmittelalter. Die Institutio sanctimonialium Aquisgranensis des Jahres 816 und die Problematik der Verfassung von Frauenkommunitäten*. Göttingen, Germany, 1998.

Schipper, William. "Rabanus Maur and His Sources." In *Schooling and Society: The Ordering and Reordering of Knowledge in the Western Middle Ages*, edited by Alasdair A. MacDonald and Michael W. Twomey, 1–21. Leuven, Belgium, 2004.

Schmid, Karl, and Joachim Wollasch. "Die Gemeinschaft der Lebenden und Verstorbenen in Zeugnissen des Mittelalters." *FS* 1 (1967): 365–405.

Schmid, Karl. "Heirat, Familienfolge, Geschlechterbewusstsein." *Settimane* 24 (1977): 103–37.

Schmid, Karl, and Joachim Wollasch, ed. *Memoria. Der geschichtliche Zeugniswert des liturgischen Gedenkens im Mittelalter*. Munich, 1984.

Schulenburg, Jane Tibbetts. "Sexism and the Celestial Gynaeceum—from 500 to 1200." *JMH* 4 (1978): 117–33.

———. "Strict Active Enclosure and Its Effects on the Female Monastic Experience (ca. 500–1100)." In *Medieval Religious Women: Distant Echoes*, edited by John A. Nichols and Lillian Thomas Shank, 51–86. Kalamazoo, Mich., 1984.

———. "Women's Monastic Communities, 500–1100: Patterns of Expansion and Decline." *Signs* 14, no. 2 (1989): 261–92.

———. *Forgetful of Their Sex: Female Sanctity and Society, ca. 500–1100*. Chicago, 1998.

Scott, Joan W. "Gender: A Useful Category of Historical Analysis." *American Historical Review* 91, no. 5 (1986): 1053–75.

Shahar, Shulamit. *Growing Old in the Middle Ages: "Winter clothes us in shadow and pain."* London, 1997.

Shaw, Brent D. "The Family in Late Antiquity: The Experience of Augustine." *PP* 115 (1987): 3–51.

Sims-Williams, Patrick. "An Unpublished Seventh or Eighth-Century Anglo-Latin Letter in Boulogne-sur-Mer MS 74 (82)." *Medium Ævum* 48, no. 1 (1979): 1–22.

Sirat, Jacques. "Le costume dans le haut Moyen Âge." In *Tissu et vêtement. 5000 ans de savoir-faire*, 114–16. Guiry-en-Vexin, France, 1986.

Smith, Julia M. H. "The Hagiography of Hucbald of Saint-Amand." *Studi medievali* 35, series 3 (1994): 517–42.

———. "The Problem of Female Sanctity in Carolingian Europe c.780–920." *PP* 146 (1995): 3–37.

———. "A Hagiographer at Work: Hucbald and the Library at Saint-Amand." *Revue bénédictine* 106 (1996): 151–71.

———. "Gender and Ideology in the Early Middle Ages." In *Gender and Christian Religion*. Studies in Church History 34, edited by R. N. Swanson, 51–73. Woodbridge, England, 1998.

———. "Did Women Have a Transformation of the Roman World?" *Gender and History* 12, no. 3 (2000): 552–71.

———. "Einhard: The Sinner and the Saints." *TRHS* 13 (2003): 55–77.

———. "Introduction: Gendering the Early Medieval World." In *GEMW*, 1–19.

———. *Europe after Rome: A New Cultural History, 500–1000*. Oxford, 2005.

Squatriti, Paolo. *Water and Society in Early Medieval Italy, AD 400–1000*. Cambridge, 1998.

Stafford, Pauline. *Queens, Concubines, and Dowagers: The King's Wife in the Early Middle Ages*. Athens, Ga., 1983.

———. *Queen Emma and Queen Edith: Queenship and Women's Power in Eleventh-Century England*. Oxford, 1997.

Steuer, Heiko. "Handel und Wirtschaft in der Karolingerzeit." In *Kunst*, 406–16.

Stevenson, Jane Barbara. "The Monastic Rules of Columbanus." In *Columbanus: Studies on the Latin Writings*, edited by Michael Lapidge, 203–16. Woodbridge, 1997.

Sullivan, Richard E. "The Carolingian Age: Reflections on Its Place in the History of the Middle Ages." *Speculum* 64 (1989): 267–306.

Toubert, Pierre. "La théorie du mariage chez les moralistes carolingiens." *Settimane* 24 (1977): 233–82.

——. "Le moment carolingien (viiie-xe siècles)." In *Histoire de la Famille I. Mondes lontains, mondes anciens*, edited by A. Burguière et al., 333–59. Paris, 1986.

Verdon, Jean. "La femme vers le milieu du ixe siècle d'après le polyptyque de l'abbaye de Saint-Remi de Reims." *Mémoires de la société d'agriculture, commerce, sciences et arts du département de la Marne* 91 (1976): 111–34.

Verhulst, Adriaan. "Economic Organisation." In *NCMH* 2, 481–509.

Vincent, Catherine. "Le cierge de la consécration des femmes: sens et fortune d'un signe au Moyen Âge. Mélanges en l'honneur de Paulette L'Hermite-Leclercq." In *Au cloître et dans le monde. Femmes, hommes et sociétés (IXe—XVe siècle)*, edited by Patrick Henriet and Anne-Marie Legras, 357–65. Paris, 2000.

Wallace-Hadrill, J. M. *The Frankish Church*. Oxford, 1983.

Wamers, Egon. "Insulare Kunst im Reich Karls des Großen." In *Kunst*, 452–64.

Ward, Elizabeth. "Caesar's Wife: The Empress Judith." In *Charlemagne's Heir: New Perspectives on the Reign of Louis the Pious (814–40)*, edited by Peter Godman and Roger Collins, 205–27. Oxford, 1990.

Warnecke, Hans Jürgen. "Sächsische Adelsfamilien in der Karolingerzeit." In *Kunst*, 348–55.

Weitmann, Pascal. *Sukzession und Gegenwart: zu theoretischen Äusserungen über bildende Kunst und Musik von Basileios bis Hrabanus Maurus*. Wiesbaden, Germany, 1997.

Wemple, Suzanne Fonay. *Women in Frankish Society: Marriage and the Cloister, 500 to 900*. Philadelphia, 1981.

——. "S. Salvatore/S. Guilia: A Case Study in the Endowment and Patronage of a Major Female Monastery in Northern Italy." In *Women of the Medieval World: Essays in Honor of John H. Mundy*, edited by Julius Kirshner and Suzanne Fonay Wemple, 85–102. Oxford, 1985.

——. "Female Monasticism in Italy and Its Comparison with France and Germany from the Ninth through the Eleventh Century." In *Frauen in Spätantike und Frühmittelalter. Lebensbedingungen—Lebensnormen—Lebensformen*, edited by Werner Affeldt, 291–310. Sigmaringen, Germany, 1990.

Wickham, Chris. *Framing the Early Middle Ages: Europe and the Mediterranean, 400–800*. Oxford, 2005.

Wood, Ian. *The Missionary Life: Saints and the Evangelisation of Europe, 400–1050*. Harlow, England, 2001.

——. "Genealogy Defined by Women: The Pippinids." In *GEMW*, 234–56.

Wood, Susan. *The Proprietary Church in the Medieval West*. Oxford, 2006.

INDEX

Page numbers in italics refer to illustrations and photographs.

death, 179, 180n24
depictions, 32, *34*, 45
Theutberga, support of, 118, 166
Charles the Fat, 110, 220, 253
Charles the Simple, 187
"chasuble of Chelles," 24
Chelles (center of learning), 162
childbirth, 216–217, 218–219
Chilperic (King of Burgundy), 179
Christina (sister of Hathumoda), 138
Chronicle (Regino of Prüm), 55
Claudius of Turin, 29
claustration
    debate over, 112–114
    preservation of family bonds, balance with,
    119
cleanliness, 212–213
clergy. *See* ecclesiastical leaders
Cneuburga (abbess), 104
Codex Forojuliensis, 78n39
Coenburga (abbess), 104
Columbanus, 78n41
commemoration, 16–17
    functions of, 74–75
    See also family bonds and memory, preser-
    vation of
Connerton, Paul, 69
Constitution of Abbot Ansegis, 264
Coon, Lynda, 233n33
Cotaniwi (nun), 111
Council of Aachen of 816, 78
Council of Aachen of 817, 90
Council of Carthage of 390, 92n116
Council of Meaux-Paris of 845, 9, 134,
    261
Council of Paris of 829, 92, 238
Council of Tribur of 895, 90
Council of Worms of 829, 217
craft production, 207–210, 211–212
    See also textile work
crysolite, 45
De cultu imaginum, 29
Cundbert (nobleman), 253
Cuniberga (abbess), 191
Curtius, Ernst, 14
Cynihild (aunt of Lull), 129
Cysoing, monastery at Flanders, 98

Dagobert, King of the Franks, 117, 219–220
dairying, 215
Davies, Wendy, 75n32
Denehard (student of Boniface), 191
Desiderius (Lombard king), 186

Dhuoda (aristocratic laywoman), 7, 10, 36,
    146, 187, 203, 219
    education, 144, 148, 273
    family bonds and memory, preservation of,
    115–117, 279
    motherhood, model of, 272
    personal troubles, 152–153
    See also *Liber manualis*
diacona (deaconess), 238
dogs, care of, 203–204
Domesday Book (Æfgyth), 230
domestic management, 177, 178–188,
    210–211, 213–214, 214–215
    administrative authority, 179–181
    craft production, 207–210, 211–212 (*see also*
    textile work)
    estate supervision, 178–179, 183–184
    female learning and instruction, 177,
    184–185
    financial management, 187–188
    hospitality, connection to, 174–178
    implications of, 175–176
    laywomen, 171–172, 173–174
    monasteries and, 177
    political negotiations, 186–187
    religious women, 175, 185–186
    royal women, 179–180, 186–187
    sick and dying, care of, 215–216
    See also food production
Donatus, 147
dress, relationship to virtue, 49–51
Dungal, 29
dyeing, 266

Eadburg (Wimborne nun), 128
Eadburg of Thanet (abbess), 234
Eberhard, Count, 264
Eberhard of Friuli, 15, 87, 134, 161
    inheritance, division of, 96–98
    library, 15, 145–146, 146–147, 196–197,
    216
    textiles, bequests of, 246, 249, 258
Eccard of Autun, 118, 216, 231, 249, 258
ecclesiastical leaders
    beauty, discussion of, 27–30
    on female beauty, 23–25, 25–26
    female learning and instruction, exhorta-
    tions on, 125–126
    lay children, on instruction of, 148–150
    marriage, support of, 71
    moral instruction, advice on, 130–131, 133
    overindulgence, warning against, 196
    vanity, concerns over, 33, 35–36, 58, 61

Paris Colloquy of 825, 28
Paulinus of Aquileia, 8–9, 196, 271
Paul of Tarsus, 58, 234
Paul the Deacon, 195
Perisinda (widow), 99
Pippinid line, 73
Pippin II, 179
Pippin the Hunchback, 164, 241
Pippin the Short, 6
pisiles (textile workshops), 260–261
Plato, 26n12
Plectrud (wife of Pippin II), 179
poetry, 14
Power, Eileen, 3
praelata, 186, 215
Prior Metz Annals, 7
proprietary foundations, 110–112
prudence, 18–19
   See also female learning and instruction;
     Liber manualis; moral exemplarity; moral
     instruction
psalters, 145, 146
purple, associations of, 22, 46

quadriga silk, 245

Raban Maur, 107, 165, 265n173, 269–270
   on beauty, 40–41, 61–62
Radegund (Merovingian queen), 24, 180
Radoara (abbess), 85
Ragyntrudis (daughter of Frankish noble-
   man), 144–145
Rastiz (duke of Moravia), 196
Rectitudines singularum personarum, 178
Regimberga (daughter of Grimald), 99
Reginhild (wife of Bernard), 141–142
Regino of Prüm, 14
Regula sanctarum virginum (Caesarius of
   Arles), 199
Reichenau monastery, 101, 110, 111
religious communities
   havens for fallen women, 118–119
   textile work, 225
religious textiles, 242–246, 249–254, 256–259
   awe, creation of a sense of, 243
   Carolingian era, survivors of, 249–252,
     253–254, 255, 256–259, 257
   economic value, 225–227, 244–245
   liturgical rites, 243, 249–250, 254
   as *memoria*, 253–254, 256–259
   religious and political bonds, strengthening
     of, 252–253

religious women
   domestic management, 175, 185–186
   food production, 206, 215
   hospitality, 191–192
   landholding options, 114–115
   moral exemplarity, 124
   textile work, 10, 225, 231, 237–238, 265
   travel, limits on, 70
religious women, Merovingian, 76
Remiremont convent, 77, 78–83
   gifts, emphasis of spiritual worth of, 82
   memorial commemoration, 79–83
   prestigious connections, 78–79
   religious reforms, 78–79
Renula, 89, 112, 135–137, 191, 224, 273
Responses (Dungal), 29
Richardis (wife of Charles the Fat), 110, 112,
   119, 220
Riché, Pierre, 146, 198n109
Richildis (abbess), 80
Richildis (wife of Charles the Bald), 58, 220,
   241, 249
   administrative authority, 179–180
Richildis (wife of Eccard of Autun), 118, 180
Rictrud, 134, 241
   beauty, 38, 49, 52, 58
   Eusebia, education and parenting of, 114,
     147, 150–151
   taking of the veil, 91, 117, 253
Riculf of Soissons (bishop), 237
Rotaldus of Verona (bishop), 260–261
Rotperga (daughter of Grimald), 99
Rotrud (daughter of Charlemagne), 221, 259
   beauty, 42, 43
   education, 144, 161–162, 273
   misbehavior, 162–163
royal women
   court authority, 181–182
   domestic management, 179–180, 186–187
   moral exemplarity, 159–161
   scapegoating of, 164–165
   targets of scrutiny, 159–160
rubies, 46
Rudolf (abbot of Cysoing), 98
Rudolf (Fulda monk), 105–107, 221
   See also *Vita Leobae*
Rudolf (son of Eberhard of Friuli), 216
Rule of St. Benedict, 78, 114

St. Gall, monastery of, 110, 111, 207
St. Gall plan, 262
Saint-Germain-des-Prés, monastery at, 263

vanity
    ecclesiastical leaders' concern over, 33,
        35–36, 58, 61
    female beauty and, 33, 35–36
    Institutio sanctimonialium, prohibition of,
        35–36, 59, 60, 186
Vatican Museum
    textile collection, 226, 250–251, 251–252,
        256
veiling, rite of, 89–93
"veil of Chartres," 239–240
Venantius Fortunatus, 41, 44n87
Verdon, Jean, 263n160
Vienna Genesis, 229
Vienna Penitential B, 218
De virginitate (Aldheim), 229–230
virgins, consecration of, 89–93
virtue
    beauty and, 38–39
    dress, relationship to, 49–51
    fertility and, 217
    gems and, 44–45, 46
    male beauty, relationship to, 45, 53
    textile work, association with, 225, 227
    See also female beauty, relationship to virtue
Vita Aldegundis (ninth-century version), 185,
    186
Vita Aldegundis (tenth-century version),
    15–16, 113, 185–186, 212, 266–267
Vita Eligii (Audoin of Rouen), 252
Vita Eusebia (Hucbald of St. Amand), 151
Vita Genovefae, 238
Vita Geraldi (Odo of Cluny), 148
Vita Gregorii (Liudger), 127–128
Vita Hathumodae (Agius), 36, 50–51, 76, 89,
    108–109, 138, 265
Vita Herlinde et Renulae (anonymous),
    135–136, 135–137, 221, 224
    on textile work, 231, 246
Vita Karoli (Notker), 196
Vita Leobae (Rudolf), 105–106, 129, 220
Vita Liutbirgae (anonymous), 139–144, 221,
    272, 278
    female supervision of family lands, 13,
        183–184
    prayer and commemoration, references
        to, 107–108
    on textile work, 231–232

Vita Rictrudis (Hucbald of St. Amand), 52, 53,
    114, 117, 134
    hospitality, on subversion of norms of,
        194–195, 195–196
    on lay to religious clothing ritual, 91, 253
    on sterility, 219–220
Vita Waldetrudis, 222
Vita Willibaldi et vita Winnebaldi, 37
Vita Willibrordi (Alcuin), 217
vitta (adornment), 59–60

Walafrid Strabo, 29–30, 205
Walburga (abbess at Heidenheim), 129
Waldetrud (daughter of Bertilla), 113
Waldo of Freising (bishop), 253
Waldrada (concubine of Lothar II), 118
Walfred (aristocrat), 111–112
Waltharius, 170–173, 209
wax, 212
wealth, 19
    beauty, association with, 31–32, 36–37
    courtyards and walled parks, 205–206
    See also domestic management; hospitality
Wemple, Suzanne, 71
Werden, monastery at, 263
wet nursing, 219
Wicharius (priest), 115
Wido of Brittany, 148n88
widows, 117–118
Wiehtberht (priest), 104
William (son of Dhuoda), 115–117, 152,
    153
William the Pious, 153
Willibald (bishop of Eichstätt), 109, 133
Willibrord (archbishop of the Frisians),
    136n42, 191
Williswind (nun), 106, 220
Wimborne, convent of, 128
Windenhausen, religious community at, 107,
    111, 142
winemaking, 213–214
Witgar (bishop of Augsburg), 258
Witgar belt, 226, 253–254, 255, 257
Wood, Ian, 73, 136

youth, association with beauty, 61–65

Zwentibald (nephew of Rastiz), 196